I0407697

ED
BROADBENT

*The Pursuit
of Power*

Judy Steed

VIKING

VIKING
Published by the Penguin Group
Penguin Books Canada Ltd, 2801 John Street, Markham, Ontario, Canada L3R 1B4
Penguin Books Ltd, 27 Wrights Lane, London W8 5TZ, England
Viking Penguin Inc., 40 West 23rd Street, New York, New York 10010, USA
Penguin Books Australia Ltd, Ringwood, Victoria, Australia
Penguin Books (NZ) Ltd, 182-190 Wairau Road, Auckland 10, New Zealand
Penguin Books Ltd, Registered Offices: Harmondsworth, Middlesex, England

First published in 1988

10 9 8 7 6 5 4 3 2

Copyright © Judy Steed, 1988

Queries regarding radio broadcasting, motion picture, video cassette, television and translation rights should be directed to the Author's representative: Peter Livingston Associates, Inc., 120 Carlton St., Suite 304, Toronto Ontario Canada M5A 4K2.

Printed and bound in Canada

Canadian Cataloguing in Publication Data
  Steed, Judy
    Ed Broadbent: the pursuit of power

  ISBN 0-670-82255-8

  1. Broadbent, Ed, 1936-   . 2. New Democratic Party — Biography.   3. Politicians — Canada — Biography. I. Title.

  FC626.B76S74 1988   971.064'092'4   C88-093005-5
  F1034.3.B76S74 1988

For Emily, my daughter,
whose shining spirit lit the way

Acknowledgements

My parents inspired my interest in politics. John Burke Ewing, my father, was a Canadian farm boy who "got educated," became Surgeon-in-Chief at the Ottawa General Hospital and was always an ardent Conservative and advocate of medicare. He greatly admired two leaders: Winston Churchill and John Diefenbaker. They shared, in my father's eyes, a passionate patriotism that taught us something about what it is to love your country. My mother, Ethel Mackenzie, is a more skeptical Scot. From her, we learned that Scotland's sad fate — being sold out to the English aristocracy and turned into a sheep run — came about because of the greed of Scottish chieftains. My mother's lesson was this: watch out for your own leaders.

This is not an authorized biography. As a feature writer at *The Globe and Mail* since 1981, I had interviewed Ed Broadbent a few times, in passing, for larger stories on Petro-Canada, the Auto Pact, free trade. But I had never paid much attention to him — until the summer of '87, when he led the NDP to an historic first-place in public opinion polls.

I want to thank Ed Broadbent for his generosity and patience in responding to a stranger's questions over a period of six months — and for his willingness to help me draw a deeper picture of his life and times. Lucille, his wife, and Velma Cornish, his sister, were invaluable sources of insight. All the Broadbent relatives — from Aunt Edna Broadbent Bice to Uncle Aubrey and Uncle Reuben, to Ed's brother David and his son Paul — were enormously helpful.

Among New Democratic Party stalwarts, Robin Sears, Gerry Caplan and Anne Carroll submitted graciously to an unending stream of queries. More than two hundred people gave me intensive interviews, and though not everyone is quoted here I want to acknowledge the density of information I received. All the errors are mine.

Thank you to Norman Webster, editor-in-chief of *The Globe and Mail*, for the opportunity to do what I do at the *Globe* — which really is a writer's paper — and for the leave of absence which allowed me time for this project. My editor at the *Globe*, Phil Jackman, is the invisible mender whose steady hand has been so helpful to me. Morty Mint, president of Penguin Books, made up his mind in five minutes to take a chance on this book, and Cynthia Good, Penguin's vice-president and editorial director, guided me through many drafts with an exuberance which made it seem almost easy. Lorraine Johnson was marvellously adept at keeping track of everything. Kathryn Maloney did the best research. Katherine Govier and Linda McQuaig told me what to expect. John Honderich kindly gave me access to the *Toronto Star*'s files. Dale Williams and our group of friends were great supports. Finally, Lankai Lamptey, my companion in life, read every word, suggested improvements, listened to me talk in my sleep and generally made the whole experience a pleasure. I couldn't have done it without him.

Judy Steed,
Toronto

Contents

ED
BROADBENT

The Pursuit
of Power

First Impressions

It is a hot day at the end of August, 1987. Oshawa's Holiday Inn swimming pool is still and empty, a startling turquoise-blue against the gray roar of Highway 401, part of the east–west transportation grid that streams with traffic pounding between Montreal and Toronto. At the far end of the pool, Canada's most popular political leader is stretched out on a lounge chair, alone, soaking up the sun. Ed Broadbent, fifty-one, is wearing beige swimming trunks and a Tilley Endurable hat — one of those funny-looking cotton-duck sunhats favoured by paddlers. He is a long-legged man who obviously tans well. Reading the Sunday *New York Times* and eating a cheeseburger, he is engrossed in an article about the Swedish economy — a favourite subject of his.

He greets me and takes off his hat; munching on his cheeseburger, he looks like a friendly, energetic, hungry bulldog. He talks about the latest developments in socialist Sweden. "The level of writing in this country about the evolution of social democratic thought is abysmal," he says. But he's not obsessed with talking politics — unusual for a politician — and the conversation glides into other fields. He chats about the books he's been reading — Michael Ondaatje's *In the Skin of a Lion*, Jay McInerney's *Bright Lights*, *Big City*, Saul Bellow's *More Die of Heartbreak*, Mary McCarthy's *How I Grew* — and the music he listens to — he adores Maria Callas, opera, Bach. Then he excuses himself to get changed.

Waiting, I ponder the puzzle of this man who has led his party to a record high of 44 per cent in the public opinion polls, threatening to change the political landscape of the country. Broadbent has been a Member of Parliament for twenty years. He first chaired the New Democratic Party's caucus during the historic 1972–74 minority government period; Petro-Canada was the NDP's biggest baby during that session. The MPs seated around the caucus table in those years were the NDP giants, and Broadbent's teachers: David Lewis, the Rhodes Scholar and labour lawyer who dedicated his life to building the party; Tommy Douglas, father of medicare, Premier of Saskatchewan for seventeen years and the NDP's first leader; Winnipeg's Stanley Knowles, the venerated parliamentarian, from whom Ed would learn the ropes.

The bare facts were on the record, but there was little insight into Broadbent's character, nothing to suggest how this allegedly unambitious man — by all accounts a solid, decent fellow who joined the New Democrats without any connection to its hierarchy — became party leader and national hero. I had caught him in action the day before, at a Greek restaurant in Oshawa. At 8 A.M., the place was packed with people and excitement. Broadbent was scheduled to speak to local NDP candidates running in the Ontario provincial election, then under way. Waitresses hustled scrambled eggs, bacon and coffee amid an extraordinary hubbub caused by a crush of reporters and TV cameras. Outside in the parking lot there were TV trucks from as far away as Ottawa. Oshawans pretended not to notice, but they knew what the fuss was about: some people were saying maybe Broadbent stood a chance of becoming the next Prime Minister.

The object of all the attention strode in and was instantly accorded a standing ovation. He was wearing a pale beige suit, hand-stitched around the lapels; brown loafers, of fine Italian leather; a white shirt and beige striped tie. He looked good, tanned, tall, solidly built, moving through the crowd, pressing the flesh, kissing ladies' cheeks, holding old men's hands, smiling at the kids, remembering his pals — the same old Ed, to his friends, except that he dressed more elegantly than he used to, and the gap between his front teeth was covered, corrected by dental surgery.

But for all his down-home amiability, Ed is a pro. As the folks finished their breakfast, Ed delivered a quick and apparently spontaneous speech. (No notes, nothing fancy, but it had all been sketched out in advance with his chief speechwriter, Hilarie McMurray.) He told his audience four things: This is a good time to be a New Democrat. We don't pretend to be perfect and we don't have all the solutions, but we're honest. We're in this to make life better for ordinary people (examples: day care, tax reform, environmental protection and, in the past, old-age pensions, unemployment insurance, medicare, Petro-Canada). And when we're in power, as in Saskatchewan, Manitoba or British Columbia, we deliver.

Then he received another standing ovation, some orange balloons were batted around, and he left the way he came, kissing, shaking hands, smiling. Outside, he plowed through a scrum of reporters: Are you afraid of complacency setting in? "No." Can the NDP expand its base and form a government? "As I've said before, my father was a Conservative for many years and a lot of Conservatives come to the New Democratic Party." Do you have any advice for Bob Rae [leader of the Ontario NDP]? "Just be himself." That's what Ed Broadbent is good at — being himself. But who is he?

My poolside musings are interrupted by the man himself. Freshly showered, in a white linen shirt and soft khaki cotton pants, Broadbent is carrying a leather suitcase. Plans have altered, he informs me, and is it all right if he hitches a ride into Toronto with me?

Heading to the parking lot, he encounters a work crew busily engaged in resurfacing the roadway. The guys recognize him immediately, surround him to pump his hand and get him to sign autographs (on paper torn from my notebook). He enjoys kibbitzing with them — you would never have guessed that ten minutes earlier he was deep into a discussion about literature and opera — and then we head for my car. It is an aging Chevette. I am somewhat embarrassed. He doesn't notice. "I love to drive," he says, "and I don't get to do it much any more." I do not realize there is a very good reason why his staff does not want him to drive. I give him the keys. We chug out of the parking lot and the gear shift knob comes off in his hand. "Great car," he says. He roars with laughter and, gesturing expansively, looking at me as he talks, steering the car by some form of blind-sight (since he hardly ever looks where he's going), he decides it would be fun to give me a guided tour of his home town. I am apprehensive.

But he doesn't hit anything and in the next two hours I am immersed in a character the likes of which I have hardly ever encountered. I started with a blank page and a bland image of a nice guy. The experience of getting to know Ed — as everyone calls him — turns out to be a bit like discovering Canada: you don't know what's here until you know what's here.

First: driving through Oshawa with Ed Broadbent is like accompanying the Prince of Wales to his birthplace. It's a sunny Sunday afternoon, so people are sitting out on their porches, walking their dogs, pushing baby carriages, and they all pop alert when Ed cruises by. They wave and call out and peer at him, a little startled perhaps to see him driving such a beat-up car; he waves back cheerfully. The image of his white-linen left arm swinging, almost regally, back and forth out his window becomes stuck in my mind. I am struck by the fact that every person we pass knows who he is — but then, I remind myself, I'm from a big city, this is a small town and he's famous.

Driving past the old landmarks, Ed points out the various generations of GM workers' houses, neat brick bungalows with pretty flower beds and carefully tended lawns, spawned in the '40s, '50s and '60s. He stops at the old Broadbent family home at the corner of Central Park and Eulalie, a modest, yellow-brick bungalow where the catalpa and willow trees he planted as a teenager now tower over the house. Past a church where he sang in the Anglican boys' choir. Past the original old General Motors headquarters with its charming art deco facade. "I love that building," he says. "Isn't it great?" He knows the town intimately, though parts have changed — a road here is wider, there a chain link fence that didn't use to be, all the new development and the massive GM installations that extend like a giant octopus through town, covering 883 acres with vast, windowless plants.

His conversation is free-form, swinging from detailed descriptions of the neighbourhoods we're passing through — "this is Polish and Ukrainian, we get 75 per cent of the vote here" — to political history. The contrast between his public populism and private intellectualism is startling. I ask him who influenced his thinking. He cites: Brough Macpherson, an internationally renowned left-wing political science professor at the University of Toronto, under whom he did his Ph.D.; a conservative British philosopher named Michael Oakeshott, who taught him at the London School of Economics; and Ted Maidman, his Oshawa boy scout leader. His boy scout leader? Yes, he loved his boy scout leader. He sees no incongruity in his list. And, he adds, "of course, my mother." Thinking it over, he decides, seriously, that his mother had the greatest influence on him of anyone in his life. ("His mother," says Mike Breaugh, Oshawa's MPP, "looked like a sweet little old lady with white hair, but she had a mental toughness about her. She could probably take Attila the Hun easily in two out of three.")

Waving, smiling, gesturing, Ed is in seventh heaven, talking ideas, from British philosophers Hobbes, Locke and John Stuart Mill, to the evolution of capitalism, the role of markets, democratic socialism and . . . girls, growing up in the '50s, going to Central Collegiate, the working-class high school that was packed with the children of immigrants, who were the non-WASP companions of his high school years. Ed was a big man on campus at Central. He won an outstanding student award four out of his five years there, was president of the Students' Council when he was only in grade eleven, was a voracious reader, class clown, regular guy — all wrapped up in one complex, funny bundle.

He doesn't mention the dark shadows, not until later. Ed once told a reporter that "mine was not a Norman Rockwell adolescence," but he never said why not. Down another street and "this is the grocery store where Dad worked nights, after a day at The Motors." Lots of fathers worked two jobs; lots of sons didn't know their fathers. Ed's father, however, was an alcoholic, which helps explain the importance of Ted Maidman, the scout leader. (Ed went camping with the scouts, not with his father.) Ed was never close to his father; his instinct for avoiding conflict — and his dislike of emotional scenes — grew out of his unhappiness with the parental battles that raged as he approached puberty, when the family was devastated by Percy Broadbent's personal disasters.

Percy's gambling and drinking would alienate him from his hard-working brothers; he would lose his job as a salesman, he would lose his car and, even worse, the family home. Ed got a frightening glimpse of the insecure underbelly. And in a small town, where everybody knew everybody else, it was hard to hide the secret. Percy's brother Reuben helped out by taking them in, for a short while. Another family friend got Percy the job as a clerk at GM. And Ed, ever more remote from his father, continued to excel. He was everything his father wasn't: a clean-living straight arrow, reliable, responsible, dedicated to holding things together. To his friends, he seemed like a regular guy, but from early on he had a deeper drive. He worked at after-school jobs to save money to go to university; he studied philosophy at Trinity College, University of Toronto, graduated with first-class honours, and proceeded to a doctorate financed by scholarships. Young Eddie was no rebel. (People thought he was a golden boy, one who'd always had it easy.) The only thing he ever did that surprised the folks back home was that he came back home and ran as an NDPer.

Ed is not a guy who shares his grief. Most people don't know he has suffered; his private feelings are hidden by his public face, by his joking manner. His close friends consider his sense of humour his most outstanding trait — next to his tenacity — and I couldn't imagine what they meant, until I drove around Oshawa with him. Being with Broadbent, I found out, means seeing the world from a wry perspective. He really loves to laugh, and he never forgets people who made him laugh. Back in the old neighbourhood haunts of his youth, he is reminded of Archie Rinker, a pal of his Dad's. "I adored Archie," says Ed. "Archie was a wild Irishman, a wild drinker and a great practical joker. I don't suppose my mother approved of him but I thought he was wonderful. One day he ordered a ton of hay and a goat and put up a post in his next-door neighbour's driveway, so when the guy got home there was a goat tethered to the post. . . ." Ed laughs uproariously, face red, delighted. "Then there was another time Archie won a live turkey and brought it home and threw it in the bedroom. His wife was asleep in bed." Ed howls. Lest I get the wrong idea, he hastily adds: "I wouldn't have wanted to be married to him, but for me, a young kid, he was a great guy."

Ed's own practical jokes will emerge as major anecdotes at every stage of his life. But we're off again. He heads over to Simcoe Street and pulls up at Colonel Sam McLaughlin's mansion. This is, after all, an important landmark not only in the economic history of Canada but in Ed's development. He stops to read the historic plaque installed next to blue spruce trees, close to the Greek columns that front the estate. When Ed was growing up, the lord of the manor, the Pope of Oshawa, was Col. Sam, whose father's carriage company built the first McLaughlin motor car in 1907. The McLaughlins' monumentally lavish home, built before they sold out to General Motors in 1918, conjures up Xanadu, immortalized in *Citizen Kane*, Orson Welles's film about U.S. tycoon William Randolph Hearst: massive archways, heavy oak panelling hand-carved in France, *trompe-l'oeil* painted walls and ceilings (vines, trellises, Roman figures, parrots), an Italianate garden featuring a pool adorned with dancing marble statues, fabulous gardens and greenhouses exotic with tropical palms, orchids and lemon trees, a bowling alley, squash court, indoor swimming pool, crystal chandeliers, Sarouk oriental carpets, giant tapestries and room upon room filled with ornate, rococo, marble-topped, curlicued Louis Quatorze hoo-ha in overwhelming profusion.

I expect Ed to toss off a few bitter remarks about capitalist exploiters. He does not. Instead, he observes that "there isn't the class envy in Oshawa that you find in other places, because everyone did all right. There was enough to go round. There's an attitude here that 'who cares about them? [pointing to Sam's mansion] as long as we're doing well.'" What bothers him most about Col. Sam is not how much money he made but that he sold out.

Since Ed was first elected to the House of Commons in 1968, concern about foreign control of the economy has driven NDP policy, dominated Canadian politics and animated his own political vision. It was expressed in the creation of Petro-Canada, the National Energy Program and the Foreign Investment Review Agency. The Conservatives subsequently attacked all three: Joe Clark promised to sell Petro-Canada, and was defeated; under Prime Minister Brian Mulroney, both the NEP and FIRA have been dumped. Again, control of the economy is the issue that lurks behind the Reagan–Mulroney trade deal, which limits the power of the Canadian government to shape economic policy; it will be one of the key issues over which the next election is fought.

Broadbent's interest in the economy arose naturally from the environment in which he was raised. He is as distinctive a product of industrial Ontario as was Pierre Trudeau of the Quebec intelligentsia. In *Grits*, Christina McCall wrote that Pierre Trudeau's "visceral response came out of his deep roots in Quebec society." Trudeau's obsession with patriating the Constitution, which dominated his leadership of the country for fifteen years, is matched by Broadbent's obsession with patriating the economy.

At the same time, Ed's tolerance of capitalists offends the socialist purists in his party; he believes that free markets are desirable. His passion for economic issues annoys party strategists who tell him voters aren't interested in what New Democrats have to say about the economy. He has been advised to stick to the social justice issues — day care, medicare, pensions, unemployment insurance — where the party has made such a dramatic impact. But he can't stop talking about industry. He comes from Oshawa, not Toronto, and there's a big difference. With three million people, Metropolitan Toronto is the nation's financial and communications centre, dominated by the bank towers, lawyers and media gurus whose self-interest, passing for the national interest, has alienated western Canada, Quebec and the Maritimes.

On the fringes of the Toronto orbit, Oshawa's 122,000 citizens live in the industrial capital of Canada's richest province, headquarters of the industry that drives the Canadian economy. Oshawans are fiercely independent, very tough and expect their politicians to live up to their credo: No Bullshit. (Oshawa language can be salty. Mike Breaugh suggested that the best title for a Broadbent biography, if the aim were to make the book a best seller in Oshawa, would be THE WORLD'S TOUGHEST ACADEMIC SHITHEAD.) It is a neat irony that General Motors of Canada, foreign-owned, resides in the riding of the one party leader who has made Canadian control of the economy his *raison d'être* — and who feels no discomfort in his friendly relations with both GM executives and the Canadian Auto Workers.

Heading out of Oshawa, the Chevette rumbles west on the expressway to Toronto, past the industrial plants, suburbs, factories and high-rise apartments that cluster around the 401. Ed is still driving and talking, gesturing and laughing. Pulling up at his destination in downtown Toronto, the ivy-covered, discreetly elegant Windsor Arms Hotel, he is looking forward to a good dinner, a glass of wine and a cigar. (His tastes are catholic and can be expensive.) He leaves me with a parting shot: "It's significant," he says, "that I'm the first leader of the New Democratic Party who was born in Canada. Everybody knows where I'm coming from."

CHAPTER ONE

Broadbent, Ontario

What is it the French say? They have a phrase for being master in your own house, Maître Chez Nous, that's it. It's like you'd rather own your house than pay rent, so you've got something to hand on to your children. I like to see us handle our own affairs. We figure we're good enough to be able to do it ourselves.

Ed's Uncle Aubrey (Curly) Broadbent.

There are no Broadbents left in Broadbent, Ontario, except buried in the Anglican cemetery. The tiny hamlet has dwindled to a dusty crossroads set in rocky farmland near Hurdville, northeast of Parry Sound on the eastern side of Georgian Bay, closer to Sudbury than Toronto. Broadbent is not even on the Ontario road map anymore, to Ed's dismay; he figures the Tories took it off just to annoy him. But this was where his great-grandfather, Adam T. Broadbent, settled in 1872 and prospered, before he fell off the roof of a house he was building and died — some said of sunstroke, others said a heart attack. He left behind a teenage son, John, Ed's grandfather. John Broadbent grew up, married Albertha — known as Bert — Tait, and the couple produced ten children who were all born up north.

The children in Ed's father's generation were: Oren (1906–1971); Edna (1908–   ); Percy, Ed's Dad, known as Ginger   (1909–1976);   Birdie   (1911–1979);   Robert (1912–   ); Aubrey, known as Curly (1914–   ); Reuben, known as Red (1916–   ); Arnold, known as Arn (1917–1975); Velma (1920–1921); Bill (1925–   ).

1

The source of the family history is Aunt Edna, Mrs Wilfred Bice, keeper of Bert's Bible — the family Bible. Now in her eighties, Edna Broadbent Bice is the oldest surviving Broadbent, the second child of John and Bert. Their third child was Ed's father, Percy. Ginger, as the kids knew him, would become the family debater, hothead, supersalesman — and ultimately the sad figure they would prefer not to talk about.

The past begins with Aunt Edna. Her presence says a lot about Ed's background, which in turn says a lot about Ontario. She and Wilfred were schoolteachers in Huntsville, near Algonquin Park, but Aunt Edna is widowed now and lives in Islington, a western suburb of Toronto, in a pretty brick house sheltered by huge oak trees. She is the youngest eighty-year-old you've ever met, with the family red hair fading to a pinkish-white. Dressed in a crisp blue skirt, blue-and-white striped blouse, white shoes and white beads, she is neat, trim and proper, happily gardening under the oak trees in her backyard, visited by robins and blue jays.

Edna exemplifies the Broadbents' respectability — which made Percy's fall from grace all the more devastating. Edna is ready for my visit. First she serves coffee, in dainty china cups and saucers, and fresh corn muffins, hot from the oven. Her house is spotless. The silver tea set is polished and on display, the broadloom freshly vacuumed, the white sheers pulled across the picture window. On the mantel, the clock chimes loudly in the stillness. Edna has gathered her collection of family documents and memorabilia from the cedar chest in her bedroom and laid them on the dining room table. There among the clippings and treasures from the past is a yellowed photo of Ed that appeared in the Oshawa *Times* more than twenty-five years ago, announcing that "J. Edward Broadbent, 24, son of Mr. and Mrs. Percy Broadbent, has been awarded a $1,500 scholarship by the Canada Council for graduate studies at the University of Toronto. Mr. Broadbent stood first in his class when he graduated in Honours Philosophy from Trinity College at the University of Toronto in 1959."

Then there's a group snapshot of the older generation, of Percy and Edna and their brothers and sisters, all nine of them, grouped around their aging mother. Percy, in the front row, is the shortest, the stockiest, with wavy red hair and a glower on his face. He had gotten so he didn't like family gatherings. For at least a year, during one of his "episodes," says Edna, Perce wouldn't show up at all. "I think," says Edna, "he was ashamed of what he'd become."

August 14, by coincidence the day of my visit to Edna, is Percy's birthday. It makes Edna think of his death, which was she says, very painful. He died from cancer when he was sixty-seven, only a year after Ed was elected leader of the New Democrats, only three months after his mother's death in 1976 — so Bert couldn't record his passing in the family Bible. (Edna filled it in.) But before Perce died, he made peace with his demons. He drank less, and he'd changed his political stripes. A rabid Tory for most of his life, he died an ardent NDPer, a switch that caused him to take considerable ribbing around town. He didn't care. If he'd done nothing right, his son had done him proud.

Edna unfolds some very old parchment documents. They are inked in ancient calligraphic script, dated 1739, 1761, 1780. These are records of real estate transactions undertaken by Broadbent relatives back in Staffordshire, where the Broadbents came from. Edna has the atlas ready and a magnifying glass, and we peer through the glass at a map of England, north of Birmingham, south of Manchester, searching out Eccleshall, Market Drayton and High Offley, tiny towns just north of Stafford, south of Stoke-on-Trent, in the heart of England's china district (where Wedgwood is made), not far from the wild Yorkshire moors immortalized in Emily Bronte's *Wuthering Heights*.

There they were, back in the 1700s, the upwardly mobile Broadbents, conscious of their superiority, adapting to the distant echoes of the industrial revolution. When Adam Thomas Broadbent, Edna's grandfather, married Ellen Brayn, the Broadbents were deeply affronted. They

ran a private school for the well-to-do gentry, after all,
whereas the Brayns were merely market gardeners. But
the Brayns would prove themselves worthy. Aunt Edna
produces a yellowed obituary from a British newspaper
recording the passing of Sir Richard Brayn, a relative of
Ellen's who was born in 1850. A medical doctor and "expert in lunacy," Sir Richard was the medical superinten-
dent of Broadmoor Asylum. By the time his fame was
adding lustre to the Brayn name, the Canadian branch
had taken root in the far-off colony of Upper Canada, out
in the bush.

Edna picks up an oval-shaped teapot, a relic of the life
the family left behind. It is a collector's item, decorated
with Wedgwood-like figures. It has been mended, and has
been in the family since at least 1630. How it survived the Brayn–Broadbent travels through the bush is
anybody's guess, but survive it did, along with the family.

The teapot made its way to Parry Sound, and likely to
Byng Inlet, a tiny spot further north on Georgian Bay,
whose ancient smooth rocks and tenacious pines would be
immortalized by the painters in the Group of Seven. One
spring day when the ice had melted from the harbour, on
May 22, 1898, Adam T. wrote from Byng Inlet a rather
self-satisfied letter (still in the family's possession) describing his prosperity, which included "six building lots
in town and a farm of 175 acres." He was doing well, and
so was the nation. Sir John A. Macdonald, the first Prime
Minister of the Dominion of Canada, had recently died
(in 1891), Sir Wilfrid Laurier had replaced him, and William Lyon Mackenzie King was grooming himself in the
wings, preparing to perpetuate the Liberal dynasty. (In
1900, King became Canada's first deputy minister of labour.)

It likely didn't occur to Adam T. that his great-grand-
son would, less than 100 years later, challenge the political heirs of King and Macdonald.

But the ambitious Adam T. would not be around for
long to expand his holdings. One hot summer day in
1898, he was hammering away on the roof of a house

and, so goes the story, was overcome by heat and exhaustion and fell off the roof and died.

His son John, known as Jack, Ed's grandfather, was left alone at fourteen — his mother having remained in England, where Jack was born in 1884, during one of his father's trips home. But Jack had no attachment to the old country; Canada was his home — so he headed to Broadbent, to stay with the cousins who had founded the town, and it was lucky he did, because that's how he met Albertha Tait. She hated her first name and nobody ever called her anything but Bert.

Bert lived on a farm outside Broadbent, closer to Hurdville, where she was born in 1886. The Taits were Irish, and Bert was a cut-up, a live wire, with a beautiful head of thick copper-red hair. (The Irish blood — the deep emotions, the lively passions, the sense of play — runs strong in the Broadbents after Bert.) She wasn't too impressed with Jack at first, though he had "lovely curly hair and the bluest eyes you ever saw," according to Edna.

Bert and Jack sat next to each other at Hemlock school, the one-room schoolhouse in between Hurdville and Broadbent. Jack was quite taken with Bert; what finally improved her disposition toward him was that he was quick with figures. He would pass her answers in arithmetic and "in return," says Edna, who got the story from Bert, "she would help him with his art work."

They looked like a handsome couple when they were united in holy matrimony on August 14, 1905. (Edna has the pictures to prove it.) Bert was nineteen; Jack twenty-one. He was a handsome, strapping (over six feet) young man who, before their marriage, had travelled as far a-field as British Columbia, timber cruising. He wasn't an ordinary lumberjack. His speciality was estimating how much lumber a company could get off a tract and, later, operating the crews that cleared the land. Eventually he would save enough money to set up his own company and take off the timber himself.

Jack was ambitious like his father, and much more prolific. Within a year of their marriage, Bert's first child, Oren, was born, in 1906. Edna came next, a year and a half later. Percy less than two years after Edna. And so it went: every year or two another child until 1920 when the ninth, Velma, was born and lived little more than a year. The only one who didn't survive infancy, Velma was buried in the Anglican cemetery in Broadbent. It took Bert another five years to have her tenth and last child, Bill, who was born in 1925.

Edna remembers that when she got married to Wilfred Bice she asked her mother, "What do you do not to have so many children?" Bert grinned and said sarcastically, "Do you think if I'd known I would have had ten?"

Bert was always quick with her tongue and good for a laugh — but her most outstanding characteristic was that she did the work of twelve people. She made her children's clothes, knitted their mittens and socks, washed and ironed their clothes, baked her own bread and packed up the whole kit and caboodle (including children) to help her husband set up lumber camps of up to 125 men, where she would do all of the above and cook for the logging crew. A formidable woman.

Jack was just as hardworking. "He'd say you don't just do your share of the work, you do more than your share," says Edna. "As little as we were, we knew that much." Jack was also a nature lover. One summer he logged Rose Island, off Parry Island in a spectacularly beautiful corner of Georgian Bay, and the family was with him, as usual. The children roamed the rocky shores of the bay, played in its sparkling waters, caught fish and were allowed to "adopt" two baby seagulls who'd been orphaned. Every night they would put them in a box, to keep them safe from harm; they looked after the seagulls until the birds were old enough to fly off on their own. The children remember walking through the woods — or what was left of them — with their father, while he named the flora and fauna. Edna vividly recalls Jack explaining how the pitcher plant lured insects which then drowned in the plant's nectar and were devoured. The woods were dangerous: the children were always on the lookout for rattlesnakes, which inhabit the region around Parry Sound, but they only ever saw dead rattlers. Their father would cut off the snake's tail and dry it for the children to play with.

But hard work wasn't enough. In the early 1920s, Jack lost everything — except his family — in a fire that raged through a tract of land he was logging. They had set up camp on one side of the river and were cutting down trees on the other side. The railway ran alongside the river.

"They thought a spark from the train must have ignited the bush," says Edna, "because a fire spread through Dad's timber and threatened the camp. He stood with a revolver in his hand and made the men, who were scared, loosen the horses and cover their heads with blankets and lead them out. We had pigs, too. They got the waste from the meals and then they were turned into a meal during the winter. The men opened their pens and let the pigs out, not thinking they'd survive. But the pigs had enough sense to burrow into a marsh, and emerged happily soaked in muck."

The fire was a disaster for Jack Broadbent. Afterward, the family stood and looked helplessly at the awful black stumps sizzling in a grotesque sort of death. It was the end of Jack's dreams. He had lost all his logging equipment as well the timber he'd paid for. He would never recover from the fire. He made one more try at logging near Hurdville, but that was the end of his independent operations.

The family moved into Parry Sound and Jack took on three jobs to feed the nine hungry mouths that were growing ever more voracious. He ran the Princess Theatre movie house; he operated a livery stable; and he opened a Massey-Harris farm equipment dealership. Bert kept on cooking and cleaning and mending; the children went to high school. Edna remembers being deeply embarrassed during this period by her younger brother, Percy. Percy was a member of the debating club, and when the big day for a debate rolled around, Edna would shrink into her socks. Sure enough, walking down the halls of the high school, she'd hear Percy's loud and determined voice echoing after her.

"At that age," says Edna, "you just hated to have a family member draw attention to himself." The Broadbents prided themselves on maintaining a proper reserve, at least in public; Percy, however, would not restrain himself. "Percy was always attracting attention," says Edna. He had a quick temper, an exuberant personality and was, perhaps, Bert's favourite. Percy was the kind of boy you could see going places. He was very aggressive and an incredible talker. His brothers and sisters thought he should have been a lawyer, which would have been something in a family where men worked with their hands. "He'd argue black was white if he could," says Edna. "He would have been a wonderful lawyer because he'd have won his case every time, just by wearing down the other side. He wasn't down even if he was proven wrong. My brothers would steer clear of discussions with him, he'd argue so."

Times were getting tough as the 1920s wore on towards the Great Depression. Jack would sell a tractor to a farmer who needed it but couldn't afford it, and he didn't have the heart to dun the man for payment. "My father wouldn't press anyone for money, and he would never say anything about how he tried to help people," says Edna. Jack didn't advertise his charity and he was known to his children as a man who wouldn't tolerate them looking down their noses at anyone, especially the less fortunate.

Gradually, his own fortunes declined. Jack gave up his businesses in Parry Sound and went to work for an American outfit, Shroeder Lumber Co., which was logging up at Lost Channel, halfway between Parry Sound and Sudbury. Edna, by that time, was looking for her first teaching job. She got it at Lost Channel, a godforsaken logging camp in the bush off the railway line where she spent the winter, when she wasn't in class, skiing without poles, strapping galoshes onto skis.

But even the American lumber company was dying, and after a year Jack lost his job. He trekked further north, his family following after him, like a gypsy caravan. He searched for work with another lumber operation. But it was all too much, and in 1927 he gave up on the north and migrated south.

"To understand Ed Broadbent," says Bob Rae, leader of the Ontario NDP, "you have to understand Oshawa."

Less than an hour's drive east of Toronto on the 401 expressway, which cuts through rich farmland that is fast being overtaken by suburban development, there rises from the blur a distinctive onion-shaped dome. It is Oshawa's Ukrainian church: to outsiders, the city's major landmark and a symbol of its mixed ethnic population. But most drivers don't stop here. Oshawa is no tourist attraction, though it is the birthplace of a famous trio: Northern Dancer, the Kentucky Derby winner; Ed Broadbent, leader of the New Democratic Party; and the Canadian automobile industry.

Broadbent's home town is a unique place, characterized by the Clark Kent/Superman syndrome. Behind its modest facade lurks an economic dynamo. Oshawa seems like an ordinary Canadian town situated in an agricultural district. There are lots of farmers and pickup trucks, young guys in cowboy boots and leather jackets and mothers pushing strollers down King Street. The old downtown core looks like it's had its teeth pulled: the charming turn-of-the-century, two-storey brick buildings that line the main streets are being pulled down, flattened into parking lots or replaced by concrete office blocks. But here and there, signs of contemporary grace blossom: tucked away beside the modern City Hall is a gem of an art gallery designed by one of Canada's most renowned architects, Arthur Erickson. And at first you don't notice GM's mammoth industrial plants that employ 20,000 people.

The Rotary and Kiwanis Clubs are active here, and the Royal Canadian Legion, the Navy Club, The Polish Veterans, the Ontario Regiment; in winter, everybody's involved in minor hockey. Oshawa's cuisine reflects the ethnic mix of its population: Ukrainian, Polish, Greek,

Lebanese, German, Hungarian and good old Anglo greasy-spoon fish and chips. Oshawa is not yuppified, and, to an outsider, is remarkably unlike Toronto — though so close. The people of Oshawa figure that Toronto knows nothing about them, and that's fine with them, but they're not in any awe of Toronto. Why would they be? In the heartland of Industrial Ontario, Oshawa is Motor City, not because of the beneficence of U.S. management, but because the industry was born here at the turn of the century.

The statistics are awesome: auto exports account for $34 *billion*, or 43 per cent of Canada's manufacturing trade with the United States. In Ontario, auto makes up 60 percent of the province's exports. General Motors has 45,800 employees in Canada, Ford has 16,000 and Chrysler 12,000. Including parts manufacturing, there are 200,000 Canadians employed in auto — more than 80 per cent of them in Ontario. Yet they are all dependent, ultimately, on U.S. bosses, U.S. plants and the exigencies of American politics. This is the troubling side of the economic boom: the vulnerability of dependence. In learning to live with it, Oshawans have evolved into tough-minded, pragmatic people, at once affectionately disposed to, and wary of, The Motors.

Oshawans understand what most Canadians may not: that the billions of dollars' worth of auto trade between Canada and the United States is not really between two different countries and does not constitute free trade. The action is generated by American automakers on both sides of the border. The Big Three — General Motors, Ford and Chrysler — ensconced in their U.S. headquarters, collect the profits, direct the R&D, and decide what they will build where. The only Canadian input into the process comes via the Auto Pact, signed in 1965. The Pact furthered the integration of Canadian production into the Big Three's global plans, giving the Americans guaranteed access to the lucrative Canadian market and the Canadians guaranteed production in Canada.

At the heart of the Pact are its safeguards, which ensure that, in effect, for every vehicle sold in Canada, one must be made in Canada, with 60 per cent of its cost spent on Canadian parts or production. Thanks to the Pact, General Motors has invested $7 billion in Canada since 1980, with $2 billion going to the Oshawa operation. Without the safeguards, auto industry experts — headed by the Oshawa-based president of General Motors of Canada — believe auto production would flow south of the border.

Knowledge of these matters informs day-to-day life in Oshawa, which makes for an alert citizenry. "Everyone in town is very tuned in to what's happening in the auto industry; they're tuned in to the big picture," says Jerry Harvey, manager of GM's truck assembly plant. That means a sensitivity to international affairs and bad weather. Auto workers have a lot in common with farmers. A hailstorm hits a farmer's field, damaging the crop, and the farmer has to sit it out; there's a problem in a Detroit plant, crucial parts don't arrive in Oshawa on time, and auto workers are laid off temporarily.

For all the billions of dollars invested in state-of-the-art technology, simple accidents frequently cause million-dollar hitches. Auto's "just-in-time" inventory system means parts come in as needed; but sometimes they don't come. The first time I visited the truck plant, for a tour of the operation, the plant was unexpectedly down and hundreds of its 3,400 workers were streaming home because of a "devastating fire" south of the border which stopped shipment of parts. The plant manager couldn't say when things would be back to normal.

Auto is a high-stakes game, delicately balanced, vulnerable to the whims of consumer tastes and subject to constant pressures — accidents, fires, strikes, transportation holdups, supplier backups — that topple its equilibrium. Auto workers, then, learn to roll with conditions they have no control over and to control what they can, producing a culture that — like Saskatchewan, where one industry also dominates — is extraordinarily cohesive. As the manager of the truck plant says: "We've got 3,400 people in here, which is a bigger population than many communities, and the chances of getting us to agree on most issues are pretty slim. But one thing we all agree on is the truck. We export 80 per cent of our trucks to the U.S. Our jobs depend on our truck selling and making people happy. The truck is the most important thing. Anything that affects the truck affects us."

"This is a practical place," says the mayor, Allan Pilkey, son of Cliff Pilkey, a former head of the Ontario Federation of Labour. "People here have a good grasp on reality. Unemployment is low — around 5 per cent — and business is booming. We all agree on one thing: for us to succeed, industry has to succeed." He adds that Oshawans also like to see their politicians win. "Anybody can run and lose," says Pilkey. "I figure it's a lot easier to effect change from within rather than without. I always thought political parties ran to form the government. Ed Broadbent is an Oshawa boy. He is definitely someone who wants to win."

"You go door to door in this town," says Alderman Brian Nicholson, "and you notice that people are independent-minded. You can't tell them what to think. They're well informed. They debate ideas. They want things to work. They're a very demanding constituency." Ed won their support the hard way. Jim Palmateer, the managing editor of the *Oshawa Times*, says that when he arrived in town seven years ago, he expected to find "an NDP hotbed. You hear that Oshawa is the heartland of the NDP. You hear that labour automatically votes NDP. None of it is true." Palmateer learned his first lesson about political voting patterns when he worked in Northern Ontario in a town that was 75 per cent unionized and elected a Liberal federally and a Conservative provincially. "That lesson was amplified here in Oshawa," he says, pointing to a city council that is dominated by Conservative politicians.

Oshawans seem to enjoy confounding outsiders' expectations. They don't care what other people think, say or do, they have their own opinions — that's how they present themselves. "Think for yourself" could well be their motto. And like the rest of Canada, they are no great admirers of Toronto, the fat-cat neighbour that looms down the road. They don't mind going to Toronto for dinner and a show, but they wouldn't want to live there.

This is the climate that shaped Ed's environment in very personal terms. He grew up in a typical Oshawa family — argumentative, bristling with different opinions about everything under the sun except one thing: they were all devoted to The Motors. Yet his grandfather and uncles participated in the historic 1937 strike against GM, and the Broadbents would later support an even more contentious action, their union's 1985 breakaway from the United Auto Workers. It was no anomaly that Ed spent his high school years here as a student politician and debater, plugged into the important issues of the day. Nor is it surprising that, Toronto being so near and yet so far away, he would later be slapped with inappropriate labels by the Toronto media — which really didn't know much about where he was coming from.

Growing up in Oshawa meant growing up in prosperity. For sheer economic clout, the massive skyscrapers on Toronto's Bay Street don't hold a candle to auto. The Golden Horseshoe, stretching around the southern tip of Lake Ontario, from Oshawa in the east, past Toronto to Hamilton, Burlington and St Catharines in the west, rolls on wheels. With almost five million people and the lowest unemployment rate in the country, the Horseshoe is the most populous, most prosperous region in Canada. Throughout Southern Ontario, from Windsor to Chatham, London, St Thomas, Sarnia, Kitchener, St Catharines, Cambridge, Oakville and Oshawa, the chain of auto towns glitters, with spillovers into glass, plastics, rubber, tires, machining, tooling and steel. Auto alone accounts for 20 per cent of Canadian steel orders. And Oshawa is the capital of this Canadian auto empire. It is also the cradle that rocked Ed Broadbent — and "anybody who thinks Eddie doesn't understand the value of industry ought to have his head examined," says Eddie's Uncle Aubrey.

September 30, 1927, is the date written in the family Bible, in Ed's grandmother's hand. That was the day Jack and Bert Broadbent settled their tribe in Oshawa, chosen by Jack as the likeliest place to find work, for him and his boys. He was right, and he wasn't the only one attracted to the place. Oshawa was already a bustling auto town of 27,000 people, dominated by two institutions: the sprawling GM factory and "Parkwood," Colonel Sam McLaughlin's mini-Versailles estate on Simcoe Street North. "Parkwood" was conceived on a grandiose scale that expressed Col. Sam's vision of his place in society: it was designed by Darling and Pearson, the firm that drew up the plans for the Parliament Buildings in Ottawa, and its palatial grandeur is vivid testimony to the massive wealth that was derived from the family business. Parkwood was finished in 1917, a year before Col. Sam sold the company to General Motors.

In Parkwood's bowling alley, next to the billiard room, is a modest display of the source of the power: the charming sleighs and carriages that were crafted by Col. Sam's father in his shed in Tyrone, a village near Oshawa, starting in the 1860s. Like Jack Broadbent, Robert McLaughlin loved wood. Jack could have happily become a lumber baron, cutting it down; Robert McLaughlin liked shaping it, making axe handles, which he sold on market day in Bowmanville. From axe handles to sleighs and carriages — it was a natural evolution.

In 1876, "the Governor," as McLaughlin Senior was known, moved the family operation to Oshawa. Within a few years, he invented the special gear mechanism that would make the McLaughlin Carriage Co. a world-famous name. He rebuffed an attempt to take over his company, and by the turn of the century McLaughlin offered 143 different models, many of them designed by Sam.

Oshawa and the McLaughlin Carriage Co. were united. A fire in the company's factory in 1899 prompted the town to lend McLaughlin $50,000 to rebuild. The Governor liked to say that his company belonged to Oshawa, and Oshawans certainly felt they belonged to the company: it was by far the largest employer in town. By

1901, Oshawa workers were producing 25,000 carriages a year and sales surpassed one million dollars annually.

Then in 1905, something happened: normal people were sighted, from time to time, bouncing down rutted roads in motor-driven vehicles. Ford Motor Co. was two years old. By 1907, Sam McLaughlin had figured out where the future lay and tried his hand at making motor cars. The McLaughlin Motor Car Co. designed and built its own bodies and equipped them with a Buick engine, imported from the United States. Business was booming on both sides of the border and the McLaughlin Motor Car Co. quickly became an industrial giant. When Buick was absorbed into the burgeoning General Motors empire, Sam McLaughlin was appointed a director of GM — though McLaughlin Motor was still an independent.

But Sam's next deal would lead to the end of the Canadian name in the auto industry, to his father's sorrow. In 1915, Sam sold the carriage company — sales were declining — and signed a contract with GM to make Chevrolets in Canada. "As with Buick, we made our own bodies to my designs," said Sam, "and we always tried to design and finish them just a little better than those across the [border] line. I remember once a General Motors executive visiting in Oshawa was particularly impressed by our model of Buick. He asked us to send one to the New York office to let the boys there see what we were doing in Canada."

He did, but the car was returned hastily from the New York showroom, where a worried GM chief had said: "Get that thing out of here, and quick. It's gathering crowds — and it's no more like one of our Buicks than a St Bernard is like a dachshund!"

Soon the McLaughlin–Buick would be gone forever. General Motors was gobbling up the independents and it wanted McLaughlin. Sam was making a lot of money out of Chevrolets and saw no reason to hold out. In 1918, Sam — with five daughters and no son to take over the family business, with the prospect of making an additional fortune — sold out, becoming the first president of General Motors of Canada.

By the late '20s, when the Broadbents settled in Osh-awa, Col. Sam had "eased off" and was more occupied with his yachts and racehorses; later he would sell his lo-cal stables to another tycoon, E.P. Taylor, who renamed the McLaughlin horseracing operation Windfields Farm, which became the birthplace (in 1961) of Northern Dancer.

But the Broadbents knew little of yachts or racehorses. Within weeks of arriving, Jack joined the 8,000 employ-ees at The Motors. Thus the Broadbent–General Motors connection was forged. For more than sixty years, there has always been a Broadbent at The Motors — and there still is. Ed's younger brother David started at GM in 1961, when he was nineteen, and is still at it after twenty-six years; he has since been joined by Uncle Aubrey's two sons and a grandson. But David's two sons won't be work-ing at The Motors — one of them intends to become a la-bour lawyer, the other a policeman.

The grand old days for the Broadbents at GM are now past: Oren, who worked at The Motors with his father be-fore the war, died in 1971, having spent the post-war years as a postal clerk. Arnold died in 1975, after thirty-six years at GM. Aubrey and Reuben served thirty-eight and forty and a half years respectively, and are happily retired, as is Bill, the baby of the family, whose thirty-eight years of service were interrupted by the war. Percy was always regarded as a newcomer, because he came to The Motors late and put in only twenty-five years. Collec-tively, the Broadbent men have more than 250 years of service to GM, and they're proud of it. At one point there were four Broadbent tool-and-die makers, then the high-est-paid job in the plant. They took pride in their work. In the early days, they built practically everything: all models of Chevrolet, Pontiac, Buick, Oldsmobile, LaSalle and Cadillac. (Since the Auto Pact was signed in 1965, production has narrowed to one Pontiac model, an Olds-mobile, a Buick, and a line of trucks.)

The Broadbents would work their way through the De-pression relatively unscathed, though layoffs were fre-quent, there was never enough cash to go around and most things were home-made. Life was plain and simple, nothing fancy; they made do. Jack bought a modest two-storey, four-bedroom house at 349 Jarvis Street, where he and Bert would live until they died. The younger boys graduated from ocvi (Oshawa Collegiate and Vocational Institute), then the only high school in town — located close to Parkwood, from whose circular driveway Col. Sam's chauffeur-driven limousine would glide out, like a monarch's.

The Broadbent home was bursting with energy, reverberating with the comings and goings of the clan and "great old discussions around the dining room table," in the words of Ed's Uncle Bill. "We always talked politics and you'd always hear fifty different opinions on every subject." (Though debates around the dinner table remained a feature of Broadbent life long after Jack and Bert passed away, the family remained reserved on a personal level. Broadbents did not talk about private feelings and they didn't talk about each other. Until I told him, Ed never knew his father had been a debater.)

Jack planted a huge vegetable garden in the back yard and evolved into what his children regarded as a "more intellectual" frame of mind. He loved to read and impressed upon the family his egalitarian, socially progressive views; at the same time, he never lost his love of the north and inculcated in his boys a respect for working with their hands.

Every year, as sure as the seasons changed, Jack would be laid off at The Motors and he'd head up north to find work on a logging crew. Reuben remembers accompanying his father to North Bay one summer. "If there was a job to be found anywhere, my father would get it. He was the hardest-working man I ever came across. We went into the bush — it was before chain saws — and my father was running the camp. I worked for him clearing brush out for the horses to come in and drag the logs out to the road."

Back at home, after work at The Motors, Jack loved to have his family around him. "We used to say," says Edna, "that Father would gather his family at home and then he'd take a book and read." While he read, the boys argued and Bert knitted, cooked, cleaned, preserved everything under the sun and made quilts with her women friends.

Into this menagerie on October 29, 1930, stepped Mary Welsh, the new bride of Percy Broadbent. Percy was the first son to get married; he and Mary lived with Jack and Bert until they found their own place, just up the street. Mary Welsh and Percy Broadbent were madly in love.

If any couple had high hopes, it was Perce and Mary. Their friends considered them an exceptionally charming pair: unlike many couples, where one partner tends to dominate, both of them were attractive, bright, high-spirited and outgoing. Mary's friends describe her as "a people person," though she was more genteel than Percy, who was a boisterous young man-about-town. The major difference between them was that Percy loved to argue and Mary did not. Mary was, says her son David, "very sensitive."

Ed's beloved mother was a complex woman. Mary was the beautiful, tiny, black-haired daughter of Patrick Welsh, an Irish-Catholic carpenter in Tweed, Ont., where she was born on August 17, 1911. Her mother, May Scriver, was descended from the Schreibers — German Palatines (a Rhine state) who had sided with Martin Luther in the reformation of the church. Ed's direct ancestor, Albertus Schreiber, a Protestant, emigrated from Germany to the United States, landing in New York City in 1709.

But another battle would precipitate another migration: during the American Revolution, Albertus' grandson, Jacob, fought for the British from 1776 to 1783, then joined the stream of United Empire Loyalists trekking north to Canada. Jacob died in 1800 in Adolphustown, the major Loyalist landing place near Kingston, Ont. The Scriver farm was established the same year in Prince Edward County, a bountiful peninsula fringed with sand dunes that abuts onto Lake Ontario just west of Kingston. This was the cradle of Ed's family on his mother's side, and it is at the Scriver family cemetery in Ameliasburg that his ancestors are buried.

Much of this Scriver lore was gleaned from Stewart Scriver, a direct descendant of Ed's mother; he and Ed are cousins but they have never met. Stewart owns Courage My Love, a funky antique clothing and jewellery store in Toronto's Kensington Market. His most surprising information is that Ed is descendend, on his mother's side, from one of the founders of the CCF in Saskatchewan — and in the NDP, that's blue blood. Stewart's grandfather Thomas Edward Scriver — Mary Scriver's cousin — has Scriver Lake in northern Saskatchewan named after him in recognition of his contribution to the province and the party.

T.E. Scriver published the *Wolseley News* in Wolseley, Sask., a small farming community 65 miles from Regina. "Tommy Douglas used to come to our house, and my grandfather and J.S. Woodsworth talked Tommy into going into politics," says Stewart. "We talked politics every day of my entire life, until I came east." At a Maple Leaf Gardens rally in Toronto in the '60s, Stewart jammed his way through the crowd to get close to Tommy Douglas. As the NDP leader passed by, Stewart said one word: "Wolseley." Tommy stopped in his tracks. "What's your name?" Stewart Scriver told him. Tommy beamed. "T.E. was one of the first ones," he said.

Ed gets his "crusading spirit" from the Scrivers, according to Marjory Scriver. (Needless to say, Ed's "fightin' Irish" side claims him too.) Mary's first cousin, Marjory Scriver is another family historian; she writes a column for the *Campbellford Herald* and the *Cobourg Daily Star*, small-town papers in small-town Ontario. "With the Scrivers, if something's wrong we can't rest until we've done something about it," says Marjory, whose own crusades concern environmental and health issues. "The Scrivers are all for justice. We believe in speaking up for what we think is right. When you look into the family history, it sounds as if we've been protesting and arguing about freedom for centuries."

But May Scriver Welsh, Ed's grandmother, would not participate for long in the family debates. She died in childbirth in Peterborough, Ont., when Mary, Ed's mother, was ten years old. Patrick Welsh was left to cope with seven children. The family was fractured, as much by religion as May's untimely death. The Scriver relatives wanted to take the children in, but Patrick Welsh wouldn't allow it. "He was a real loyal Irish Catholic," says Marjory Scriver, "and it seems he didn't want his children brought up Protestant." The local Catholic priest put a lot of pressure on Welsh to ensure that the children weren't lost to the faith; so severe were religious divisions in Ontario that a Roman Catholic orphanage was deemed a better place for Catholic children than a Protestant aunt or uncle. The youngest child was put up for adoption, the two older boys boarded in Peterborough, two younger boys were put into an orphanage; the middle girls, Mary and her sister Rosaline, were sent to foster parents and then on to a Roman Catholic orphanage in Cobourg. It was a traumatic separation for the children after the loss of their mother; subsequent events only increased Mary's yearning to reunite her family.

Within a few years, Patrick Welsh migrated to Oshawa and got a job at The Motors. He took Mary and Rosaline out of the orphanage and brought them to live in Oshawa. At first they boarded in a rooming house close to their father and later, when he could afford it, they lived with him in a small flat. The sisters, by now teenagers, did housework and homework, looking after their father and going to OCVI. Mary felt a constant, anxious responsibility for her siblings, who remained scattered. Her character was shaped by adversity; she evolved, against all odds, into an optimistic woman, devoted to family, determined to hold things together. "She never let life get her down," says Ed. (As her marriage deteriorated, Mary concealed her anger and depression from the world; only Velma, her daughter, knew the depths of Mary's pain.)

Mary's childhood, then, was a Dickensian struggle against loneliness, poverty and loss; it's not hard to imagine the appeal of Bert and Jack Broadbent's warm home. The Broadbents were a deeply rooted family, exuding an aggressive self-confidence that came from surviving tough conditions — in the bush and in The Motors. They believed in the Canadian dream, and they had what Mary wanted more than anything: security and love. At the same time, they took some getting used to. Mary never did feel fully comfortable about their taste for hot discussion, and she passed on to Ed her dislike for emotional confrontation. When Percy would get ranting, she would leave the room. The only way she got back at him — publicly — was by supporting the Liberals, which outraged his Tory passions.

When Mary met Percy, he was a stocky, red-haired dynamo, a hotshot young salesman at Oshawa Wholesale, selling groceries to retail stores. The drudgery of The Motors was not for Percy; he was going to make something of himself. Women were impressed; he was considered a great catch. "Percy was such a gentleman," says Mary's sister Rosaline Maddill, who is now in her seventies. "He was so successful. I would never have guessed how he was going to turn out." Marjory Scriver remembers the young Percy as "a charming man, the type you couldn't help but like. He had a good brain, and he was very thoughtful."

Mary was a secretary in Oshawa Wholesale's warehouse, still living with her father and Rosaline. Percy would come in to the office and flirt with her; she was shy and delighted by his attentions. He couldn't help but notice her. Less than five feet tall, with blue-black hair, freckled skin and the sweetest spirit, Mary was a charmer. He was twenty-one, she was nineteen, when they married in 1930 in the Anglican church. A Roman Catholic, Mary "converted" to Protestantism and raised her children as Anglicans. Deeply religious, she was active in the church all her life. The early years of the marriage were wonderful. Velma, their eldest, was born on August 10, 1931, named after Percy's baby sister who died in infancy. John Edward came along five years later, on March 21, 1936; and the baby, David, was born on October 10, 1942.

Mary is described by all who knew her as "a great woman." Since she lived her life in the obscurity typical of women of her generation, it is difficult to extract the record of her achievements. She was the sort of woman who, unacknowledged, did things for people in the community; she took a special interest in disadvantaged children, though she would never have called them that. One story: Ed's Uncle Reuben has a mentally handicapped, diabetic daughter. Elinor, who is now in her twenties, seems much younger than her years, speaks in a loud staccato voice and does not have an extensive social life. But Aunt Mary was Elinor's special friend. For years they had a regular luncheon date whereby on alternating turns each would play hostess, pick a restaurant and pay for the meal.

Elinor's lunches with Mary were a highlight of the girl's life, but one date landed Mary in a terribly embarrassing situation. (This story comes from Ed, who eventually got his mother to see the humour in it.) Once, when it was Elinor's turn to pick, she spotted an ad in the *Oshawa Times* for a restaurant that featured "exotic dancers." Elinor had no idea what exotic dancers did — nor did Mary — but they agreed this was a lovely idea, to eat lunch while enjoying unusual artistic entertainment. They traipsed down to the restaurant, where a man at the door tried to discourage them, but Elinor and Mary were not to be dissuaded. In they marched, sat down, ordered lunch and then were treated to the spectacle of strippers removing their clothes. Mary was mortified, frozen in her seat while Elinor loudly laughed her head off throughout the entire entertainment — to the consternation of the strippers and their male audience. "My mother didn't want anybody to know what happened," says David, "but she made the mistake of telling one of us, and we told the others." It became a family joke.

"I loved Aunt Mary," says Elinor, beaming, showing off her scrapbook. She has painstakingly cut and pasted pictures of her favourite pop stars — Michael Jackson and Michael J. Fox — next to newspaper photographs of her Uncle Ed, Aunt Velma and Uncle David planting a tree in memory of their mother at Oshawa's Boys and Girls Club, where Mary dedicated many years of work.

Mary died in 1983, yet to this day Velma, Ed and David become very emotional talking about her, their eyes filling with tears. Ed was devoted to her; he says that she was "without a doubt the most important influence on my life. She was a wonderful, warmhearted, generous woman — she was the same way with her children and her neighbours' children. She made no distinctions. She loved people." Mary, who sought love so keenly as a child, was deeply loved as a mother.

Velma and Mary: the two women who strongly influenced Ed during his formative years, are very different women. Ed learned his feminism early, from Velma, though she wouldn't have used the word back then and he wouldn't have known it; he also picked up his voice inflections from her. Jay Scott, *The Globe and Mail*'s film critic, recalls that when he moved in next door to Velma and her family in Toronto's Riverdale district, he didn't know who she was. "But I used to hear her all the time, in the garden, calling out to Barry [her husband] and her kids. I got used to her voice. She likes to talk. One day the TV was on and I heard Velma's voice. I looked out in the garden, to say hello, but she wasn't there." Scott was puzzled, until he noticed that Ed Broadbent was on TV, with Velma's voice emanating from her brother's mouth.

Called Judy as a kid, Velma is a nurse and a long-time NDP activist, deeply involved (as is David) in local riding politics. Five years older than Ed and further to the left than either of her brothers, she is the family radical. She has short, reddish hair (like her father's) faded to pale blond, and a lively, freckled face, shadowed by sudden sadness when she talks about her parents' troubles. The most outstanding feature of Velma's personality is her creative spark. She communicates a keen insight into the characters who inhabit her life and, at the same time, strong political convictions.

Velma was a tomboy who grew up something of a rascal and never quite curbed herself. She figures she disappointed her ladylike mother. "I was the first child, and my father took me fishing and bought me hockey skates and a puck," says Velma who, unlike Ed, enjoyed a warm relationship with her father in childhood. "I always felt I was as good as any boy. But I felt I failed my mother. I never lived up to her nice, genteel image."

Velma remembers her childhood as a comfortable time. Growing up in Oshawa, she says, Percy Broadbent's children didn't identify themselves as working class. "Dad was a salesman, and we were well off compared to a lot of people. We went up to the cottage in the summer, we were a close family, we felt we could do anything we wanted to do. Ed's very best quality comes from our father. Dad taught us that everybody is equal, that nobody was better than us and nobody was beneath us." Except perhaps the union members whom Percy looked down on.

Percy the Golden Boy: by the late '30s, selling groceries for an aggressive, expanding company, Percy was the Broadbent who had it made. He was a young businessman with a pretty wife and three children. He had a good job, a shiny new car, a promising future. He dressed conservatively and smartly, his shoes were always shined, he liked to smoke cigars, vote Tory and play the big-shot — all of which may help to explain why his brothers, except for Reuben, weren't inclined to help him when he later fell on hard times.

During the war years, he lived the high life, working and playing hard — the Great Gatsby scaled down to Oshawa, Ont. With Mary in tow, Percy and his gang would go dancing, take weekend trips to Detroit and Buffalo — Toronto was too dull — and go sailing on Lake Ontario. The house was always full of people and Percy and Mary generously shared what they had. But Percy was running with a crowd that drank and gambled, activities that increasingly took up his spare time and excluded his wife. Somewhere along the way, he lost control.

But before he did, family life was happy. "We were well nourished," Velma laughs. "Mother was a Jewish-mother type — you know, big dinners, dumplings, three types of dessert at every meal." Mary also waited on her men hand and foot, which annoyed Velma and instilled in her the resolve to bring up her own sons differently — which she did.

"Summers were incredible," says Velma. "Father would come in with crates of strawberries and raspberries and Mother's preserving and cooking would go on and on. Chili sauce, pickles, grape jam, never one pie but two. Ed and Dave must miss it. They loved her grape jam and her pies." Yes, Ed loved the pies and his mother's devoted attention when he came home from playing hockey or boxing at the Oshawa Boxing Club, with his younger brother David tagging along after him.

Percy's children adored their grandparents. Going over to Bert and Jack's house on Jarvis Street, they would be absorbed into the action. "Gran was always hanging out clothes on the line, ironing, preserving, knitting us socks and mittens," says Velma. "Grandfather would be digging in the garden, or reading." Bert would invite everybody to stay for dinner; Velma and Ed would see their Broadbent uncles in action. "As adults, they weren't that close," says Velma. "They're reserved but argumentative, all of them very assertive." Perce was the most argumentative, the most gregarious. And always, in the background, loomed The Motors.

In 1936, the year Ed was born, General Motors earned $200 million in profits, the largest in its history, according to the *New York Times*. The company then tried to reduce wages for the fifth consecutive time; GM's Oshawa employees got mad. In March of 1937, they joined the United Auto Workers, affiliated with the Congress of Industrial Organizations (CIO), led by American labour leader John L. Lewis. A month later, The Motors was hit by its first major strike, precipitated by a combination of lousy working conditions, corporate profits and wage cuts. 3700 MOTOR WORKERS STRIKE AT OSHAWA blared a *Toronto Star* headline on April 8, 1937. One hundred RCMP officers were sent in from Ottawa (where Prime Minister Mackenzie King complied with a request from Ontario Premier Mitch Hepburn) in addition to 100 Ontario Provincial Police officers; both the federal and provincial governments promised to throw their resources behind

General Motors in its fight against John L. Lewis, the CIO and the auto workers' union.

It was not an easy time to go on strike — not that it ever is. "Things were hard then," says Ed's Uncle Aubrey. "The average man on the line in '37 made between $500 and $700 a year — in a good year." Most workers could count on being laid off regularly for long periods; by the early '30s, the workforce had been slashed from 8,000 to 4,600 — and if you had a job, you were supposed to be grateful. Aubrey and his wife Evelyn lived in a couple of rooms, in a flat in a house. When the strike began, Evelyn was just home from the hospital with their first baby. How did they survive? Aubrey and Evelyn shrug. "You just existed," says Evelyn.

Aubrey, now in his seventies, is a large, pink-cheeked, white-haired gentleman who still plays golf and goes moose hunting in the fall. He wears the heavy gold GM ring that signifies twenty-five years' loyal service; his ring has two diamond chips, each representing five years of extra duty. "It was a good job," Aubrey beams. Yet in his own quiet, self-deprecating way, Aubrey was a tough character. He is distinguished in the family for having been the only CCFer in the bunch, which contributed to the heat around the family dining room table. Not that he's militant, he says mildly. "We're all anti-communists. We're middle-of-the-road people. But back in 1934, in Depression days, I saw men crying on the line, afraid they'd lose their jobs. The line was speeded up — conditions were terrible, that was before the union came in — and the men couldn't keep up. They were desperate. Desperate for work, desperate for food. I didn't like the way a lot of people weren't taken care of and it wasn't their fault. I felt the CCF was a little more for the underdog. I guess I was the first in the family that considered them a reasonable party."

The Broadbent boys and their father, who was a strong union man, were all out on the picket line — except for Percy. They were confronted by some frightening prospects. Premier Hepburn (a Liberal) had come to power promising "to swing well to the left," but he swung hard right against the strikers, sending a specially formed, 400-man militia known as Hepburn's Hussars (or Sons of Mitches, as they were called in Oshawa) to take up machine-gun positions against the workers, to guard Canada against the threat of U.S. union organizers working "hand-in-glove with international communism," so Hepburn told the press. The militia was "issued live ammunition with instructions to shoot the strikers at the knees if ordered to fire," wrote Bob Linton in *A History of Local 222.*

But the men stood their ground, maintaining peace on the picket line. An American newsreel cameraman, desperate for some action, tried to bribe a couple of strikers, for five dollars each, to stage a fight. There were no takers. No one was shot and public support gradually mobilized behind the workers. Twenty-five thousand people marched on Queen's Park in support of the strikers, and Mackenzie King, in Ottawa, strove to disassociate himself from Hepburn. Two Ontario Cabinet ministers resigned from Hepburn's Cabinet — Arthur Roebuck, attorney general, and David Croll, labour minister — in opposition to the Premier's handling of the strike. They accused Hepburn of being undemocratic. Roebuck reminded the Premier that in a democracy the state must necessarily remain impartial in an industrial dispute and that labour has a clear right to organize. *The Globe and Mail*, published by George McCullagh, a close friend of Hepburn and an ardent supporter of Hepburn's strategy, hit back at Roebuck and Croll, asserting that they should "fall in line enthusiastically or give way . . .".

Yet it was the Premier who had to give way, in more ways than one. Fifteen days after the strike started, the UAW won its first contract; the Broadbent boys went back to work. Hepburn's Liberal Party subsequently declined as a power in the province for almost fifty years. The Oshawa strike was also a turning point for the CCF in Ontario. In the 1943 election, the Liberals won only fifteen seats compared to thirty-four for the CCF and thirty-eight for the Conservatives.

"As a landmark in the history of the Canadian labour movement, the Oshawa strike of 1937 stands next only to the Winnipeg General Strike," wrote Irving Abella in *On Strike*. "The achievements of the Oshawa strikers in fighting and defeating both the power of big business and the provincial government inspired workers throughout the country." Without a penny of aid from the CIO, "the Oshawa strikers had won a great victory for themselves but, even more important for the CIO, they had created the psychology of success and the enthusiasm needed for a massive organizing effort."

Those were heroic days, but the Broadbents downplay their part. They weren't union leaders, they say; they were just ordinary men out on a picket line. Aubrey thinks it's more important that "we'd already gone on strike before the CIO ever organized the plant." Gentle Aubrey gets serious. "I was in the body shop then and it was a nasty place, a rough place to work. We were working with molten lead, covering welding joints with lead, and conditions were so bad that things reached a boiling point when the company speeded up the line on us." In February of '37, sixty-eight men in the body shop, Aubrey among them, walked out. "We shut the plant down. We were on strike before the UAW ever came near us." That is a point of pride. He does not add that the body shop was the most militant unit in the company and that he was a strong force within it. He was his father's son, and the Broadbent men didn't kowtow to anybody.

But Jack had little more than four years to live. He would die young, in 1941, at the age of fifty-seven, of the family scourge: cancer. There's a picture of him taken that year, shortly before his death. Oren, his eldest son, is home on leave from the war, standing stiffly in his army uniform. Bert is stout and determined next to Oren, and then Jack, looking frail and handsome, is smiling into the camera. From a fourteen-year-old orphan in Parry Sound, he had come a long way, with great spirit, and he was proud of his family. He didn't live to see the downfall of his son Percy — that was left to Bert, who had had such high hopes for her third child. She was protected, however, by the attentions of her other children, and after she died in 1976, shortly before Percy's death, they contributed money for a stained-glass window in her memory, that's now in the chapel of Christ Church, where she was a driving force in the women's auxiliary. Percy would not be so honoured.

By the late '40s, Percy was hiding rye bottles around the house. Still a jovial figure in public, behind closed doors he was becoming hostile, verbally abusive and drunk; his wife suspected he was unfaithful to her. Their battles increased in intensity, frightening and involving Velma, who would try to protect her mother and fight with her father.

Speaking about this period of his life, Ed seems distressed and baffled. His memories of his father are "overlaid by Dad's alcoholism," says Ed. He was afraid of his father's "drunken rages" and remembers feeling threatened by a sense of dread "about what he might do." Ed was hit, "but I'm not even sure about that, I recall one occasion, but I don't know . . . maybe I've blocked it out." His reaction was typical of many children of alcoholic parents. He withdrew, occupying himself with school, studies, friends; and he would buy his mother little presents from money he saved up from his paper route. He felt bad that he couldn't do enough for her, guilty that he couldn't protect her.

Even before Percy's drinking got out of hand, Ed was not close to his father. Casting back over his childhood, he recalls only one happy moment with Percy, and even that is poignant: "Dad was pushing me on a swing and I was in a state of near-ecstasy. You see, it thrilled me so much that he was doing something with me." This is the only father-son scene he is able to recreate, and he does so with painful clarity. "I can visualize it still, my father pushing me on that swing, as one of the happiest moments of my life."

Ted Maidman, the scout leader, remembers the young boy who was so eager for paternal attention. Now in his sixties and a little stooped over, Ted has retired from The Motors after forty years and works at Canadian Tire "just for the fun of it" when he isn't cycling in marathons. He lives with Joan, his wife of forty years, in an Oshawa apartment, where they collect treasures from their travels — one china cabinet is filled with hedgehogs from around the world. Hanging on the wall, visible from the front door, is a Picasso print of a child tenderly holding a bird. "That's Ted's favourite," says Joan.

The Maidmans are the kind of people who are always helping out in the community. Ted started up one scout troop and led another — the Third Oshawa Troop, to which Ed belonged — for ten years. The troop met every Tuesday at Oshawa United Church, from 7 P.M. to 9 P.M. Ted taught his boys signals, knots and games, and took them out on hikes and camping trips in which Joan often participated. "When I think back on all the time Ted spent with us when I was a kid," says Ed, "how he put himself out to do those things with us, I really appreciate his generosity of spirit."

The Maidmans had a keen appreciation of Ed's spirit. As a fourteen-year-old boy scout, Ed intrigued them. "Some kids tend to rush in fast," says Ted. "Not Ed. He would hold back and figure out what we were doing and wait until he could do it right. You could see the wheels turning. We'd have a game, say a scavenger hunt, and you'd tell the kids 'go' and they'd be off like a shot, except Ed. You'd see him standing back, thinking, putting himself in your shoes and figuring where you would have hidden the clues. He was clever."

Joan says, "He could read people."

Ted agrees. "He was one step ahead in his thinking. Even in those days, you'd never want to get into an argument with him. Ed was just one of the boys in the troop, but he was . . ." Ted turns to his wife, seeking her assistance.

"He was a shining light," says Joan.

Ted nods. "Didn't you always say he was a kid who'd go places?"

"No," says Joan, who considers herself psychic. "I predicted he'd be known throughout the land." She blushes, and crosses her arms defensively over her Mickey Mouse t-shirt. "Don't get us wrong. We're not political. When Eddie first ran we helped him because we figured he'd be a good politician, that's all, because he's a good person. I'm interested in the person, not the party."

As for Percy's broken dreams, the pragmatic Joan Maidman says bluntly: "That was the story in every other household in the '30s. The things we never got because of the Depression, the things we couldn't do — well, we all had it tough. But Eddie now" — she looks at an old photo of Ed — "his mother *loved* him. You can see it in his face. I was in their house once, and I felt it — his mother's warmth and love for him. The loved children are the ones who can leave home and go out into the world. He's fuelled by love, not anger."

Ed did everything he could to avoid his father's anger. By the time Percy was hitting rock bottom, Ed was busy elsewhere, absorbed in adolescent activities. As he says, he is "good at repressing bad news." He learned to do it early in life, just as he seems to have been driven to excel — though always under cover as "just one of the guys." But he was different.

The bucolic '50s, the era of *Father Knows Best*, was not a period of domestic contentment for the Broadbent family. Ed likes to say that he loved growing up in the '50s, but he's talking about the culture, not the home life. "It was a very, very emotional time for Mary," says Rosaline. "She said she never thought of such things happening to her. She was such a good wife." For Mary, the options were limited: she was wedded for better or for worse, divorce was unthinkable, and she had to keep her problems to herself.

Even her best friends were never fully aware of what was happening to Mary's marriage. Marjory Scriver was so close to Mary that "we had mental telepathy going — we'd get the feeling to call each other up, and sure enough something would be bothering one of us." Yet Mary would refer only "obliquely" to her troubles, says Marjory. "She was loyal to Percy. She wouldn't spill over to anybody. And in her childhood Mary had seen men drink. She knew what it was like. Her own father drank quite a bit, like a lot of Irishmen. But Mary knew how to get along." She did rely on her sister Rosaline, and would take Percy up to visit Rosaline and Murray Maddill in Peterborough. The Maddills ran a strict Christian home, no smoking, no drinking, but Rosaline was aware that Perce brought along a bottle of booze on his visits. "He hid it outside," says Rosaline, "but we knew." Marjory Scriver remembers one time when Mary brought Perce up to the Scrivers' cottage on the Trent River. "We were sitting around at the beach, having a barbecue, and you could see that Perce was . . . well . . . you didn't actually see him drink, but he was dozy and happy, no trouble to anybody."

As Mary struggled to maintain respectability, Percy's gambling became compulsive. He lost their home, to gambling debts, and in 1950, the year Ed started high school, Percy lost his job at Oshawa Wholesale. "My father's decline was hard on us," says Ed, with an awkward tilt of his head, looking suddenly very vulnerable. "Yes, it was traumatic. The psychic sense of damage . . . they say the longest drop is from the lower-middle class to below . . ."

Percy was taken on, almost as a favour, as a clerk at The Motors, in the department that made seat covers; a family friend, a GM executive, kindly "made the arrangements" that braked Percy's descent. Still, it was a terrible come-down for a high flyer. Percy was only forty-one years old but his bright future was eclipsed; he would take a night job stocking shelves at a grocery store he used to sell to, in an effort to stay away from drinking, and he would remain at GM until he retired at sixty-five. By then his life was brightened by his sons' accomplishments; he lived to see Ed leader of the NDP, with his own Tory rantings transformed quite comfortably into ardent defences of New Democratic policy. "Perce was so wonderfully proud of Ed," says Marjory Scriver, "that it was beautiful to see. Ed was the greatest thing in his life. He'd always say, 'Ed did it on his own. We never had any money to give him. We couldn't help him.' Perce was amazed at what Ed accomplished. He couldn't get over it." But it wasn't until his father's death that Ed was able to come to terms with Percy.

Reuben was the only brother who stayed close to Perce and Mary. There's a sense that the other brothers, strait-laced in their own fashion, avoided Percy, out of shame or impatience with his dissolute ways. But as Percy deterio-rated, Reuben helped out. He is said to be the spitting image of Percy, short and square and a little "portly," as Reuben would say, with the Broadbent red hair faded to white. Now in his seventies, he lives in a big, solid, two-storey brick house with his second wife Dorothy and their daughter Elinor. The house, just around the corner from The Motors, looks like a doctor's house, not a worker's bungalow. Inside, Reuben's carpet is plush and new, his furniture French Provincial, his standard of living upper crust — though not his manner. Reuben points out, mod-estly, that he is the only Broadbent who has three dia-mond chips in his GM ring. He's also very specific about his "forty and a half years" service to The Motors. (Ed's uncles talk about their "service to The Motors" like sol-diers devoted to the army; this attitude seems to have carried over to Ed, who spent years during high school and university in military training, which he loved. The GM connection also forged a spirit of corporate loyalty that survives in Ed today.)

Like Aubrey, Reuben is a genial philosopher who looks as if he had worked outside on a tractor all his life, but for many decades at The Motors he hardly saw the out-doors, let alone his children. Looking back, he regrets all those weekends and double shifts he worked, but he did it for the money — which came in handy for his investing.

"They call me the capitalist," chuckles Reuben. "I've al-ways had that stigma. I used to take a lot of ribbing." He didn't mind. "I've always been better off than the rest of them," he says. During the '37 strike he walked the picket line with his brothers but spent more time in his broker's office. "I was a steward in the tool-and-die de-partment but I wasn't too active in the union. I didn't smoke and I didn't drink and I'd go to those union meet-ings and sit in a roomful of smoke and someone would get up to speak who was half-cut and I thought it was a waste of time. But I learned something from that strike."

And what was that? Mischievous grin: "How to play crib." Pause. Eyes twinkle. "But the union was necessary." Isn't that a big admission for a capitalist and a conservative? Shrug. "Oh, I can afford to be a New Democrat now. But the real Conservative of all of us was Perce. You should have heard him." Shakes his head. "Perce was always anti-union." Then a new admission: "I was as strong a Conservative as Perce," says Reuben, "and I had my misgivings when Ed went NDP." But now Reuben's got an NDP sign up on his lawn. Why did he switch? "Because the other guys are so rotten. I thought Stanfield was an honest man, and Dief was quite a speaker. I had no use for Trudeau. Mulroney and Turner . . . . Well, all I can say about politicians is that a man's word should be as good as his bond. If his word's no good, if you can't trust him, what's the use? Ed's an honest boy, and he hasn't changed."

Reuben figures he and Mary had a bond: they were both married to alcoholics. Reuben, however, did what Mary couldn't. He divorced his wife after twenty years of marriage in 1958, and "around that time I spent many a Sunday night with Perce and Mary, playing rummy for nickels." Their companionship helped Reuben through hard times. He got custody of his three children and two years later married again, happily.

"I was the first Broadbent to get a divorce," says Reuben, "and I should have done it years earlier. Mary and I had a lot in common. Nobody wants a drinkin' person around. And she couldn't stop him from bringing it in the house." But still, says Reuben, "Perce wasn't so bad. No one can say he was anti-social and he never did a mean thing that I knew of. He had an independent spirit. He had a lot of friends. He knew everybody in town — but that was part of the problem. He was a salesman, and salesmen have to travel a lot and they have to drink. That's how it started. Perce had a problem. And Mary was a brick."

Though Percy tried Alcoholics Anonymous, he didn't stick with it, and family life was grim during Ed's high school years. Velma and David, the eldest and the youngest, were the most obviously affected. They had been closer to their father as children and were more involved with his decline. Ed, the middle child, had come along during Percy's early career highs, when he was on the road most of the time. Later, when the storms hit, Ed cleared out. In the evenings, he would go down the street and knock on the door of Jim Carson, one of his high school teachers. Carson remembers Ed asking to baby-sit in return for a quiet place to work. Or Ed would call up his pal Reg Gutsole to do homework with him at the *Oshawa Times*, where Ed had a part-time job in circulation.

"I was a paperboy for five years," Ed told *Today* magazine in 1981. "I signed up the most new customers several years in a row and won trips to Buffalo with other paper carriers. Once, three or four of us slipped away from the others — a little free enterprise on our part — to our very first burlesque show. My reaction was like that of any other healthy twelve-year-old boy seeing for the first time the substantial, unnamed parts of the female anatomy. It was quite exciting. Buffalo always symbolized the high point of an evil, but essentially attractive, existence." The other memories Ed recounted for public consumption were more Norman Rockwell-ish: singing the *Messiah* at St George's Anglican Church, where he was a choirboy and acquired his love for classical music; buying a set of encyclopedias with his paper-route money; working after school in a men's-wear shop; being chosen by the Rotary Club for an Adventure in Citizenship program which took him to Ottawa, when he was thirteen or fourteen, to be photographed standing beside the Peace Tower with Oshawa MP Mike Starr, whom he would defeat in 1968; helping write Central Collegiate's student constitution when he was the grade nine class president; belonging to a current affairs club "where we all read *Time* magazine, god help us."

Ed gave no sign of the family turmoil at home, but Velma was deeply torn by her mother's suffering and her fractured loyalty to her father. David, the youngest, afflicted from birth with a muscular problem that made his legs weak, was in many ways the most vulnerable. (He chooses not to discuss these years.)

"Ed wasn't aware of a lot of what was going on," says Velma. "He has the protective veneer, many men do, that lets them shut out the things they don't want to see." She pauses, her eyes watering. "It's still hard to talk about it." Velma was caught in the middle between her parents. She was her mother's confidante; she knew too much for her own good, and it took her years to let go of the pain of those years. "I begged Mother to leave Father but she wouldn't," says Velma. "They were so different in personality and I didn't understand then that they loved each other deeply. Mother was such a gentle woman, yet ours is a debating, argumentative family, Ed included. Even a friendly political discussion bothered her. She hated scenes. She didn't like any kind of confrontation. When Ed went into politics, she was very affected by how the media treated him. Whenever anything negative was said about him, she would take it personally. She was always there to stroke him and defend him. I used to call him up and give him shit if I was mad at something he'd said, but I don't do it anymore, not since Mother died." (If anyone tries to criticize Ed in her presence, Velma leaps to his defence.)

Mary's dominant instinct was to keep things going, and she did. Through the worst period she remained, to the outside world, cheerful and energetic, active in the community, in the church, in the Boys Club. If her husband was a profound disappointment, her son Ed could not have pleased her more: he was chosen an outstanding student four years in a row, he was president of the Student's Council when he was only in grade eleven, class valedictorian in grade thirteen. "Ed likes to do well," says Velma. Indeed: he is remembered vividly by his high school teachers as "an overachiever," according to Jim Carson, who taught English at Central Collegiate and later became principal. Carson is now retired from teaching but still active in the United Church. "Ed was a deep thinker," says Carson, "but I wouldn't call him a sobersides. He was always a popular kid." Carson lived close to

Ed's home on Central Park at Eulalie, and "in those days," he says, "that was the wrong side of the tracks, populated by the European immigrants, the lower-middle class and the labourers. The doctors and lawyers lived in the north end and sent their kids to O'Neill [formerly called OCVI], which was *the* school, but I preferred teaching at Central. Our kids worked harder."

Ab Robins, Ed's math teacher, concurs. Now retired, he taught at OCVI from 1939 to 1950 and moved to Central the year it opened in 1950, which was Ed's first year in high school. "Our kids were working class, maybe, but they were smarter than up at O'Neill," says Robins. "I shouldn't say this, I'll get in trouble, but in my subject, maths and physics, we turned out more engineers and doctors than they did at O'Neill. And we had great school spirit."

The kids at Central were hungry for knowledge, and Ed was one of the hungriest. Robins still remembers the stir when Ed was elected student council president when he was in grade eleven, "because presidents were always in grade twelve or thirteen. Ed just had an unusual talent," says Robins. "He had leadership qualities. It's funny. Me, I'm a Liberal, and my wife's a Liberal, and Jim Carson is a Tory, but we all vote for Ed. We vote for the man." Jim Carson added: "We've educated our children to think for themselves. They don't vote for a party just because their parents did. Times have changed. I don't think it makes much sense to vote for a party with a lousy leader."

Ed's friends from Central Collegiate aren't surprised by his current popularity. "Ed was a superachiever and I think everybody recognized it," says Reg Gutsole, "but it didn't alienate him from people. Superachieving came easy to Ed, but he never got a big head." Reg's comedic soul still shines brightly, though moderated by the responsibilities of an Oshawa elementary school principal. Reg's Dad worked at The Motors for forty-seven years, and Reg was the first in his family to go to university, as were many of Ed's friends.

Reg and Ed were a team: they were the voices from Central Collegiate on *High Time for Teen Time*, an Oshawa radio show, and they were masters of ceremonies for Central's Christmas Capers. Reg remembers one of their gags. "I came out on stage carrying a cardboard box dripping wet at one corner. Ed would say, 'Where are you going with that box? What's that dripping? Cider?' And he'd put out his finger to taste the stuff. Then I'd take a puppy out of the box." Reg laughs. "Real cornball stuff."

Reg's wife Marlene, also a teacher and a former student at Central, remembers looking up to "Ed and Reg and those guys: they were the ones who came up with the laughs and kept the school going. They were our idols. They were the exciting people."

With Bev Bennett, his girlfriend in grade thirteen, Ed co-authored Central Chatter, a column for the *Oshawa Times*, signed Benny and Ed. Benny was like Ed: she was involved in everything and she even — unusual for a girl in that era — became president of the student council, though the principal advised her not to run because of her gender. Today, Bev is divorced from Toronto movie producer and promoter Bill Marshall (who also attended Central Collegiate), and works at a Toronto non-profit housing agency. Though she hasn't seen Ed for years, except to wave at him once at a political picnic, she remembers him with fondness.

Benny met Ed in the debating club and she managed, she says, "to make myself obvious." Ed was tall and skinny with a brush cut and a gap between his two front teeth. He was her first real boyfriend and she was crazy about him. Ed was a good dancer and a nifty jiver; they grooved to the Four Aces and Johnnie ("Cry") Ray and Fats ("I Found My Thrill On Blueberry Hill") Domino. At home, Ed played "Cry" over and over and over again on his record player, memorizing the words, acting out Johnnie Ray's tremulous, melodramatic delivery; he drove his father mad. But Ed also had a passion for the big bands. On every record, he knew which musician played what. Benny remembers dancing with Ed, feeling romantic, and he'd be whispering in her ear: "That's Joe Schmo on the sax and so-and-so on the clarinet . . ."

But Ed has expressed other memories of dancing: "There used to be a regular Saturday night dance called the Get-together Club at the other high school," Ed told *Today* magazine. "The highlight of dancing, of course, was to be able for the first time to gently touch a girl's breast. All adolescents know what the real function of dancing is."

The dominant impression of Ed in his final year of high school, Benny says, was that of a very political person. "He always talked politics and debated ideas. It got kind of boring hanging around with him if you weren't interested in politics." Ed wasn't attached to any political party then, though Velma figures that he likely would have thought of himself as a Liberal — an allegiance Ed disputes. He is adamant that he was never a Liberal. Reg remembers being surprised at the political direction in which Ed eventually moved. The two boys spent one summer together at Camp Borden, as army officers-in-training, shooting machine guns, driving tanks, throwing hand grenades, firing rocket launchers, having a great time — and talking politics. They had one friend who was, says Reg, "as far left as you can be. It wasn't Ed. Eddie was a more middle-of-the road type."

"I knew Eddie'd be a leader," interjects Reg's wife Marlene, "because he was always a leader, but I was really surprised he went NDP."

Reg nods. "I always looked upon the NDP as being extremely left wing. My background, the way I was raised, taught me that. My father was a labourer and he was a staunch Conservative. I've heard people say Ed is as far left as you can be, but I don't see it. I don't think Ed's left at all. I still have some difficulty voting NDP, but I guess I've moved towards them and in my mind they've moved toward me."

"It would be no surprise to me," says Marlene, "if Ed became the next Prime Minister." The Gutsoles are "getting so bad thinking this way" that in the summer of 1987, up at their cottage, they painted a huge sign saying

ED FOR PM and nailed it over their neighbour's dock. "He's a staunch Liberal," says Reg, "but he didn't take it down. He said to me, 'You might not be wrong.'"

In 1955, Ed graduated from Central Collegiate. He enrolled at Trinity College, University of Toronto. Oshawa's big-man-on-campus became a poor unknown in the big city, struggling to find his feet at a college dominated by the haut-WASP sons of the Toronto establishment, in a wider university environment that produced such future superstars as Peter Gzowski, Barbara Frum, Stephen Lewis, Michele Landsberg, Stephen Clarkson, Christina McCall, Margaret Atwood — the new generation of Canadian nationalists who emerged from the University of Toronto in the late '50s and early '60s. They would later be amazed to discover that a small-town kid had grown, unnoticed in their ranks, to a position of political prominence and even — was it possible? — national leadership.

Ed, meanwhile, an outsider to their groups, had moved into a Campus Co-op residence where he encountered the first political movement that would consciously shape his ideology: self-help capitalism.

CHAPTER TWO

Toronto, 1955: The New Generation

Ed, in his somewhat plodding way, in a somewhat plodding country, best repre-sents what Canada is all about. He worked very hard to get where he is. Nobody, not even his worst enemy, questions his sin-cerity. His views were formulated during this period, at U. of T., and they evolved, and they represent, I think, the highest as-pirations of our generation. A man, his country and a time have come together; whether it will lead to anything, I don't know.

Doug Marshall, Ed's U. of T. peer.

Enrolling at Trinity College, University of Toronto, in September, 1955, Ed Broadbent joined what author Christina McCall terms "Ontario's first post-imperial gen-eration." Another alumnus, the iconoclastic Howard Adel-man, who became a philosophy professor, real estate investor and defender of refugees, observes: "This was the generation that broke the colonial mould. Up until then, we celebrated the British empire or aped the Americans."

Toronto was emerging from the colonial cocoon. An ar-tistic community led by painters Joyce Wieland and Mi-chael Snow had blossomed in the lofts and cafés along Spadina and Gerrard. In the basement of the Royal Ontario Museum, Herbert Whittaker — *The Globe and Mail*'s theatre critic for over twenty-five years — was mounting plays and promoting a theatrical troupe of actors, directors and writers who felt, says Whittaker, "that we had to speak with our own voice. We *needed* to be ourselves, not copy." Post-war waves of immigrants had settled in, establishing businesses and restaurants that shot vivid, cosmopolitan flares through a dull WASP city — to such an extent that it's hard to imagine, now, how eagerly Torontonians used to head out of town in search of excitement, how Buffalo was such a glamorous lure. It was Toronto's brewing culture — the theatre, music and street life — that seems to have ignited the spirit of the young man who arrived from Oshawa that fall of '55.

Ed joined a diverse throng of well-fed, ambitious, fledgling patriots, attracted to the University of Toronto by its sterling reputation. Reared in economic prosperity, impatient to shed their banana-republic inhibitions, they would go on to form a virtual who's who of English Canada's cultural elite: there was Peter Gzowksi, editor of U. of T.'s student paper, *The Varsity*, now host of CBC radio's *Morningside*; Barbara Frum, host of CBC-TV's *The Journal*, was then Barbara Rosberg, wondering what she was going to be in a decidedly sexist world, where *The Varsity* frequently ran front-page photos of pert co-eds being auctioned off to engineers. There was Julian Porter, son of Ontario's Provincial Treasurer, Dana Porter, who outraged *The Varsity* when he said university fees were too low; Margaret Atwood, a fledgling writer, was under the influence of Victoria College lecturer Jay Macpherson, who won a Governor-General's award for her poetry but was not allowed to address a mixed audience at Hart House, the cultural centre that barred women; Dennis Lee, author of *Alligator Pie* and a whole raft of children's books; Adrienne Poy, vice-president of Students Administrative Council, who would marry Rhodes Scholar Stephen Clarkson (they are long divorced) and become president of McClelland and Stewart Publishers; Barry Callaghan, writer, son of Morley; actress Jackie Burroughs, who was then living in St Hilda's residence; Mildred Istona, editor of *Chatelaine*; David Lewis's son Stephen, former leader of the Ontario NDP, most recently Canada's ambassador to the United Nations; Gerry Caplan, Stephen's backroom Machiavelli, creator of the Waffle Manifesto (with Ed), later federal secretary of the NDP; Michele Landsberg, National Newspaper Award-winning columnist, renowned feminist and author, married to Stephen Lewis; Christina McCall, political journalist and author of *Grits*, a best-selling examination of the Liberal Party; Liz Binks, as she was known when she was a reporter for *The Varsity*, whose alumni included her future husband John Gray — as Elizabeth Gray she became host of CBC radio's *As It Happens*; Mr Gray, the Ottawa bureau chief of *The Globe and Mail*, now that paper's European correspondent; Michael Cassidy, now an NDP MP, was managing editor of *The Varsity* under Gzowski, then editor, followed by Doug Marshall, who became entertainment editor of the *Toronto Star*. The list goes on. Maturing in this milieu, soaking it all up, was Ed, the kid from Oshawa. None of them knew what they were part of.

Generations make a difference. The Trudeau/Pelletier/Marchand forces, fifteen years older, were merely the tip of the iceberg, the Quebec figureheads of a movement that would dominate the national stage for two decades, while Ontario's junior class matured. But coming from English Canada, U. of T. undergrads had a long way to go to catch up with the French-Canadians.

"We were brought up that nothing Canadian was interesting," says Michele Landsberg. "We were colonial. English Canada seemed so pale, pallid and unfocussed. The French at least had the power of a clear identity — oppression gave them that — but we didn't know who we were. Then we got to university and we started to wake up. We began to sense our intellectual power. Many of us were the first generation born in Canada, the first to get to university, and we started paying attention to Canadian politics."

And there they all were, not necessarily knowing each other — in '55, U. of T. had 12,189 students, the vast majority men (8,615 males to 3,574 females), but dreaming the same dreams; at least, the men were. Ed matured in an era of clear-cut male dominance.

"I personally approve of keeping women out of these things," Senator John F. Kennedy told *The Varsity* in 1957 after a few women tried in vain to get in to Hart House to hear him debate. "It's a pleasure to be in a country where the women cannot mix in everywhere." Stephen Lewis was debating that night, asserting his support for women's rights; Ed was in the audience, watching. Feminism would not break upon his consciousness until much later. Ed was not at university to protest; he was there to soak up all the learning he could get. And Trinity College was an imposing place.

"Coming from where I did, I suppose I might have been freaked out by the whole scene," he told Sandra Gwyn, who observed that, "Trinity, in those days, was the cashmere-sweater-and-blue-blazer pinnacle of the Upper Canadian WASP ascendancy." Ed, however, said: "I never felt any sense of inferiority. I simply fell head over heels in love with the whole ivy-covered intellectual atmosphere."

Situated across Queen's Park Circle from the massive pink sandstone buildings of the Ontario Legislature, where Tory Premier Leslie Frost reigned in complacent assurance, the campus sprawled through downtown Toronto, its grassy common enclosed by the Romanesque splendour of University College, the Sigmund Samuel Library and Convocation Hall. Its students could not be blamed for believing they would inherit their world. "If there was a Periclean age in Canadian education, the University of Toronto, in the last half of the 1950s, was Athens," wrote Gwyn. "In the last precious years before mass education turned all our universities into factories, before campus radicalism put to death the old idea of a community of scholars, this was *our* Oxbridge. As gurus, among others: E.J. Pratt, Northrop Frye, Emil Fackenheim, Edmund Carpenter, Marshall McLuhan." And, most important for Ed, during his postgraduate years, C.B. Macpherson, the political theorist whose influence would mark his thinking forever.

In their search for a culture they could claim as their own, Ed's generation faced formidable obstacles. Robert Weaver's *Tamarack Review* was first printed by U. of T.

Press in 1956 as a vehicle for Canadian poetry and fiction, but the little magazine's very existence was questioned by condescending critics who couldn't imagine there was enough good Canadian work to merit inclusion. Asked in a patronizing fashion how the *Tamarack Review* compared with "the real thing" from New York or London, Jay Macpherson shocked Canadians with her bold response: "I don't particularly care," she said, "how it compares with outside work, because I live in Canada and am primarily concerned with Canadian writing."

This was the backdrop against which Ed's assertive nationalism developed. During the same period, Christina McCall, a student at Victoria College, wrote an essay on Canadian novelist Morley Callaghan and submitted it for an important prize. She lost out, however, to an essay on Christopher Fry, a British dramatist.

"My professor told me — he was a Canadian for Christ's sake and he spoke with a mock-English accent — he said, "I'm sorry, Miss McCall. The problem with you is that, though you write brilliantly, your subject is folkloric." McCall rolls her eyes, her anger rising at the memory. "Folkloric!"

It was hard to be a Canadian, then. Even now: when C.B. Macpherson died on July 21, 1987, *The Globe and Mail* ran an obituary that demonstrated an awesome ignorance of Macpherson's stature by highlighting his chairmanship of a committee that "sought to reshape the role of the undergraduate student" at U. of T. and missed the fact that Macpherson was internationally regarded as one of the pre-eminent political theorists in the world.

"Typical," Ed fumed. "Canadians don't know anything about our own great people." So Ed wrote a letter to the editor, published in the *Globe* on July 28, 1987. "The loss of this great man leaves a void in Canada and in most other parts of the world where his superb work is known and studied . . . He was among the intellectual giants of our age. I know of no other twentieth-century theorist who has thought more ably about the interconnected meanings of freedom, equality and democracy."

These were the themes that absorbed Ed throughout his eleven-year connection with the University of Toronto. His intellectual quest was at odds with the conservatism of the era. Dwight Eisenhower had been elected president of the United States in 1952, and would preside until 1961, when John F. Kennedy's Camelot vision dazzled the world. In 1955, the American empire was at its height and the Canadian inferiority complex rampant. Official Canada was represented by dull old Louis St Laurent, who was Prime Minister. There was no Canadian flag, no "made-in-Canada" Constitution, no Quiet Revolution in Quebec, little national self-esteem, just another branch-plant society groping for an identity.

In the pages of *The Varsity*, Peter Gzowski promoted Pogo for President — Pogo was an American cartoon character drawn by Walt Kelly — and complained in an editorial: "What bores we all are." Right or wrong, he wrote, "students have led demonstrations in Ireland, Cyprus, Poland, Japan, Egypt and Algeria. But in Canada we are afraid of our own opinions."

The big movie of '55 was *Rebel Without a Cause*, starring James Dean. His existentialist *angst* was a pop American version of French author Albert Camus's meditations on the meaninglessness of life. Ed loved the bleak romance of Camus, who was a precursor to Jack Kerouac's Beat Generation. Elvis Presley was gyrating for screaming teens — not Ed's style, he preferred Fats Domino for dancing; and Ernest Hemingway was the most famous writer in the world, having won the Pulitzer Prize in 1952 for *The Old Man and the Sea*. Radios jingled to the tunes of "Que Sera Sera," "Unchained Melody" or "Love is a Many Splendored Thing," and Pat Boone recorded a more popular, white-bread version of Fats Domino's sassy black song "Ain't That a Shame (My Tears Fell Like Rain)." New York was the capital of the world and who wanted to be Canadian?

Liberal External Affairs minister Lester Pearson would win the Nobel Prize in 1957 (for mediating the 1956 Suez Crisis), and John Diefenbaker became Prime Minister, but compelling Canadian role models were few and far between.

Nineteen fifty-five was a seminal year. Innocent Ed, fresh out of a summer at Camp Borden, as part of his military training, settled in at Trinity, flapping across campus to classes wearing Trinity's traditional black gown — an English affectation, as it appeared to students at other colleges, matched by the British drawls affected by some of Trinity's Upper Canada College types. But there was another side to Trinity: its spiritual, anti-materialistic Anglican aspirations were best reflected in its highly-thought-of philosophy department, where Ed was content, pondering the great moral questions.

Dr George Edison, then head of Trinity's philosophy department, now retired to Elora, Ont., remembers that Ed was "reserved in class. He was a quiet boy. But after he'd given a paper, he used to come round to the office to see me. I'd question him and we'd talk back and forth. I got to like him very much. He was a faithful student, a good scholar, very competent. I've watched him handle himself as a politician, and I have to say I agree with him on most things. He is basically sound in what he's advocating. He has a profound social commitment; that's what motivates him, and I'm proud of him."

Not all Ed's teachers were so favourably disposed. Emil Fackenheim, the renowned philosophy professor and Hegel scholar, taught Ed and wasn't overly impressed — though Fackenheim had a huge impact on Ed. "I was incredibly lucky to get him in first year," says Ed. "It was a turning point in my life." Ed had been planning to major in political science, but the intellectual excitement generated by Fackenheim's philosophy course convinced him to major in philosophy. "Fackenheim had a great gift," says Ed. "He interested us in thinking." Ed beams. "I hit university at the right stage in my life — I really *hit it*," he says, eyes shining.

Fackenheim, something of a superstar in philosophy circles, is now in his seventies; he retired from the University of Toronto in 1983 and lives in Jerusalem, "so it's hard to recall students from the '50s," he says. The great man is also, one must add, well aware of his own genius and not given to praising neophytes. "Ed did not stand out as a profound student," says Fackenheim. "He would be the first to admit, I think, that his prime ability lay not in philosophy. He was more interested in political science." (Not to hear Ed tell it, not then. "I got A's in every course I took from Fackenheim," he says.) But Fackenheim does praise the institution. "The philosophy department at the University of Toronto was the best in North America. I was never tempted to leave."

Outside the philosophy department, Ed's real life existed far beyond the Buttery, Trinity's cafeteria, where Ed "passed" for a square. If he was looked down on for his cheap tweed jackets and unchic attitudes — he didn't play soccer, he had no friends in Rosedale — he didn't notice. He was too busy exploring the city, soaking up everything: foreign films, pubs, concerts, plays, endless discussions, limited only by his meagre financial resources.

Ed was poor, but he found "culture." Oshawa hadn't much to offer in that line; Toronto was heaven, for him. There was the Crest Theatre, where Ed saw Barbara Chilcott, Murray Davis and Donald Davis, of the famous acting family, perform on stage; a year after the Stratford Shakespearean Festival opened in 1953, the Canadian Players were touring bare-bones Shakespeare across the country. A peak experience of those years was "when Maria Callas filled Maple Leaf Gardens." Ed was there. "It was one of the great moments of my life," he says. (He even remembers who he went with: a passionate Eastern European woman who was enraged by Callas's refusal to perform an encore.)

But not all his activities were so genteel. Most Friday nights he would wander in to the King Cole Room in the Park Plaza Hotel "to drink beer and solve the problems of the universe. Other times we hung out at the Silver Dollar, which was the ultimate dive — a bar and strip joint just a few hundred yards from the co-op [where he lived]. Every night around midnight we'd go to the nearby Crescent Grill: the hookers and gamblers would come in for their midnight snacks and so would we. It was great. I suppose it was at the Silver Dollar that I laid the foundation for my later belief — not always shared by my socialist colleagues — that socialism and pleasure are not necessarily a contradiction in terms."

His innocent pleasures stand in stark contrast to the troubles that were brewing south of the border. In the winter of '55, long before Vietnam was an issue, before Black Power was chic or feminism had been reborn or radicalism was a possibility, one black woman named Rosa Parks refused to go to the back of a bus in Montgomery, Alabama. Martin Luther King led a protest and a movement was born that was destined to radicalize America — and hold Canadians in thrall.

It came as quite a surprise, like a tornado out of a clear blue sky. Those were, after all, The Eisenhower Years; they were smug years. From the ragged vantage point of the late '80s, plagued by AIDS, illiteracy and the decline of the American empire, it is hard to picture the triumphant, patriarchal middle-class vision as it existed in the heyday of American dominance: the booming economy, the two-car, four-children, two-parent family with Mom at home baking apple pie and Dad proudly surveying his domain. Order prevailed. Or so they thought.

Life magazine, in '55, described America as "a nation up to its ears in domestic tranquillity," enjoying the highest standard of living in the world, "embroiled in no war." Yet an internal war was raging that would kill off America's left wing — from which, ironically, Canada would benefit. "Senate Votes Unanimously to Extend Investigations of Domestic Communism, Thousands of Federal Employees Dismissed as Security Risks," ran a *Life* headline. The most powerful nation in the world was eating its own. That greedy gobbler of lefties, the infamous Senator Joe McCarthy, was searching under every bed for dreaded commies, purging universities, bureaucracies and Hollywood.

Within a year, Martin Luther King was arrested, police dogs were attacking black protesters and America was turning ugly. Slowly, a trickle of disillusioned — or frightened — academics started streaming north, many of them to U. of T., to be joined later by a wave of anti-Vietnam Americans. Their patriotism was transferred to their adopted country; they were amazed to discover Canadians so timid in expressing themselves, so lacking in self-confidence, and unleashed on this rather passive crowd a more aggressive version of what it means to love your country. Doug Marshall remembers an American prof at Trinity sputtering in shocked dismay that "this is a *country*. You should be studying *some* of your own writers and thinkers in your own country. If you don't pay attention to yourselves, who will?"

Ed was paying attention, but no one noticed him. Oshawa's superachiever was anonymous in a crowd of well-connected, left-wing urban sophisticates. The spotlight was clearly fixed on Stephen Lewis, whose father was already a legendary figure. David Lewis, national secretary of the CCF for fifteen years, at the centre of the party since 1936, was a Rhodes Scholar, a labour lawyer and intimate friend of such giants as F.R. Scott, the Montreal poet and law professor who co-authored the Regina Manifesto, acted as chairman of the CCF during the '40s, and had a profound influence on Pierre Trudeau. This was the big time.

Gerry Caplan, initiated into the campus CCF by Stephen in 1956, remembers the first time he went to the Lewis house. "It was like a model of socialist realism," says Caplan. "David Lewis, my hero, the martyr and brain of Canadian socialism, was wearing an apron and washing the dishes. The twins [Stephen's younger sisters] were dressed alike, playing classical duets on the piano, surrounded by books, culture, commitment, devotion. Sophie [the mother] was organizing everything — taking proper care of her remarkable family. I couldn't believe it."

Stephen was the Judy Garland of Canadian socialism, virtually born in a trunk and trained to politics since his youth. "Stephen was a child of destiny, a man of history, growing up in that family," says Caplan. (Ed, the son of nobody, was unmarked by destiny.) Barbara Frum remembers that "when we were all wondering what we were going to be, Stephen already *was*. He was a politician." Doug Marshall recalls that "at every opportunity, Stephen was honing his skills as an orator, shaping every syllable, and to us he was spellbinding."

Gerry Caplan, the son of a Toronto accountant, had wasted his adolescence on the pursuit of cute girls, cherry Cokes and convertibles. But now he'd seen the light, thanks to Lewis; Caplan was hooked — by the son, by the father, by the dream. He was not the only one. An extraordinary group of fellow student CCFers dominated campus politics: there was Michael Cassidy, son of Harry Cassidy, head of the School of Social Work; John Brewin, son of Andrew Brewin, Q.C., the lawyer and civil rights activist who would become a long-term NDP MP; Terry Grier, grandson of a Tory MP, later chairman of the NDP's election planning committee, now president of Ryerson Polytechnic Institute in Toronto; law student Harry Arthurs, who became dean of Osgoode Hall Law School and is now president of York University. They were a powerfully persuasive bunch: by 1960 Gerry Caplan became president of the campus CCF, which won model parliament elections for the first time in the history of U. of T. It was a victory in which Ed played no part.

"It's funny," says Doug Marshall, "that Ed, who came from Oshawa and knew what socialism was all about, at a gut level, was submerged by the middle-class, academic socialists on campus."

"I got taken up with ideas," says Ed, explaining his lack of interest in campus politics. "I grew out of student activism, I guess. I did so much of it in high school, I was sick of it." When he came to Toronto, living away from home for the first time, he entered a new and marvellous realm, far from the family troubles. "Right now I'm reading Mary McCarthy's autobiography [*How I Grew*]," he says. "She talks about getting to university and sitting in the library and feeling like she has arrived in heaven. That's how I felt. For me to go into Sigmund Samuel Library, and wander through the stacks, and look at all the books, all the knowledge — I loved it." Friends remember seeing him at his favourite carrel, his books and papers laid out in an orderly fashion, head bent over his work. This was a serious young man. He was president of Trinity's Brett Philosophy Club. The rivalry of partisan politics didn't appeal to him — it was too confining. He was free to roam the intellectual universe, and he was utterly absorbed, like a kid travelling through outer space. "I loved learning," he says simply.

The image of pugnacious Percy, his Dad, trapped at The Motors, disappointed in life, was no doubt a keen if unconscious spur — and Ed's commitment was intense. He had not been raised "surrounded by books, culture, commitment," like Stephen. It is worth noting that Stephen never did graduate from university, a prospect that would have dismayed Ed. Their patterns of development stand in stark contrast: whereas Ed took his time, feeling out his own path, Stephen was already shaped by the great expectations that propelled his youth. It is mysterious: by the time Stephen would burn out and quit politics, in his forties, Ed would begin to hit his stride; and Ed, not Stephen, would inherit the torch from David Lewis.

In the '50s, while Stephen's political commitment drew him inexorably into the real world of politics at an early age, Ed was content with his scholarly pursuits — though he never had any doubt about where his sympathies lay. "To me, to be intelligent and thoughtful meant you were on the left," says Ed, while acknowledging that his stance was, at that time, relatively bereft of ideology. "All the people I became close to were left-wing. If you wanted the improvement of mankind, you were on the left." The decision, he feels, about which side people choose, left or right, stems from gut reactions and attitudes that are "established well before university level. Because of your family situation or social circumstances, you either want basic continuity of institutions as they are or you want to improve things. But the motivations of all of us are complex. You have careerism on the left and on the right. You have people in all parties who seek change, and people who want to maintain the *status quo*."

Michele Landsberg also believes that "people's emotional stance toward society is formed early in life. The big lie perpetuated by the establishment is that those who hold establishment views are neutral. Political choice reflects an emotional bias. Unfairness makes me mad, and that's why I'm a New Democrat. Conservatives defend their privilege, Liberals are out for power, and New Democrats talk about collective responsibilities and redistribution of wealth, clinging to romantic ideas of justice and fairness."

Michele was on campus then, and she admired David Lewis "extravagantly" long before she met Stephen. Lewis senior was struggling to keep the party alive, building the infrastructure that would one day serve Broadbent so well. The NDP had not yet come into being, but David Lewis was forging the links between eastern unions, western farmers, old-time CCFers and urban activists that would, in 1961, produce the NDP. Yet the prospects were bleak for left-wingers in the '50s. Aside from the government in Saskatchewan and the official opposition in British Columbia, the CCF had only a couple of provincial MPs in Ontario and not a single federal MP from southern Ontario until 1962. The CCF had been virtually wiped out in Ontario by a vicious red-baiting campaign financed by big business conservatives who had targeted Lewis as their victim. Anti-Semitic cartoons coupled with truly dreadful propaganda linking the CCF to Hitler's Nazis resulted in a relentless anti-CCF barrage, supported by the media, that was racist, slanderous, untrue, a blot on Canada and as bad as anything U.S. Senator Joe McCarthy dished out.

Writing about this period in his memoirs, *The Good Fight*, David Lewis detailed how the Canadian Underwriters Association instructed its salesmen to inform clients "that if the CCF came to power they would lose their life insurance and their savings." Similar scare tactics were engaged in by the country's major corporations — Bank of Montreal, Royal Bank, Imperial Oil, CPR, Power Corp., Massey-Harris, Imperial Tobacco, Bell Telephone, Hudson's Bay, Inco, Noranda Mines, Hollinger — which paid for anti-CCF pamphlets, one of which, "Social Suicide," was mailed to every household in Canada, costing its publisher more than one million dollars. Lewis was appalled that the country's newspapers perpetuated the business community's slanders and refused to report CCFers' attempts to set the record straight. It is a sad and shameful story. David Lewis, the great believer in democracy, considered this whole period "monstrous," and he was right.

Not that it couldn't happen again. In the summer of '87, when Broadbent and the NDP topped the polls as the most popular leader and party in the country, with the Tories trailing at 23 per cent, the president of the national Conservative party, Bill Jarvis, wrote a four-page letter seeking to raise money for an "NDP opposition fund," implying the NDP is a communist front that, in power, would subject Canada to totalitarian control. Jarvis spoke about "the political gangrene" that was poised to "infiltrate" Canada, to nationalize everything, eradicate the profit motive and generally impose total government control over everyone.

The difference this time around was the reaction of the press. The *Globe*'s Ottawa columnist Jeffrey Simpson, who had been a parliamentary intern to Broadbent, led off: "The New Democrats must have the Conservatives spooked. How else to explain the piece of garbage masquerading as a fundraising letter recently published by Conservative Party headquarters?" Simpson quoted Jarvis: "Imagine our nation governed by the leaders of the radical, hard left." Said Mr Simpson: "Imagine, rather, a nation governed by a group that would send out this letter."

Why did the CCF receive such vicious treatment in the '40s? Its crime was the same as the NDP's in '87: the party was popular. In 1943, in Ontario, the CCF came close to forming the government and was, briefly, first in a federal Gallup poll. In 1944, Tommy Douglas led the CCF to victory in Saskatchewan; across the country, the party was on the move. By the mid-'50s, it seemed half-dead, owing to a curious phenomenon that has persisted to this day: its opponents at once borrowed its policies while scaring the living daylights out of voters who would dream of voting for the party that originated those policies.

The dirty tactics paid off. In the Diefenbaker sweep of 1958, the CCF was reduced to eight seats, 9 per cent of the vote, and lost its most respected leaders, M.J. Coldwell and Stanley Knowles. Ed was by this time a CCF voter but still, he displayed little interest in the party. "The political clubs on campus seemed to be extensions of the House of Commons," he says, "and the level of debate was awfully partisan." He was also turned off by what he thought were stupid, sophomoric pranks perpetrated by campus politicians. One year university CCFers carted around a huge poster displaying a voluptuous Swedish athlete imprinted with the slogan: "This is what socialism did for Sweden." It didn't do anything for Broadbent. "I thought it was abominable. It personified student games to me." He had no thoughts of becoming a politician — and nobody else predicted a starring role in politics for him. As his brother-in-law Barry Cornish jokes, "When I knew Ed at U. of T., I never detected signs of greatness in him."

Ed stayed at U. of T. a long time. His Ph.D. thesis — *The Good Society of John Stuart Mill* — is housed in the university's archives, where an official file outlines Ed's U. of T. career: 1959, B.A.; 1961, M.A.; 1961 to 1966, School of Graduate Studies; Ph.D., 1966. Major: Modern Political Thought and Seventeenth-Century Political Thought (Prof. C.B. Macpherson). First minor: Government of Canada. Second minor: Philosophy.

The B.A., M.A., Ph.D list is then followed by: MP, 1968. An *Oshawa Times* clipping for May 6, 1968, from the U. of T. file: "In his nomination speech, Mr. Broadbent concentrated on what he called the problem of the transfer of power in society from elite groups to the majority. 'No boy or girl should begin life,' Mr. Broadbent said, 'with a political or economic advantage over others.'"

In his thesis, Ed describes the typical person in the Good Society as conceived by John Stuart Mill, the liberal British philosopher and economist who was sympathetic to socialism, supportive of women's rights and trade unions and who died in 1873. Such a citizen, wrote Broadbent, "should express a collective interest in the well-being of the group" while maintaining a strong individual identity, and should be "co-operative in the sense that his participation in work, politics and other social activities should be entered into with a sense of community."

This is where Ed's ideology begins, consciously: at the Campus Co-op residence. From small town Oshawa, he moved in his first year into Webb House on Huron Street, close to the university. The rambling old home, buzzing with the energy of its cosmopolitan extended family, was named after Sidney Webb, a British economist, and his wife Beatrice. For Ed, who was interested in the impact of ideas and intellectuals on the world, the Webbs were icons: they founded the Fabian Society in 1884, helped create the British Labour Party, the London School of Economics (where Ed would later study), the *New Statesman* magazine; they also influenced Canada's League for Social Reconstruction which helped write the 1933 Regina Manifesto, the intellectual cornerstone of the CCF.

Not that Ed chose the co-op for its politics. "I went there for economic reasons," he says. "It was the cheapest place to live." Room and board cost $15 a week at a time when university fees cost $335 for a year's undergraduate tuition. At the co-op, in return for low-cost accommodation, students had to do four hours of work a week. They lived in doubles or triples, about twenty people crammed into each house. The large living rooms were turned into bedrooms, and the only common room was the kitchen. There were five houses for a hundred people; the women were segregated into one building, but they mingled freely with male co-opers in a relatively egalitarian atmosphere that was unusual on campus.

They all ate together at Rochdale House, where Elsie Cader, a German cook, served meals that were gourmet feasts compared to residence sludge. And there was an active social life of calypso parties, folk music evenings and discussions that absorbed co-op members and created a strong group loyalty — partly in defence against the outside world.

"The co-op was regarded as a second-class society on campus," says Lyla Barclay, who was doing a Master of Social Work at U. of T. and living in the co-op when Ed was there. "We were all poor or immigrants or refugees or DPs but we felt, 'To hell with them, we know we're bright and we can do as well as the rest of them.' And we did. The co-op was full of political people, fascinating people from all over the world — Africans, Indians, Brits, Scots, Americans, Scandinavians, Germans, Czechs — and it was very common for us to spend hours talking and arguing. It was heady stuff."

Lyla remembers once sitting with Ed for a few hours, trying to explain "first co-op principles" to him, with the help of Ron Burrows, a physics whiz who had been a co-op president. Today, Dr Burrows heads the Solar-Terrestrial Physics Department of the Hertzberg Institute of Astrophysics at the National Research Council in Ottawa. He remembers Ed as "a serious, purposeful person but not a drag." And here it is again: "Ed was a regular guy." For Lyla Barclay, an American, Ed had what she described as "a real Canadian personality. It's hard for Canadians to see what's great about Ed because he's so much what you know. It is easy to underestimate him, because he doesn't oversell himself, but if you underestimate him you do so at your peril. He is very much a product of his time and place and generation."

Most of Ed's time outside class was taken up by the co-op. "It had an enormous influence on me," says Ed. One of the dominant figures was Griff Cunningham, a co-op activist who was back at U. of T. doing an M.A. when Ed met him. Cunningham grew up, like Ed, in a small auto town (St Catharines, in the Niagara Peninsula). His father was "a real, honest-to-goodness cowboy" who'd been a Methodist missionary to the Indians in North Dakota before migrating east via Saskatchewan. The only baggage he brought with him to Ontario was intellectual: he was a socialist and an activist in the farmers' co-op movement.

"My father was the first president of the CCF in St Catharines," says Cunningham, "and he started a farmers' co-op in town. He was the kind of man who worked eighteen hours a day for the cause — and never made any money." Cunningham, now a gray-haired professor of social science at York University, spent ten years in socialist Tanzania and was, for eight years, principal of an adult education college in Dar es Salaam. Today he lives with his feminist partner, Rusty Shteir, on Albany Avenue in Toronto's radical-chic Annex district. They shop at Karma Co-op, the food co-op Griff helped found almost twenty years ago, and have renovated their house in a splendid fashion typical of the neighbourhood; their living room walls have been specially "washed" to resemble a tawny Florentine villa.

Griff remembers: "One of the first things I did when I got back from Africa in 1971, after being debriefed by CIDA (Canadian International Development Agency), was to call up Ed. He had just lost a leadership bid against David Lewis and he invited me to a party to celebrate his defeat. I was just off the ship so I remember this great wake which was more of a bash." Was Griff surprised by his friend's evolution? "No. I detected a note of statesmanship in Ed Broadbent as an undergraduate. He had an aura of promise."

Ed was a "comer," according to Griff, "not because he was a flaming radical; he was a straight, responsible young man, and that was what we needed — Ed knew how to work." For his part, Ed admired Griff, who was older (by six years) and had impeccable co-op connections; Griff would pursue a Ph.D on the English co-op movement and was a handy source of history.

Co-op businesses, Griff explains, are owned and controlled by the people who use their services, and tend to flourish in regions — the Canadian prairies, the Maritime provinces — where capitalism has failed or never bothered to show up. "Once you've had the co-op experience," says Griff, "you're never a simple-minded capitalist again. You cut out the middleman and return the profit to yourself. It's self-help capitalism, and it's one of the major economic forces in the western world. It's what the social democratic movement in the west is all about, and social democrats are the best friends capitalists ever had."

The co-op movement began in Britain. In 1844 in the town of Rochdale, just north of Manchester in the industrial heartland of Northern England, a group of weavers started a retail co-op to sell their wares. The idea caught on, was adopted with particular success by farmers, and carried to Canada in the early twentieth century by English and Scandinavian immigrants who settled on the western prairies. It is no coincidence that, in Saskatchewan, the 1933 Regina Manifesto kicked off the aptly named Co-operative Commonwealth Federation, the precursor of the NDP. To this day, in Saskatchewan, Alberta and Manitoba, prairie farmers belong to powerful co-ops which in turn function as enormously influential political forces; the Saskatchewan Wheat Pool, for instance, owned by the farmers who supply it, is one of the country's major corporations, with $2 billion in annual sales.

The co-op movement also put down tenacious roots on the Atlantic coast and spawned its own share of political activists, among them Cape Breton's Allan MacEachen. The son of a coal miner who rose to become a Liberal finance minister in Pierre Trudeau's Cabinet, MacEachen was influenced by the Antigonish movement, centred at St Francis Xavier University in Nova Scotia, led by Roman Catholic priest Moses Coady. Dr Coady developed "a system of worker-run co-operatives that would free the individual farmer, miner and fisherman from the domination of a small economic elite," wrote Linda McQuaig in *Behind Closed Doors*. Like the prairie co-opers, the reformers in the Antigonish movement became a powerful force because, McQuaig noted, they "didn't just confine themselves to debating the great political and theological questions. They wanted to *change* things."

(Today, co-ops are a significant economic force in the three prairie provinces, Quebec and the Maritimes. Seventy per cent of Canada's grain trade and 50 per cent of its dairy industry are co-operatively organized. Almost 43 per cent of Canadians belong to at least one co-op, and total co-op assets exceed $51 billion. In Quebec, the Desjardins *caisse populaire* — a co-op credit union — has 1,381 branches and total assets of almost $24 billion, representing one of the most powerful financial institutions in the province.)

Back in the '50s, Ed absorbed this history, living at the co-op, washing dishes, peeling potatoes and working his way up to president of Campus Co-op by his third year. A chief attribute of co-opers was frugality; they had to be thrifty — Ed especially. He was working his way through school on the URTP — University Reserve Training Plan — which required weekly attendance at various military training sessions and lectures in return for a guaranteed summer job in the air force, his chosen branch of the military — another reason why he couldn't hang out on campus. But Ed enjoyed the lectures, which featured speakers like James Eayrs talking about international affairs, and he loved the summers: his first, in Cape Breton, on a radar base, allowed him enough free time to hitch-hike around Nova Scotia, which he found incredibly beautiful; his second, on a jet training base near Winnipeg, saw him as assistant to the adjutant and flying T33 jets (with a pilot), doing loops and rolls and dives over Lake Winnipeg, "scaring the bejeesus out of some poor guy fishing;" his third year he ended up at air force headquarters in Ottawa, "which was a bizarre experience," working on Treasury Board submissions to justify expenditures.

Returning each fall to the co-op, Ed took on an increasing load of co-op business. Griff Cunningham and Howard Adelman, who became a founder of the infamous Rochdale College, organized education sessions and attracted politicians to speak to their group — though socialism as a clearly articulated philosophy was not then popular. "We had a hundred or so members but not many socialists," says Griff. "I knew who they were because I was one of the few." But even then, "I was into girls more than I was into politics."

Ed's relationship with Bev Bennett, his Oshawa girl-friend, had tapered off, and he was a regular at the King Cole Room, the "in" pub for hanging out. "Ed was very partial to the KCR, but he stayed aloof, somehow," says Terry Hollands, who was a close friend of Ed's in the co-op. Now director of the Solar Thermal Research Centre at the University of Waterloo, Hollands remembers Ed being attracted "to lots of girls, but we all suffered from that: you'd be attracted, but there was no birth control pill, and marriage was out of the question, so you had to abstain." Doug Marshall remembers many who didn't abstain. "Just about every second woman I knew had an illegal abortion. You were always hearing about someone who did them, out in some town, and people were always driving off somewhere for a nasty job on a kitchen table by an ex-nurse or something. It was rough."

Ed's sexuality appears to have been sublimated into his work — at least his co-op friends remember his major passions being intellectual. "I was studying science, math and engineering," says Hollands, "but I found philosophy fascinating. I used to get Ed to explain it to me. Hegel, Kierkegaard, Kant — he was keenly interested in what he was reading and loved to talk about it. He'd started at the beginning, with the Greeks — Aristotle, Plato — and as he moved through it we'd discuss it. Oh, he *loved* Bertrand Russell — he had pictures of Bertie up on his wall — and John Stuart Mill. Ed's political consciousness seemed to evolve with his studies and he had a big influence on me. I became a socialist too."

What impressed Hollands, he says, was that "Ed came to see things in a broad context. He'd talk about a specific issue in relation to history. And I think it's a great credit to U. of T. that it nurtured people like Ed. He is a classic example of someone who responded deeply to education."

Hollands was another bright kid out of a small-town background similar to Ed's: his father ran a dry cleaning store in Thorold, Ont., and Terry was the first in the family to go to university — on scholarship. Together, Ed and Terry moved in second year to Owen House, on Spadina just north of College Street, named for Robert Owen, a Welsh socialist reformer who set up a model co-op community in Indiana in 1825. Though the trappings were serious, the students were not always.

"Ed had to have his record player set up, and he was very fussy about his music," says Hollands. Ed was listening, then, to Puccini, Verdi and Handel, he had discovered jazz and he loved Billie Holiday — all of which was, to Hollands, "different." Hollands and his girlfriend Mara, now his wife, were struck by Ed's personal contradictions. Mara was surprised that Ed the serious student was also Ed the prankster. "Ed has always been a livelier person than his image led you to believe," says Mara. Ed was the best man at the Hollandses' 1961 wedding and was, as usual, the life of the party — though Mara found him, on other occasions, "somewhat intimidating. I felt like a second-classer with Ed sometimes — if you told him that he'd be shocked — but you'd say black and he'd challenge you and I don't like going all night long having to defend myself." Mara turns to her husband. "You liked that, the debates."

Terry Hollands shrugs. "Ed could be pugnacious, like his Dad. But he's mellowed. And there was another side to him. He enjoyed good discussions and you'd think he was being really serious and then he'd surprise you with his pranks; you didn't expect them from Ed. Things like a pail of water over the door." Or, a dirty joke that Doug Marshall says Ed told him about a whore in a brothel being instructed that she'd never succeed in business until she realized the customer always comes first. Or, in the *Torontonensis* year book for his graduating year, his statement that he hailed from "Pincher Creek, Alta.," which infuriated his mother. Or, calling Buckingham Palace to speak to Princess Margaret. Barry Cornish, then a co-op resident, now Ed's brother-in-law, describes this scene. Ed was always carting his co-op pals home to Oshawa for big Sunday dinners, cooked by his mother. One Sunday evening Barry, along for the ride and also, by this time, interested in Ed's sister Velma, was telling a tale Ed had heard too many times: about how Barry was born on August 21, the same day as Princess Margaret Rose, sister of Queen Elizabeth, and how "but for the fickle finger of fate and a few genetic twists and rearrangement of chromosomes, I might have been the Princess."

Ed asked Barry if he'd ever informed Princess Margaret Rose of this fascinating possibility. Barry had not. Ed said he thought it was about time. "Let's phone her and tell her," said Ed. And sure enough Ed got through to Buckingham Palace, though not to the Princess, and tried to explain to a befuddled British secretary the genetic dance that could have transformed Barry Cornish into Princess Margaret Rose. "That shut Barry up, for a while," says Velma, chuckling.

Ed's weekend visits home became famous in Oshawa because, says Uncle Reuben, "you never knew what Ed would bring home next." What Reuben means is that Ed's co-op friends were a polyglot crew, the likes of which Oshawans had never seen before: there were young men wearing turbans, people from Africa and Japan. Once he brought Henry Shapiro, an orthodox Jew, home for dinner, and his mother was in a flap trying to figure out how to prepare and present a kosher meal. "Both my parents were totally open to other racial groups," says Ed. "Whoever was my friend was a friend of theirs."

Ed was experiencing, in his own modest way, the revolution that was occurring across the continent. In 1957, Stephen Lewis borrowed his father's car and drove south with Gerry Caplan to Little Rock, Arkansas, which was swarming with National Guardsmen. Arkansas Governor Orval Faubus had rejected a federal order to integrate the school system and the Ku Klux Klan was burning crosses. Caplan and his pals insinuated themselves through the gates of the governor's mansion, heavily guarded by the tanks and guns of a well-trained riot squad. The National Guardsmen, Caplan found out, were patriotic American boys — and simple racists of the purest kind.

Back in Oshawa, Ed and Velma tried to train their parents out of using language that was now considered objectionable. They would hear their mother talking on the phone, describing someone as a "Polack," and they would jump on her. "I'm not bigoted," Mary would respond. "That's what they are: Polacks." Velma was particularly sensitive to racist issues: she was working as a nurse for a Jewish doctor in Oshawa who was excluded from the local golf club because he was Jewish; his exclusion appalled Velma.

To Ed and Velma, their father was a loose cannon on deck, and they always worried that he might burst out with his redneck, anti-union views among the wrong company. Percy, who was still drinking but able to hold down his job at The Motors, was "argumentative and bumptious," says Hollands, "but I don't think he ever really said anything awful, at least not in front of me." Hollands was aware Ed had difficulties with his Dad. Percy would settle into his special chair, with a drink and a cigar, but he didn't really participate in the fun. It was Ed's mother who welcomed them, cooked for them, laughed with them, and Ed never stopped bringing his friends home to meet her.

In third year, Ed became president and Hollands general manager of the co-op. What Ed loved in the co-op was the combination of philosophy and action. "I liked *doing* things," he says. Ed and Terry were in charge of management, finances, maintenance and education. They brought in a speaker from St Francis Xavier University to talk about the Antigonish co-op movement, and had special evenings with federal and municipal politicians. Everyone ate together at Rochdale House, on Huron Street, and in the evenings, after doing chores and studying, they'd head over to the KCR.

The highlight that winter was the big debate on co-op expansion. Howard Adelman was wheeling and dealing on behalf of the co-op, scouring the university area for new houses to rent or buy to accommodate long waiting lists of students looking for rooms. Ed and Howard became the major opponents on how the co-op should grow.

"We'd go to the kitchens of the houses at 10 P.M. for coffee break, and debate," says Adelman. Seated in the book-lined study of his magnificent midtown Toronto home — whose skylights, art works and Oriental carpets are the sumptuous evidence of his real estate savvy, which started in his co-op days — Adelman remembers engaging in "a good, tough, honest fight" with Ed. "He set a standard he's adhered to. Ed's a fair debater, reasonable at all times, no personal attacks, nothing underhanded. We just had a legitimate difference of opinion, that's all." The difference was this: Ed believed in expansion but not in expanded bureaucracy; he wanted more co-op houses, but thought they should be independent and run themselves. Howard envisioned, on the other hand, a more corporate-style expansion that eventually resulted in a deal to build the massive, high-rise co-op on Bloor Street which became the infamous, drug-ridden Rochdale College.

Ed remembers the debate clearly. "I said that no matter what your ideology, the circumstances of living in a twenty-storey building would destroy what we were trying to do." He was right. Rochdale self-destructed in 1975, when its last residents were evicted, and is now a senior citizens' residence. Though Adelman disassociates himself from the Rochdale fiasco — "I left in 1966 when it was only three storeys high" — he concedes that "Ed discovered 'small is beautiful' before it became trendy." And over the years, Adelman has observed that 'Ed hasn't changed much. I don't think he was ever ambitious for power; he's not driven by personal ambition. He's a thoughtful, considerate guy, driven, I think, by his humanitarian instincts. I'm not a socialist, though I tend to vote NDP because I really think Ed wants to make the world a better place for most people. My only reservation about him is that I don't think he understands the workings of capital too well."

Ed did understand the workings of academia. If he didn't get good marks, and if he failed to win a scholarship, he wouldn't be able to afford graduate studies. By fourth year, he decided to leave the co-op. "There were too many interruptions," says Terry Hollands, "and I guess we'd done our thing there, we'd run it, so we got an apartment." The new place was on Kendal, north of Bloor, just south of a little park. Five co-opers moved into its three bedrooms and entertained. Anyone living with Ed learned that Ed's friends were always dropping in, even if Ed disappeared after a while, retreating to his bedroom to study.

Ed McFarlane, one of Ed's Trinity friends, was a regular visitor to the Kendal apartment and, like Hollands, was a scholarship student studying science — math, physics and chemistry. His memories of Ed are not of a serious student but of a gregarious extrovert. "Ed was definitely not shy," says McFarlane. "He likes meeting people and he always liked a big party, which was a major difference between us. I prefer small gatherings." Ed also had a great appetite for trivia. "We'd drive down to New York for a weekend, and to pass time on the road we'd play Twenty Questions. Ed always won. He could remember everything. He was born to play Trivial Pursuit." But their major disagreement concerned the American conductor and composer Leonard Bernstein.

"I didn't like Leonard Bernstein and Ed loved Leonard Bernstein," says McFarlane, a soft-spoken, very gentle man who gets all het up thinking about HOW MUCH ED LOVED LEONARD BERNSTEIN. "Bernstein was a flashy extrovert, and Ed enjoyed that. To me, Bernstein was just too much. He was showing off. Ed would say he was bringing joy to people. That's a key difference between us." But that too was Ed: full of unrestrained enthusiasms, attracted to people who expressed *joie de vivre*.

But Broadbent and McFarlane had more in common than not. McFarlane was a mathematician, as was Bertrand Russell, one of Ed's idols, so they talked about Russell, science and philosophy and went to movies together. Ed was a film buff; he still is. He liked intellectual French films and the works of brooding Swedish director Ingmar Bergman — as well as the Marx Brothers and, later, Monty Python, the crackpot British comedy outfit. Broadbent and McFarlane frequented the old Alhambra

Cinema on Bloor Street (now the Bloor Cinema) and the Christie Cinema, which started showing foreign films. They also haunted Palmer's Drugstore on Bloor Street, where they would read *The New Yorker* (still one of Broadbent's favourite magazines), in whose pages they first discovered J.D. Salinger, before he became famous for *The Catcher in the Rye* — a controversial novel Ed taught a few years later to Oshawa high school students, arousing the wrath of some parents.

McFarlane was another (relatively) poor kid who'd made his way in the world by doing well in school. He grew up in Toronto's Beach district, where his uncle inveigled him into the dangerous act of campaigning for the CCF. The Beach was not then receptive to CCFers (though it now elects New Democrats federally and provincially). "A lot of people would chase me off verandahs when they saw me with my CCF literature," says McFarlane. "They acted like I was spreading communism."

As the '50s wore on, the world was changing. The pages of *The Varsity* were filled with stories of student protests against the Duplessis regime in Quebec, the Hungarian uprising against Soviet opression — and laments about the lack of excitement in Ontario. After the Tory convention that chose John Diefenbaker as the party's new leader, Peter Gzowski wrote in *The Varsity*, on February 26, 1957, that "the drabness of Canadian politics lies not in our stars but in ourselves. If a politician were to speak out frankly, he would lose more votes than he would gain. And so we shall probably have to keep choosing between different shades of gray."

Marshall McLuhan had not yet enunciated his concept of the global village, but Ed's generation was the first to experience the all-encompassing power of the tube. TV images of American race riots prompted U. of T. students to incinerate an effigy of Gov. Orval Faubus of Arkansas in October, 1957; and in the '60s, TV would bring home the horrors of the Vietnam War, precipitating worldwide student protests. U.S. television dominated Canadian airwaves, from the Ed Sullivan Show to Jackie Gleason to American politics — which fascinated Ed, a great fan of

Adlai Stevenson, the Democratic presidential candidate defeated by Eisenhower, for the second time, in 1956.

At home, in the late '50s, Ban the Bomb peace activists were on the march, conferences and discussions on world disarmament were popular, folk singer Pete Seeger was strumming his banjo at protest singalongs in the JCR at University College, and Quebec was erupting. "Quebec Storm Gathering" said a *Varsity* headline next to a photo of a haughty Premier Duplessis, who would soon be replaced by Jean Lesage and the Quiet Revolution. There was definitely no revolution about to happen in staid Ontario. When university model parliament elections rolled around, Doug Marshall, as editor of *The Varsity*, wrote an editorial recommending that students take the risk and vote CCF. His suggestion was couched in cautious, apologetic tones: "While we would vote Conservative or Liberal as normal and responsible citizens, because both are experienced parties, on Wednesday we will vote CCF and we urge you to do the same. Where else except at a university will the CCF be given a chance to act on its policy . . . ."

"Normal" people, apparently, were not CCFers, nor were U. of T. students about to break with tradition: despite Marshall's urging, they continued to vote Conservative. Activists despaired. Ontario was immoveable, though on its eastern and western flanks, in Quebec and the prairies, vast changes were brewing. Then there was Cuba, where all eyes focussed after the 1959 revolution led by Fidel Castro. That January, reported *The Varsity*, a U. of T. dentistry student, one Jerry Becker, was vacationing in Cuba and stumbled onto the revolution. While sitting beside a pool in Havana, he heard "a lot of fuss," he said. He ran out to take a look and a Cuban revolutionary, running by with a gun in his hand, told Jerry to "get off the streets. This is for Cubans."

Like most young idealists, Ed was fascinated by Fidel Castro — never dreaming that twenty-two years later, as the head of the New Democratic Party, he would engage in a seven-hour, oftentimes heated discussion with the dictator who, in Ed's view, was guilty of having infringed human rights — though he had great cigars.

While the Cubans were rebelling, in Toronto the toga parties and calypso parties continued and one brave woman, dressed up as a man, insinuated herself into a Hart House debate, from which she was rudely ejected. (Women were not officially admitted to Hart House until 1972.) And in 1959, at the last meeting of the Philosophy Club, to which Ed belonged, Professor Bruno Morawetz expressed his outrage (as reported in *The Varsity*), that "contemporary philosophers are still asking the question of Achilles and the tortoise while they are being threatened by the hydrogen bomb."

"Music is a fine thing," Prof. Morawetz continued, "but fiddling while Rome is burning is not." Ed was impressed by the professor's anger and despair but he didn't quite buy it. Morawetz was older, he was sick and tired of philosophical games in the face of global unrest; he wanted action. Ed, on the other hand, was young and eager to think. He wasn't ready to *do* anything. "Morawetz was a very moving guy," Ed says. "I'd had him all the way through. He was emotionally very engaging and he cared deeply about ideas and their relevance to action. He wasn't the kind of intellectual who treated ideas as a game. But I remained intellectually skeptical."

When he graduated "first in his class in honours philosophy for the whole university," as he puts it, with pride, the year was 1959. Ed was twenty-three years old, and he was still a skeptic about most things. His passions were to find their anchors in the next decade.

CHAPTER THREE

The "S" Words: The Sixties, Sex and Socialism

Question: You seem like such a moderate guy and you never were a radical, so everyone wants to know why you didn't run for the Liberals?

Ed (somewhat offended): Running for the Liberals was never a consideration. I was a socialist before I became a New Democrat.
October 19, 1987.

The '60s dawned for Ed Broadbent in Oshawa, back in his old room in the family home at Central Park and Eulalie. After graduating from U. of T., he spent the summer of '59 at the Ontario College of Education, taking the short course that allowed university graduates to become high school teachers; the first wave of the post-war baby boom generation was flooding into the schools, and teaching jobs were easy to find. Ed's plan was simple: he would work for a year, save money, and return to U. of T. for postgraduate studies. Far from the hotbeds of activism, he watched as the world transformed itself. While the fireworks were going off, he was digging away at his own foundations.

John F. Kennedy's glittering inauguration as President of the United States in 1961 kicked off a decade of turmoil and upheaval. In America, the civil rights movement fuelled the counterculture revolution and the anti-Vietnam marches that swept university campuses and spread around the world, spewing drugs, rock and roll and idealism in its wake. Ban the Bomb, black power and women's liberation produced a tattered army of activists. Tom Hayden, now Jane Fonda's husband, had visited Berkeley in 1960 for a student conference and came away, according to *Esquire* magazine, "infected with a political virus." Politics was a fever, then. Hayden went on to become president of SDS (Students for a Democratic Society) and co-authored the 1962 Port Huron Statement, which called for reduced military spending and increased worker participation in government and business. The publication of the Port Huron Statement signalled the official birth of the American New Left, as the Waffle Manifesto was to do in Canada in 1969 — with Ed as one of its advocates, along for the radical ride, briefly, with Gerry Caplan, Jim Laxer and Mel Watkins.

"All over the world there was rebellion," says Caplan, who was outraged by Canadian complacency. "The U.S. was burning down. France and Germany were going crazy. In Canada, we had Expo '67 and the flag. It depressed me. The NDP was so ineffective. The real test, to me, was action. What could we accomplish?"

Picture Canada in the early '60s. Prime Minister John Diefenbaker, the prairie populist, has alienated the eastern elite that runs the Conservative Party and is on his way out. The Liberals are grasping for alliances, primarily in Quebec, that will keep them in power for another twenty years. And the newly formed, under-funded New Democratic Party is hammered in two consecutive federal elections.

In 1963, President Kennedy is assassinated and Lyndon Johnson takes over, embarking on the War on Poverty inspired by Michael Harrington's controversial bestseller, *The Other America*, which exposed the rotting underbelly of American affluence. (Harrington will later become a great friend of Ed's, through the Socialist International.) The Vietnam war heats up, as does the anti-war movement, and the agitation spreads to Canada. By 1965, the Quiet Revolution in Quebec is steaming ahead, Cabinet minister René Lévesque has created Hydro-

Québec and economic nationalism is an issue across the country. That year, Walter Gordon, the pin-striped finance minister from the Toronto establishment, resigns from Pearson's Cabinet in a dispute over foreign control of the economy and soon after publishes a denunciation of Liberal policy in *A Choice for Canada: Independence or Colonial Status.* The same year, George Grant, a rumpled, chain-smoking philosophy professor at McMaster University in Hamilton, publishes a slender, ninety-seven-page book called *Lament for a Nation: The Defeat of Canadian Nationalism.* Grant's eloquent *cri de coeur* was triggered by Lester Pearson's acceptance of nuclear warheads for Canada — a move sought by President Kennedy, fought by John Diefenbaker and denounced by a noted Quebec intellectual. In 1963, Pierre Trudeau had written scathingly in *Cité libre,* a left-wing magazine he helped create: "The philosophy of the Liberal party is very simple — say anything, think anything, or better still, do not think at all, but put us in power because it is we who can govern you best." A year later, nuclear warheads had moved across the border to North Bay, Ont.

George Grant, a Tory who favours the New Democrats and despises the Liberals, wrote in *Lament for a Nation:* "It was under a Liberal regime that Canada became a branch-plant society. It was under Liberal leadership that our independence in defence and foreign affairs was finally broken." Grant wholeheartedly supports Quebec's struggle for survival and once asked: "Why should Quebec want to be part of Canada when Canada has no interest in being Canada?"

Enter Jim Laxer, a significant force — and rival/irritant — in Ed's career. A graduate of the ultimate WASP high school, North Toronto, Laxer is a history student specializing in French-Canadian nationalism. He was born in Montreal, and his hero is Henri Bourassa, founder of *Le Devoir,* grandson of the great Quebec patriot Louis-Joseph Papineau, who led a rebellion against the government in 1837.

Laxer reads George Grant's little book one night in a horrible room at the old Y in Ottawa, and is overwhelmed. Grant's conviction that Canada has been sucked into the U.S. empire hits Laxer between the eyes. "It's the most important book I ever read in my life," says Laxer. "Here was a crazy old professor of religion at McMaster University and he woke up half our generation. He was saying Canada is dead, and by saying it he was creating the country. The book's an epic poem to Canada, a magnificent statement written with incredible energy and anger."

Broadbent, completing his Ph.D at the University of Toronto under C.B. Macpherson, is among the crowd — along with Laxer and Mel Watkins, who don't know each other at the time — that attends a huge anti-Vietnam teach-in at U. of T. Grant delivers a powerful tirade against the American empire. Mel Watkins, too, is overwhelmed. Brought up on a farm near Parry Sound in the heart of Tory Ontario, near Broadbent, Ont., Watkins had done his postgraduate work at the Massachusetts Institute of Technology. He considered himself an Americanized liberal. "I was your standard anti-nationalist, neoclassicist economist," says Watkins, now a U. of T. professor. "But I was radicalized by Vietnam. The anti-war movement in Canada developed into anti-imperialism," he explains, "and for me that translated into nationalism."

For Ed, all this excitement was merely a distant echo. In the fall of '59, he had been hired as an English teacher at Oshawa's O'Neill Collegiate, the upper-crust high school that was the rival to his alma mater, Central Collegiate. Back on his old turf, at a new school, riding his bicycle to work (which marked him as something of a hippy in Motor City), Ed was not dramatically different from his Central days but more evolved, more polished — and head-over-heels in love with his own intellectualism.

Hugh Winsor, *The Globe and Mail*'s national political columnist, was then a junior reporter for the *Oshawa Times*. "I was a little in awe of Ed," says Winsor, who was a few years younger and quite a lot greener. "Ed was a Fabian socialist in those days — and maybe still is — and he was very philosophical, very political, though not

in a partisan sense. He had obviously read all these people — Kant, Hegel, Heidegger — and I couldn't keep up
with him." If Ed was safely absorbed in the intellectual
past, he was at the same time keenly interested in the
politics of the day, especially the American variety. His
hero was still Adlai Stevenson, the Democratic statesman.

Winsor, along with Ed's usual raft of friends, spent
many an evening at the Broadbent home, being fed by
Ed's mother and watching political events on TV, accompanied by Ed's younger brother David, who was still in
high school. The son of a New Brunswick doctor, Winsor
came from a middle-class family and was struck by what
he saw as the stark contrast between Ed's working-class
environment and Renaissance personality. "Ed seemed an
unlikely product of that home," says Winsor, still puzzled
twenty-five years later by Ed's development. "His family
was *very* modest, not intellectually inspiring. Yet Ed was
clearly an intellectual, interested in classical music,
ideas, worldly far beyond his origins." Where, Winsor
wondered, did Ed get it?

Ed and his brother David were so different from each
other that Winsor found it hard to believe they came
from the same family. It was David, however, who was
more "normal," who "fit in" to the Oshawa environment
better than Ed. David, seven years younger than Ed,
didn't like school — and he felt the pressure of following
in the tracks of a superstar brother. While Ed was teaching at O'Neill, David was struggling through grade ten.
"That year," says David, "one of my teachers [at Central]
said to me: 'Why aren't you more like your brother?' That
kind of bullshit — that bothered me." A year later, David
would drop out, quitting school when he was nineteen
years old. David preferred coaching junior hockey and
working. He went straight into The Motors. His mother
didn't approve, but his father didn't mind — David and
his Dad were close and they took to driving to the plant
together. Through it all, the two brothers remained
friends — though David's life would later be complicated
by Ed's growing fame.

In '59, bored at school, sick of being forced to study stuff he wasn't interested in, David was hanging out with his friends, going to hockey games and dances, working at part-time jobs — anything to avoid the books. Coming home or going out, he would look at his brother in amazement. "Ed was always *reading*," says David. Ed had subscriptions to left-wing American magazines — *The New Republic*, *The Nation* and *Partisan Review*; he devoured European writers Albert Camus and Arthur Koestler, whose skepticism he admired; he was up to his eyebrows in the works of French intellectuals Jean Paul Sartre and Simone de Beauvoir; and he was always talking about international politics. One of the big events during this period was the revelation of Stalin's brutality in Russia. Ed was strongly anti-communist and would hold forth on the errors of totalitarian regimes. His interest in such issues was still, however, academic. His real life was more mundane: living at home, teaching high school students, saving money, dreaming dreams.

In the fall of '59, Louis Munroe, an English teacher at O'Neill, came home one day and told his wife Lucille that there was a new teacher on staff. "He wears these nice woolen ties and corduroy suits," said Louis, "and he enjoys having discussions. Let's have him over for dinner."

"So we had him over for dinner," says Lucille, "and debated the existence of God." The Munroes and Ed hit it off, discovering shared passions for literature, music and philosophy. "On Saturday afternoons," says Lucille, "we got in the habit of listening to the Metropolitan Opera broadcasts from New York on the radio. We'd drink a vodka and orange juice, we wouldn't talk much, we'd just sit together and listen to the music." The Munroes became "family friends" with the Broadbents, visiting their home for frequent dinners and travelling, on a few occasions, up to the family cottage at Pine Lake, near Gooderham, Ont.

Lucille was active in the community, acting in amateur plays (Hugh Winsor remembers reviewing one of her performances) and working as a nurse at the Oshawa General Hospital (where she met Velma Broadbent).

Then she moved to a job at the Oshawa Clinic, where she stitched cuts, set casts on broken bones, and assisted in minor surgery.

Ernie Winter, then head of the English department at O'Neill, remembers Louis and Lucille vividly. "Louis was a brilliant teacher, a fine fellow," says Ernie Winter. Lucille was "a charming, effervescent type."

And so Ed encountered the woman who would become, according to his friends, the best thing that ever happened to him; but neither of them knew it at the time.

"We'd never had a teacher like Ed Broadbent before," says William Hanley, then a fourteen-year-old grade ten student. They sure hadn't. They thought he looked like Steve McQueen, the sexy Hollywood actor who projected a tough-guy image; they thought he was a beatnik. "O'-Neill was upper-middle-class and conservative," says Hanley, "and Ed Broadbent stirred things up. He was skeptical about everything and he discussed ideas with us in a very adult manner. It was fun. In its own small way, it was revolutionary what he did. He was the first, and probably the last, high school teacher I had who was so challenging. To us, he was a radical. He pushed us to think and ask questions, which was unusual in our sedate community. Our teachers were good, academically, but not at all interested in rocking the tiniest little boat."

Hanley, whose father worked at The Motors, was another in a long line of Broadbent friends and students who would be the first in the family to go to university, and did so on impressive scholarships. Hanley took his B.A. at U. of T., his M.A. at the Sorbonne in Paris, his Ph.D. at Oxford. Today he is a professor of French at McMaster University in Hamilton, specializing in eighteenth-century literature, notably Voltaire, "which continues the skeptical, radical tradition," Hanley laughingly observes. Hanley has never forgotten Ed's parting gesture. "At the end of the year, when he left, he sent me and my friend a joint subscription to *The New Republic*, which was *the* avant-garde left-wing magazine.

It was a big deal, to us, and it was extremely kind of him."

Ed enjoyed teaching almost as much as he loved learning. He had a knack for stimulating students and took tremendous pleasure in triggering their imagination. He was the kind of teacher who, above all, encouraged his students to think for themselves. He organized a philosophy club for grades ten to thirteen. "We went through the standard questions — ethics, the Good, freedom, does God exist — and the kids loved it," says Ed. He remembers once joking with some students: "Does God exist? Where is He? Is He here in this room with us? Is He sitting with us?" Then Ed clapped his hands together, squeezing an imaginary object, acting out the scene. "There, I've got Him," he said, as his students' eyes popped in amazement. It is no surprise that some of the more conservative parents didn't appreciate his efforts in regard to religion and literature.

With the approval of his English department head, Ernie Winter, Ed was guiding his grade twelve class through J.D. Salinger's novel of teenaged *angst*, *The Catcher in the Rye*. One evening in 1959, Barry and Velma Cornish, now married, were sharing the traditional Sunday night dinner at Mary and Percy Broadbent's. Ed was called to the phone and detained for a long time by one of the parents "complaining that Ed was teaching this filthy book," remembers Barry. "But typical Ed, he got into a long discussion about the merits of *The Catcher in the Rye*, being really serious about why it was a good book, patiently explaining on and on . . . Then he'd hang up and the phone would ring again and it was another parent fit to be tied about this dirty book and Ed would start the discussion all over again. He was always like that. He'd explain anything to anybody, to the village idiot, about why he did what he did and thought what he thought."

What Ed remembers about that year at home, besides listening to opera with Louis and Lucille, was that finally he was able to speak, a little, to his father. During the winter, when Ed couldn't ride his bike, he would borrow

his father's car and drive his father to work, dropping
Percy off at The Motors before heading over to school.
Those short rides allowed an intimacy to grow that had
never been present in their twenty-four years' awkward
acquaintance. And the son who was in so many ways like
his Dad — argumentative, pugnacious, ambitious —
started to know his father, a little. "Most of my recollections of my father are of him as an alcoholic," says Ed.
"That permeated the family. I never knew him in his exuberant, joyful period."

In the fall of 1960, back at U. of T. for his M.A. in the philosophy of law, the proud recipient of a Canada Council
scholarship, Ed moved into an apartment near Spadina
and Dupont with Terry Hollands. It was a momentous
autumn for both Ed and for Canadian socialism, in quite
distinct developments. Ed fell in love and the CCF was on
the verge of uniting with major unions and "New
Generation–New Party Clubs" to form the NDP. In an October 31 by-election, Walter Pitman won Peterborough
for the New Party, an interim step between the CCF and
NDP, and Ontario socialists were jubilant.

But Ed was more absorbed by money and love. Before
Christmas, he was broke; he tried to get a bank loan,
using Hollands as his reference — which Hollands
figured was pretty useless, since he didn't have much
more money than Ed. Ed's loan application was turned
down and he had to move back home, commuting every
day to school for the rest of the year. But the pain of pen-
ury was offset by the adrenalin rush of advanced passion.
Ed was madly in love with Yvonne Yamaoka, and she
seemed equally keen.

Yvonne was a compelling attraction for a young intellectual who understood little of his own deeper complexi-
ties; besides, he was horny. Ed met Yvonne at a party.
Ed McFarlane, Broadbent's Trinity friend from his undergraduate days, was back at U. of T. doing graduate work
in physics and remembers the night it happened. "I
bumped into Broadbent on the way home. He was dancing down the street. He told me all about this fascinating

woman he'd just met." Ed was then twenty-four years old and though he'd had crushes on girls and women all his life, going back to grade two, this was his first great love.

"Ed didn't really have a steady girlfriend when he was an undergrad at U. of T.," says his sister Velma, who figures Ed fell hard for Yvonne. A few years older than Ed, Yvonne had graduated from U. of T. and was already working as a city planner at City Hall. Japanese-Canadian, sophisticated, independent and elegant, Yvonne was tiny, with long black hair and a reserved manner that intrigued men. Michael Cassidy was just one of the swains at U. of T. who had yearned after her in vain. "Yvonne was my heart-throb," says Cassidy.

But Yvonne Yamaoka's life had been deeply marked, like most Japanese-Canadians of her generation. She was born in British Columbia, the daughter of an industrious immigrant who came to Canada in 1904, penniless, and worked the whaling ships off the Pacific coast before an accident landed him in Vancouver. Seitaro Yamaoka then sold Christmas trees from a downtown corner and eventually bought his own woodlot, cut down his own trees — a lot like Ed's grandfather — and operated his own saw mill; later, he developed a process for re-using rejected lumber that made him a small fortune. Through the Depression he kept people on his payroll who would otherwise have starved, and by the late 1930s had established himself as a patriarch in the Japanese-Canadian community. "He was a man to be feared," says his eldest daughter, Setsu Weldon, an optometrist. "He roared like a lion. He expected people to obey. I had a brother who was disinherited because he didn't obey my father." But Seitaro Yamaoka looked after the people who worked for him, and he was successful. Before the Second World War, he was exporting one million dollars' worth of lumber a year.

Then the war came, and the Yamaokas were trapped in the snares of one of the worst injustices of Canadian history: the internment of Japanese-Canadians, followed by the confiscation of their property, in 1942. Shortly after Japan bombed Pearl Harbor and entered the war against the Americans in 1941, Japanese-Canadians were treated like dangerous aliens and traitors. Yvonne was a child when her family, among 21,000 Japanese-Canadians, was rounded up in Vancouver and shipped off like cattle into the interior, where they were held for the duration of the war. In effect, they were incarcerated for seven years, lost their civil rights and were not given the freedom to travel — or vote — until 1949. By 1950, the Yamaokas were settled in Toronto, attempting to survive the trauma. At the age of sixty-five, Seitaro Yamaoka went to work stoking coal on barges that were dredging Lake Ontario. He lived to be 103.

The Canadian government, then headed by Liberal Prime Minister Mackenzie King, had justified its actions against Japanese-Canadians by invoking the War Measures Act — a procedure repeated in 1970 by Liberal Prime Minister Pierre Trudeau, to "deal with" Quebec. In 1942, the CCF stood alone opposing the treatment of Japanese-Canadians, and was vilified by Liberals and Tories; in 1970, sixteen New Democrats, Ed Broadbent among them, rose against the majority to defend democracy and the human rights of the Québecois, and were again denounced.

The imposition of the War Measures Act against Japanese-Canadians was, says Roger Obata, the first president of the National Association of Japanese-Canadians, "a totalitarian horror. Only the CCF supported us." (Foremost among their defenders was Toronto lawyer Andrew Brewin, a civil rights lawyer and CCF activist.) The psychological damage continues, Obata says, to this day. "People were in a state of shock. It took decades before we could even speak of what had happened." Joy Kogawa, author of *Obasan*, says: "No democratic country in the world did what Canada did to us. The government stole our property and exiled us. The dispersal policy was dedicated to destroying our communities, and they did it. They would not allow us to go home."

The Yamaokas' experience had a huge impact on Ed. He was outraged, years later, by Prime Minister Trudeau's response to Japanese-Canadians' quest for restitution. "Trudeau used one of his *reductio ad absurdum* arguments," says Broadbent, mimicking Trudeau's cool, haughty tone: "If we do this for Japanese-Canadians, we'll have to do it for every aggrieved group, and yes it was unfair but life is not fair and all kinds of Canadians have experienced unfair things . . ." Broadbent shrugs. "Trudeau refused to recognize the unique nature of the Japanese-Canadians' circumstance. They never did anything wrong and they lost everything."

The case also haunts Ed because it demonstrates, he believes, one of the great twisted myths about Canadian political parties. "These yahoos," he says, referring to the perpetrators of 'commie-pinko' innuendoes in relation to the NDP, "I find them deeply morally offensive." If any party is opposed to any sort of totalitarian regime, he says, it is the New Democrats. "Who stood up for the Japanese-Canadians? Who was against the War Measures Act? The NDP has a distinguished civil libertarian record. Freedom and individual rights are distinguishing characteristics of social democratic parties. To suggest otherwise is malevolent."

Preoccupied with his relationship with Yvonne, preparing for their marriage in September, Ed did not attend the New Democrats' founding convention at the beginning of August, 1961. The convention drew avid CCFers and New Party members from across the country, while Ed and Yvonne visited Velma and Barry at the cottage at Pine Lake. When they weren't swimming, they listened on the radio to the excitement generated by 2,084 delegates who gathered in Ottawa to approve a socialist program, pick the name for the party and choose a leader.

At the five-day meeting, Saskatchewan Premier Tommy Douglas defeated Hazen Argue, then Saskatchewan's only CCF MP, for the leadership, and the freshly christened New Democratic Party (which won out over New Party or Social Democratic Party) adopted a liberalized program that erased the rhetoric of the Regina Manifesto — to the outrage of Saskatchewan's purists.

The New Democratic Party stood for economic planning, a Canadian Development Fund, control of multinationals, medicare, portable pensions, tax reform, protection for farmers, fishermen, credit unions, small business and the CBC, withdrawal from NORAD, support for NATO, and a promise to give Canada its own flag. Hardly radical; this was the modern face of democratic socialism, with a commitment to a mixed economy and no more talk about wholesale nationalization. The NDP's proposals seem all the more moderate because most of them were subsequently implemented by Liberal and Tory governments: medicare, the flag, the Canada Development Corporation, the Foreign Investment Review Agency. (The Mulroney Government has since dismantled the levers of economic control, bargained away in its search for a trade deal with the United States.)

But Ed Broadbent was in love; politics was a minor concern. The wedding was small, conducted by a Unitarian minister, attended by Yvonne's family, the Broadbents and a few friends. The Yamaokas accepted Yvonne's choice of mate; if they wanted her to marry within her own race, they knew enough not to force the issue. "Yvonne broke the ice even before her marriage by bringing all kinds of people home," says Setsu. Yvonne had many admirers, and "most of them were Canadian." For their part, the Broadbents quickly fell in love with Yvonne.

The newlyweds moved into an apartment on Collier Street, a secluded dead-end street just a few blocks north of the busy intersection of Yonge and Bloor. Their apartment, overlooking the dappled green forest of the Rosedale ravine, became the local drop-in centre for any of Ed's friends who happened to be in the neighbourhood.

No problems were visible at first — indeed nobody ever really knew what happened to Yvonne and Ed; most of their friends were shocked when they broke up six years later. Yvonne and Ed: they were considered the perfect couple, at the centre of an intellectual, artistic, left-wing circle that included anybody who liked good discussions, good music, good food. Yvonne was a marvellous cook.

She prepared Japanese meals long before Japanese cuisine was fashionable. A skilled hostess, she looked after her guests in traditional Japanese fashion, with great care. Percy, Ed's Dad, came to adore her attentions; David and his future wife, Sharon Kinsman, frequently drove into Toronto from Oshawa and always felt welcomed by Yvonne. "She tried very hard to do things right for the Broadbent family," says her sister Setsu.

One of Yvonne's friends says she was "difficult to get close to, hard to get to know," a description that some people would apply to Ed himself. Yvonne was a woman of contradictory qualities — as was her husband. They sound, in fact, like they might have had too much in common. He was very Canadian, and she was very Japanese; they were both reserved and quite stubborn when it came to "private" family matters and personal judgements, yet given to playful amusements and a common desire for adventure.

Yvonne needed a sense of humour to be married to this domestic klutz. Ed's first efforts at house-husbandry were hilariously inept. His sister Velma and her husband Barry Cornish remember visiting the Collier Street apartment one afternoon when Ed had manfully hung new kitchen cabinets. They were all sitting in the living room, having a drink to celebrate his endeavours, when a great crash shook the place, accompanied by the sound of breaking glass and china. Ed's cabinets had fallen to the floor, demolishing all their plates and glasses.

He also tried sanding the floors with an electric sander while wearing a tie. He nearly choked to death when his tie got caught in the machine and twisted around his neck tighter and tighter . . . until he was saved at the last minute by Yvonne, who pulled the plug.

Barry remembers that Ed had acquired expensive tastes — like his father: a penchant for Havana cigars, good clothes, good Cognac, and, soon, a motorcycle and a leather jacket—a brown bomber jacket he still wears. He was also developing a reputation as a wild driver, noted for talking with his hands and looking at his companions as he drove very fast. (Today, his handlers decree that Ed does not drive on official party business.) He dreamed of inventing an invisible device that would alert him to the presence of police speed traps; he was always getting caught and losing points, which threatened the loss of his driver's licence.

"Ed never has any points left," Velma says bluntly. Ed admits it, and cheerfully tells stories of showing up at court to fight speeding tickets. But it was not only his driving habits that were less than genteel. Ed also had a somewhat vulgar sense of humour, which conflicted with his high-minded intellectual attitudes, and he could tell sexist jokes along with the worst of them. (His earnest feminism came later, though Velma must be credited with having been the first woman to struggle to get her brother to see the light.) Ed could be bawdy and rowdy — qualities Yvonne would not have appreciated — and he was the kind of man who gets along well with men — even businessmen. Teaching at York University a few years later, he was invited to speak to a men's dinner and discussion club run by Harry Rosen, whose business selling "gentlemen's apparel" made him a millionaire. Every session, Rosen's group would pick an interesting expert to function as a catalyst. One year they chose Ed Broadbent, who came to their dinners, spoke to them about political theory, and generally "shot the shit," says Rosen — who was surprised at what a nice guy Ed was. "It was fun to sit and have a beer with him. He explained Marxism to us — you could tell he wasn't a Marxist — and he was an intelligent guy. What I didn't expect was his great sense of humour. He was a lot of fun."

Then there were all the parties. Velma remembers cutting up fruit for a batch of sangria that filled a plastic garbage can for a huge crowd that packed the Collier Street apartment one night. There were always people visiting, even — occasionally — Louis and Lucille Munroe, who maintained their friendship with Ed and sometimes had dinner with the Broadbents when they visited Toronto. "Any of us, if we were downtown for a movie or a concert, we'd all go over to Ed's and drop in for a coffee or a beer," says Velma. "Ed loved it."

Yvonne was not enamoured of the open-house policy, according to some friends who sensed her resentment at having her privacy constantly invaded, though she was unfailingly polite in public. She would come home from a hard day at work, looking forward to a little peace and quiet with Ed, only to find his friends already occupying the apartment. Ed's gregariousness may have initially attracted her but over time seems to have aggravated her. For his part, he seems to have found her formality and reserve, once so enticing, increasingly alienating. Besides this inevitable clash of wills, there was another factor: Yvonne didn't know it at the time, but she was suffering from hypoglycemia, a malfunction in her blood-sugar level which caused fatigue and irritability. "Yvonne is very kind and very conscientious," says Setsu. "She took on too much and sometimes felt the strain."

But early on in the fall of 1961, while the honeymoon period was still glowing, Ed's intellectual quest became focussed. He switched from philosophy to political science in order to study with Crawford Brough Macpherson, who must be credited with lassoing Oshawa's roaming intellectual cowboy and reining him in. Macpherson's influence on Ed would be enormous — he stands as a giant figure in Broadbent's development. It was almost as if Ed had been holding himself aloof in a skeptical posture, until Macpherson came along with the analysis that articulated Ed's instinctive politics. Before Macpherson, Ed was engaged he says, in "trying to understand life." After Macpherson, Ed would be drawn towards "trying to *act* in life." Ed reached a kind of intellectual and spiritual fulfilment in the work of Macpherson; he found the roots that would sustain him throughout political battles as yet undreamt of.

At the Macphersons' house on Boswell Avenue in Toronto, up on the third floor, Brough's study remains as it was before his death on July 21, 1987, at the age of seventy-five. The room is a serene and spartan space, the walls painted a soft yellow, a faded oriental carpet on the wooden floor, with an old footstool close to a comfortable chair, a little bed for a nap, bookshelves filled with books:

the *Collected Works of Karl Marx and Frederick Engels* (three volumes), next to Disraeli, Pepys's *Diary*, Darwin's *Origin of the Species* and John le Carré's *The Little Drummer Girl*. And crammed in profusion are a vast array of translations of his own books into Japanese, Italian, French, German and Spanish, among other languages.

Above his plain wooden desk hang three old engravings: portraits of seventeenth-century English political theorists Hobbes and Locke, and an interior of the Bodleian Library at Oxford University, where Brough studied and taught. There is a letter on his desk, received shortly before he died. His wife Kay shows it to me. It is from the Minister of Education, Bangkok, Thailand: "We are pleased to inform you that *The Real World of Democracy* [Brough's book] has been recently printed in Thai for free distribution to our schools, libraries and organizations concerned."

Above the bookshelves there hangs a Picasso print. Kay says it was Brough's favourite picture. It is a tender, poignant image of a young child holding a white bird — the same picture that hangs in the Oshawa apartment of Ted Maidman, Ed's boy scout leader. Kay says: "Brough was a peacemaker. A gentle man."

The gangly, hook-nosed Macpherson was a professor of political science at the University of Toronto. He was born in Toronto and had taught at U. of T. since 1935, but his increasing renown had taken him, on visiting professorships, to practically every great university in the world. He was a left-wing Canadian socialist, he was famous and revered, and he was entitled to a certain self-importance, but there was no pomposity with Brough. Until he retired in 1977, he continued to teach undergraduate courses, because he loved nothing more than stimulating young people to question the world around them. Ed used to sit in on Macpherson's undergraduate classes and saw the master at work. Under Macpherson's guidance, Ed, with five years of philosophy under his belt, was doing "make-up" courses necessary to fulfil political science requisites. "There was just a handful of students in Macpherson's political theory seminar," Ed says. "The experience was intense." Macpherson was reaching the height of his power. "I became very involved in his interpretation of the foundations of democratic theory. I spent more and more time with him." Macpherson became Ed's intellectual role model.

"He assumed . . . that his job was to engage the student's mind in the real task of critical thinking," Ed wrote in *This Magazine* (November, 1987). "He would look for assumptions, stated or unstated: assumptions about human nature, about the economy, about history. He would analyse and conclude; never intellectually vulgar, always critically appreciative of the great contributors to our common heritage. The final effect was as satisfying as variations on a theme by Bach. Like all great political theorists, his goal was not merely to understand but also to change. He sought to influence our decisions about the future by forcing upon us a morally critical assessment of the past and present. . . . [He] longed for the kind of society in which all men and women would have equal opportunity not to climb up a class-divided ladder but to exercise their creative potential. . . . He correctly saw that the main body of liberal freedoms and political institutions must be an essential element of a socialist society."

Describing Macpherson, Broadbent seems to be describing himself. Ed was not alone in receiving the full impact of the professor's formidable gifts. Macpherson's personal magnetism was unforgettable. His lectures were famous for drawing huge crowds of students who silently absorbed everything he said and then, at the end, burst into applause — an unusual phenomenon at university.

"We were on the edge of our seats, enthralled, feeling that first flush of intellectual discovery, listening to Macpherson," says Lynn King, a student of Brough's in the '60s, now an Ontario judge. "Even writing his exams was exciting, if you can imagine that, because you knew you could write what you really thought, instead of having to regurgitate what some professor wanted to hear."

Macpherson's political stance was clear to his students. "It was in his classes that I got my first inkling of what socialism was all about," says King. "He presented it in a very simple way, as something positive and desirable. The capitalist assumption, he explained, is that man is acquisitive and greedy, that consumerism is the driving force of society; the socialist assumption is that man is co-operative, sharing and creative. Of course this was the '60s and we all wanted to be creative and sharing." Macpherson's message was well-suited to the idealistic '60s, and it is not surprising that he turned out a lot of activists.

Rosemary Brown, a former Vancouver MLA who would run against Ed for the party leadership in 1975, was a close friend of the Macphersons. When she came to Toronto to visit, she would stay with them. "Brough would knock on my door at 7:30 in the morning," says Rosemary. "He coddled an egg very well, and he loved to sit with a cup of coffee and a cigarette and talk." Did you debate ideas with him? "Yes, but he wasn't one of those people who made you argue about feminism or equality. They were givens for him. He believed in the inherent equality of persons. He was involved in the issues of the day. He talked about the Constitution and the Meech Lake Accord — he shared my indignation at the lack of democratic process involved in Meech Lake, at how a handful of individuals made profound changes to the Constitution without input." And he talked about war and peace. "He and Kay were committed to the peace movement, he was an ardent environmentalist and very concerned about how our selfishness has become destructive. About how all the little nations were getting into the nuclear race — it's madness. About poverty and the Third World. He talked about everything."

Macpherson's most famous book, *The Political Theory of Possessive Individualism: Hobbes to Locke*, was published in 1962 to worldwide acclaim. "It is rare for a book to change the intellectual landscape," said *The New Statesman*'s review. "It is even more unusual for this to happen when the subject is one that has been thoroughly investigated by generations of philosophers and historians. . . . Until the appearance of Professor Macpherson's work, it seemed unlikely that anything radically new could be said about so well-worn a topic. The unexpected has happened, and the shock waves are still being absorbed."

An analysis of the evolution of the liberal-democratic state, *Possessive Individualism* is one of Macpherson's many books that have been translated into more than ten languages. In it, he argued that Hobbes and Locke, founders of western liberalism, based their thinking on a questionable assumption: that people were by nature acquisitive, self-centred and greedy. Macpherson argued that society could be organized in a manner that promoted people's inherent sense of co-operation. What it boiled down to, says U. of T. political scientist Peter Russell, who studied and taught with Macpherson, was that "Brough thought human nature was not fixed. I don't agree with him. I'm more of a historical pessimist, which makes me a liberal. Liberals, you could say, believe in original sin — that there's a nasty streak in humans. Marxists — and I would call Brough an intellectual Marxist — are optimists." Russell insists on defining the term Marxism, because, he says, it is misunderstood. "To be a Marxist does not mean you're in favour of totalitarian government or pro-Soviet Union — Brough was very critical of the Soviet Union. Essentially, a Marxist believes that the economic relations in society determine the opportunities people have, that when wealth and power are unevenly distributed, working people cannot fully develop themselves." Like economist John Kenneth Galbraith, Macpherson argued that the modern liberal-democratic state was afflicted by "the ability of a possessing class to keep the effective political power in its hands in spite of universal suffrage." The task for democrats, he said, was to break this logjam.

Brough was not a rigid ideologue. When Peter Russell wrote a critical review of *The Political Theory of Possessive Individualism*, Macpherson said to him, "You've made some interesting points that I'd like to discuss with

you." Above all, says Russell, Macpherson was open-
minded. "That's why I call him a gentleman. He was a
truly liberal man in his interest in other people's ideas.
We co-taught a course together for fifteen years, and we'd
argue out these differences with our students. We had a
ball."

Although he was not a member of the NDP, Brough was
keenly interested in its politics. A few years before his
death, he hosted a dinner party at which Ed was a special guest. "Brough was worried," says Kay, "that the NDP
was moving to the right." Certainly that's Kay's perception; she sits on the party's left flank and is impatient
with the leadership's moderate ways. It was an interesting evening: Ed, party leader, a disciple of Brough's, was
being challenged by his teacher. "It was a wonderful discussion," says Dorothy Inglis, a New Democrat from
Newfoundland, who was there. "Brough was talking as
he always does about the integrity of the party, the need
to keep to our socialist goals, that we shouldn't be
tempted by good fortune to water down what we stand
for. Ed was listening carefully, he was really absorbed.
Brough believed very strongly that the way is not to be a
liberal party but to be a socialist party concerned with
changing the system — that's what makes us different,
that's what attracts people to us."

Behind Macpherson's remarks was an implied criticism
that the party was watering down its socialist convictions
in order to reach for power. Ed, however, was undaunted.
He defended the role of the socialist politician dealing in
the real world, seeking to persuade people to make
changes. He talked about the pragmatic problems facing
the NDP but "seemed," says Inglis, "not unmindful of the
truth running through Brough's statements. I felt, listening to Ed, that — removed from the constraints of office
— he would share Brough's views. Ed was very open to
Brough, and clearly had tremendous respect for him. But
we knew that some of the people Ed would go back to in
Ottawa wouldn't be as keen on following Brough's
course." Ed understood only too well the gap that existed
between the role of the thinker and the job of the politi-

cian, but he sincerely felt he had not betrayed the Macpherson convictions. Kay remained skeptical.

But Brough had more on his mind than political theory. Herbert Whittaker, *The Globe and Mail's* drama critic for twenty-five years, now retired, was friends with Brough since 1949. "I never had a political discussion with Brough, ever," says Whittaker. Seated in his Rosedale apartment, which overflows with framed stage and costume designs, artworks, books and plants, Whittaker remembers Brough as having, even in old age, "a youthful receptivity. He was never a retired authority. You know, I became part of their family. We did a lot of things together. Kay would come to plays with me — Brough preferred music — and she was the organizing force." An ardent feminist and, by the '70s, an involved New Democrat, Kay Macpherson was the activist partner to an intellectual husband. "Brough was able to live happily in a whirlpool of women's liberation," says Whittaker, "approving it, supporting it and letting it flow over and around him, while pursuing his own equally important work." Kay was charging full tilt at the "men-only" system that infuriated her. "I think Brough had a rotten time with me, a lot of the time," Kay says. "I would get enraged at what was going on and I'd take it out on him." But most importantly, he "looked after the household while I politicked." Basically, they agreed, even though she jokes that the few times she attended his lectures she couldn't understand what he was talking about. Herbert Whittaker was similarly unable to appreciate Brough's scholarly intentions.

"Was I aware of Brough's deeper purpose?" asks Whittaker. "He inscribed me a copy of *The Political Theory of Possessive Individualism*, of which I couldn't get past the first page — though I offered to design a lurid cover for its paperback edition."

Whittaker was asked to define Macpherson's politics on a sad occasion. "I was abroad in July [1987] at the time of Brough's death. When I was informed, I was determined to get an obit into *The Times* [of London, England], which is not an easy matter. I wrote the obit and phoned it in. They called back to check and asked me some questions. One was: "Would you say he was a rightist?" I said, "No, I should think he was the opposite. Some people thought he was a Marxist." And so *The Times* of Tuesday, August 25, 1987, reported in its obituary of Macpherson that "he was a scholar of international repute . . . who elaborated theories which were regarded as Marxist by some, but which, in fact, tended to see the salvation of socialism as lying in its embracing liberal-democratic values."

Did young Ed think of Macpherson as a Marxist? "Macpherson escapes categorization, as all great thinkers do," says Ed. "Clearly he was profoundly influenced by Marx, but he went beyond Marx as Marx would have gone beyond Marx. C.B. Macpherson lived in the twentieth century. He was a modern thinker. He believed very strongly in human rights, the growth of the human personality and the freedom that's necessary for personal fulfilment. He built a socialist theory that combined individual rights with community needs; he kept, if you will, the best of both liberalism and socialism." It was this blend that touched Ed at such a deep level, and would forever separate him from Canadian socialists of an earlier generation. "I think that David Lewis and Tommy Douglas viewed the [free] market as a necessary evil," says Ed. "I see the market as desirable. We've got to accept the market and enhance it. I also think you take certain things out of the market — education, health care, child care — so people don't have to compete for them."

At the University of Toronto's tribute to Macpherson on September 30, 1987, former students Ed Broadbent and Bob Rae, leader of the Ontario NDP, sat in the front row of Convocation Hall listening to such luminaries as Nobel Prize-winning scientist John Polanyi express fond feelings for the great man. Polanyi and Macpherson shared an ardent commitment to the peace movement. "Brough was my colleague for over three decades," said Polanyi. "He was ambitious out of love for life. He moved far beyond the academic confines. He cared mightily for mankind."

The last word was Brough's. In 1965, CBC radio recorded Macpherson delivering, for its Massey Lecture series, "The Real World of Democracy," since published as a book. At the end of the tribute, the tape was played. Macpherson spoke: "If you want an operative conclusion, it is this: tell your politicians that the free way of life depends, to an extent they have not yet dreamed of, on the Western nations' remedying the inequality of human rights as between ourselves and the poor nations. Nothing less than massive aid, which will enable the poor nations to lift themselves to recognizable human equality, will now conserve the moral stature and the power of the liberal democracies." This was Macpherson's message, writ large: selfish greed is ultimately destructive; the only salvation is to share the wealth.

Macpherson's message to Ed, in the fall of '61, was that Ed should consider a period of study at the illustrious London School of Economics. Embarked on his doctorate, in his sixth year at U. of T., Ed was attracted to the idea of a change of scene, and so was his bride. London, the cultural centre of the English-speaking world, was a great lure to the young couple.

But before going to England, Ed got involved with the New Democratic Party, gingerly dipping his toe into the murky waters of partisan politics. There was no glamour attached. The Diefenbaker era was dissolving, Lester Pearson's Liberals were gaining strength, and the NDP was struggling to expand its base. Guided by the impassioned oratory and pragmatic politics of its leader Tommy Douglas, strengthened by the unremitting back-room slogging of David Lewis, the party still needed all the help it could get. During the federal election campaign in the spring of '62, "while Pearson and Diefenbaker traversed the country in chartered aircraft, surrounded by staff and reporters," wrote historian Desmond Morton, "Douglas and a couple of aides waited at airports for commercial flights or drove with local supporters . . ."

Under siege in Saskatchewan, where the province's doctors were waging war against the NDP medicare system,
Tommy Douglas would lose his Regina seat. Yet there
were a few glimmers of hope: Gerry Caplan and Stephen
Lewis had teamed up to run David Lewis's campaign in
Toronto's York South and got David elected for the first
time. He joined eighteen New Democrats in the House of
Commons. Still, there was a widespread feeling, wrote
Desmond Morton, that "the New Party experiment had
failed. The NDP had lost the farmers' support without col-
lecting the workers. A Gallup survey after the election
reported that voters from trade union homes had split 23
per cent for the NDP, 25 percent for the Conservatives,
and an overwhelming 38 per cent for the Liberals."

John Valleau, Ed's neighbour on Collier Street, remembers how bad it could be for New Democrats: "Ed and I
got involved around the same time, working for the NDP
in Rosedale in '62," says Valleau. If ever there was a losing cause, this was it; not many people even knew there
was an NDP candidate in Rosedale. Here's how Valleau
found out about him: "I was in my kitchen one dull and
dismal day, minding my own business, when I heard a
very loud noise coming from the street. I went out to
look, and there was this fellow, a small, thin Brit, all
alone, making a theoretical, intellectual speech to Collier
Street through a loud-speaker. I felt so sorry for him —
the poor man had no audience at all — that I asked him
if I could do anything to help him."

The lonely NDP candidate was an English Fabian socialist by the name of Des Sparham. Voluble, charming and
annoying, he was a tireless organizer of New Party clubs,
slogging across the country, rounding up tiny groups of
mostly younger, middle-class urban professionals who often knew nothing about the CCF but were interested in
progressive politics — the yuppies of their generation.
They were neophytes, but Sparham eagerly latched on to
anyone who'd give him the time of day. His own Rosedale
campaign was organized by "this little group of haggard
people," according to Valleau, that included Valleau and
his wife Liz, Lyla Barclay (Ed's pal from co-op days), her

husband Tony Barclay, another Brit, and Ed Broadbent. Ed's sister Velma came along to help canvass, and remembers that campaign as her baptism; she also recalls that Ed became president of the riding association, though his achievement was hardly remarkable, given the few members in the group. The connections he made, however, were enduring.

Valleau is an important link in the Broadbent network. With a Ph.D. from Cambridge, Valleau is now a professor of theoretical chemical physics, working at U. of T.'s Lash Miller Chemical Labs — the headquarters of John Polanyi. Valleau shares more than a building with Polanyi. They are both members of an organization Polanyi helped create called Science for Peace. The peace movement is one of the major feeder groups into the New Democrats, and it is a movement to which Ed is closely bound through personal friendship.

"The weapons of mass destruction now threatening the survival of civilization and, perhaps, of the human race itself were produced by sophisticated technology," states a Science for Peace brochure. "Because of the role science has played in putting this destructive technology in man's grasp, the image of science, once regarded as a source of abundance, comfort and health, has been tarnished. . . . Science for Peace is an organization devoted to exploring ways of putting science in the service of peace instead of war."

Stretching in the sunshine of his U. of T. office, his desk littered with Science for Peace newsletters, Valleau looks like an amiable, aging hippy. "My father was a Conservative but he was a Red Tory," says Valleau. "He had a social conscience so it wasn't that big a move to vote CCF." By the time the NDP was founded in 1961, the Valleaus were so keen on the party that they both remember, the night their second child was born, rushing back to Liz Valleau's hospital room after her labour in time to listen to Tommy Douglas's victory speech celebrating his leadership of the newly christened NDP.

The Valleaus and the Broadbents, neighbours on Collier Street, became friends, visiting back and forth at each other's apartments. After a while, "Liz and I realized there was some tension between Yvonne and Ed, but there was tension between Liz and me too." Both couples would split: "Our generation had lots of firsts, and one of the areas in which we broke new ground was getting divorced," says Valleau. But the friendship between the Valleaus and the Broadbents — incorporating politics, music and literature — was enduring; it did not end when Ed and Yvonne left Collier Street for London in the summer of '62.

Journeying to the London School of Economics was, for a Canadian socialist, like trekking to Mecca. "It was still, for us, the mythical place," says Gerry Caplan, "the home of the Fabian Society, of the Webbs, of Harold Laski. One had a sense of returning to one's spiritual home."

In the fall of 1962, Ed enrolled at the fabled LSE, a college of the University of London located in Houghton Street, off the Strand. Ever resourceful, Yvonne found a job as a town planner. They rented a cheap, unheated flat in Chiswick and every morning rode into the city on their Lambretta scooter, chugging through Oxford Circus to the offices of the London County Council, where Yvonne worked. "She'd bang her helmet against mine," says Ed, "disputing the route I was taking." His scholarship and her salary afforded them a little extra money to attend concerts and plays and soak up the culture. They were a happy, if tense, adventurous pair.

Ed was deeply immersed in his Ph.D. thesis on John Stuart Mill, the nineteenth century English liberal who evolved into a non-Marxist socialist. Struggling with Mill's search for the proper balance between individual liberty and social justice, blending what he had learned from Macpherson, Ed honed the themes that would provide the foundation for his political career. Mingling in the polyglot student body — LSE attracts huge numbers of Third World students, Africans and Asians as well as Americans and Australians — he loved the sense that he was at the hub of a global network; he could also be found, on a regular basis, at pubs near the British Museum in Bloomsbury, where he met with Gerry Caplan,

Giles Endicott and other Canadian expatriates who formed a New Party Club — London chapter. Like similar groups that had sprung up across Canada, the LSE gang focussed on developments in the newly created New Democratic Party. Dull, stodgy, colonial Canada would be transformed — in their minds at least — into a dynamic, independent nation.

"We all knew we were going back to Canada," says Giles Endicott, an early CCF activist during student days at U. of T., later a founder of the Waffle. "We knew we were going to be involved in the political scene somehow. I had decided to run but I don't recall Ed saying he was interested in being a candidate. He seemed to see himself as more of a thinker or an adviser. He was very serious about the issues but he wasn't one of the hotshots. He wasn't a Stephen Lewis, he wasn't born into it."

Ed was not dreaming of becoming Prime Minister. Though his peers remember him as a serious scholar, he remembers having fun in the European playground. Ed and Yvonne rode their motorcycle through Scandinavia. For a winter holiday, they drove south to Spain with Gerry Caplan, who was studying for a doctorate at the London School of Oriental and African studies. Along with Gerry's wife Ann, they joined Velma and Barry in Barcelona. The trip was a fiasco. As a navigator, Ed was considered by some members of the party to be stubborn and pigheaded. He bickered with Yvonne there and back about which route was the best. It snowed in Barcelona and Gerry caused a serious accident. "I almost killed Velma and her kids," Gerry admits, "when I went off the road." Velma thought Gerry was a neurotic troublemaker and they were all stuck in Valencia for a week while the car was repaired and friendships strained.

Back in England after the Spanish sojourn, Caplan was persuaded to return to Canada to manage David Lewis's re-election campaign in the '63 federal election. It was, for Caplan, a terribly disappointing outcome sharpened by a greater blow: Lester Pearson won a minority government and Lewis lost his seat. Depressed, Caplan returned to London, his marriage broke up, and he remembers a visit from Ed: "He found me sitting alone in the kitchen, eating cold baked beans out of a tin, drinking gin from a bottle and feeling sorry for myself."

Caplan then headed for Rhodesia and Zambia, and found himself, at the age of twenty-five, continuing his doctorate at the University of Rhodesia, "teaching African history to Africans," he says with a note of irony. Caplan says he left Ed "with never any sense that Ed would become a politician." To this day, Gerry remains somewhat astonished by Ed's political career.

For Ed, the enduring legacy of LSE was the influence of Michael Oakeshott, a conservative philosopher who became famous during the era of student protests for refusing to submit to a strike by student radicals. Praising Oakeshott's brilliant lectures and clear analysis, Ed is conscious of the irony of his absorption in a conservative thinker while studying in one of the world's socialist centres. "Oakeshott was appallingly right wing," says John Wilson, a political scientist, who had also graduated from Trinity College and studied with both Brough Macpherson and Oakeshott. "But Oakeshott was a great teacher," Wilson adds, "and of course Ed would have been interested in him — Ed wanted to understand conservatism. Oakeshott was the kind of man you could learn a lot from. He was a clear thinker and very articulate."

Oakeshott's teachings had, for Ed, a practical application. "Oakeshott caused me to understand the relevance of persuading people to change," says Ed. "He argued that politics is by definition a conservative enterprise; the idea is not to pursue pre-selected goals, but to keep the ship afloat. As a leader, Oakeshott would say, you're the captain of a ship without charts; there is no harbour." Ed rejected the chartless ship notion. He believed in socialist goals, in a better society. "But Oakeshott compelled me to think about the conservative nature of human beings. People are slow to change. If you're a democrat and a socialist, as I am, you have to meet people half way. You have to respect where people are, you must respect their identity and not denigrate them if they have different values. I have learned that you have to persuade people to shift to where you are, if you hope to have any influence. If you don't respect them, they won't listen to you."

Oakeshott, then, taught Ed his fundamental strategy, and Ed was considering completing his Ph.D. at the LSE. But he decided, finally, to come home — a decision that still means a lot to him twenty years later. "I came home to work with Macpherson. He was the best in the world. This is it. We've got as good as anything you'll find anywhere. My generation — we were the lucky ones. We didn't suffer the Depression, we didn't fight a war, we just reaped the benefits of economic prosperity. We grew up confident in ourselves. I listen to Glenn Gould play Bach, I read Margaret Atwood, Alice Munro, Richler, Ondaatje; in painting, architecture, academics — we're second to none. We are the confident generation. We aren't deferential to the British nor do we feel inferior to the Americans. We are Canadian, and we can do our own work at the highest levels. The tragedy is that just at the time when we can really come into our own economically, there's a political leadership at the top that wants us to become integrated with the U.S."

In the fall of 1963, returning home to be with the best — Brough Macpherson — Ed settled in at the University of Toronto and concentrated on completing his thesis on John Stuart Mill. Ed would formally conclude his working relationship with Macpherson when he underwent his oral examination before seven professors prior to the official receipt of his doctorate in 1966. Peter Russell, a University of Toronto political scientist, was one of the committee that questioned Ed for the standard two-hour period in which the doctoral candidate must defend his thesis — always a nerve-wracking experience. Ed was comforted by the presence of Macpherson, his thesis supervisor. Then at the pinnacle of his fame and influence, Macpherson had already placed his stamp of approval on Ed's work, which applied Macpherson's critique of Hobbes and Locke to John Stuart Mill. "Ed found that Mill's liberalism was built on the same fallacious view of human nature as was Hobbes's and Locke's," says Russell. Ed came down, then, on Macpherson's optimistic side, opposed to the liberals' "original sin" notion of human nature. Though Ed's approach was largely derived from Macpherson, "Ed was a good scholar," says Russell.

Ed was content with the pleasures of academic life; he was still not thinking seriously about electoral politics. Nor were the NDP's prospects alluring: in Saskatchewan in 1964, with Tommy Douglas out of provincial politics, the venerable NDP government fell to Ross Thatcher, a former CCF MP who led the Liberals to victory. It was a terrible blow: "The NDP might stagger, stumble and even split in the rest of Canada," wrote Desmond Morton, "but always there was Saskatchewan — powerful, efficient, perhaps a little smug but invariably generous and perennially willing to help beyond its own borders." Though the party lost "less than a percentage point in its popular vote," it lost power. "The NDP was at its nadir." A year later, Pierre Trudeau would be elected a Liberal MP from Montreal — after supporting the NDP in previous elections — and Trudeaumania was around the corner. Ed's life was about to change dramatically, but he didn't know it.

CHAPTER FOUR

A Political Career

*It's good to have a guy of his calibre repre-
senting us. He can speak both tongues. He
can talk to the hierarchy on that educated
plane of his, and he can talk to ordinary
people. Ed comes from a working family.
He knows what his mother and father endured. He understands what it's all about.*
Abe Taylor, former president of Local 222.

As an adult, nothing Ed Broadbent touched ever turned
immediately to gold, and his professorial career was no
exception. In horse racing parlance, he was a slow starter
— and a strong finisher. In 1965, he began teaching political science at York University, then a fledgling institution with 3,000 students (full- and part-time) and 128
faculty members. The new university was like Ed's Oshawa high school, Central Collegiate: an aggressive up-
start determined to challenge its establishment rival, the
University of Toronto.

The York population congregated at the lush Glendon
campus at Bayview and Lawrence, trekking northward to
the barren lands above the 401 expressway, where the
sprawling new campus was being built in a sea of muddy
farmers' fields. York was created to take the burden off
U. of T.; it vowed to be "accessible," and attracted a
bumper crop of baby boomers, among them vast numbers
from working-class and immigrant families. Today the
university is a mammoth institution, with 40,000 students and 2,000 faculty members. Broadbent is not the
only political figure to have emerged from its hive. Murray Ross, York's first president, remembers Ed as "one of

101

a group of bright, young political scientists we brought in." But Ed was not spotted by the authorities as the brightest light. "The one we had our eye on," says Murray Ross, now retired, "was Thomas Hockin. There was also a student radical named John Bosley." Today Hockin is not exactly a household name though he is a Tory Cabinet minister, and Bosley, another Conservative MP, is the former speaker of the House of Commons.

York's political science department was then headed by an American, Robert Presthus. When advised that a young member of his staff was thinking of running for the House of Commons, Presthus told Ed: "Why don't you do something useful? If you want to go into politics, why waste your time in Canadian politics?"

At that point, Ed's political career had consisted of working for his provincial riding association (St David's, in Rosedale, where he lived). After canvassing for the invisible NDP candidate in Rosedale federally in '62, he decided, on his return from LSE, that he might as well get involved; it seemed like a natural thing to do. Old friends from his U. of T. days, such as Giles Endicott, were active in the association; someone called him up and asked him to help; he said yes. He sat on its executive and did his share of routine duties in a constituency that was uninterested, to say the least, in New Democrats. (One NDP canvasser remembers knocking on the front door of a Rosedale mansion whose owner exclaimed, on being informed about the New Democratic Party: "You must want the servants' entrance.")

Even though the party had so few people to choose from, Ed was not tapped as a future star. Mostly, he was absorbed by his academic career. He officially received his Ph.D. in 1966, and at last the years of earnest study were paying off. He loved academic life. He related well to students; he treated them like intelligent people, which they appreciated. He was hip. He wore turtleneck sweaters when most professors wore ties, he enjoyed having a beer at the Jolly Miller pub after class, and he just plain loved teaching. But unlike his mentor, C.B. Macpherson, he was not known as a charismatic prof. He didn't perform well in front of crowded lecture halls. He told jokes that fell flat, students dozed when he read from notes and they didn't applaud at the end. But in smaller groups, he came alive. His forte was seminars, where he felt more relaxed, let down his guard and his humour came through. He had a knack for stimulating exciting debate and took pride in demanding a lot from his students. "I worked them hard," he says.

Ex-students confirm it. "He was strict and he was tough — we had to read a book a week and he made us write essays all the time," says Richard Keshen, who ended up with a Ph.D. from Oxford. Now teaching philosophy at the University College of Cape Breton, Keshen attended Ed's seminar in political philosophy in 1966-67. The students knew Ed considered himself a socialist, "but he didn't impose his ideas," says Keshen. "He was even-handed in dealing with the conservatives and liberals amongst us. He didn't push ideology. He was keen to talk about John Stuart Mill and he explained the Marxist critique of Mill. But he belonged in the liberal tradition that emphasized individual freedom. A typical Marxist would have seen that as a bourgeois sham. Looking back, I can see the influence of C.B. Macpherson which resulted, I think, in Ed's efforts to bring together liberalism and socialism."

"Broadbent was a lousy lecturer but he was excellent in seminars," says Paul Grayson, now a York sociology professor. "Broadbent's seminar on political theory was one of the most instructive courses I ever took. Dealing with the modern theorists, from Mill to Marx, Lenin, Macpherson and Oakeshott, he made us get down and analyze their assumptions and logic in a very critical fashion. He criticized both Marx and Lenin for their neglect of the individual. He was mightily hepped up on Mill's essay "On Liberty" and he was concerned that the state should not impinge on individual freedom. And he was tough, let me tell you. But we really loved his seminar. It ran for three hours in the evening and the time flew past." Grayson had another reason for liking Broadbent: "He was one of the few academics who realized Canada was a separate country. The big concerns on campus were American — Vietnam, black power. I thought, 'This is horseshit.' There's something happening in Canada."

Grayson was right. It was an intense time. In 1965, Canadian nationalism was at its peak. George Grant had published *Lament for a Nation*, Walter Gordon had resigned from Pearson's Cabinet and was using his personal clout and wealth to expose the vulnerability of an economy dominated by foreign-owned multinationals. The Ontario government under Tory Premier John Robarts was maintaining the *status quo* with tiny twists of progressivism mixed in to keep the opposition at bay. But across the province's eastern border, there was unbridled lust for change: in the next fifteen years, Quebec would be transformed by Lesage and Lévesque's leadership, and would come to dominate national politics, thanks to Trudeau, Marchand and Pelletier — Quebec's three wise men who decided to run for the Liberals in the '65 election. In his memoirs, Gérard Pelletier acknowledged that they considered the NDP a much more reasonable party, in terms of its policies, but they had no choice but to go Liberal if they wanted to effect change in Ottawa.

In Quebec, "the climate of urgency," in René Lévesque's words, was heightened by the Parent Report on education, which revealed that as of 1964, "four-fifths of our adult population hadn't gone beyond, and many hadn't even finished, elementary school!" But the Quiet Revolution would change that, and Quebec was striding ahead by leaps and bounds, asserting an aggressive control over its destiny. Robert Cliche, the brilliant lawyer from the Beauce region and a close friend of Lévesque's, became Quebec NDP leader in '65 — but his efforts to build the party were stymied by the social democratic slant of Lesage's government. In '65, Quebec refused to join the new Canada Pension Plan, and instead created the Caisse de dépôt et placement du Québec, to invest the province's pension funds in the Quebec economy. Within two decades, the Caisse de dépôt became an economic giant, with assets of $28 billion and a strong track record for propelling an industrial strategy that worked.

In the United States in '65, the war in Vietnam had escalated under President Lyndon Johnson, and anti-Vietnam rallies spread like wildfire across North American campuses. The violence of American culture was shocking: two years after John Kennedy's assassination, black activist Malcolm X was shot dead in New York in 1965 at the age of 40. Three years later, Martin Luther King, the youngest person ever to win the Nobel Peace Prize, was shot dead in Memphis; two months later, running for the Democratic presidential nomination, Robert Kennedy, 42, was shot dead.

And some Canadian activists were still battling it out on the frontlines. For instance: in 1965, at six o'clock one hot and humid morning in Rhodesia, Gerry Caplan was arrested and thrown in jail for supporting black student demonstrations against Ian Smith's white regime. Seven days later, Caplan was deported to Zambia, and eventually arrived home to a hero's welcome. Ed, in contrast, was an interested observer, participating in his own scholarly way in the sweeping changes that carried his generation forward. More than two decades later, when *The New York Times* ran a front-page story headlined A LEFTIST LEADER SURGING IN CANADA (November 8, 1987), one had to laugh. The image of Ed the rebel charging down from the Gatineau Hills was at odds with the reality of a man who matured in the most protest-prone era of modern history and never once got arrested, which in those days was almost a cause for shame.

In 1965, Brian Mulroney became a full-fledged lawyer in Montreal. He boasted of his close relationship with John Diefenbaker and told friends that he was going to become prime minister one day. Ed Broadbent, meanwhile, knew no important politicians, and when he thought about politics — which he did, all the time — it was in terms of ideas: the evolution of democracy, the role of the market, individual rights, community needs, economic development, and so on. If Mulroney was occupied with dreams of power, Broadbent was absorbed in shaping his own political vision. Liberty, equality, fraternity — the goals of the French revolution transmuted into contemporary terms were Ed's passion. (Later, those who didn't like him would say that he was just a guy who lacked fire in his belly, who never had the guts to put himself on the line. He didn't see it that way.)

There he was, at the height of the '60s, struggling through a declining marriage, teaching, drinking beer and talking politics at the Jolly Miller pub in North York with Harvey Simmons. The son of a Boston private eye, an occupation that intrigued Ed no end, Simmons was a political scientist with a Ph.D. in government. He arrived at York in 1965. Ed, unlike some of his more nationalist colleagues, was not alienated by Simmons's American passport. (If anything, Ed is pro-American in terms of authors and left-wing thinkers, despite his nationalism — an irony pointed out to the *Wall Street Journal* reporter whose first question about Ed was: "He's anti-American, isn't he?")

The Simmonses and the Broadbents socialized frequently. Ed played with Erica, the Simmonses' little girl, who has never forgotten that he taught her how to blow bubbles in bubble gum and that he saved his aluminum cigar cylinders for her. But Ed was no domestic marvel. Eileen Simmons, Harvey's wife, observes that "Ed missed women's lib, so did Harvey. This business of men cooking and pushing baby carriages is very recent. In the '60s, men devoted themselves to their careers, and women devoted themselves to men. Of course," she adds, "Yvonne was different. She had her own career." Nor was Yvonne interested in having children.

Eileen and Harvey were not aware of the problems Ed and Yvonne were having, though the Broadbent–Yamaoka marriage was close to the breaking point. Harvey did notice, however, that Yvonne didn't appreciate Ed's sense of humour. "Ed can be very silly. He likes to kid around. If your wife doesn't appreciate your silliness, it can lead to a lot of distance."

Ed and Harvey had a lot in common. "The thing with Ed and I was, we always agreed," says Harvey. "I was what's called a liberal democrat, a left-wing one, though I consider myself a socialist now." He explains the differ-

Percy Broadbent, 1938.

*Ed Broadbent at 16
months old.*

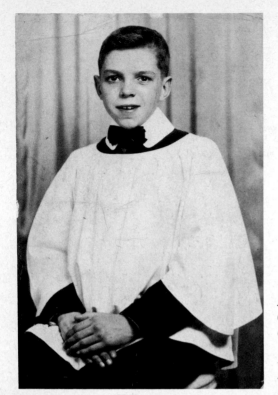

Ed when he was a choirboy at St. George's Anglican church in Oshawa.

Ed (right), visiting his M.P., Michael Starr (middle), whom he later defeated.

Ed with Bev Marshall in Oshawa, 1956.

Christmas 1956, with brother David (left) and sister Velma.

On graduation day, University of Toronto (B.A.), 1959.

Ed with his father, after receiving his M.A. in 1961.

Percy and Mary Broadbent at home in Oshawa, 1975.

Ed with energetic supporters at Local 222 in Oshawa.

1968: Ed becomes a Member of Parliament.

Tommy Douglas campaigning for Ed.

*A typical playful
pose.*

*Ed and Lucille at the
St. Andrew's Ball in
Oshawa, 1968.*

ence. "Liberal democrats believe in equal opportunity for everybody and assume there's a level playing field. Socialists believe it's more complex, that to create a level playing field which allows for equal opportunity, you have to use the powers of the state in a more forceful way to narrow the gap between rich and poor." Yet Simmons feels that there's a fuzzy gray area between the two groups: "Socialists have moved to the right, relying less on state intervention, and liberal democrats have moved to the left, allowing for state intervention." He defines Ed as "a pragmatic socialist. I consider myself a Broadbent socialist."

Simmons was sensitive to the perception that, in the words of Paul Grayson, "the issues and priorities at York were defined by Americans with American interests." As a student, Grayson was enraged by the condescending attitude to matters Canadian. "We'd get Ed to come out and talk to the NDP club on campus, to discuss Canadian perspectives. He was one of the few who was interested in Canada. It was easier in those days to get people to talk about Selma, Alabama. The classic line was 'there's no radicalism in Canada,' but for Christ's sake, we had Quebec, René Lévesque coming out as a separatist, Trudeau as justice minister, Walter Gordon trying to get someone interested in this country . . ."

Grayson's picture is reinforced by university officials. Harold Kaplan, the man who, as head of York's political science department, approved Broadbent's leave of absence to run in the 1968 federal election, was an American from New Jersey. "The political science department was packed with Americans," says Kaplan. "Our students were undergoing the late '60s revolt and they were keen Canadian nationalists." Robin Matthews, a Carleton professor, stirred things up by releasing a report on the Americanization of Canadian universities. Matthews was hopping mad and travelled across the country drumming up support for his cause. Ed says he "shared Matthews's concerns" but he bore no antipathy to his American friends. He did not like personalizing battles. And though he occasionally engaged in heated debates on various

issues with colleagues, he was able to do so, Simmons observed, without blowing up. "I tended to get hot under
the collar but Ed never lost his cool." Simmons had a particularly hard time controlling his temper with right-
wingers. "I'd get really mad but Ed would stay reasonable. I was impressed."

If ever Ed had a good reason to get mad it was at his
department head, Kaplan's predecessor. Robert Presthus
was "a real ugly American," Kaplan says. "He was a big
name, of sorts, with good credentials and published arti-
cles, but he would go on and on about how everything
north of the border was third-rate and amateurish. If it
was Canadian it wasn't any good, as far as Presthus was
concerned." John Saywell, York's first dean of arts and
science, defends Presthus. "He wasn't alone in feeling Canadian political science hadn't grown up. Twenty-five
years ago, we didn't have the people and we didn't have
the intellectual technology. But that's all changed now."

Ed says that Presthus was "completely insensitive to
the feeling we had of being threatened when the majority
of our teaching staff was not Canadian. One of the functions of a university is to pass on the nation's cultural
traditions, and it was becoming tough for us. At the same
time, there were a lot of good Americans around, people
like Kaplan and Simmons, who accepted the Canadian
tradition."

True: in '68, Kaplan had a job offer back in the United
States. He returned to his old New Jersey stamping
ground for a visit and realized he'd become a Canadian.
"Politically, I couldn't go back to America; I couldn't face
it," says Kaplan. "I resented the hawkish atmosphere so
much. It was awful. Vietnam was polarizing the country,
bringing out the kind of chauvinism that re-emerged
under Reagan, that came out over Nicaragua, that I de-
spise. I really distrust American hawks. I'm scared of
them."

At that period, Ed was more concerned with the deteri-
oration of his marriage. He and Yvonne separated briefly,
got back together, and struggled to make the marriage
work. They went to see a marriage counsellor; their best

efforts failed. "Ed was devastated that the marriage didn't work," says Harvey Simmons. Yet Ed was the one who initiated the final split in 1967. "He phoned us the day he told her," says Simmons. "He was really broken up about it." Yvonne was shattered; she had a nervous breakdown.

Yvonne's bitterness about the disintegration of her relationship with Ed, says one of her friends, came from her conviction that Ed had fallen in love with Lucille Munroe. "I understood why the marriage broke up," says Setsu Weldon, Yvonne's sister. "Ed already had soft feelings for Lucille, and his marriage to Yvonne was weak. There was nothing anybody could do about it. It's just one of those things that happen in life. But I think it's all worked out for the best. I don't think Yvonne would have liked a political life, and for Ed, it was the right thing." Still, the family pressures against the divorce were enormous. "I was heartbroken," says Setsu, a born-again Christian who believes "marriages are committed — no matter what." Ed's family was shocked; his parents adored Yvonne. "Yvonne was a great person," says David, Ed's brother. "I was devastated. I never saw her again. It was like somebody passing away — it took me a long time to get over it." Indeed, it would be years before David could wholeheartedly embrace Lucille.

Lucille Munroe, meanwhile, had moved to Kanata, an Ottawa suburb, where she was living in a rented townhouse with her son Paul and teaching French at his elementary school. Her husband Louis had died on February 16, 1965, and within a period of three years she had also lost her mother and father. Ed, who had remained close to Lucille and Louis since meeting them in Oshawa in 1959, had tried to help her through these terrible times. And if he did fall in love with her, she was in no condition to respond. "I had enjoyed my marriage," Lucille says, "and I felt I could never go through that horrible pain [of loss] again." She was slowly recovering, relieved to be back in Ottawa, living among her Francophone relatives.

Lucille had straddled two cultures all her life. Her father, John Charles Allen, was an Anglophone from Port Colborne, Ont.; her mother, Stella Brunelle, a Franco-Ontarian from the village of Lafontaine, close to Penetanguishene, in a French-speaking district of Ontario. The six Allen children were raised bilingual in Ottawa. They spoke French at home all day with their mother and, when their unilingual father came home at night, English. J.C. Allen was a travelling insurance man with Guaranty Trust, a member of the Catholic Order of Foresters, the Knights of Columbus and a prominent Liberal. (Keith Davey remembers seeing Ed and Lucille at the opera one night in the '70s and suddenly realizing, with a jolt of recognition: "That's J.C. Allen's daughter who's married Ed Broadbent.")

J.C. Allen ran unsuccessfully for the Liberals and became president of the Ontario Liberal Association in the late '50s. But he was not, says Lucille, hostile to socialism. "He called the CCFers Liberals-in-a-hurry." She switched her allegiance from the Liberals to the New Democrats before she was involved with Ed. Prime Minister Lester Pearson's decision to allow nuclear weapons on Canadian soil in 1963 triggered the switch, and she has been an active NDPer ever since. "I think I was a socialist all along," she says.

The trail that led Lucille to Oshawa, to cross Ed's path, was marked by tragedy. She was reared a proper Catholic girl at the Gray Nuns' Rideau Street Convent in Ottawa. She proceeded into nursing, training at the Ottawa General Hospital, an old gray stone institution on Bruyère Street, also run by the Gray Nuns.

She met Louis Munroe through his sister, who'd been a patient of Lucille's at the General. Louis was French-Canadian, educated in English schools; he was teaching high school in Arnprior, in the Ottawa Valley, when his sister arranged a blind date with Lucille. They went out with each other for two years and were married on December 29, 1956. "Louis was a very gentle man, very loving, dedicated to his students," says Lucille, smiling, her bright blue eyes shining. She loved him.

She and Louis adopted their son, Paul, in 1962, when he was two-and-a-half years old. But already the dark shadow had fallen: Louis had just found out that he had multiple sclerosis, a degenerative disease that attacks the nervous and muscular systems. "His symptoms," says Lucille, "were that he felt tired, nauseated, and sometimes his eyesight bothered him." Gradually, he declined, losing a sense of feeling in his fingers, walking with a limp (and a cane), becoming more dependent on Lucille than either of them liked. "People teased him and said I waited on him — they didn't know he was sick," says Lucille.

In December of '65, young Paul got chicken pox. "Louis had never had it," Lucille explains, "and he got a bad dose. He went into the hospital, but when he came home he didn't seem to pick up. One day he got out of bed and vomited all over the bed. He went into hospital again, was transferred to Toronto, and the doctors told me he had a brain tumour. They operated and he never regained consciousness." Ed attended the funeral; as an old friend, Ed did what he could for Lucille.

Less than a year after his final break from Yvonne, Ed told Simmons that he'd been approached to run for the NDP in Oshawa. (Ed didn't know it, but he wasn't the party's first choice.) The New Democrats were gearing up for the 1968 election and they wanted a strong candidate for the Oshawa riding, which was held by the Tories. "Ed wanted to know what I thought," Simmons recalls. "I said, 'Don't do it. You won't win and if you do, you'll be a lousy politician. You won't like it.' I thought Ed was a serious intellectual and that politics would bore him. But now I think he's happier as a politician than he would have been as an academic. University life can be isolating. He likes the rough and tumble of politics. He's a gregarious guy. He's engaged in the world. And I think he likes being the head of a big organization. He likes being the boss."

Historian Jack Saywell remembers Ed coming to see him, to talk about the possibility of running. "It was a real dilemma for Ed," says Saywell. "He was torn. He liked academic life. He wanted to know if we had provisions allowing him to take a leave, give it a shot, and return if it didn't work out. I was surprised that he was thinking of running at all. I hadn't thought of him as engaged in activist politics." Saywell had taught at the University of Toronto from 1954 to 1963, during the period when Ed was an undergraduate. One of the most influential of the new, post-war generation of historians, Saywell knew Gerry Caplan, Stephen Lewis and John Brewin, "and they lived for politics. Ed was a different kind of person."

Fascinated by Quebec politics, Saywell had met "Mulroney and his gang in Montreal, hanging around the Union Nationale [the party of Maurice Duplessis]. Mulroney was one of those young hotshots. I don't even think you can call him right wing. He isn't any wing. His motivation was always sheer, unprincipled ambition. Ed, on the other hand, was a political theorist of the left. He was motivated, I think, by his sense of wanting to participate, by his egalitarian convictions."

Against the advice of friends and family — his mother worried about Ed's giving up academic security, his colleagues thought he was wasting his time and that he'd never defeat a Tory incumbent — Ed decided to run for the NDP nomination in Oshawa–Whitby. He was thirty-two years old. Suddenly, Ed was on the front lines — where he had never been before. Leaving behind the safe shores of academia, he roared off to Oshawa on his motorcycle. His life would never be the same again.

Ed's political career began on a downbeat note. For his nomination speech at Oshawa's Carousel Inn on Sunday, May 5, 1968, Ed delivered a lecture on John Stuart Mill's concept of liberty to a crowd of about 250 people — many of them union guys who'd come off the assembly line at The Motors to hear him speak. They were not amused. Though Ed grew up in Oshawa, now that he'd come back, armed with all his degrees, he was painfully out of place. He was just another "academic shithead," a phrase that would dog his early years as a politician. Ed's nominator, Abe Taylor, a big, tough, experienced union boss, sat with his head in his hands, in despair, thinking: "What have I done?" Taylor considered taking back the nomination, but it was too late. John Valleau and Harvey Simmons were there, squirming in embarrassment for their friend. "I was appalled," says Simmons, who thought: "My god, he'll never win if he keeps lecturing like that."

"It was hilarious," says Valleau, who has a quirky sense of humour. Abe Taylor didn't think it was funny; he knew he would have to teach Ed how to talk to "real people." But Ed had the Broadbent name on his side — all those uncles plus his mother's reputation for good works — and there was something people liked about him. He won the nomination handily over a local school trustee. The next day the *Oshawa Times*'s front page was dominated by a big headline, BROADBENT PICKED BY NDP DELEGATES, and a picture of Ed. He looked like a kid dressed up for church in a sports jacket and tie.

Ed got lucky: he had Abe Taylor for a mentor. Though he'd made a lousy speech, he'd won the nomination, mostly because of Abe. Throughout his life, Ed seems to have had a knack for finding the right people at the right time to bring him along. From Ted Maidman, the scout leader, to C.B. Macpherson and later, David Lewis, Ed got the attention he needed; his sister Velma says "it's because people saw something in him. Things were never easy for Ed, but he's always had support and help. It's because he is what he is. He's a very complex person. He has his faults and failings, and he's been protected from a lot of things, but he *is* special — that's not to say there haven't been times when I've wanted to kick his ass."

Abe Taylor did kick ass, and Ed was the beneficiary. Abe was *the* man at The Motors, the godfather of the union; his shrewd negotiating skills would result in breakthrough achievements. "Because of Abe, we opened the first dental clinic in the basement of the union hall, we got an optical centre and we bought a building for a retirees' centre that became the largest of its kind in North America," says David Broadbent, who would sit on the UAW executive with Taylor for a decade.

Abe started at The Motors in 1947 and retired in 1978. "I saw a lot of friends of mine get caught on that treadmill, working seven days a week," says Abe. "Some of them are dead today because of it. You could call them sleepwalkers. If customers are screaming for cars, then dealers are screaming at GM, and the company pushes the guys. The company would say, 'If you don't work the hours we need you, we'll get people in who'll do what we want.' GM doesn't care about the human or the family side of things, all they care about is the economic side for themselves. Then, of course, a worker who's been pushed too much becomes a liability to the company because he's not working at full efficiency, so they want to get rid of him."

Ed knew all this by osmosis — his father having worked two jobs at the same time, his Uncle Reuben having been caught on the overtime treadmill, the Broadbent men with 250 years of collective service to The Motors — and he knew the town. But still the election was going to be a tough fight. The Oshawa–Whitby federal seat had never been represented by a New Democrat and Ed was up against a popular incumbent, former Tory labour minister Michael Starr, who to this day refuses to comment on Ed Broadbent. ("Mike feels he was robbed," says a friend of Starr's. "He never got over it.") Ed's biggest problem, however, was with the group that supposedly formed his base: Local 222. The union was caught up in an internal war between rival factions that threatened to mash the neophyte candidate to a pulp. Right off the bat, Ed learned one of the most important lessons a politician can learn: don't stick your head in a trap.

The UAW in Oshawa was split between the Autoworkers and the Democrats, who had been feuding with each other since the early 1950s. Abe Taylor, president of the local from 1963 to 1978, explains: "The International [headquartered in the U.S.] supported a 'right-wing caucus,' called the Autoworkers, that was the dominant force in the union. You couldn't get elected if your name wasn't on their slate. Their machine would just run over you — but I wouldn't join them. In 1950, they negotiated an ill-fated five-year agreement that ran until '55, when the economy was booming, cars were selling, but our men lost money by the time the contract was up. That was the cause of the '55 strike — we had so much catch-up to do."

The first major revolt against U.S. domination was led by Cliff Pilkey in 1952. Then a young repairman at The Motors, Pilkey was opposed to the way the union's leadership was "dictated to" by the American head office. "We were calling for greater Canadian autonomy," says Pilkey, who later became head of the Ontario Federation of Labour. Pilkey, Taylor and their friends formed a "ginger group" to oppose the establishment. "We were called the Young Turks, then the Right-wing Democrats," says Taylor. They accepted the right-wing label because they were being red-baited; they figured they'd confuse the opposition by adopting one of its own labels.

In 1957, Pilkey became president of the local and the Democrats trounced the Autoworkers. By then, Pilkey says, "we were into the McCarthy era. Geez it was vicious, the red-baiting. It was carried into Canada by the International and they tried to rub us out. There had been a tiny group of communists in the union. All you had to do to finish someone off was to label him a commie. That was enough. Nobody would go near you. We were all labelled communist. A lot of innocent people were damaged. But we were able to battle back by pointing out that our right-wing opponents were captive of the International leadership and didn't have a thought of their own."

In 1959, Pilkey took on the legendary U.S. labour leader Walter Reuther in a debate over control of the union. Pilkey recalls that Reuther, whom he admired tremendously, "wouldn't look at me on stage, even though I was president of the local." Reuther and Pilkey had to debate twice: at 7:30 P.M. and again at 2:30 A.M. for the second shift that got off in the early hours of the morning. "You should have seen the guys out on the streets at three o'clock in the morning," says Pilkey. "They were buzzing." Opposed by Dennis McDermott, Canadian head of the UAW, Pilkey argued that "we wanted more control over

where we were going. We felt we shouldn't have to buy
the American pattern — it's just what Bob White says
now — and that we had different needs from the Americans. We wanted to negotiate our own pattern." Little did
Pilkey know he was laying the groundwork for a massive
breakaway that would occur twenty-five years later with
the support of both feuding factions. Though they would
coalesce behind Bob White to create the Canadian Auto
Workers in 1985, the Autoworkers and Democrats would
remain rivals. The trouble with the Autoworkers today,
according to Taylor, is that "they're puppets of Bob
White. They support whatever he says. I don't like that. I
keep my independence. Bob White — he's very ambitious.
That's okay, so long as it doesn't go to his head, so he
doesn't forget what he's there for. That's the danger of
power. You gotta watch these guys." How about Broadbent? "It's not a danger with Ed. To me, he has his feet
planted on the ground."

What was Abe's advice to Ed on how to deal with Local
222 back in '68? "Ed doesn't go in and say, 'Are you a
Democrat or an Autoworker?' He says, 'What is the problem?' He doesn't get into the middle of other people's politics. It wouldn't do him any good. The only way for him
to survive in this game is to keep his nose out of the in-
fighting." Abe's counsel would prove remarkably sound,
but it was easier said than done.

Prime Minister Pierre Trudeau, elected leader of the
Liberal party in April, called an election for June 25. The
summer of '68 was a hot season. Upheaval was rampant
around the world. Students were rioting, shutting down
universities in New York, Paris, Berlin, Frankfurt, London and Rome. Martin Luther King had been shot dead
in Memphis and in Chicago, at the Democratic Convention, National Guardsmen rolled down the main street in
jeeps protected by barbed wire. "The world was blowing
up," as Gerry Caplan said.

Canada's federal election took place against the backdrop of the counterculture revolution, Expo '67 in Montreal and French President Charles de Gaulle's infamous
outburst: "Vive le Québec libre." Quebec nationalism was

surging: René Lévesque, having quit the provincial Liberal Party, had formed the Parti Québecois and would be elected leader in October, '68.

The NDP had been struggling to keep up with developments in Quebec. At its 1967 convention in Toronto, Claude Ryan, the editor of *Le Devoir*, had advised the party that it must reach out to Quebec nationalists. "Although Ryan made no acknowledgement," writes Desmond Morton, "the convention had already endorsed a specific constitutional resolution which his own newspaper was currently urging: 'special status.'" Recognition of Quebec's distinct culture, contained in the 1987 Meech Lake Accord, was, in 1967, a controversial proposal that resulted in a shower of attacks on the NDP. Eugene Forsey, a former research director of the Canadian Labour Congress, quit the NDP over the issue and supported Trudeau's fight against concessions to Quebec. Trudeau was fixed on the conviction that Quebec must be an equal partner in a bilingual Canada. In Oshawa Ed spoke out in favour of bilingualism and showed sympathy for the Francophones' cause, but he was still a long way from fully appreciating the Québecois's struggle, according to Lucille.

Ed was off and running, aided and abetted by a motley crew of hippy students and tweedy academics who made the trek from York University to Motor City, mingling with Oshawa's cowboys, farmers and union types who didn't know what to make of Ed's Toronto gang. After a hard day knocking on doors, they'd all gather in a local pub for a beer and a chat — "to shoot the shit," as they say in Oshawa. Gradually a sense of camaraderie developed. Ed remembers seeing one of his students, a young female intellectual in a mini-skirt — she was initially regarded as something of a weird case by the local UAW guys — engaged in an animated discussion with a hoary old, pot-bellied auto worker. "They found out they could talk to each other," says Ed. Without planning it, he had brought together the disparate groups that would provide him with an enduring base.

Slowly, Ed began to get a feel for politicking, though he was not consciously aware of what was happening. He believed he would make a good MP because he had thought so deeply about fundamental democratic principles; instead, his intellectual pronouncements turned people off. What they liked about him was that deep down, underneath all the learning, was a nice warm guy. At a deeper level, he was what they wanted their children to become. "Everybody in Oshawa has that dream," says Mike Breaugh, "that my kid will get the education I never had, my kid won't have to face working in a factory for forty years. Ed is a very popular manifestation of the dream. His father was just an ordinary guy at The Motors, and Ed proved you could make it, you could get past the barriers."

Still, Ed had his handicaps. It would take him years to simplify his convoluted, philosophical rambles — "he sounded like he was talking backwards," said an Oshawa friend — but gradually his academic veneer wore off as Abe Taylor reminded him "to speak without using 50-cent words." Though Ed wasn't a great orator on occasions when he had to address big crowds — a persistent limitation that has dogged his career — very quickly he became a superb campaigner, exuding a warmth and ease mainstreeting with voters that made him the darling of party organizers. "He's a down-to-earth individual, now that we've educated him," says Taylor. "It's good to have a guy of his calibre representing us. He can speak both tongues. He can talk to the hierarchy on that educated plane of his and he can talk to ordinary people. Ed comes from a working family. He knows what his mother and father endured. He understands what it's all about."

The 1968 election remains famous for Trudeaumania. Smiling bashfully, submitting to kisses from an endless stream of smitten women, oozing sex appeal and a self-conscious self-confidence, Pierre Elliott Trudeau, at the age of forty-nine, more than seventeen years older than Ed, stumped the country and seduced it — despite scurrilous rumours, spread by right-wing opponents, that he was either a communist or a homosexual or both. Evidence cited as examples of his "dangerous tendencies" were visits he had paid during his globe-trotting years to Cuba and China. As a left-leaning French intellectual, Trudeau aroused the vicious attacks that were usually reserved for New Democrats, but he ignored them, and so did the rest of Canada.

Tory leader Robert Stanfield could not compete with Trudeau's charisma. With his bony head and drooping eye, Stanfield emerged as a stiff and stuffy relic of times gone by. Though he was a charming, progressive man who belonged in the Red Tory camp, Stanfield wasn't good on television — and this was the first election in which TV came to dominate the public's perception of politics. NDP leader Tommy Douglas, whose old-fashioned oratory had shaken the rafters of countless arenas in the past, had the same problem: a lousy media image. Stanfield and Douglas "were written off by most commentators," writes Christina McCall, "as the plodding politicians of Canada's yesterdays. Trudeau was the man for tomorrow." And he captured the pent-up mood for change that was sweeping the country.

Tommy Douglas tried to take the spotlight off Trudeau by focussing on two key economic issues that are as relevant today as twenty years ago. Indeed the next election is likely to be fought over the same ground: foreign control of the economy and tax reform, issues that were imprinted on Ed Broadbent in his first election. At the heart of the free trade debate of the 1980s is the question that dominated the political agenda in the 1960s: how can Canada function as an independent nation if it is unable to control foreign investment and must submit to U.S. law?

Fighting these battles in the '68 election, Tommy Douglas relied on two high-profile studies. The Watkins Report, directed by economist Mel Watkins — soon to encounter Ed in the Waffle — had been initiated by Walter Gordon. Released in '68, the Watkins Report was a highly critical, well-documented account of Canada's branchplant status, and it created a furor. "It was not radical," says Watkins, "but it was nationalist. It said we had to do what countries like Japan and West Germany have done: bargain more effectively with the multinationals and regulate and control foreign investment."

The Carter Commission, in a different vein, attacked a taxation system that favoured the rich and penalized the poor. In her 1987 book, *Behind Closed Doors: How the Rich Won Control of Canada's Tax System . . . And Ended Up Richer*, *Globe and Mail* reporter Linda McQuaig describes why Kenneth Carter, a conservative Bay Street accountant, incited a ferocious response from his business colleagues. The Carter Commission, appointed by Diefenbaker, in 1967 delivered its findings to Pearson who passed the buck to Trudeau. Carter discovered, says McQuaig, "that powerful interest groups had won concessions that enabled them to pay unfairly low rates of taxation, shifting the burden to the middle-class and the working poor. Carter wanted to eliminate these special privileges."

The NDP championed both Carter and Watkins, while the Liberals and Conservatives retreated in the face of fierce opposition from the business community. Trudeau, not particularly interested then in economic matters, concentrated on spreading charisma. In *Grits*, Christina McCall quoted Keith Davey on Trudeau's election strategy: "All he had to do was show his face and make his speech about the Just Society and participatory democracy and all that jazz. He didn't need the Liberal Party to win and he didn't know what the Liberal Party was all about."

The NDP stuck to the issues, confident that it had attracted an impressive slate of candidates who represented a new leadership generation: in Toronto, journalists Doug Fisher and Bruce Rogers, and John Harney, the bilingual secretary of the provincial party; in Quebec, philosopher Charles Taylor, Trudeau's friend; labour lawyer Robert Cliche, whom Lévesque supported; and Laurier LaPierre, who made his name as co-host of CBC-TV's *This Hour Has Seven Days* and had already been touted in *Maclean's* magazine as possibly Canada's first socialist Prime Minister.

No such predictions were made about the NDP's low-profile candidate in Oshawa–Whitby. The Conservatives, and almost everybody else, thought Mike Starr was invincible: a former Oshawa mayor, he'd first been elected MP in a 1952 by-election, and he'd worked his constituency diligently. He had run for the Tory leadership in 1967, losing to Stanfield, but was a popular man about town. "Starr had a hammer-hold on the riding federally," says Cliff Pilkey, who had won provincially for the New Democrats in 1967. But Pilkey's Machine geared up for Broadbent; the driving force behind it was Vi Pilkey, Cliff's wife, who was largely responsible for creating the organization. It embraced local supporters as well as Ed's alliance of students, academics and family — sister Velma, brother-in-law Barry Cornish, brother David, sister-in-law Sharon, Mum and Dad and assorted relatives and friends, including Lucille Munroe and her son Paul, who was then eight years old. "We travelled to Oshawa (from Ottawa) practically every weekend because my mother was canvassing for Ed," says Paul, who remembers the campaign vividly. Lucille and Paul would stay with Ed's mother and Paul would go out with David, putting up Broadbent signs.

Ed's team built up a groundswell of support that began to worry Starr's Tories. Starr's only hope was that Ed would be crushed between the Autoworkers and Democrats, or that he'd turn off people who wanted to vote for him because his speeches were so boring. Just to rub in the "academic shithead" label, Starr's supporters would refer to Ed as "Dr Broadbent," which was the kiss of death in Oshawa.

"Ed had the damnedest time learning to deal with Local 222," says Mike Breaugh, Oshawa's MPP since '75. "He'd go to a meeting and talk to one guy from one faction, then he'd get hell from the next guy, who was in the other faction, then both caucuses would take a run at him." Cliff Pilkey helped Ed manoeuvre. They'd go to the plant gates at 5:30 in the morning, and then they'd have coffee at the restaurants where the truckers hung out, and Ed began to get a feel for it. The guys "tell you exactly what they think," says Breaugh. "They give you shit if they feel you deserve it."

"Oshawa," he adds, "is a great learning place. It sure isn't Toronto. Oshawans are very straightforward. You have to be tough to take it."

Where Ed shone — "his greatest strength," according to Breaugh — was in the kitchens of ordinary voters. "Ed's ability one-to-one at a kitchen table is better than any politician in the country. People love talking to him." But he was a pain to go canvassing with because he'd get into a deep discussion and "would spend half the morning with one voter if you let him, when he was supposed to do an entire poll," says Breaugh. And in the evenings, there were his lectures. He would be up at the front, declaiming about economic policy and redistribution of power, while his father would be at the back, selling lottery tickets for the Canadian Legion and interrupting Ed's flow by whispering proudly: "That's my son Ed up there." Percy was by then a well-known local character whose personal problems were considered no worse than those of lots of other guys. "The town's full of people like Ginger, who've been derailed," says Breaugh. "Ed's family situation was not uncommon. You'd see Mary [his mother], and she seemed like such a sweet woman, super polite, very friendly, but she had a sense of mental toughness about her. She wouldn't have survived without being tough, and there are a lot of women like that, who dragged their families through the shit successfully."

In a sense, Ed's first campaign was Mary Broadbent's finest hour, the vindication and reward for everything she'd gone through. She had thrown herself wholeheartedly into the election, stuffing envelopes and phoning volunteers (while Percy constructed home-made signs and then drove around town with David and Paul to hammer them into people's lawns). She was beside herself with excitement on the night of Tuesday, June 25, 1968, when they managed to pull off a cliff-hanger victory. The UAW hall on Bond Street was packed to the rafters with a few thousand supporters and a lot of tension. Mary clutched the hand of Uncle Aubrey's wife and wouldn't let go. Her eyes shone, watching her son mount the stage. She was thrilled.

"It was a shambles," says Velma. "We had a victory party with a lead of seven votes. It had poured rain all day and all night the returns seesawed back and forth so we really didn't know if we'd won." The next day, *The Globe and Mail* reported that "Michael Starr, the nice guy of the House of Commons for the past sixteen years, lost out by 113 votes to Edward Broadbent, the New Democratic Party's professor of political science with somewhat of a swinger's image." The result was due to Trudeaumania, says Cliff Pilkey. "The Liberal candidate drew enough votes from the Tories to let Ed go up the middle and win." If Ed was grateful to Trudeau, he never let on.

But Mike Starr would not concede; a recount was held. Ed was on tenterhooks for almost a month, not knowing whether he'd be back teaching at York in the fall or going to Ottawa. On July 13, the results were released: Ed Broadbent was the new MP from Oshawa–Whitby. He won with a fifteen-vote margin. Meanwhile, the four bright NDP leadership hopefuls — Fisher, Harney, Rogers and LaPierre — had been defeated.

Doug Fisher, now a conservatively inclined newspaper columnist, says Ed was lucky. In early '68, Stephen Lewis had asked Fisher to consider running in Oshawa. Fisher had turned down the offer "because I wanted a big city riding where you wouldn't have to do too much work when you'd won. That's why I picked a Toronto riding [which he lost.] But I asked Stephen who else he had in mind for Oshawa. He said there was a York professor whose parents lived in the riding. I asked, 'What's in his disfavour?' Stephen said, 'Oh, he's a Brough Macpherson disciple.' That meant, to the Lewises, that he was a Marxist, and they were jumpy about Marxists." Lewis disagrees with Fisher's interpretation: "I liked Brough Macpherson's analysis. I'd read him, I'd sat in on his classes at U. of T. I certainly wasn't worried about his Marxism and I didn't know anything about Ed. The only thing I would have been concerned about was getting someone who could appeal to GM workers in Oshawa." In other words, Ed's reputation for boring speeches preceded him.

According to Fisher, the party had reason to be concerned about Ed's appeal, but not on ideological grounds. Ed's early performance in the House of Commons "was so painfully awkward and academic that you almost choked on it," says Fisher. "And he made so many mistakes — signing the Waffle Manifesto without thinking and then turning around and reneging on it — that if I'd been him I would have slunk out the back door and not come back. The only thing Ed had going for him was a Ph.D. and a nice face. But he's turned out to be durable. He wears. He's had the boots put to him by a lot of people and he's had the resilience to hang in. He's no giant, but he's grown. It's the rare ones in this business that come along, and he has really come along."

With mixed feelings of trepidation and excitement, Ed moved out of his university office, gave up his apartment, packed his books and belongings and carted his worldly goods to Ottawa. He had no sense that he was embarking on his life's work. "I was determined to stay only as long as I enjoyed it," he says. In Ottawa, he settled into an apartment at Bronson and Laurier, asked Lucille Munroe out to dinner, and tried to get used to his new milieu.

In the green glory of a late Ottawa summer, walking along the canal with Lucille, Ed still hadn't quite caught up with himself. He rode his bicycle to the Hill, where the Parliament Buildings, in their gothic grandeur, were poised on the bluffs above the Ottawa River, with magnificent views northward to Quebec and the Gatineau Hills. Seated in the House of Commons, beneath its stained-glass windows, surrounded by the stuff of history, he was moved by powerful emotions. If politics is the secular religion of our time, Ed was like a junior Jesuit. A passionate student of democracy, he had spent more than a decade exploring an intellectual world whose finest — flawed — creation was this: a system of government based on a vision of equality, justice and rule of law. Now he was part of it. A player. But he didn't talk about these feelings in public. His first speech in the House of Commons was delivered in a joking spirit. NDP MP John Gilbert, now a judge, remembers Ed's debut well. "It happened at four o'clock on a Friday afternoon," says Gilbert. "No one was there — just a bare quorum. Ed got up and said, 'I'm delighted to see such a crowded gallery. They're hanging over the banisters . . .' It was typical of Ed."

He needed his sense of humour. Entering the New Democratic caucus in 1968 was like joining an elite team of formidable pros. It was like going to the rink and getting to play in a Montreal Canadiens lineup in the days when Jean Beliveau was captain. Just as Guy Lafleur stumbled for a couple of years after he was brought up from a junior team to play with the Canadiens, so Ed underwent an awkward transition from professor to student. He was playing with three of the great masters of Canadian politics, as even members of the other two parties would agree: Stanley Knowles, Tommy Douglas and David Lewis. The saints.

Ed was taken under the bony, capacious wing of Stanley Knowles, a tall, cadaverously thin, greatly beloved figure. "Stanley was it. Stanley knew it all," says Eugene Forsey, an expert in Parliamentary procedure. "Nobody in the House could match his knowledge, except perhaps Arthur Meighen [former Tory Prime Minister]. Not only does Stanley know the rules but he has experience of how the rules work. He used to spot mistakes in Beauchesne," referring to Arthur Beauchesne's 900-page *Rules and Forms — A Compendium of Canadian Parliamentary Practice*. "In Beauchesne!" Forsey's voice rises in amazement. "Beauchesne was the authority, and I spotted one mistake in Beauchesne, I might add, but Stanley, he knew the whole thing so well he could take me through the book and show me 'here's a mistake and over here and there and there . . .' "

Knowles was first elected CCF MP for Winnipeg North Centre in 1942, taking over the seat held for the previous twenty-one years by the founding saint of Canadian socialism, J.S. Woodsworth, an Oxford-educated Methodist minister whose credentials included an arrest for seditious treason during the Winnipeg General Strike of 1919. Woodsworth's political model was the British Labour Party; he was a mainstream democratic socialist, much feared and grudgingly admired by Prime Minister Mackenzie King, who offered him a Cabinet portfolio. Woodsworth rejected it "and used his bargaining power with a minority government to extort Canada's first old-age pension legislation," wrote Desmond Morton.

In 1942, when Woodsworth was dying, he was taken by train to Winnipeg for a last meeting with his constituents. "Winnipeg North Centre must be held," he said. "Oh, yes, J.S.," they said. "The choice of a candidate must be absolutely democratic," he said. "Oh, yes, J.S.," they said. "And the candidate must be Stanley Knowles," he said.

Knowles, a United Church minister, sixty years old when Ed encountered him, had seen five prime ministers in action: Mackenzie King, Louis St Laurent, Lester Pearson, John Diefenbaker and now Pierre Trudeau — a special favourite. (Knowles always regretted that the NDP had failed to persuade Trudeau to join its ranks.) Knowles had fought and won landmark battles on social issues, particularly pension reform. NDP MP Max Saltsman once joked that all he had to do to win his Waterloo, Ont., riding was to get Stanley to drive around with him and wave at senior citizens. "When I'm dead," Stanley interjected, "you can stuff me and prop me up in your car and keep on winning." Stanley knew the value of loyal constituents. The day after every election since 1942 he had returned to the CN shopgates in Winnipeg to thank the people for voting for him. Ed admired him enormously — but then there were Tommy and David.

Tommy Douglas and David Lewis: two more intense and different personalities would be hard to imagine. Loveable Tommy, hard-nosed Lewis: they were a stereotyped couple, Lewis the tough cop who made the hard decisions that freed Tommy to fly on his charisma. They couldn't have done what they did without each other, yet they were not close personal friends. "There was a lot of tension between them," says an intimate observer, "but they didn't explode at each other. They carved out different domains." Ed, it should be remembered, did not know these people. He didn't belong to the network. It was all new to him.

Tommy, the tiny, passionate orator, was, despite his nice-guy image, a hard-driving politician who had headed the first social democratic government in North America. As NDP leader, he presided over Ed's entry into political life and had an enormous influence on the Oshawa neophyte. Tommy was no pious sissy. A former boxer with a photographic memory, during his teenage years he won the Manitoba Lightweight Boxing Championship (he weighed 135 pounds) and took lessons in the art of public speaking, delivering dramatic monologues and reciting Robbie Burns, the Scottish poet. He had studied for his Ph.D. in a Chicago ghetto. He discovered, he said, that the only difference between Chicago's homeless transients and himself was that they didn't have jobs. A Baptist minister, he was competitive, ambitious and aggressive. On the value of doing political battle, he said: "I don't know whether it increases the adrenalin in my system, but a fight always makes me feel better." He was not a pacifist; he did not believe in rigid ideology. "I'm afraid I'm not an intellectual," he said. "I'm a pragmatist."

He disapproved of censorship: "You don't make a good man or a good woman by prohibiting or refusing them. On this continent we have inherited the mores and social attitudes of the Puritans, who tried to make people good by legislation. Determining how long skirts should be, how many square feet of cloth had to be in a bathing suit, whether certain words in a play were obscene, or whether people could drink or smoke or swear didn't work. Even if it had worked, I wouldn't give a five-cent piece for any person who was good because he had been prevented from being bad. There's no credit in that."

On June 15, 1944, he led the CCF to victory in Saskatchewan, winning forty-seven of fifty-two seats and 53 per cent of the popular vote. As a young premier, he was invited to dinner by Mackenzie King. Expecting a party, he found himself dining alone with the elderly Prime Minister in the lugubrious gloom of Laurier House, where King lived alone amid an astonishing profusion of rococo antiques and historical bric-a-brac — including a "Wanted: Dead or Alive" poster seeking his outlaw grandfather, William Lyon Mackenzie, a leader of the 1837 rebellion against the Family Compact in Ontario. Little Tommy, taking it all in, was overwhelmed. The two men sat beneath the portrait of King's dead mother, whom King "contacted" through occult seances. Douglas was unnerved by the "weird vibrations" and astounded by King's revelations. The Prime Minister spoke frankly about the individual idiosyncrasies of his Cabinet ministers, revealing secrets that Douglas almost blushed to hear. He came away with an uncanny sense that King had chosen him as his spiritual heir.

But Douglas remained Premier of Saskatchewan for the next seventeen years, transforming his province from a bankrupt backwater into a prosperous region that was, said the *Toronto Star*, "the flagship of social change in all of Canada." The obstacles were horrendous: the departing Liberals had not only left a destitute government, but they had stripped the filing cabinets of crucial documents. And the red-baiting never stopped. When opponents charged that Douglas's socialist hordes would turn the province into a Soviet dictatorship, Tommy responded that they were insulting the intelligence of the people of Saskatchewan. Tommy believed that socialism was Christianity in action, and he understood that people's basic needs came first. He was a canny politician: among his first moves were the Farm Security Act, which prohibited banks from seizing a farmer's home quarter section; public insurance for homes, farms, vehicles; sewers, which allowed farmers to burn their outhouses; and electricity — the CCF took power to 60,000 farms in fourteen years. It was all done without creating a deficit "in a province that had no Alberta oil to fuel it, no Ontario industrial grease," observes Cliff Scotton, who became federal secretary at Tommy's request in 1965.

Tommy ran a tight ship, balancing the budget, developing the best civil service in the country. Among the crew he promoted were Al Johnson, his deputy treasurer who was later brought to Ottawa to direct the implementation of medicare; and Tommy Shoyama, chief economic adviser who became federal deputy finance minister. Douglas established a department of co-operatives and a group of Crown corporations that were run on a determinedly businesslike basis. Under his rule, Saskatchewan prospered. The best argument in favour of social democracy, he said, "is to make it work." He did, and then he moved to the national scene in 1961, to lead the newly created New Democratic Party for ten years.

Everybody who knew him cherishes Tommy stories. NDP MP Les Benjamin: "The first time I heard Tommy speak was in 1944 in Yorkton, Sask. I was wandering around with nothing to do and I saw posters plastered all over, 'Hear Tommy Douglas.'" It was like a rock star had come to town. "So I went down to the skating rink with my friend. It was jammed to the rafters. He had the place howling. He could wring tears out of a juryful of bankers. The last time I saw it happen was at the '83 convention in Regina, for the party's fiftieth anniversary. He went through all the good things we had done, how we had influenced government, and he attacked the right wing's crass appeal to selfishness and greed. Well, he got the longest standing ovation — twenty minutes — I've ever heard, and people were crying. I told him, I said, 'Tommy, I learned my politics at your knee.' And Tommy said, 'Yeah, and a few other low joints.' Every election year we'd have a campaign management school and Tommy would give us tips on public speaking. He had three principles: stand up, speak up and shut up."

Tommy was a mesmerizing figure — but then there was David Lewis, equally fascinating, just as powerful. Tommy and David: everyone talked about them, analyzed their differences. Scottish-born Tommy, prairie evangelist, business-minded socialist; Polish-born David, urban intellectual, labour lawyer, backroom organizer.

Tommy could be a harsh taskmaster, impatient, irritable; David could be manipulative, arrogant, rigid. Others considered both men warm and loveable. "Tommy had a good visceral sense of politics," says Terry Grier. "He wasn't much for intellectual strategizing. He was a kind of natural politician. David was more sophisticated, but he wasn't a natural like Tommy. David was thin-skinned — I revered David, I have to tell you — and most people didn't realize how sensitive David was. He wasn't as tough a guy as Tommy. Tommy could be a tough bugger to work for. He could be miserable, nag you to death. David was a nicer person." Yet ask another NDPer and you'll hear that Tommy was nicer, David was a tough bugger. On one thing everyone agreed: Tommy and David were deeply respected for their dedication to the party. Tommy was its public face, David its organizational guts.

David Lewis was born in Svisloch, in Imperial Russia (now part of Poland) in 1909. He was eight years old when the Russian Revolution erupted in 1917. Two years later, Svisloch was occupied by the Bolsheviks for six months; they arrested Lewis's father and threatened to execute him. "It was an unforgettable experience," Lewis wrote, "which evoked a deep and lasting animosity toward all communists." Fighting communism in Canada became one of his life's works. The other was to build a social democratic party that would form a government.

The family emigrated to Montreal in 1921. David, a twelve-year-old, was placed in a grade one class with six-year-olds. It was the typical immigrant experience. Humiliated, he decided to teach himself English by studying a novel he'd bought at a second-hand bookshop: Charles Dickens's *Old Curiosity Shop* provided his entree into the English language.

A brilliant student, six years later he enrolled in political science at McGill University. There he made friends with Eugene Forsey, a political science professor, King Gordon, who taught Christian Ethics, and F.R. Scott, a poet and law professor. Forsey, Gordon and Scott were the Three Musketeers of Early Canadian Socialism, each one a Rhodes Scholar, as David would become. Frank

Scott was on his way to becoming the nation's foremost constitutional lawyer and civil liberties activist. David was thrilled when they invited him to join a study group that later formed the League for Social Reconstruction, which would have a hand in shaping the CCF Manifesto. These were historic connections. Tommy and David belonged in the history books; they were, in short, a legendary pair.

Ed was excited by his sudden immersion: the switch from the relatively serene life of a political science professor to the intensity and often uncontrollable demands of politics was an abrupt one. It took Ed some time to find his feet. As in his early years at the University of Toronto, he was an anonymous figure; he didn't have any important connections to the party's hierarchy, and he wasn't a naturally imposing presence. "Ed seemed like a decent guy," says Tony Penikett, leader of the Yukon NDP Government, who met Ed in the early '70s, "but he had this unfortunate academic tendency to modify every statement before it was out of his mouth. He wasn't particularly charismatic."

Ed found a measure of stability by travelling to Oshawa every weekend, where he stayed with his parents. "On Saturdays I had office hours and met people with concrete problems," says Ed. "It wasn't abstract. It was real. I'd stay overnight and have a good time. I took a remarkable degree of satisfaction from this part of being an MP." And so he dug in to his constituency and extended his support.

The person who spent the most time with Ed in those days was his personal secretary, May Gretton. She knew the intimate details: the Ed whose Volvo was always breaking down and she would have to rescue him; the Ed who'd play practical jokes, phoning her up and pretending to be an outraged constituent: "You mean to tell me Ed Broadbent's not in the office? It's 9:30 in the morning and what are we paying these lazy oafs for anyway?" The anonymous caller would blast May, she'd defend the MPs — "I'd list off all the hundreds of things MPs had to do besides sit in their offices" — and then Ed would burst out laughing on the other end of the line "and I'd realize he'd got me again."

Ed was lucky to get May Gretton. He arrived, a rookie MP on the Hill, and if there was one major reason he didn't fall flat on his face it was May. Today, in her late sixties, she is still the character she always was, and she's still in touch with Ed and Lucille. May does not look like a senior citizen, nor does she act like one. Wearing an elegant dark wool dress and a long string of pearls, her hair a subtle reddish-blond, she talks with ease about the politicians she's known in thirty years on the Hill.

May grew up in Ottawa and started working on the Hill in 1947. She wastes no time describing the hazards of her career. "I was a secretary for George Cruickshank from Fraser Valley. He was a Liberal, and I was more inclined, then, to be a Liberal. But I hated working for him. I was twenty-five years old, I was shy and I couldn't cope with his drinking. I wouldn't go near him. Sometimes I'd go to the Gallery [in the House of Commons] and look at old Mackenzie King. He was so sick he could hardly hold up his head, let alone pay any attention to what was going on. Anyway, I quit Cruickshank's office. I said I want a nice, quiet old gentleman who won't chase me around the desk, and they gave me Joe Noseworthy." Noseworthy, the CCF giant-killer who had knocked off former Tory Prime Minister Arthur Meighen, became her boss for almost a decade, followed by M.J. Coldwell, the party leader. Noseworthy and Coldwell were polite, reserved gentlemen of the old school, she says, so she was content. But she continued to observe the dark shadows behind the bright lights of politics. "I liked Pearson, but his wife was a drunk. He'd sit in his office and watch the baseball game and she'd get bored. She'd wander the halls and get lost. Security would find Mrs Pearson and they'd direct her back to the Prime Minister's office. Didn't bother him a bit."

Something of a skeptic by the time the 1968 election rolled around, May vividly remembers her first glimpse of her new MP. "Ed arrived at the House of Commons look-

ing so young and handsome, all tanned, wearing a pale
beige suit. He wasn't married. I said, 'Get a young chick
to work for you who matches you. You're so young and
handsome. I'm too old.' But he said he wanted to work
with me, so we did." Right away, May noticed that
though Ed was flirtatious with women, he wasn't a
lecher. "I saw the women coming on to him, all right, but
he didn't take them up on it." Anyway, there was Lucille.
Ed and Lucille were "keeping company"; though they
weren't formally engaged, they were accepted as a couple.

May soon got to know Ed's parents, who travelled to
Ottawa for Ed's investiture in the House of Commons,
where they got to shake hands with Stanley Knowles.
"They were so proud," says May. "Of course some of their
relatives were jealous, and they started calling Mrs
Broadbent 'Mrs Ottawa,' 'Here comes Mrs Ottawa,' they'd
say — oh, she used to get mad — but that's the way families are, if one gets ahead of the others."

Ed's working habits, May noted, were fastidious. "Tidy
and exact" are her words, the same adjectives used by
Ed's old friend Joe Levitt to describe Ed's carrel in the
University of Toronto library. Just as Ed lined up his student notes precisely, so did he handle his House of Commons business. Says May: "Every day his desk was piled
high with messages and papers and he insisted on dealing with everything immediately so that his slate was
cleared for the next day. He's organized. He's the type of
person who likes to get his job done, leave his desk clean,
go home and enjoy life."

Ed was particular about everything, especially his appearance. "His mother said he was always the same." His
shoes were always polished and he was fussy about his
clothes. "In those days they had a tailor in the House of
Commons, and when Ed bought a new suit, he'd have the
tailor in to hem the pants. If his pants came back one-
eighth of an inch too long or too short, he'd send them
back to get them fixed." Despite the attention he paid to
his grooming, he was criticized for the academic, tweedy
look he favoured, with leather elbow patches on his
jackets. Ed in his favourite brown corduroy suit looked

dull in comparison to the more sophisticated, eclectic elegance of Pierre Elliott Trudeau, whose sandals, cravats and increasingly long hair made him look like a hippy Prime Minister. But Ed was not impressed by Trudeau. "Pierre Trudeau," he wrote in the *Toronto Star* in 1970, "is the darling of all those who prefer the illusion of change to its reality." He was appalled that Trudeau, who "had acquired more influence and power than any other leader in Canadian history, did nothing with it." Trudeau could only be described, he said, "as a Mackenzie King who likes girls."

Still, says May, "Trudeau was a spellbinder. Ed doesn't ooze charisma the way Trudeau did. You have it or you haven't. I look at Ed in a different way. He's a nice, homey, reliable guy. But let's be honest. Ed's not a very good public speaker. He gets into this 'speech' mode and his voice goes up. He's like someone who yells on the phone and doesn't really trust the phone to carry the sound of his voice. And he's not exciting like Trudeau. After all, Ed comes from Ontario. He's what Ontario is all about. Trudeau is what Quebec is all about. They're different cultures."

Solid, reliable, moderate Ed: but there were other sides to his character. Lucille Munroe says that "what attracted me to Ed was his idealism." Their relationship was founded on a shared passion for what Lucille terms "moral issues." As the years went by, she would become concerned "that his idealism was being corroded — perhaps that's too strong a word — by the compromises of political life." Gradually, as his ambition grew, she would have difficulty accepting "his pursuit of power."

Then there was his silly side. The stress of being a Member of Parliament triggered a veritable avalanche of Broadbent pranks. Earnest Ed concealed Ed the trickster, and May Gretton had to learn fast to recognize which mode her boss was in. "I was very businesslike," says May, "and I'd be in taking dictation — I responded to most of the letters myself, he dictated only for technical details — and in the middle of it he'd say something, trying to embarrass me. One day he said he'd been to an

MP's wedding. Everybody knew that the groom was very tall and the bride was very short. He looked me right in the eye and said: 'How do you think they'll make out in bed?' He didn't blink. I thought, 'He's trying to get my goat, he wants me to blush and stammer. I won't do it. So I just said, 'Oh they'll find a way.' "

Another time, she had just bought a brand new yellow convertible. "Ed knew I was very pleased with it. One day I got a call from a Bell Telephone man who said he was flying over my area and saw a yellow convertible going off the cliff. (I lived near the river.) He wondered if I knew the owner of the car. My heart flipped and I tore outside to look — of course my car was safely parked. It was Ed."

Practically everybody who was at all friendly with Ed was at one time or another a victim of his pranks. But his joking around relieved stress, which was endemic. "If you can't be silly, you'll go crazy," says Willy Parasiuk, Manitoba's former health minister and a friend of Ed's. "It's the silly times you remember more than the momentous ones. Otherwise all you ever think about is, 'the party's going to collapse, the government's going to collapse,' and it's too heavy." Politicians who drank too much and had affairs with secretaries, assistants with bleeding ulcers, marriages on the rocks, nervous breakdowns, these were the common hazards of the business. Ed coped with the pressure by switching roles: at caucus Christmas parties he was a hit, one year playing Snow White to Stanley Knowles's Prince Charming, with the seven dwarfs performed by seven short MPs, including Tommy Douglas and David Lewis; the next year Ed was the Pope, pulled in on a furniture mover's dolly, sprinkling holy water on the MPs. "We had the best Christmas parties of any caucus," says MP Les Benjamin, who has never forgotten how funny Ed looked as Snow White, wearing a costume from the National Arts Centre and a mop for a wig. "No prima donnas were allowed in our outfit."

But Earnest Ed was never off stage for too long, and friends were often amazed by how quickly he'd resume his serious self, hammering away at his favourite subject, industrial democracy. "Industrial democracy. Worker participation." May shakes her head. "He had files and files and files of it. That was all he ever wanted to talk about. It never went over. Nobody ever paid any attention to it, but he just kept banging away at it. He probably still has it in his mind — it's a belief he can't shake. That's the way he is." She's right. "I still believe in the vision of industrial democracy," Ed says in the spring of '88.

Industrial democracy is an idea that is coming around again. In the '60s, worker participation was the clarion call of American and European progressives. Scandinavian and West German socialists were giving workers more input into their patterns of work, moving away from the dehumanized assembly-line model of mass production. The Japanese would advance the concept, particularly in the automobile industry, demonstrating that workers who took pride in their work were more productive, making their companies more profitable. But in North America, the adversarial union–management relationship proved stony ground for industrial democracy. Unions feared giving up hard-won rights and being co-opted into sweetheart deals; management feared sharing power and could not envision bringing workers onto boards of directors. Neither side could imagine changing.

Yet Ed fervently embraced the concept. "Ed must be credited for the work he did on industrial democracy," says Jim Laxer. "It was his major contribution to the party, and it grew out of his belief in a broader sense of egalitarianism." Broadbent pitched it on every possible occasion, and developed reams of policies around it. In an article for the *Toronto Star*, published on August 13, 1969, Ed wrote — still very much the academic: "Drawing on our socialist tradition and such liberals as John Stuart Mill, we New Democrats must present to Canadians a richer view of democracy." He talked about equal opportunity for self-development — a favourite theme of C.B. Macpherson — about extending democracy in the workplace and redistributing not just wealth but power. The NDP, he said, had succeeded in its primary mission: gaining acceptance for the welfare state. It must now blaze a new trail, confident that the other parties sooner or later would follow the path. Electoral risks were involved, he acknowledged. "But if we New Democrats don't take those risks we will likely lose out in any case to those cynical politicians who have mastered the art of expediency. We must not succumb to the Utopian temptation to create a program whose message is socialism now; nor must we yield to the impulse to play it safe. Ours is the unromantic middle road. A road which Canadians respect."

He could not have written a more appropriate epitaph for his own political career. Dennis McDermott, then head of the United Auto Workers (Canadian branch), would have liked to deliver Ed's epitaph back in 1969. "McDermott thought Ed was a cow's ass, an academic shithead who was floating up in the clouds, with no idea what the real world was all about," says an NDP insider. "Ed was peddling worker participation and McDermott said Ed didn't know what a factory floor looked like." Thus Ed infuriated the union power brokers who worked so closely with David Lewis. The party establishment was angry that an MP who represented an industrial riding would so quickly alienate its union constituency. Ed became the target of harsh attacks. It was hard on him. "Ed doesn't like criticism," says May Gretton. "He doesn't handle it well."

But he did have his supporters, Jim Laxer for one. "Worker control seemed pie-in-the-sky, it's true; I guess it wasn't real to people, then. Now I understand it. A lot of other countries have done it and it's clear that you can't run an intelligent economy without worker participation. Ed was just ahead of his time." Almost twenty years later, General Motors in Oshawa would spend millions of dollars in an effort to implement industrial democracy in its plants, doing away with assembly lines, trying to involve workers in designing their work patterns, re-educating supervisors to play a more supportive role.

Ed now admits that he made a mistake — a tactical error — in his approach to the issue. "I didn't work out the policy with the people who would have to live with it," he says. "I learned a great lesson. I would no sooner develop a policy on agriculture without talking to farmers or on women's issues without talking to women. . . . Although I got Cliff Pilkey to give me verbal support for what I was doing, I was out of touch. Well motivated, but out of touch. Olof Palme [former Prime Minister of Sweden] later talked to me about how they'd implemented industrial democracy in Sweden. The way they did it — this sounds obvious now — is that they got the leadership of the trade union movement to take the initiative and develop the program. That's the way it should be. That's where it has to come from, not from the top down."

But in June 1969, when Ed introduced his five-point program for industrial democracy to the NDP's federal council, he was startled by what was reported as a "bitter attack" from union leaders. His proposal, published in *Canadian Forum* that year, would radically restructure management–labour relations. Undaunted by the howls from both sides, he persisted, holding belated discussions with hostile unionists and revising his program, which he presented in a watered-down version at the NDP convention in Winnipeg in '69. He called for unions to negotiate in areas traditionally regarded as prerogatives of management: technological change, production, pricing and profit policies — which meant, he said, that corporations would have to open their books and provide fuller disclosure on profits, investments and product research.

His vision of industrial democracy supplanting the welfare state as the party's primary goal was shot down by all sides. And he was already getting into hot water on another front: the Waffle. Born of the activist spirit of the '60s, promising to lead an invigorated party into the '70s, the Waffle's short life span paralleled the experience of the American New Left as it was shaped within SDS. The American left, cut off from the Democratic Party, was cast adrift to fight its battles in single-issue movements — civil rights, anti-Vietnam war, feminism; in Canada, the Waffle drew radicals to the New Democratic Party and then imploded. Ed, the idealist, would learn another painful lesson: "When the party polarizes, no one's happy.

When there's no compromise to be made, you're in trouble."

CHAPTER FIVE

The Perils of Politics

*The political immaturity Ed displayed, dur-
ing the '71 leadership contest, could have
destroyed his career — had he not put his
head down and gone to work. . . . Ed has a
bulldoggedness, a staying power, that I
think is his strongest characteristic. He
didn't have the intellectual polish of David
Lewis but I came to realize he has a
deeper understanding of Canadian life than
Lewis.*
Murray Weppler, David Lewis's chief-of-staff.

It is a sunny day in New York City, October, 1987. Stephen Lewis, then Canada's ambassador to the United Nations, is eating lunch at a Greek restaurant across the
road from the fluttering flags of the United Nations. He
is reminiscing about the Waffle era, back in the late '60s,
when he was one of the group's chief opponents. An attractive, intense man whose leadership of the Ontario NDP
from 1970 to 1978 carried the party to the heights of official opposition-hood, Lewis now relishes his non-political
life. This is the kid, after all, who was born in a trunk,
who was performing in the political arena as soon as he
was old enough to shake hands, running campaigns when
he was a teenager, crisscrossing the country as the NDP's
first national director of organization in 1961 when he
was in his early twenties.

Though he still bites his nails to the quick, he is learning to relax. He occasionally wakes up in the middle of
the night in a cold sweat, dreaming that his father wants
him to return to the partisan fray, but he is resisting the

call. And when Ed Broadbent came to New York to woo him to run federally in the next election, Stephen promised Ed that he would do anything for him except one thing: run for office. Stephen's wife, Michele Landsberg, approves. Stephen burned out in 1978. Ten years later, rejuvenated but withdrawn from active involvement in the party, he has developed a Garbo-esque allure. His international exposure has added to his charms, and admirers continue to yearn for his return to the political stage.

His time at the United Nations has been a mixed bag. "I'm more and more jaundiced about ideology," says Lewis. "But I still insist on the distinction between democratic socialism and communism." This distinction was, of course, his father's driving passion, in a continent awash in anti-communist sentiment. The brutality of Stalin's regime in the Soviet Union, combined with the hysteria of the McCarthy anti-communist witchhunts in the United States, smeared without distinction leftists of all stripes.

Democratic socialism has nothing to do with communism. It can't be said often enough, Lewis asserts. In Sweden, Norway, western Europe, the United Kingdom, Australia, New Zealand and even Canada, social democracy and its practitioners are mainstream forces. The Scandinavian countries lead the world in advances relating to equality, child care and full employment, while their socialist governments cohabit with such home-grown capitalist corporations as Volvo, Saab, and Ikea, the largest furniture retailer in the world. "The terms of the cohabitation are crucial," says Lewis. "The key to Scandinavian success is that their socialist leaders work with corporations but they have the power of government."

Social democracy, in Lewis's world view, is the middle ground between capitalism, Reagan- or Thatcher-style, on the right and totalitarianism, Soviet- or Chinese-style, on the left. "The extreme left and the extreme right tend to converge, which reminds me of the Waffle. The Waffle had nothing to do with democratic socialism and everything to do with acting out a pathological aggressiveness."

The Waffle was Canada's answer to America's New Left, and Stephen's best friend, Gerry Caplan, was one of its instigators. Ed, too, was in on its creation, though he didn't hang around for long.

The product of a generation formed in the shadow of the Vietnam war, determined to confront the hypocrisy of the establishment, the Waffle "followed in a tradition of noisy dissent on the party's left going back to the Regina Convention of 1933," wrote the McLeods in their biography of Tommy Douglas. A radical precursor was the "Socialist Fellowship," formed in British Columbia in the '50s and more revolutionary than the Waffle. CCF leader M.J. Coldwell, a gentleman of the old school, banned the group from the party, terming it "a threat to liberty and freedom in Canada." Twenty years later, the Waffle's lifespan was equally fiery, and almost as brief. And on both sides of the Canada–U.S. border, the New Left — at once a source of new ideas and old conflicts — met the same fate: confrontation, disillusionment, fragmentation, dissolution.

The Waffle began in the early spring of 1969 when Gerry Caplan and Jim Laxer had lunch in Ottawa and talked about the stagnation of the NDP. "We had to do something about the future of the party," says Laxer. With Mel Watkins, whose description of the country's "branch-plant economy" had defined the particular vulnerability of Canada's business sector, they planned action.

Picture the fixers: Laxer, today the fit, attractive chairman of the political science department at Atkinson College, York University, was then an overweight, rumpled, long-haired twenty-nine-year-old history lecturer at Queen's University. He was married to the activist-feminist Krista Maeots, and together they were regarded as the leading contemporary egalitarian couple. Caplan, thin and wiry with dark hair and an intense manner, renowned for his quick wit and hypochondriac tendencies, was installed at the Ontario Institute for Studies in Edu-

cation (OISE), where he taught Third World development
and Canadian political culture. Their economic guru was
Mel Watkins. Famous for his 1968 Watkins Report on
foreign control of the economy, Watkins was almost ten
years older, a skinny, moody, brilliant economist with
badly arranged teeth (which limited his TV appeal), who
more than any of them had thought out a vision for an
independent Canada. This was what drove the Waffle: independence, the very issue that was pushing Quebec politics towards the brink of separatism.

Laxer was the passionate romantic who loved his country, Caplan the edgy activist oppressed by Canadian complacency, Watkins the specialist who spoke the technical
language that unlocked the economic secrets of foreign
domination. They were inspired by a fierce conviction
that Canada was being sucked into the American empire.
Laxer remembers the sense of urgency. "I had a burning
feeling Canada might cease to exist. The colonial mental-
ity had crippled us. We couldn't act and live as full human beings because the centres of power, the real
decision makers, weren't here. We were at the end of the
cafeteria line. In our own country, we got the dregs."

Fired up by their mission, Caplan and Laxer paid a
visit to Broadbent in his Parliament Hill office. They
needed an MP on side, to give them credibility in the
party, and Ed seemed the likeliest prospect. Certainly he
was sympathetic to their views. Elected less than a year
before, Broadbent was a fresh-faced hope for the new generation, even if he was still a political neophyte. "Ed invited us to come and sit in on a caucus meeting," says
Laxer. "We didn't think they'd allow us to, but Ed assured us there'd be no problem. Sure enough when the
time came, and we were waiting outside, Ed appeared
with his face as red as a beet. 'They won't let you in,' he
said. So Gerry and I went to the Sparks Street Mall and
had a coffee and planned our agenda."

In Toronto, Caplan called a meeting at his house on
Boswell Avenue, and Broadbent came, along with Watkins, Laxer, Krista Maeots, Giles Endicott and some
others. Ed was the only MP in the group, Endicott the

only member of the party's federal council. Seated in Caplan's living room, surrounded by the vivid African sculptures he had collected in his travels, they debated their ideas. They dreamed of joining forces with Quebec and delivering to the party — and the nation — a vision of Canada that would transform the country.

For Giles Endicott, "a large part of what we were doing was the generational thing. The new generation wanted to flex its muscles and gain some power. We looked on the old guard — David Lewis, Donald MacDonald [Leader of the Ontario party] — as right-wing. We thought they weren't paying enough attention to the Americanization of Canada." Yet foreign control of the economy was being studied by a policy committee of the party, Tommy Douglas was making speeches about it, and union activists like Cliff Pilkey had already challenged international control of Canadian locals. Cliff Scotton, the party's federal secretary, saw the Wafflers as "dissidents, out to defrock the establishment." Endicott admits: "The Waffle whiz kids didn't invent the issues." But they took their name from a slim conceit: they saw the party waffling to the right, and joked that they would rather waffle to the left; legend has it that Ed said the words that gave the group its name, though this is in dispute. At any rate, the label stuck. Only in Canada, wrote Norman Snider in a *Toronto Life* profile of Broadbent, "would a movement of flaming radical intent be christened with such a deadly name as The Waffle, instead of The Northern Panthers or suchlike."

Over a period of weeks, they produced the Waffle Manifesto, "Towards an Independent Socialist Canada." It focussed on three major areas: foreign control of the economy (Watkins's specialty), Quebec (Laxer's) and industrial democracy (Ed's). Laxer's passion for Henri Bourassa had evolved into his absorption with Quebec's Quiet Revolution and his identification with the struggle of the Québecois to become masters in their own land. *White Niggers of America*, the English title of Pierre Vallières's best-seller published in 1968 as *Nègres blancs d'Amérique: Autobiographie précoce d'un "terroriste" québecois,* exemplified the radical spirit of the times. Written in prison after a twenty-nine-day hunger strike, the book was infused with anger and hope. Despite his "short but brutal experience of life," Vallières was filled with a "boundless conviction that it is possible to build a better world *now*, if we all agree to roll up our sleeves and set to work. The world is waiting to be transformed." Some of the transformations he envisaged were contained in Ed's articulation of industrial democracy — giving power to workers by involving them in management decisions that affected their lives — borrowed from Europe and Japan.

The first draft of the Waffle Manifesto was written mostly by Laxer, the second draft by Watkins. They were thrilled with their work. "We had the spirit of the New Left," says Laxer. "The Manifesto was an expression of the youthful radicalism of the era, but it was Watkins who made it a brilliant document. Watkins was my idol. I thought he was the greatest guy. I loved what he stood for. I looked up to him. I would have done anything to get him elected leader of the party."

Ed, however, was alarmed by Watkins's rhetoric. He called Laxer. "I'm worried about where this is going," Ed told Laxer. Then Ed showed the Manifesto to Marc Eliesen, the party's research director. An economist from Montreal, Eliesen had worked for the federal finance department in Ottawa; his first boss was Simon Reisman, then deputy minister of finance. They would both go on to greater things; as chairman of the Manitoba Energy Authority, Eliesen supervised construction of Manitoba's $3 billion Limestone hydro-electric project. "The art of governing," he says, now that he knows something about it, "is the art of choosing priorities within a context of competing demands." Even in his leftist youth, he was a pragmatist; he was not impressed by the Manifesto. "They were into 'smash capitalism,' which was mentioned 832 times," says Eliesen, exaggerating. "The Manifesto was written for the converted. As a communications piece, it didn't work." Nor had Eliesen been much impressed by Ed, when they first met in '68. "Ed was an inward, intellectual guy, a poor communicator. It was odd

— a guy like that representing a worker constituency. But as I got to know him, he dropped his guard and opened up."

Together, Broadbent and Eliesen rewrote the Manifesto. Their version was presented to Laxer at Scott's Chicken Villa on the Sparks Street Mall. Laxer read it with dismay. "You've taken all the juice out of it," he complained. "The guts are gone."

Ed tried to convince Laxer that a more moderate document would reach more people; as the only elected politician in the group, Ed was learning from bitter experience about the kind of language that turned off audiences. But his Waffle colleagues had little respect for his perspective. Laxer thought Ed lacked imagination and was a bad writer. For his part, Ed thought Laxer was out of touch with the reality of the party. How easy it is, in politics as in life, to fail to connect: these two men liked each other, shared a vast range of similar interests, but could not agree on tactics. (They would again try to collaborate, as party leader and research director in the early '80s, with a more hostile outcome.)

At subsequent meetings of the group, Ed tried to persuade the Waffle to support the Broadbent–Eliesen version of the Manifesto. Endicott, for one, read it and approved: "Ed softened the language and I think he improved it." Says Ed: "I toned down what I had come to regard as foolish rhetoric, stuff about American imperialism that turned off working-class families. I still believe that if the Manifesto had been rewritten not only would I have stayed in but we probably would have passed it at the convention." But the Waffle wasn't interested in what it considered a tame and muted statement. And Ed wasn't interested in their tactics. "They wanted to polarize the party," says Ed. "That was the Left thing. I wasn't interested in polarization. I wanted to move the party as a party. We disagreed on style, not on substance. I wasn't bitter. I just left."

Ed wasn't alone in withdrawing from the Waffle; within six months, Endicott had backed out too. "I was a party hack," says Endicott. "My whole life was bound up in the structure of the party. I tried to persuade Laxer and Watkins that we must not be seen to be creating a party within a party. They didn't seem to realize the damage they could do to the organization. But then, neither of them was a party person and they really didn't care about the party. Jim was out of the New Left and Mel was out of the Liberals. They were declaring war on the NDP and it had to react. It was war."

Ed, back in the bosom of caucus, helped draft an official statement that reflected many of the Waffle's stands, backed away from its call for "public ownership of the means of production," and eschewed its rhetoric. But the less radical document, "For a United and Independent Canada," received little attention. Tommy Douglas promoted it, explaining that nationalization "can be a very blunt instrument that can lead simply to greater bureaucracy without necessarily solving the economic problems that you're trying to solve." But his voice was drowned out by the Waffle fireworks.

"The reception of the Manifesto far exceeded our expectations," says Watkins, and he does not lie. "It is a brilliant document, frankly," Watkins adds. "It was really advanced in its perceptions of issues — not only nationalism but Quebec's right to self-determination, feminism, the environment and support for independent Canadian unions. Mostly it touched a powerful nationalist chord. To be a Canadian nationalist was still, however, perceived as an anti-American aberration. The joke was that in every other way we aped the Americans, who are the most profoundly nationalistic people."

The controversy and excitement surrounding the Waffle spread across the country, attracting a particularly strong group in Saskatchewan. As well, Laxer admits, it drew "some crazies. There were Trots [Trotskyists] in the Waffle and other assorted loonies but that's like saying there are mosquitoes in Muskoka. So what? They didn't control the Waffle. Watkins and I always controlled the Waffle, and I can tell you honestly I was shocked by David Lewis's reaction. We thought of ourselves as good people. We looked up to David. We were surprised the party's leaders disliked us."

The New Democratic Party gathered in Winnipeg in October, 1969, for Tommy Douglas's last convention as leader. Delegates arrived at the historic gateway to western Canada in a celebratory mood. At the Manitoba Legislature, two mammoth bronze buffaloes flanked the magnificent marble entrance; the Golden Boy flashed his gleaming presence from on top of the highest dome — to which perch he was moved, having stood naked and offensive, on the Legislature's front lawn after his arrival in Winnipeg in 1918. Half a century later, New Democratic hopes were soaring — and their presence in the Premier's office was almost as offensive to some Manitobans as the Golden Boy's naked body had been.

Ed Schreyer, a thirty-three-year-old MP who spoke five languages, had won the Manitoba NDP leadership that summer and moved directly into a provincial election. His breakthrough victory, which preceded the convention, was not unanimously welcomed. Sipping Scotch in the exclusive sitting rooms of the Manitoba Club, the provincial ruling class was disturbed. The significance of Schreyer's win, says *Winnipeg Free Press* columnist Val Werier, "was not that Schreyer was a so-called socialist, but that he didn't belong to the Manitoba Club. It wasn't that the NDP was so radical, it just represented a different power base. For the first time you had a Premier and a Cabinet who didn't fit in with the WASP elite." Eyebrows were raised. The name of the Legislative Speaker — the Hon. B. Hanuschak, son of the former Anna Bartikw, married to Nadia Stechkewich — was "unpronounceable in certain circles," says Werier, with a wry grin.

The party's spiritual homeland was here in Manitoba and next door in Saskatchewan, in a land of vast skies, rich soil, sweeping rivers and frozen winters; in the Ukrainian, French, Scandinavian and native Indian communities that dotted the prairie, belying the Anglo image that outsiders had of the region. "But don't think the Manitoba and Saskatchewan groups are the same," warns

Michael Decter, a Winnipeg-born, Harvard-educated economist and later a close adviser to Broadbent. Decter explains: "The CCF was the Saskatchewan party, born of the rural, populist movement. The mainstay of the Manitoba left was the radical labour movement, which was closer in spirit to the British Columbia party, allied with middle-class intellectuals. The marriage of the Manitoba party and the Saskatchewan farmers produced the NDP." Decter's version is a decidedly western viewpoint — it was, after all, David Lewis who masterminded the new party's alliance with the nation's trade unions. But then, western New Democrats figure they hold the key; and the key is power. Central Canadians, accustomed to viewing the NDP as a minor player, had never come to terms with the party's strength in the west.

When *The Globe and Mail*'s Jeffrey Simpson dismissed New Democrats as "the chattering classes [who] run nothing but comment on everything," he was betraying his eastern bias. "This may be the one criticism of the party that does not hold water," wrote Robert Bott in *Saturday Night* (January, 1988). "The NDP and its precursor, the Co-operative Commonwealth Federation, have more than half a century of cumulative experience in running governments..."

In Winnipeg, prairie radicalism was front and centre — only in Winnipeg does the government distribute a brochure for a walking tour of the city titled "1919: The Winnipeg General Strike," directing tourists to visit such sites as the location of Bloody Saturday. The excitement of Winnipeg's historic past could still be felt in the city's old industrial quarter near Portage and Main, where the Wheat Board and the wheat pools, the financial houses and the transportation centres were located in magnificent turn-of-the-century buildings that still exude pioneer drama.

To Winnipeg in '69 came a motley crew: the eastern establishment headed by David Lewis and labour leader Dennis McDermott; the Ontario radicals in the form of the Waffle, including Jim Laxer, Gerry Caplan, Mel Watkins and, on the fringe, Ed Broadbent; the western establishment headed by NDP leader Tommy Douglas, Saskatchewan's Allan Blakeney (soon to become Premier), Manitoba Premier Ed Schreyer, B.C.'s Dave Barrett (who would defeat B.C.'s Social Credit government in 1972). And, by no means least, Canada's socialist elite: the Saskatchewan activists. They had long ago vaulted the party into power provincially; they had seen their hospitalization and medicare battles result in a national health care system. They had watched eastern politicians turn on a dime: warning one day that medicare would destroy the moral fibre of the nation, crowing the next that it was the crowning achievement of democracy. They were sophisticated, pragmatic, tough-minded — the western equivalent, according to native son Bill Knight (now federal secretary of the NDP), to Quebec's new generation of activists spawned by the Quiet Revolution and the Parti Québecois. Like their peers in Quebec, they didn't take kindly to outsiders (especially ones from Ontario) coming in and telling them what to do.

It is not surprising that the convention turned into "a nightmare," in Desmond Morton's description. For Ed, it was a baptism by fire. Despite Tommy Douglas's opening-night speech reminding delegates that "we are not a philosophical society but a political party," forces were unleashed that could not be contained, arguments erupted that could not be resolved. David Lewis, having slogged for years, riding endless milk trains across the country to remote towns to meet with a handful of CCF and NDP recruits, working to establish the party as a living entity, was like an ox gored. "David Lewis felt that he was the party," says a delegate, "so he interpreted any criticism as a personal attack." It's true that Lewis exuded "an état-c'est-moi attitude," says Terry Grier, who'd started working for the party in 1960 at the age of twenty-four, had apprenticed under Lewis and deeply respected him. Yet David's sense of personal power outraged many westerners who could not abide the establishment's inability to deal with criticism. They felt David's rigid authoritarian manner had contributed to the crisis. David felt they were hell-bent on tearing the party apart.

Many of Lewis's allies saw the Wafflers as destructive, irresponsible, hysterical, even anti-Semitic. Jim Laxer, who is half-Jewish, says David mistakenly perceived a more familiar — more dreaded — enemy. "David Lewis spent decades fighting the commies," says Laxer, "and when he saw us coming he thought, 'Here they come again — the commies.' Because my father had been a commie, maybe he suspected me, though he remained friendly with me afterwards. But there was no commie conspiracy. I had never been active in left-wing politics before. I was never in the CP [Communist Party]. I hated the CP." It is one of the great ironies of the party's history that it fought communism so strenuously from the inside — in the process alienating thousands of well-intentioned Marxists who had no wish to replicate the Soviet Union in Canada — while being attacked from the outside as a commie-sympathizer. Yet there was no greater enemy to communists than David Lewis.

Over the next two days, with an ever-widening base of support — and a generally negative reception from the media, but lots of attention — the Waffle gained strength. It succeeded in polarizing the debate. Delegates "haggled over such terms as 'imperialism,' 'exploitation,' and 'socialism,'" wrote the McLeods. Ed was dismayed; he considered wrangling about rhetoric an exercise in futility. He also disliked the way Wafflers "insulted ordinary people who had worked all their lives — and made many sacrifices — for socialism."

Gerry Caplan was perceived as a real militant. "He was a very angry guy. He was not interested in keeping the convention running smoothly," says Norm Simon, now a close friend of Caplan's. Then a director of public relations for the Canadian Union of Public Employees, Simon had been assigned to manage the pressroom; he was not impressed by the Waffle. He responded just as Ed had: "I'm a nationalist," says Simon, "but I thought those guys were impractical politically. It wasn't so much what they were saying as how they were saying it, the strident nature of their language. They alienated a lot of us."

Ed, a young politician lacking any obvious base of support outside his constituency, devoid of powerful connections, stuck to his own agenda — though the pressure to swing right into the establishment camp or left into the Waffle enclave was enormous. The radicals figured he didn't have the guts to take a stand either way; the moderates thought he was mixed up. But Ed was determined to straddle their differences and stay friends with all of them. If he ended up looking downright ridiculous, it was partly attributable to the Oshawa lessons of Abe Taylor. Ed's political character was forged by the internecine warfare at Local 222. In his experience, everybody fought, all the time; the party's divisions were no shock to him. If he lacked finesse, he knew something about long-term survival. Rule number one: when two sides are head-bashing, keep your distance. Rule number two: maintain friendly relations with opposing forces.

There was an additional force at work in Ed: the negative influence of his father. The legacy of Percy Broadbent, it seems, was to have created a son whose behaviour was utterly opposed to the father's model. Having experienced his father's alcoholic rages, which pushed his family to the brink of disaster, Ed had no perverse urge for destruction — unlike some middle-class radicals who'd been reared in a suffocating, hypocritical security that they felt compelled to smash.

Ed understood David Lewis's gut anxiety about the Waffle tearing the party apart, and at the same time he shared the Waffle's policy goals. This contradiction, which he would later attempt to resolve, seemed to neutralize him, to some observers.

"The Waffle had a meeting room at the convention," says Carol Sigurdson, a Saskatchewan Waffler, "and I'll never forget seeing Ed Broadbent standing in the doorway, with one foot on the inside of the room and one foot on the outside, as if he was wondering, 'Which way am I gonna go?' Dave Barrett did the same thing." Fred Gudmundson, Carol's husband, observed: "What I saw in Barrett and Broadbent was a complete vacuum as far as theory was concerned. They're guided by humanitarian instincts and the herd instinct."

Harsh criticism, but Sigurdson and Gudmundson, then in their early thirties, were typical Saskatchewan radicals from Mozart (pronounced Mose — as in nose-art). "Everybody was involved in politics," says Fred. "It was what we did when we weren't farming. In Saskatchewan, you don't hold big public meetings; everything goes on underneath." And out in the open, all the time. Saskatchewan MP Lorne Nystrom, who comes from Wynyard, near Mozart, remembers that families bought their groceries, banked their money and sold their grain according to their political convictions. "The Liberals shopped at the OK Economy store," says Nystrom, "and they wouldn't go to the co-op store or the credit union or the wheat pool, where all the CCF families went. I didn't enter a privately owned chain store until I went to university. And we all grew up attending political meetings. It was a way of life."

The Saskatchewan activists — and most Wafflers — were not kind to Ed, though he felt little hostility toward them. "Wafflers maintained they were the real socialists, and that anyone with different views was a bourgeois sellout," says a delegate. Ed was considered one of the sellouts. He wasn't a radical, he wasn't "pure," he was a working-class guy with an academic veneer and a ponderous speaking style who'd latched on to John Stuart Mill (sneer) and didn't have the guts to be a Marxist. As for his precious industrial democracy, "the trade union movement thought Ed didn't know what he was talking about," says Giles Endicott. "He'd put his foot in the camp of the New Left — in the U.S. you had Tom Hayden attacking the conservatism of American unions — so they figured Ed was an enemy like Hayden. They thought his ideas would lead to labour being co-opted and sold out. The UAW hammered Ed."

As Ed's grand vision was being squashed, he looked, to some delegates, like a kid walking through a field stepping in every available cow pie. Dennis McDermott was increasingly annoyed by the Oshawa MP's pursuit of "stupid-ass ideas." And David Lewis's doubts about Ed increased. For David, the battle lines had been drawn, and the marks went deep. Anyone who wasn't with him was against him; Ed's refusal to take sides made him seem useless.

Fred Gudmundson and Carol Sigurdson appreciated the clarity of Lewis's stance, though they didn't agree with it, and were disappointed that Tommy Douglas failed to speak out on their behalf. Says Carol: "Tommy believed what the Waffle was saying — that our land base should be generating wealth for us, not for Americans — and he knew the Waffle was important to the cause, but he wouldn't stand up for us. That's why I respected David Lewis more. I didn't agree with him, but at least he spoke clearly for his position. I don't mind that. It's the fudging I can't stand."

Among the party's power brokers, however, Tommy Douglas expressed an acid view of the Waffle. Bill Knight, soon to be elected to the House of Commons from Saskatchewan, knew that Tommy's amiable facade hid a very tough core. "Douglas was every bit as tenacious in his opposition to the Waffle as Lewis," Knight told the McLeods. "If he'd stayed on, he would have put the sword to them just as Lewis did." (No one could have predicted that less than ten years later, Ed Broadbent would try to bring them back into the fold.)

When it was all over, little had been resolved. Mel Watkins was elected a vice-president of the party, the Waffle won seven seats on the National Council, and policy resolutions moved left — but harmony did not prevail. Carol Sigurdson was, finally, disgusted with the atmosphere of compromise. "Let the Liberals make the compromises, they're good at it," she said. Fred Gudmundson added: "If you're going to transform capitalism, which is exploitive, then you turn to socialism. If you're going to have a socialist government, you don't sneak it in by compromising your principles. You have to educate people. The CCF was elected in 1944 because of forty years of educating people. The Waffle was our last chance."

That notion amuses Saskatchewan MP Les Benjamin: "Our party has been around since 1933. It started in radical Saskatchewan, and we still have our radical traditionalists. It's a good thing, because they make sure we don't forget what it's all about. They can't have us doing things for practical reasons; they want us to do everything for philosophically correct reasons. Sometimes it's hard to live up to them. Some of them say we're not socialist anymore. But it's not us who've changed, it's the other parties. Our worst and meanest opponents have kept pensions, unemployment insurance, hospitalization, medicare, auto insurance — all the things we fought for. Any party that tried to get rid of those things would commit political suicide. Property rights: some people say we don't believe in private property. I say, 'Where the hell were you guys when the Japanese Canadians lost their property? We stuck up for them and we were treated like traitors. Who opposed the War Measures Act? You guys allowed it — you allowed the government to seize private property.' More than any other party, we've changed the political agenda of this country, and don't you forget it."

Between the '69 "Waffle" convention and the '71 leadership convention all hell broke loose in Quebec. October, 1970, had started "sunny and cheerful," wrote John Gray in *The Globe and Mail*. "The country still carried the sweet innocence of the aftermath of Centennial year [1967] and the strange phenomenon of Trudeaumania which had so titillated the land in 1968." But the mood was shattered by the infamous October Crisis of 1970, triggered when British trade commissioner James Cross was kidnapped in Montreal on October 5 by members of the FLQ — Front de libération du Québec. Five days later, Quebec labour minister Pierre Laporte was kidnapped. On October 16 — "the day of shame," in René Lévesque's words — Prime Minister Trudeau imposed the War Measures Act, sending in the army, in effect, to occupy the province. Supported by Justice Minister John Turner, Quebec Premier Robert Bourassa and Montreal mayor Jean Drapeau, Trudeau raised the spectre of an armed insurrection and terrorist bloodbath (for which he had no evidence). More than 450 people were arrested, many of them held without charge. The next day Laporte's body was found in the trunk of a car. "Indiscriminately," wrote Lévesque in his memoirs, "union leaders, artists, writers, whoever had dared cast doubt upon official verities, or simply those the unleashed bloodhounds didn't like the look of, were thrown into the paddy wagons and put away. Deprived of all their rights, beginning with *habeas corpus*, a great many of them were to remain in custody for days and weeks . . . the whole of Quebec found itself behind bars as Trudeau and company now attempted to justify their act before Parliament . . ."

Approval for invocation of the War Measures Act was given in the House of Commons on October 19. Voting in favour were 128 Liberals, fifty-two Conservatives, six Créditistes and four New Democrats. The only opposition came from sixteen New Democrats, among them Ed Broadbent. While the rest of the country heartily approved Trudeau's firm hand in dealing with Quebec, Ed was appalled that the government would suspend the civil rights of an entire province — and in hindsight, many observers decided Trudeau had indeed over-reacted. John Gray noted that a few years after the event, James Cross described the crisis as "a case of six kids trying to make a revolution."

At the time, however, the New Democrats were lonely opponents to the War Measures Act. "David Lewis decided it was wrong and that we'd fight it," says Ed. He remembers that "the party dropped to 6 and 7 per cent in the polls, because practically everybody else in the rest of Canada thought it was a good idea to put the boots to Quebec." The Gallup poll published on December 12, 1970, showed that 87 per cent of Canadians supported the federal government's actions — though a few newspaper editorials were opposed. "This War Measures Act," stated *The Globe and Mail* on October 17, 1970, "is not only drastic and dangerous, it is in itself a denial of the very rights which Mr. Trudeau once wanted to enshrine in the constitution."

The New Democrats' opposition was a classic case of the party standing alone in the political arena for what it believed, and losing support among the electorate. Ed, calling home to his brother to check out the mood at The Motors, was informed by David that "a lot of the people think the government did the right thing and they don't support the NDP." David, however, was on Ed's side. "The War Measures Act reminded me of what they'd done to the Japanese-Canadians and I was dead set against it," says David.

As the NDP sank in the polls, David Lewis was undeterred; he won the admiration of even his Waffle opponents for his immediate, continuing, day-after-day, passionate condemnation of the government's action. But Quebeckers seemed not to notice his lonely quest for justice on their behalf.

The refusal of the Québecois to embrace the New Democrats plagued Lewis. His dreams of victory were, he knew, empty without Quebec on side — a conviction he would brand into Ed's consciousness. Partly because of his Francophone wife-to-be, Lucille, Ed was becoming more sympathetic to Quebec's aspirations — though Lucille says "it was a slow process." Ed supported David's efforts to direct resources to Quebec. It was a hard sell: the party never had any money to begin with, and when there was a little extra cash or an organizer to spare, they were directed to regions where officials argued the party could reasonably win, which was not in Quebec. David insisted on trying. Fluently bilingual, with close ties among his old Montreal childhood friends, he visited, met, talked, discussed and tried to break down the barriers, but with little result.

The NDP was so marginal in Quebec that in the 1970 provincial election, Desmond Morton reports, "the party's thirteen candidates collected a derisory 4,130 votes — 0.15 per cent of the total." The Quebec wing, wrote Morton, was exposed "as the Potemkin village it really was." (A facade designed to deceive visitors.) Since René Lévesque's resignation from the Liberal government in order to found the Parti Québecois in 1968, Quebec nationalism had heated up, excluding any and all outsiders — including Tories and New Democrats.

On other fronts, however, there were glimmers of hope. Allan Blakeney, a lawyer from Nova Scotia who had served in Tommy Douglas's provincial Cabinet, led the Saskatchewan New Democrats to a smashing victory in the 1971 provincial election. Next door in Alberta, NDP leader Grant Notley was elected in the Lougheed sweep that overthrew the Social Credit regime. Lougheed proceeded to develop an interventionist government that far exceeded, in its string of Crown corporations and government-owned airlines, anything any socialist government had ever done. Lougheed, a Tory, justified the state's activities not in the name of socialism but "because it's good for Alberta." There were also negative signs: that same year in Ontario, Bill Davis — replacing Tory Premier John Robarts — swept Ontario, embarking on a ten-year reign. Ontario's NDP leader, Stephen Lewis, guided by Gerry Caplan, realized victory was not close at hand.

Federal New Democrats, meanwhile, were preoccupied with the search for a new leader. Tommy Douglas was stepping down — he had overstayed his welcome by a few years — and David Lewis, at sixty-one, was eager to take his rightful place at the head of the party. But the first candidate to throw his hat into the ring — quite presumptuously, Lewis thought — was Ed Broadbent. This was an interesting move from a young man who had not met with great success at the previous convention, and stands as the first clear sign of Ed Broadbent's ambition. It was announced by the publication of *The Liberal Rip-Off*, which Ed says "was written in a dash prior to the leadership convention." His book was a critique of the Liberal government and focussed on Trudeau's failure to advance any policies related to industrial democracy.

Why Ed decided to enter the fray remains a bit of a mystery, since he had no widespread support. He remembers that Jim Renwick, a Toronto MPP who was pushing for fresh leaders, suggested he consider running, as did John Gilbert, another Toronto MP. "Tommy Douglas, too, was discreetly encouraging," says Ed. "He wanted a

leader from the new generation. But I'm not blaming
Tommy or Jim for what I think in retrospect was a mistake. If I'd foreseen the consequences, which you can't, I
wouldn't have run." Ed's friends and acquaintances seem
to agree. Says Desmond Morton: "Ed was impossible, full
of himself." Gerry Caplan observes: "Eddie blew the leadership. Made a fool of himself. His run was wildly premature." Murray Weppler, then a senior aide to David
Lewis, figures, "Ed was politically immature. He misread
the party, he misread it all." An anonymous delegate, not
an Ed fan, said: "Instead of taking stands — Quebec was
hot, the Waffle's economic proposals were hot — Broadbent tried to slide through the middle. Instead of showing
he could build bridges, he managed to piss off everyone in
sight."

Yet a *Globe and Mail* editorial, published April 22,
1971, just before the Ottawa convention began, conveyed
great expectations for Ed. It began by describing the party's strength, which

> it might almost be said, has been moral rather
> than political. [New Democrats] have often been
> able to recognize, ahead of others, the basic needs
> of the people; they have often been motivated by
> compassion more often than by a desire for power;
> principle and philosophy have played a greater
> part in shaping their policies. . . . Moving on to
> the matter of leadership: Mr Lewis spoke the most
> logical condemnation of his candidacy when he
> said, some two and a half years ago, "The next
> leader of the party should come from its new gen-
> eration of members, both inside and outside the
> House of Commons." . . . Ed Broadbent, of the
> younger contenders, has come across most clearly.
> He can win an election: he demonstrated that by
> beating the odds-on favourite, Conservative La-
> bour Minister Michael Starr. He sees the whole
> party as the instrument which the leadership must
> lead: he would not join in a compact against the
> Waffle; but he rejects the extremist aspects of the

> Waffle. He has precise and understandable poli-
> cies. . . . He would nationalize the petroleum in-
> dustry because it is almost totally foreign-owned
> and costly in lost profits; and because it is an in-
> dustry that is growing in importance to the world
> economy and could enable us to develop our own
> research and develop our own independence in
> world trade. Finally, he is people-oriented, in the
> most   valuable   of   New   Democratic   Party
> traditions . . . .

This rational analysis by an outside observer gave no
hint of what was about to happen. The Waffle, at the
peak of its power, again polarized the convention, with
David Lewis and Jim Laxer carrying their battle to a
bloodier plain. "I can't describe how horrible that convention was," says Liz Valleau, Ed's neighbour from his Collier Street days. "There was intense bitterness among the
[leading] candidates, dirty dealings, backstabbing and a
sort of psychological violence to it. Everyone was frightened — by what? By the strength of their emotions, I
guess." Liz was attracted to the Waffle initially — "it
seemed exciting but dangerous for the party" — and
ended up supporting Ed because he looked like a good
compromise between Jim Laxer and David Lewis. But the
convention was not in the mood for compromise.

As usual, however, it started off on a high note, with
Tommy Douglas's retirement speech as party leader.
"There is little value in making programs that appeal
only to ourselves," warned Tommy, ever the pragmatist,
with an eye on the party's radicals. "There is nothing to
be gained unless we take a large segment of the population with us." He also rejected expressions of anti-Ameri-
canism which were coming from the Waffle camp. "Our
quarrel is not with Americans. . . . Our quarrel is with
successive Canadian governments which have supinely
acquiesced in the steady erosion of our economic independence."

But as soon as his speech was finished, the fighting
erupted. During one policy debate, Terry Grier, a Waffle

opponent, was "hissed and booed by hordes of young people who hadn't been anywhere in sight two years earlier
and weren't in sight two years later. I wasn't elderly then
— I was only thirty-five — and I was really turned off by
them. I had joined the party at their age and I had stuck
with it, working to build it. I was getting ready to run in
'72 and was worried that relationships with my own constituents would be poisoned by their shenanigans."
Though the party professionals felt their own careers
threatened, they didn't dream how close the Waffle would
come to winning the day.

For the leadership, Laxer wanted Watkins to run but
Watkins felt he couldn't handle it — he was plagued by
mood swings — so the Waffle torch passed to Laxer. Saskatchewan's Carol Sigurdson, running for party president
on the Waffle slate, was still hoping Tommy Douglas
would throw a little support their way. She was again
disappointed. At a backroom meeting during the convention, she sat beside Tommy and watched him play his
cards. "He wanted to keep the left in the party — he
knew they were the thinkers with the good ideas — but
he wanted the left subservient," she says. Still, to Lewis's
intense displeasure, Tommy supported the Wafflers' right
to speak out. Tension between the party's two reigning
saints was palpable.

Re-elected by a small margin in Toronto's York South
in '68, David Lewis was looking for the recognition that
was his due. No one could deny that he had held the
party together for decades. He had done all the unglamo-
rous backroom slogging that gave the NDP a firm foundation. Inevitably he was deeply disappointed that when his
time finally came it was marred by the Waffle battle that
dominated the leadership race.

Still, Lewis was a clear front-runner, with Laxer nip-
ping at his heels. In the secondary ranks, Broadbent's
main competition was John Harney, who was egged on by
"moderates who saw Lewis as too old, Broadbent as too
woolly and Laxer as political suicide," writes Morton. The
fifth candidate was British Columbia MP Frank Howard,
who was never in the running.

John Harney was the party's Québecois hope. An Irish-Francophone, born near Quebec City, descended on his mother's side from French ancestors who landed in the 1600s, Jean-Paul (as he was called in Quebec) had made his way to Queen's University in Kingston and then to York University, where he taught political culture. But despite his charisma and his oratorical powers, Harney had a problem. Perhaps it was his years in Ontario that alienated him from his Quebec roots; for some reason no one can quite nail down, the potential of John Harney would not blossom. Luck and timing: where Ed Broadbent had won his seat by fifteen votes in '68, Harney had experienced a bitter defeat; in '71, as appealing as he was, Harney was seatless, and that worried delegates.

On one of the major policy battles — the fate of Quebec — Ed was promising a "renewed commitment to federalism" as well as a recognition of Quebec's right to self-determination — a position he defends ardently today. "I wanted Quebec to have the right to choose its own destiny," says Ed, "but I wanted to promote federalism and encourage Quebec to stay in Canada. That's in essence the party's position now. But David opposed me. He thought my position would be used to fuel separatism."

"Ed really tried," says Watkins, "to hold things together." For the Quebec debate on the convention floor, Watkins, managing the Laxer group, and Charles Taylor, managing the Lewis group, agreed on two microphones for pro and con arguments. "Ed didn't want to speak at either mike," says Watkins. "He wanted a third mike for his position. Maybe it wasn't such a bad idea, but no compromise was possible." Even Ed's leadership team was at odds: Terry Grier remembers stopping by Ed's campaign room one night and witnessing Broadbent's advisers "at the eleventh hour engaged in a ranting argument about what Ed should say next." Critical delegates said Ed didn't make sense, that he had an inflated regard for his own importance and was speaking gobbledygook out of both sides of his mouth at the same time. "Sometimes you can say the wrong thing but you can say it damn good," observes Gordon Brigden, a long-term party organizer. "But Ed didn't even do that."

Still, Ed believed he was occupying the party's middle ground, and so did his supporters. MP John Gilbert, a Broadbent delegate, had high hopes for his man. Gilbert predicted that Ed had "a good chance" to become Prime Minister in '76 and "an excellent chance" in '80. Ed's hopes were not quite so high. He believed, he told the *Toronto Star*, that he was running "a strong second in the leadership race."

It didn't turn out that way. On April 24, the day the convention voted, the first ballot results were a shock: Lewis was first, predictably, with 661, Laxer second with 378, Harney third with 299, Ed fourth with 236, Frank Howard last with 124. Howard dropped off. On the second ballot, Ed was down to 223, Harney up to 347, Laxer at 407 and Lewis still led at 715. Ed dropped off. On the third ballot, half his vote went to Laxer.

> Shouts of wild jubilation erupted from the Laxer group when the results of the third ballot were announced," reported the *Globe*, "showing that Mr Lewis had added only twenty-seven votes while Mr. Laxer had added 101 from the Broadbent supporters. . . . The atmosphere was charged as the delegates tore the orange slips from their ballot books for the final vote in a two-way contest between Mr. Laxer and Mr. Lewis. . . . When the final results were announced, a forest of Lewis placards was raised [in victory]. . . . While members of Mr. Lewis's family hugged and kissed him . . . the chant of 'Power to the People' could be clearly heard from the Laxer section.

The final vote was 1,046 for Lewis, 612 for Laxer. Laxer moved to make Lewis's win unanimous and at the end, Lewis promised to work with Laxer. Carol Sigurdson lost the party presidency to Donald MacDonald, though she won 33 percent of the vote. Liz Valleau was depressed. "The back-stabbing got to me. I hated the way the Lewis faction treated the Waffle. I felt the party wasn't open to new ideas, and I've never felt the same about the NDP since. It's still the only party I can work for, but I feel more cynical about it now. The only good thing about the '71 convention was seeing Ed mature as a politician. He maintained his morality. He didn't stomp on anyone."

Candidates' reports on leadership expenditures showed that Laxer had raised the most money ($8,346.49) and had the second-highest costs ($10,368.94). Lewis had spent the most ($11,108) and was left with a $3,416.15 deficit. Except for Howard, who raised only $1,891, Broadbent had raised the least ($2,531.30) and was left with the biggest debt ($6,913.52).

Ed came out of it poorer but wiser, with a bruised ego, some good reviews and a conviction that it had been an unpleasant experience which he would not repeat. Liz Valleau remembers his last words on the leadership race: "Never again." Norman Snider observed in *Toronto Life* that Ed emerged from the convention "looking like an ambitious opportunist and did himself a lot of harm in the process. But, typically for Broadbent, he learned from the experience."

Giles Endicott was just one of Ed's supporters who saw a future for their man. "I always thought David Lewis would win in '71," says Endicott, "but I backed Ed because I thought it would be a good idea to set up a moderate person to succeed David when the time came. Ed fits right in to the mainstream of the party; he represents the party to an astonishing degree."

Six months after it was all over, Ed had bounced back and proposed to Lucille Munroe — to her surprise, she says — in the back of a taxi somewhere in Toronto. Though they had been courting for three years, since Ed had first come to Ottawa as an MP in 1968, Lucille wasn't sure she wanted to get married again. Her recovery from the deaths of her husband, mother and father within a few years of each other had been slow. "I told Ed I'd think it over," she says.

In the autumn of 1987, I first met Lucille in Ottawa at the rambling Tudor-style house she shares with Ed and their daughter Christine, now a teenager. Lucille had hot muffins cooling on the kitchen counter and fresh-ground coffee ready to perk. A year older than Ed, slim and attractive in a chic Alfred Sung outfit, Lucille has short, wavy brown hair, big blue eyes, a slight French accent when she speaks English, an utterly unpretentious manner — and a hint of steel. Though she feels free to express her feelings and opinions, she's very firm about setting limits. Beyond a certain line no journalist will ever go.

She padded around in stocking feet, exuding vivacity and warmth, making sure everything was just so — coffee, cigarettes, muffins. Then she curled up in a blue leather chair in her blue-and-white living room, and talked. Exotic fresh flowers — bird of paradise, ruby-red scalloped ginger — were artfully displayed; everything shone — the piano, stereo equipment, small tables. In the bookcases, the books are arranged in alphabetical order, by author. Beyond the baronial fireplace and leaded-glass windows overlooking Laurier Avenue, traffic rumbled by.

There is no point asking Lucille about her husband's personal life. Lucille describes Ed as "a very private person. There are certain things — like his divorce — that he won't discuss with anyone, not even me. But that's fine. I respect his privacy. I would never intrude." And the strong suggestion is felt: don't you intrude.

What she did reveal: since Lucille Munroe first met Ed Broadbent in 1959 in Oshawa, she had watched his political instincts develop. "Ed had a thirst for knowledge," she says. "He was engrossed in sorting out his own ideas in conjunction with other thinkers. He was committed to a society that would develop people's potential, so it didn't surprise me, finally, when he turned up in Ottawa as an MP." Lucille, too, had a thirst for knowledge. In the early '70s, living in the Ottawa suburb Kanata, she was teaching at her son Paul's school — her day job. At night, she would attend university courses in political science and sociology. She was a keen student and loved her studies.

She had also grown accustomed to accompanying Ed to political events and campaigning for him in Oshawa, which she became so good at that she would be described in newspaper reports as "a hidden asset." Like Ed, she is gregarious and outgoing, for the most part untroubled by the role of political companion, though she disliked the times she had to "just sit there and do nothing." She had worked as a nurse and a teacher for many years and she had her own interests — like Ed, she is an avid reader and music lover. Opera, she has said, is "one of the few things that moves me to tears." Above all, she is a woman with deeply held convictions; conversations with Lucille usually lead into thick forests of discussion about complex moral issues. She has the mind of a philosopher, pursuing arguments with taut logic. At the same time, she grasps life with great vigour. "Lucille has a strong sense of her own identity," says Ed. May Gretton concurs: "She feels every bit his equal. She's never been 'left behind.' "

It didn't take long for Lucille to make up her mind about marriage. Within weeks of the proposal, she arranged to take a day off from teaching and on October 29, 1971 — the same day that Mary and Percy Broadbent were married — she and Ed slipped into the office of a Justice of the Peace in Ottawa and tied the knot. Then they went to the suburban St Laurent shopping centre and had a hot dog, visited a jeweller about their wedding rings, and dropped in on Lucille's brother for a glass of champagne. A photograph of Ed and Lucille toasting each other shows her looking like Leslie Caron in *Gigi* — slender, big eyes, short dark hair, wearing a bridesmaid's dress she'd bought for her sister's wedding which she'd altered for her own marriage. At her side, beaming, is her prince, who looks like a big happy goof, with his gap-toothed grin and long hair straggling over his ears. That evening, they drove to Oshawa for a previously scheduled dinner and dance at the Polish Club. There was no honeymoon. Ed moved into her townhouse in Kanata, shared with Lucille's son Paul, then twelve, and a boxer dog named Hamlet. (Ed didn't like the dog.) On Monday, Lucille was back teaching and Ed was in the House of Commons.

If Ed had ever harboured romantic visions about the life of a politician, such notions were entirely shredded by sheer hard work. "When I went to Ottawa, I soon found out why Canadian politicians seem dull," he told *The Globe and Mail* in October, 1972. "They haven't got time for anything but politics. You realize that we work every night but Wednesday until 10 P.M.?" He was also adjusting to family life, trying to juggle the needs of his wife and son with the demands of the job.

For Paul, who had been an only child for twelve years, it was a difficult transition, though he had known Ed since he was a little boy. Paul was now sharing his mother with a permanently installed stepfather and, within a year, a new sister. Christine was a year old when the Broadbents adopted her in 1973. She needed a great deal of care and attention; her babyhood had been severely disrupted and she was an anxious child. Lucille understood that she was making a special commitment to her daughter and, as required by the conditions of the adoption, quit work to stay at home for a minimum of six months. At the same time, Lucille was studying for her B.A. at night while Ed was travelling back and forth to Oshawa, preoccupied with the upcoming '72 election. The children often went with them, to visit Ed's parents, while Ed hustled round his riding, dealing with constituents' problems and making speeches. The Broadbents experienced the same problems that afflict all political families — trying to maintain a stable home for their children while coping with extraordinary demands. Lucille decided that her own ambitions for a career would have to take second place; she chose to normalize life as much as possible for her children and didn't return to work — though she did, with a considerable sense of accomplishment, complete her B.A.

The Broadbents' extended family in Ottawa included Lucille's relatives as well as May Gretton, Ed's secretary. May and her husband Richard had a sailboat they anchored on the Rideau Lakes near Portland, south of

Ottawa. They would take Paul on weekend sailing and camping trips. Ed tried to stay close to Paul, and together they went to old movies on the revival circuit, but as Paul entered his teenage years he became more interested in friends, music and cars — he was a typical teenage boy with an old jalopy dripping oil in the driveway.

"Paul was a good-looking boy, an avid reader, interested in news and current events — he wanted Ed to think well of him," says a family friend. "He was a good student but somehow, as his father became more famous, he lost interest in academics. He joined the army and didn't go to university, which I think disappointed Ed and Lucille. Paul grew up seeing his father on TV and that's hard on kids. He wanted to live up to Ed's image, and win Ed's approval, but finally he had to break away. The best thing for him, I think, was getting away, and I guess that's what the army did for him."

Paul Broadbent, now nearing thirty and living in the north of England with his wife Eileen, a medical doctor, disputes some of this interpretation. "When I was growing up, Ed wasn't famous. During the '70s, he didn't get that much attention. Until 1974, when he became interim leader, he was just a backbencher, quiet and awkward." Did Paul spend much time with his father? "It varied. Everything went in cycles. Once an election was over, he had more time; we'd go to the cottage for a week with a pile of books and read, we'd go skiing in Quebec for the Easter weekend, but then gradually the political machine would gear up for the next election and he'd be gone." Did Paul regard his father as a workaholic? "That's not the right word. He would throw himself into everything with a great deal of enthusiasm. He tends to expect everyone else to have the same drive and enthusiasm he has — of course most people don't, and that definitely causes a clash. I was a classic underachiever, bored at school — I suppose it was the typical teenage rebellion. Ed being the perfectionist that he is, he had high standards and I suppose I failed to achieve just as a reaction to his expectations."

Fluently bilingual, Paul is articulate, thoughtful, well-read — yet he seems to have felt a bit overwhelmed by his father, though they have a lot in common. "We have the same sense of humour and our reading tastes are similar," says Paul. As well, neither of them was crazy about sports and both loved films. But where Paul was mechanically gifted — he could take car engines apart and put them back together — Ed was all thumbs around tools. Paul remembers Ed struggling to assemble an Ikea bookcase set in Christine's bedroom, "and he couldn't follow the instructions. He got very frustrated." Finally Christine built the bookshelves herself.

As a teenager, Paul rebuilt cars in the driveway and stayed out late at night. "Ed would tell me to be home at ten and I'd come back at midnight, with no gas in the car. He'd get mad." How does he get mad? "He glares, he has a way of staring at you to give the impression that 'that's not good enough,' only stronger. He's good at making people feel guilty — you've let down the family, the party, the country." Paul struggled through his last years at a French high school and joined the Armed Forces in 1980, working in the communications command for five years before quitting to move to England with his wife, whom he married in November, 1985. He is now running the computer operations of a five-man medical practice.

Christine, the blond, blue-eyed little girl, grew up in the whirlwind of politics. Unlike Paul, she never knew another life. Indulged by her mother — "Lucille is the nicest person I've ever met in my life," says May, "and she's not one to discipline children" — Christine became an outgoing, energetic, strong-willed child with a love of sports and horseback riding. She was so fluently bilingual, slipping back and forth between French and English, that her grandfather Broadbent was amazed and loved to show off her linguistic talents to his Oshawa neighbours. But at her French school in Ottawa, Christine didn't always impress her teachers, because she wasn't keen on doing homework — which caused some conflict with her father. Ed sometimes bristled at his daughter's recalcitrance, but hating any sort of confrontation tried to keep off the topic. "Ed's frightened of his temper," says Lucille. "He gets impatient and then he clams up." Lucille, in contrast, is known for her patience and openness. "Lucille and Ed complement each other beautifully," says a friend. "She picks up where he leaves off."

In the Broadbent relationship, Lucille is always the one to bring up issues and keep the lines of communication open. "Some people call me blunt," she says. "I would prefer to say I'm frank." In her marriage to Louis Munroe, she had been more volatile. "I can remember slamming kitchen cupboards because I was mad at something Louis had said, but that doesn't happen with Ed. There's not much to fight about." Their favourite time, as a family, comes on Sunday mornings when Ed prepares breakfast. On sunny days, they trek up to the rooftop deck and stretch out in the sunshine, reading the Sunday *New York Times* and listening to classical music.

Ed and Lucille were always a harmonious couple, says Paul. "They fit together very well. What's nice is that they have different opinions about things and that's acceptable. They are two totally different personalities who work well together. My father is a very honest person, very feeling. He tries to approach everyone with the same warmth and enthusiasm — it's easy for him to be out there campaigning, smiling and shaking hands with people. My mother sometimes finds that hard. She is more of a quiet person, very thoughtful — she's as dynamic as he is but in a different way. My father has developed a very dominant personality, and my mother sometimes finds it hard to accept his drive, drive, drive attitude. The tougher things get for him, the more he drives, and he's been getting stronger over the years, not weaker, gaining momentum as he goes."

The period of intense political activity during the early '70s set the pattern for the Broadbents' private life. "Sometimes you have to make tough choices," says Lucille, talking about her decision to take on the full load of running the house and looking after the children. "Someone has to go to the parent–teacher meetings and buy the groceries and shovel the snow. If you can do it all and have a job, fine. I know some political wives who work full time but it's a very heavy load — because they have the responsibility for the home and children too." Getting a political spouse to share domestic duties is, she says, almost impossible. "A politician feels his responsibility is to his constituency — that always comes first and you have to accept it." What made it easier for Lucille was her conviction that "if Ed weren't in politics, there would be an egalitarian sharing of the workload." She had some evidence in his favour. "I saw Ed when he was married to Yvonne, when Louis and I would visit them. I remember Ed was doing his thesis and Yvonne was working; Ed did the laundry and prepared the evening meals. They divided the tasks and Ed was sensitive about sharing housework." Robin Sears, who later worked closely with Ed for seven years, observes that "Lucille hates the servile 'waiting-on-the-leader' syndrome. She's snapped at me and others when Ed is babied or has his bags carried. It's her way of keeping a sense of proportion, I think."

The winter of '71, immediately following Ed and Lucille's wedding, was rough. Trouble was brewing — as usual — in the union, between the Autoworkers and the Democrats. David Broadbent, first elected in 1968 to a position in Local 222's hierarchy, was a Democrat, "but Ed and I started getting threats from both caucuses about my participation. People said I was running on my brother's name and that if I didn't get out, they wouldn't support Ed and they wouldn't vote NDP." Ed learned, fast, how to deal with such pressures, as did David. They discussed the situation, "and I told Ed," says David, "that I had my own life, separate from him, and that I wanted to continue in the union. Ed stood by my decision. It was hard for him, in his position, but he respected my life." (After twenty years of union activism, David Broadbent has gone on to a prestigious spot on the CAW's national executive.)

There were other issues that tested Ed's judgement. Mike Breaugh, now Oshawa's MPP, was then on the executive of the Ontario English Catholic Teachers Association. At a convention in Ottawa, the teachers were all steamed up: they were contributing to the Unemployment Insurance fund but didn't qualify for payments. They decided to lobby the MPs and Breaugh went to see Ed. Breaugh has never forgotten Ed's response — which was not what he wanted to hear. "Ed told me he appreciated our problem but he said the UIC fund was in trouble and needed the money." Breaugh was "pissed off. I thought, 'What the hell,' but then I had to appreciate that he'd levelled with me." Other MPs soft-soaped their responses, leading the teachers to believe the MPs were going to support them, only to back down later. "We didn't like what Ed said, but at least he told us the truth," says Breaugh, who learned a valuable lesson that he carried into his own political career. "It's part of the Oshawa climate," he says. "People would rather hear a negative response that's straight than a positive response that's crooked."

Even more contentious was a threat to the Auto Pact. Ed charged that the Liberal Government was preparing to ignore the Pact's safeguards, which guaranteed Canadian production. It was a hot issue in Oshawa. With the local mayor, he set up a committee that organized a 30,000-letter write-in campaign, spreading the word throughout the Golden Horseshoe, from Windsor to St Catharines, Oakville to Ste-Thérèse in Quebec. The campaign was successful. The safeguards were saved — and Oshawans approved of their MP's success in what was his first serious test.

He was not successful, however, in his efforts to mediate the continuing battle between David Lewis and the Waffle. "I couldn't see then, and I don't see now, how the final split could have been avoided," says Watkins. "There were people — Ed, again, was one — who tried to find a peaceful solution. But both sides were intransigent. Our greatest victory, and our greatest undoing, was Laxer's strong showing at the leadership convention. We were too strong to be tolerated and not strong enough to win. So we left the party, finally, rather than be expelled." Watkins ended up spending a few years in Yellowknife, working for the Dene Nation on its land claims in the Northwest Territories, and then returned to teaching economics at the University of Toronto. Looking back, he observes: "I have no regrets about the Waffle. It was appropriate for its time and place." He also recovered from his disillusionment with the New Democrats and rejoined the party in the early '80s "because it was a luxury to stay outside. And the NDP has changed. It's more nationalistic than it used to be. I like to think that what we did had an impact."

As for Ed's role in the Waffle affair, Watkins says: "Ed is a decent man, and it wasn't a time for decent men. The kind of politics he practices works very well most of the time, but it didn't work that time."

Facing the 1972 election, the NDP was divided and dispirited, but so was the Liberal party. Trudeau did not understand, wrote Christina McCall in *Grits*, what Canadian politics was all about. "He had not recognized that the two old-line parties were loose aggregations of people held together by little more than their hopes for personal advancement through the electoral and patronage systems, their feelings of friendship for each other, and the vicarious excitement to be derived from being close to power. . . ." Having failed to oil the party machinery, Trudeau was subjected to a less than adoring reception from party hacks; nor was the public swooning. "You didn't have to be a cynic to realize that the attainment of power had altered Trudeau's character," wrote McCall. "Now the sweet reticence had vanished and was replaced by a display of overweening pride that astonished his old friends."

Married to twenty-two-year-old Margaret Sinclair in 1971, Trudeau, fifty-two, embarked on the '72 election campaign with an arrogant hauteur that chilled voters and an advertising slogan — The Land is Strong — that elicited sneers. Inflation was soaring. An economic recession fuelled by OPEC price increases was looming. The country's vulnerability to multinational oil companies was never more apparent: as of 1971, Canada's energy sector was 90 per cent foreign-controlled.

David Lewis charged out of the gate on a fine shot of adrenalin vicariously derived from NDP leader Dave Barrett's stunning upset over "Wacky" Bennett's Social Credit government in British Columbia in August, 1972. The new NDP government in Victoria gave the New Democrats a triple crown, with the party holding power in three western provinces: Manitoba, Saskatchewan and B.C. Elated, Lewis headed the party's most successful federal campaign ever. Criticizing finance minister John Turner's tax concessions to corporations, Lewis attacked the "corporate welfare bums," a phrase that attracted headlines and revved his campaign into high gear. Tory leader Robert Stanfield, in his second try against Trudeau, "shortened the slogan and used it as a sadly effective weapon against the poor and the jobless, insisting they lived on government largesse," wrote Desmond Morton. Stanfield also got into trouble by announcing that, in order to hold down inflation, he would impose wage and price controls, which the Liberals denounced (and later imposed).

Stanfield was still staggering under the burden of a lousy media image. "As the public sees him, [Stanfield] is about as lively as a grave-digger on the night shift and about as entertaining as a hangover on a Monday morning," wrote Geoffrey Stevens in his biography of Stanfield. Yet this was the same man who turned up at a 1971 NDP Christmas party, Stevens noted, "roaring on stage as a knight in shining armour to rescue the fair Guenevere from a fate worse than death, and uttering these immortal lines: 'I represent help for the helpless, hope for the hopeless, and bras for the braless.'" In addition, he told the NDP party-goers: "Tonight is . . . a time for a summing up of my four years as Leader of the Opposition — years of remarkable development for me. Four years ago, I was certainly not a national sex symbol, and as some of you may remember, I was not always the witty and spontaneous master of repartee that my aides and other paid advisers now assure me that I am today. I have become eloquent in French and fluent in English."

But this was the private Stanfield. Publicly, though the Conservatives were well prepared for the campaign, and well-financed, with their own DC-9 jet just like Trudeau's, Stanfield did not generate as much enthusiasm as David Lewis. Despite his more penurious circumstances — the NDP could not afford to rent a jet — Lewis "waged the most effective campaign of all the party leaders by concentrating almost exclusively on a single issue," wrote Stevens. Ironically, Lewis's exposure of the "corporate rip-off" probably benefited the Conservatives more than the NDP. "Lewis 'loosened' thousands of government votes by causing Liberal supporters to question seriously the Government's policies," wrote Stevens. "Once loosened, these votes were swept up by the Conservatives . . ." Which is doubly ironic: disapproving of government taxation policies, voters turned back to Conservatives who would only reinforce the corporate tax concessions and loopholes which are still, in 1988, the target of NDP — and now Liberal — opposition. One wondered whether Canadians would ever tire of this predictable drama, wherein Liberals and Tories exchanged roles in government, while the critics pronounced that the bit players were doing the best job.

In Oshawa, facing a rematch against former Conservative MP Michael Starr, Ed was in trouble. The Tories, convinced they could win back the seat they'd lost in '68 by only fifteen votes, went into battle with a vengeance for which Ed was unprepared. Two weeks into the campaign, the Oshawa New Democrats were in disarray, reporting a lot of damage to NDP signs and a lot of bad blood aimed at Ed by his major opponent. NDP headquarters, having decided to concentrate resources in winnable ridings, targeted Oshawa and sent in one of its legendary fixers: Jo-Anne McNevin rushed to the rescue.

A partial list of election campaigns McNevin has worked on includes: British Columbia provincial '69, Alberta by-election '69, British Columbia provincial '72, Canada federal (Broadbent) '72, Manitoba provincial '73,

176 ED BROADBENT: THE PURSUIT OF POWER

Canada federal '74, Alberta provincial '75, Broadbent leadership '75, Ontario provincial '75, Director of Federal Organization based in Ottawa '76-'82 (27 by-elections, 5 provincial — Ontario, Saskatchewan, B.C., Manitoba, Yukon) two federal elections. Then Saskatchewan '82, B.C. '83, Canada federal '84, Yukon '85, Manitoba '86 . . .

Now working out of Winnipeg, in charge of western organization for the party, McNevin remembers the '72 campaign. "I was tired. I didn't want to go to Oshawa," she says. She had just finished the '72 British Columbia election, where Dave Barrett slew the Bennett–Social Credit regime. B.C. was her home turf — she was born in West Vancouver in 1939, the year the Lions Gate Bridge was built — and she wanted to enjoy the view and spend time with her husband and five children. B.C. politics was also her first love. "People say we're the Canadian Californians, lotus land, laid back, zany politics, polarized, us against them — and it's all true. But B.C. New Democrats are incredibly hard working and long suffering. We had struggled against the Social Credit phenomenon for thirty-five years."

She deserved to celebrate, but the call to Oshawa was urgent. "I'll never forget it. It was not a pleasant campaign, there were a lot of threats against our committee rooms, that kind of thing — it was such a close fight."

In his book *Discipline of Power*, *Globe* columnist Jeffrey Simpson wrote about McNevin's arrival in Oshawa: "One of the smartest and toughest political organizers in Canada, McNevin studied the polling sheets pasted on the wall of Broadbent's committee rooms, asked a few questions, and declared: 'This campaign is a disaster.'" Simpson should know: he was then Ed's parliamentary intern, and within hours of her arrival McNevin had roped him into answering phones and stuffing envelopes. "Within seventy-two hours, she had stared down the chauvinist reaction to her arrival, issued instructions on every aspect of the campaign, reorganized the polling and generally, by a combination of sweetness and sarcasm, galvanized the reluctant and shocked the complacent into a disciplined, inspired campaign team." Stories are legion, and legendary, about McNevin leaping up on a table in front of dozens, or hundreds (depending on who's telling) of hardboiled union types and shocking them into action by swearing at them (ladies don't swear).

Her job was to get Ed elected. Was she tough? "My father was upset that Jeff Simpson described me as tough. But other people have said that about me too. Maybe it's a confidence that you know what you're doing." What is it that she does? She shrugs. "Organizers give people the confidence to carry out the work to be successful. We're running a series of pre-election workshops across the country now — there's nothing mysterious about it. Organizing is common sense. You take the statistics and demographic information, analyze it and organize yourself based on your findings." She laughs. "Then you have to keep everybody happy."

She pulled it off; she squeaked Ed past Mike Starr with an 824-vote margin, a feat that prompted Percy Broadbent to get up on stage at the victory party and say a few words — a move that had Ed, sister Velma, brother-in-law Barry Cornish and mother Mary holding their collective breath. "Perce was anti-union and he was right wing," says Barry. "And Ed was uncomfortable with him." At his moment of triumph, Ed watched with alarm as his father opened his mouth to speak. "Pappy got up there," says Barry, "and made a good little speech about how proud he was of his son." Velma nods. "We were terrified about what he might say. Barry was down in front of the stage, ready to catch him in case he fell." But Percy didn't fall and the family was relieved. Reminded of the scene, Ed blushes. "It's true," he says. "I was very moved by it. Dad was saying to me that he was proud of me."

Ed's '72 victory "cemented his hold on Oshawa," wrote Simpson. The cement didn't harden, however, until the next election in '74, when McNevin took charge of his campaign from the beginning and drove him to a 10,000-majority triumph. And Ed held on to her: she would run his '75 leadership campaign and a year later she would be appointed national director of organization, working

with him out of Ottawa. From the debacle of the '71 leadership convention to running the party took only three
years. May Gretton must have been right: "Deep down,
underneath, Ed's an ambitious man," she said. "But he
doesn't let it show."

"Look at it," says Paul Broadbent. "In his early political years, in his first attempt at the leadership, the personality wasn't there, he was reading speeches straight
from notes, it wasn't working too well. Then the big
break came: he was made interim leader, thrust in the
job as a stop-gap, and he grabbed it. From that point on
he gained momentum and he never stopped. He has this
incredible determination. This drive. Look at what he
made out of the disaster of '74."

CHAPTER SIX

The Boss: Rebuilding the Party

Believe it or not, Ed's idea of a good time is an election campaign. He's like a rock star who loves touring. And he had high hopes, he had great expectations — but then he always does. He is convinced the breakthrough is out there, just around the corner.

Robin Sears

Parliament was a house divided after the 1972 election. Winning 109 seats, Trudeau's Liberals were facing a 107-seat Tory opposition. David Lewis's thirty-one New Democrats suddenly loomed large in the Liberal leader's eyes. With the strongest caucus the NDP had ever had in the House of Commons, and the Tories refusing to negotiate, it was left to Trudeau — and primarily his Liberal colleague, Allan MacEachen, who conducted the manoeuvring — to form a shaky alliance with the New Democrats.

"David Lewis and his colleagues had a well-known model for how they should behave in such circumstances," wrote Desmond Morton. "There was no more precious document in the NDP's archives than the 1926 letter from William Lyon Mackenzie King formally committing his minority Liberal government to introduce old-age pensions in return for support from [CCF leader] J.S. Woodsworth. . . . Nearing the end of his political career, David Lewis was entitled to a comparative legislative landmark as a testament of his service to ordinary Canadians."

And David got it, forcing the '72–'74 minority government into passing "more progressive legislation in eighteen months than had been passed in the previous four years," wrote Christina McCall. This period was the crucible that forged Broadbent as a serious politician. Again, Ed got lucky. He had David Lewis as his teacher.

Ed's first step was to run for caucus chairman. His opponent, the incumbent chairman Alf Gleave, was a grain farmer from Saskatchewan. "Alf was likeable and irascible — a kind of crank — but I was very fond of him," says Ed. "When I ran against him, he was offended — it's a small family, eh?" (Gleave denied that Ed's challenge bothered him. "That's democracy," he said curtly). Again, Ed threw himself onto an opportunity, and this time when he grasped it, it was not beyond his reach — though David Lewis was not initially pleased about the situation.

Lewis had serious reservations about Ed's political future: where Ed's supporters viewed him as a diamond in the rough, Lewis saw an immature jokester who had lurched from one bad cause to the next, from the Waffle Manifesto to industrial democracy to a premature run at the leadership. "David told me once that he felt he couldn't trust Ed," says Marc Eliesen, the party's research director. "He couldn't see Ed assuming responsibilities." Ed's joking behaviour was part of the problem; one oldtimer who's worked on the Hill for a quarter of a century thought that Ed, in his early years as an MP, was a "spoiled brat." Not everyone was amused by his pranks. He was too boisterous for the more sedate New Democrats. Yet he was still prone to making long-winded philosophical speeches which bored even partisan listeners to sleep. It's no wonder David Lewis was concerned about his new caucus chairman.

Ed's memories of this time are dominated by his relationship with Lewis. "I had a caricature of David, and it was a very important part of my life to get to see the complexity of that man," says Ed. "Tommy Douglas was loved, more, and David was respected. David was a man of passionate social democratic convictions, but I had seen

him as too much part of the establishment, as not wanting to change. I came to understand why. He had made
all the tough decisions for Tommy; it had fallen to David
to do the internal fighting."

Ed's job, he says, "was to bridge the gap between leader
and caucus." He took a deep breath, and dove in. "I didn't
know David well and as caucus chair, I had to explain his
thinking to caucus members and their thinking to him. I
had to bring both sides together." His most difficult task:
to understand David — a tall order for an inexperienced
MP accustomed to spouting off his own theories with some
degree of youthful arrogance. It was almost as if Ed's ca-
reening career screeched to a halt, confronted by Lewis's
stature. Just as most Liberals felt somewhat diminished
in the presence of Pierre Trudeau, most New Democrats
were overawed by Lewis's sophisticated erudition and su-
perior intellectual skills. Lewis could be intimidating and
unapproachable. "He kept his own counsel pretty much,"
says Alf Gleave. Yet to the surprise of many observers,
Ed increasingly felt comfortable with Lewis as Lewis
warmed to him. The chemistry between them worked; a
bonding took place. Ed was in the right place at the right
time, and he had found another crucial mentor. "During
this period Ed retrieved his political future," says Murray
Weppler, Lewis's chief-of-staff. "The political immaturity
Ed displayed during the '71 leadership contest could have
destroyed his career — had he not put his head down and
gone to work." And so Ed rebuilt his credibility.

Broadbent's rival, John Harney, who had the potential
to shift the spotlight away from Ed, had at last succeeded
in winning a seat in the House. But Harney proved a disappointment to senior caucus members. Andrew Brewin,
a Toronto MP from 1962 to 1979, was particularly distressed by Harney's poor performance. "Andy Brewin had
promoted Harney," says a party insider, "but Harney
didn't deliver; he had a casual approach to his duties."
Says another observer: "Harney liked to go sailing." Ed,
in contrast, was a workhorse. Harney and Broadbent did
not become bosom buddies; to this day, they politely
conceal in public their private dislike for each other.

Ed dug in and took on his responsibilities in such a strong fashion that, says Weppler, Lewis came to rely heavily on the young MP. "Ed has a bulldoggedness to him, a staying power that I think is his strongest characteristic. He didn't have the intellectual polish of David Lewis but I came to realize that he has a deeper understanding of Canadian life than Lewis. The Lewises were like impoverished aristocrats; their politics was a high calling. David was at Oxford at twenty-three, he was the first Canadian president of the Oxford debating society. Ed had none of that. There's no glibness in Ed Broadbent. He never made a fast move in his life. But David saw that Ed was tough, and that's a quality you need for political leadership. I don't mean the vicious streak of Trudeau, I mean the capacity to take the crap that comes with the job, the physical and emotional stamina, the toughness of soul to take the daily pressure. Ed's got it, he got it in childhood, and Lewis saw it. He began to see in Ed a political heir. It's to Ed's credit that when he does suffer a setback, he's not decimated by it — and at the same time he's capable of admitting his mistakes."

The price paid for political leadership: Lewis paid in spades. "There was incredible pressure on David for the entire two and a half years," says his press secretary Jean-Guy Carrier. "Every day he had to keep on justifying his decision to prop up the Liberals in return for remarkable legislative achievements." The cost of the NDP's support included raising old-age pensions and family allowances, the establishment of a Food Prices Review Board, a new energy policy which resulted in the creation of Petro-Canada, the national oil company, and a major inquiry headed by Mr Justice Thomas Berger, a former NDP MP from B.C., into the proposed Mackenzie Valley pipeline. In addition, the NDP gained significant changes to the Election Expenses Act that allowed contributors to national parties to deduct a large portion of their donations from income tax. This measure was especially important to New Democrats' smaller donors — the NDP does not accept corporate contributions. With all parties benefiting, in effect, from an influx of greater public support, the NDP would, by the 1979 election, be better prepared to compete against its wealthier rivals.

Despite the gains, NDP caucus members were extremely nervous about "being in bed" with the Liberals. New Democrat MPs from western Canada were especially jumpy, while the Tories made hay — and a lot of obscene bedroom jokes — about Lewis's support for Trudeau. "For Saskatchewan, the very thought of us agreeing with the Liberals on anything was anathema," says Les Benjamin. "It was an article of faith to hate Liberals, so you can imagine what a ball the Tories had at our expense."

Stephen Lewis, then leader of the Ontario NDP, was in constant contact with his father during this period. Part of the tension for David, says his son, arose from David's feelings about Trudeau. While David Lewis was one of the few people Trudeau showed any respect for, "David disliked Trudeau intensely," says Stephen. "David detested Trudeau as an arrogant son-of-a-bitch who had no respect for working people. He personally rather liked Stanfield, and he recognized Trudeau's intellectual capacity but he couldn't stand Trudeau's contempt for the underdog. David really felt buffeted. He felt badly that people in the party thought he was selling out, that he was keeping Trudeau in power, but he was focussed on what he could extract from a minority government."

David's strategy demonstrated, says Stephen, how New Democrats can best handle a minority government — an issue of great consequence as the party faces the possibility of another minority regime after the next election. "The beauty of the party is the strength of its principles," says Stephen, "its commitment to principles. As long as we have a democratic socialist left to influence policy, that's enough. You don't need to exercise power." David Lewis, however, and the junior leader he was grooming in the wings, were not content playing "conscience of the nation." Indeed, Broadbent was being nurtured by two men — Lewis and Douglas — whose goal was to exercise power.

On October 25, 1973, Tommy Douglas, the party's energy critic, stood in the House of Commons and moved a resolution calling for "a publicly owned National Petroleum Corporation." The timing was right: "In the Middle East, war broke out," wrote the McLeods. "The Arab oil states announced a 25 per cent production cut and a boycott against Israel's strongest allies, the United States and Holland. Because there was no eastern pipeline, Canada too was vulnerable, and the government began to draw up rationing and emergency oil-shipping plans. Energy Minister Donald Macdonald spoke of 'a breakdown in the private supply system.' "

Still, the Liberals did not act; so the New Democrats threatened to pull the plug and force an election. "The condition for our support in a pre-Christmas confidence vote was that the Liberals make an announcement to create a publicly owned petroleum company," says Ed. He met with the Liberals to hammer out an acceptable deal; and Trudeau finally made the announcement that would result in the birth of Petro-Canada. Terry Grier remembers the subsequent NDP caucus meeting was filled with "absolute elation. It was the cleanest and most complete capitulation by the government to any of our demands." It came at a propitious time. The OPEC price of crude oil was escalating — along with inflation — from a 1970 rate of $2.50 a barrel to almost $30 a barrel by 1980, the year after the Iranian revolution which saw the overthrow of the Shah of Iran and the installation of the Ayatollah Khomeini. Nightmares loomed: the price of oil was forecast — incorrectly — to hit $79 a barrel by 1986. The industrialized world, dependent on stable energy supplies, was reeling. Alone among oil-producing nations, Canada had neither control over this crucial energy sector nor any policy to develop it in the national interest. "Foreign-owned companies produced about 90 per cent of the country's oil and gas," wrote the McLeods. "With a few exceptions, they used foreign-designed and foreign-built equipment to funnel raw resources out of Canada. Canadians missed out on management, research, manufacturing and processing jobs. Even jobs in the oil patch were less secure than they might have been, since the foreign-owned companies often used their Canadian profits to explore elsewhere."

"The seven sisters," as Anthony Sampson labelled the major multinational oil companies, overwhelmed national interests by their sheer size and power. By 1981, Exxon, the biggest of all and parent of Imperial Oil in Canada, had revenues of $115 billion — more than double the $54 billion revenues of the entire Government of Canada that year.

Ed felt a tremendous sense of pride when, in 1976, Petro-Canada's "window" on the oil industry opened with the purchase of Atlantic-Richfield for $343.4 million. It was a small stake in a multi-billion dollar industry, but it gave Canada a presence. Petro-Canada grew rapidly into one of the country's largest energy corporations, taking a leading role in developing Canadian suppliers and promoting health and safety issues. But "as it matured," wrote the McLeods, "Petro-Canada came more and more to resemble its private competitors. . . . It followed passively behind Esso and Texaco in setting retail prices and copied their marketing gimmicks. It shipped large volumes of sulphur to South Africa, despite Ottawa's alleged opposition to apartheid. It joined in pillaging the lands of Alberta's Lubicon Cree, an exercise the World Council of Churches condemned as 'cultural genocide.' " For New Democrats, it was like seeing a beloved child grow up into a delinquent.

But by then, David Lewis's political career would be finished, and he would be dying. His efforts during the minority government period cost him a great deal, in personal and political terms. "David believed," says Jean-Guy Carrier, "that the party had to wrench progress out of the government and be more concerned about making gains for Canadians than about partisan politics. I like to think he felt it was worth it." David didn't know the sorrow that awaited him down the road.

In the spring of '74, finance minister John Turner's budget became the issue that brought the government down. "That budget was a brilliant set up," says Robin

Sears, who attributes to Liberal advisers Keith Davey and Jim Coutts the strategy that "trapped" the New Democrats at a time when party coffers were empty and the leadership worn out. David Lewis was forced to rake Turner over the coals. He charged, wrote Desmond Morton, that Turner's tax concessions were the work of "a wrong-way Robin Hood, taking from the poor and giving to the rich . . . There are some people in this country who suggest that the time has come for a Tory government," Lewis declared. "I want to say to the members of this Parliament and to the people of Canada that a Tory government has already arrived." It was almost over. It remained for the Prime Minister to ridicule David for all his sabre-rattling, election-threatening speeches. "David the daisy," mocked Trudeau, "picking his petals one by one: will we have an election; will we not have an election.' "

They had an election, set for July 8, 1974. Cliff Scotton, federal secretary for almost ten years, knew the NDP was in trouble. "The party was coming out of my finger tips, it was what I ate and breathed, my whole life was absorbed in it. I was out, across the country, talking to people, and I was convinced nobody wanted an election. They were saying to me, 'Jeezus, what do you mean, call an election? No way. We'll never survive.' But David said, 'I've done soundings across the country,' and he was convinced he was right — that's what David was like. He said, 'We've got to get out of this appearance of propping up the government,' and he said he needed my help. It was the only time he ever said he needed anything. I'm a marshmallow. Though I didn't want the election, and I didn't think it would turn out well for us, I went along with him."

"There is a fine madness to a national political campaign," wrote *Globe and Mail* reporter Norman Webster. "It is early calls and missed meals, seventeen-hour-days and having to check your hotel key to know which town you are in. One French-language journalist calls the whole thing 'barbarous.' " There was also a fine malaise to the '74 campaign that was characterized, among voters across the country and in all three parties, by a mood of ambivalence and uncertainty.

Yet the New Democrats' hammering away at energy policy had produced a great change in their opponents. Reporting from Sault Ste Marie, Ont., on June 29, Norman Webster wrote that, "Prime Minister Pierre Trudeau promised last night that a re-elected Liberal government would require Canadian ownership of at least 50 per cent — and preferably 60 per cent — of major new natural resource projects. . . . The Conservative Party's natural resource policy goes further. It calls for Canadian ownership of more than 50 per cent of Canadian non-renewable resource industries." Finally, foreign control of the economy was an issue that Liberals and Tories were — at least during this campaign — prepared to embrace, especially if it would defuse the New Democrats.

David Lewis was exhausted by the balancing act of the previous two years, wrung out by the internal wrangling and external fighting. In public, he looked as strong as ever, leading yet another New Democratic campaign centred on "Who Controls Canada?" But it didn't take off, the party's financial resources were paltry, and Lewis endured a gruelling schedule, labouring under the terrible burden of his secret illness. He had recently found out that he had leukemia, a blood disease that is usually fatal; he did not inform his children, at his wife's request. Weppler, one of the few colleagues who knew, remembers seeing David, on rare occasions throughout what would be his last campaign, looking ashen and frail. Weppler recalls those times with emotion. "I felt as close to David as I did to any man, the warmth of that man . . ."

Meanwhile, back in Oshawa, Ed Broadbent's third campaign was gearing up. Ed was nervous, though Jo-Anne McNevin was at the helm, "convinced," says Michael Decter, "that she could drive Ed to a massive victory. We had no idea the rest of the world was going to hell in a handbasket." Decter had been pulled in from Harvard, where he was finishing an economics degree. In the middle of exam period, he was in the shower one day when Ed called. "I'm going to lose this election," Ed said. "I'm running against Harvey Kirck (the broadcaster) and I need your help." Decter was amused that Ed perceived "old Harvey" as a threat — Kirck finally decided not to run — but Decter hustled up to Oshawa, where McNevin took one look at this hippy socialist whiz kid — who would later become head of the Manitoba civil service before his twenty-eighth birthday — and shuddered. "Michael's hair was very long, down his back," says McNevin. "I made him put it in a pony-tail. I was worried the UAW guys wouldn't appreciate him."

Decter's memories of that campaign mainly involve "how hard Jo-Anne drove us. It was a wonderful organization, so we were all the more shocked by the results outside Oshawa." Decter won his bet with David Lewis — "David said we wouldn't win by more than 2,000 votes" — as Ed piled up his 10,000-vote majority. "But we watched in total horror," says Decter, "as practically everybody else vanished, as David lost his seat." Watching the returns on television, the *Globe*'s Stanley McDowell wrote that, "The most moving moment of the evening must have been the sight of David Lewis, defeated in York South after forty years of work for the CCF and the NDP, telling his supporters, 'Don't feel too sad. This is just one battle lost. There are many more to come.'" Dennis McDermott was not consoled. On July 9, McDermott was fit to be tied: "It's absolutely sickening, absolutely repugnant, it's absolutely nauseating," McDermott told reporters. Regrets were also expressed by Conservatives and Liberals, but McDermott outdid them all. "This man could have been one of the most successful and wealthy lawyers in Canada, but decided instead to devote himself to the people. . . . It's tragic when you have this decent man . . . repudiated by his own constituents. The people in York South ought to be ashamed of themselves."

What a difference a few percentage points in the popular vote make: though the party attracted only two per cent fewer voters — down from 17.2 in '72 to 15.2 in '74 — it lost fifteen seats. The NDP caucus shrank from thirty-one to sixteen, Lewis was finished, and Trudeau's Liberals had regained their majority, with 141 seats compared to the Tories' ninety-five. David Lewis, wrote Morton, "had led his party back into the wilderness and he had been chief among those who had suffered its humiliation."

Within a year, the party would be gearing up for a leadership contest that offered up no viable heroes. Writing in *The Globe and Mail* a month before the leadership convention, on June 7, 1975, dateline Sudbury, Christina McCall presented a long analysis of the New Democrats' dilemma. "The federal party has been unable to look like an alternative to anything. It has been outmanoeuvred by the Liberals' continuing brilliance in straddling the centre through co-opting the social democrats' best ideas and electing as its leader Pierre Trudeau, who drew, through sheer flash, the fervid admiration of the restless voters of the sixties who might have turned to the New Democrats but for him; bruised by its terrible internal fight in the early seventies with the far left in the shape of the Waffle; and laid low by the minority situation of the '72–'74 period which left it looking foolish — accused of complicity when all it was attempting to do was show some responsibility, like some hapless fundamentalist preacher caught as a found-in while passing out tracts during a raid on a rundown bordello."

None of the four leadership candidates, she concluded, "has anything like the commanding aura of the four prophets who went before." She was right.

It is a bitterly cold day in the winter of 1987. Inside a red-brick row house in midtown Toronto, Robin Sears has just arrived home from work and from the babysitter, where he picked up his little boy, Matthew. Sears is making dinner for Matthew, who is three years old and is upstairs constructing a Lego train set. Classical music fills the downstairs living room, its walls hung with paintings, its bookshelves filled — George Orwell's *Collected Essays*, John le Carré's spy novels, Eldridge Cleaver's black American *angst*, the I Ching's Eastern path to serenity.

After dinner, Sears will go back to Queen's Park — where he is principal secretary to Ontario NDP leader Bob Rae — for yet another of the unending meetings that have knitted his life into a political patchwork quilt. Only thirty-seven years old, tall, sandy-haired, conservatively dressed in gray flannels and a gray shetland sweater — he used to wear his hair long, in a pony-tail down his back — he is one of the most seasoned social democrats on the continent. In 1974, at the tender age of twenty-three, he was brought to Ottawa by veteran federal secretary Cliff Scotton; a year later, Sears took over Scotton's job, and remained in charge of running the party for seven years. Those were tough times.

Mushing tomatoes and mushrooms into a pot full of pasta, Sears thinks back fourteen years to the "unforgettable experience" of attending NDP caucus meetings after the July, 1974 election. "It was like going to a funeral," he says. He was a neophyte, though he was "born to the cause," being the grandson of British Columbia's flaming CCFer, Colin Cameron. But even with the radical Cameron blood coursing through his veins, he was temporarily overwhelmed by the gloom that pervaded his political world.

Surveying NDP territory that summer of '74 was like looking at burnt-out land after a fire. It was hard to see the shoots of green beneath the charred remains. Though Ed's personal victory was outstanding, he could hardly rejoice. Now he knew how his grandfather felt all those years ago, north of Parry Sound, when he lost his lumber operation to a forest fire. Pierre Trudeau had emerged triumphant while the New Democratic Party, once again, received no credit from the public for the sterling legislative achievements of the minority government. The payoff landed in the laps of the Liberals, not the New Democrats — a scenario that would be repeated thirteen years later in Ontario, when provincial Liberal leader David Peterson swept from a minority to majority government on the strength of a legislative agenda developed by NDP leader Bob Rae. It was the same old story:

voters liked the reform package but wouldn't vote for the party that devised it.

It was a lesson Ed would not forget. Holding the balance of power had been an exciting and frustrating experience; the gains were real, in terms of the nation's well-being, but so were the losses, in terms of the party. David Lewis had been defeated. Gone were Toronto's Terry Grier, and the young MP from Saskatchewan, Bill Knight, and John Harney, Ed's old leadership rival. Stanley Knowles, Tommy Douglas and Andrew Brewin were hanging in, approaching their eighth decade. As Sandra Gwyn observed in *Saturday Night* magazine, "the NDP section [in the House of Commons] has been easy to spot by all the silver up front." Of the younger generation, Saskatchewan's Lorne Nystrom had survived, and Bob Rae would enter the caucus in a 1978 by-election.

For Ed, chosen by caucus to act as interim leader, the prospect of heading a drastically weakened and demoralized party was not exactly thrilling. Yet it was the terms of his takeover that, in many senses, would eventually give him real power. He who gets to rebuild, gets to re-shape. "There are times I think he forgets the party isn't his," says Ed's son Paul. "His attitude sometimes annoys people in the party — but it's easy to understand his proprietary feelings. He rebuilt the party, and he's a party man." But Ed's rise would be accompanied by many falls; only what Murray Weppler termed his "toughness of soul" enabled him to survive.

Within six months of becoming interim leader, Ed's hold on the party was weakening day by day. He was disillusioned and depressed, flirting with a return to what he calls, with a sense of irony, "the real world of the university." Nothing was working. The great opportunity for the NDP in Quebec was being blown away by the growth of René Lévesque's Parti Québecois. In Ottawa, the mood in caucus was not uplifting. "We'd been hyped up through the minority Parliament, and now we had reduced members, reduced research, everything seemed to have shrunk," says a staff member. "As interim leader, Ed seemed to lack confidence. There was an uncertainty in the party about how Ed would work out, about where to go from here. Tommy and David had been fatherly men of great stature and vision; Ed was this neophyte in a chocolate-brown corduroy suit with leather elbow patches who was trying desperately to learn to speak French. His accent was atrocious."

Ed also had difficulty dealing with the sticky personnel problems that came with the leader's job. "Ed was too nice a guy," says Michael Decter, who for a few months worked as Ed's executive assistant. "He didn't like firing people. We had to clean house in the research department — we were back in real opposition and we needed people who could dig down for strong issues. But it wasn't working. So when it came time to get rid of some people, Ed couldn't do it. I had to put my own job on the line and visit Lucille. Lucille is very realistic and she can point out certain hard facts to Ed. She doesn't interfere, but she can be tough-minded."

Another problem Ed faced was that "outside Oshawa, nobody knew who the hell he was," says Decter. "Ed had no national profile. So we lived out of suitcases, driving across the country, making pit stops. I was a novice as executive assistant, he was a novice leader. I'd write speeches, he'd deliver them — more or less. There was no bullshit, no pomp, we were just trying to build the party. When we'd get back to headquarters [in Ottawa], Cliff would haul us in and we'd submit expense accounts, $11 for a motel, $6 for hamburgers. Cliff suggested we should be travelling on a slightly grander scale."

Ed remembers the shock of the job: "There was a lot of conflict, a lot of travelling. The travelling . . ." he rolls his eyes, remembering. "The party had been wiped out, we had to get out there, from Newfoundland to B.C., hanging around airports, staying in motels, renting cars to drive through blizzards to arrive at meetings where a handful of people would show up . . . I hadn't been married long, I had a baby daughter, a teenaged son, I missed my family, my friends — and all for what?" For a lot of hassle and a lukewarm reception from the people he was doing it for.

Unaccustomed to the role of party boss, Ed discovered that the political landscape had suddenly become a more treacherous domain, mined with a whole new range of demands and expectations that could blow him away at any moment. Now that he was the party's official spokesman, the heat was on. He was compared, unfavourably, to Tommy Douglas and David Lewis. Critical eyes suddenly spotted defects that hadn't bothered anyone when Ed was just another caucus member. The "image-makers" set to work — a term used caustically by Anne Carroll, who become a secretary in Ed's office in 1975. "A lot of people started to take credit for improving Ed," she says, "for changing his clothes, his hair, his teeth. Sure he matured — haven't we all? — but he's still the same guy. He still wears corduroy suits." And he'd already had his teeth fixed, by Lucille's dentist during a routine visit a couple of years earlier — a fact Ed wants squarely on the record.

Ed was not what you would call a malleable property. He resisted being packaged. He refused to allow his handlers to take over his private life. While some aides considered him difficult, he was struggling to maintain his identity. Even his sense of humour came under attack. Ed made faces for the cameras, walked backwards off planes, and found ways to enjoy himself. "He thrives on the antics," says Anne Carroll, "he *needs* the fun times. They're the key to his survival."

Yet Ed was told by his advisers, among them Robin Sears, to quit joking around in public, a recommendation that Sears now regrets because it produced "a dissonance between Ed Broadbent the serious public person and his private persona, which is full of humour, jokes and charm."

Curbing Ed's fun-loving nature, especially when he was with Tony Penikett, a senior aide and an expert practitioner of practical jokes, was difficult. A typical story: one evening, out for dinner during the '75 leadership convention in Winnipeg, where Rosemary Brown was making a strong impression, Ed fell into Penikett's trap. As they all sat down around a large table in a crowded restaurant, Penikett had a private word with the waiter,

telling him that Ed Broadbent would order steak and potatoes. Posing as Ed's personal physician, Penikett explained that Ed's digestion was in a delicate state and
that as his doctor Penikett was directing the waiter to ignore Ed's order and bring him a bowl of barley soup and
nothing more. Penikett knew that Ed hated barley soup.
And so they settled in to their meal — Ed loves to relax
over a good dinner and a bottle of wine — and sure
enough Ed ordered steak and potatoes. As the food was
served, Ed found a bowl of barley soup plunked down in
front of him. Penikett quickly interjected, "Ed, that's
been sent to you by constituents of yours who are sitting
over there, just across the room. Smile at them." Feeling
trapped — after all, he needed every delegate vote he
could get, given Rosemary Brown's momentum — Ed
smiled feebly across the room and began to eat the awful
barley soup. When he finished, Ed told the waiter to
bring him his steak and potatoes. "I'm sorry, sir," said
the waiter, "but your doctor said you can't have it."
"What doctor?" Ed exploded — and the jig was up.

Another time, Ed and Tony were kibbitzing in a union
hall in Moose Jaw, during the era when Quebec Premier
Robert Bourassa had received a lot of bad press for travelling with a hairdresser and a bodyguard. "So when
someone asked me who Tony was," says Ed, "I explained
that I'd fired my research director to hire a hairdresser/
bodyguard." At that moment, Tony flirtatiously wet one
finger and ran it along his left eyebrow. Ed roared. It was
stories like these that made Robin Sears blanch.

In the attempt to mould Ed into a serious politician,
"we tried to inject some theatre into his style," says
Sears. "I said, 'You don't have to *be* angry, you just have
to look it.' Ed said, 'I can't do that.' He was really uncomfortable with the ritual of presentation." But then Ed
overdid it, coming across in Question Period in such strident tones that Trudeau once called him "a hyena." Sears
also saw Ed as "a man of heated but transitory enthusiasms, for certain foods, or socks, writers or singers." His
impulsiveness had to be tamed. Sears remembers that Ed
would call him at midnight — "Sorry to call so late, but I

was thinking. . . ." — and then again at 6 A.M. — "Sorry to call so early, but I had another thought . . ." Ed's boundless energy had to be curbed. "When you're exhausted at the end of a twelve-hour day, and he keeps on coming, you'd think: would somebody get a baseball bat?" Bill Knight recalls that when he moved from Saskatchwan to Ottawa to work for Ed, "I was a night person. I had to change my entire lifestyle working for him. That maniac is up at the crack of dawn having good ideas which he wants to share."

Then there was Ed's attitude to speeches. His writers would cook up what they thought was a finely scripted work, only to find Ed with a pair of scissors, carving up the whole thing, diligently cutting and pasting it back together to suit himself. They despaired of controlling him, and they struggled to educate him. "Ed knew nothing about popular culture," says Sears. "He couldn't tell Mork and Mindy from Laverne and Shirley if they bit him. And he knew nothing about sports." In this respect, however, Ed was a whiz compared to Trudeau. Christina McCall tells the story of Trudeau phoning Keith Davey. "Davey told him he was watching hockey [on TV] and added that the Buffalo Sabres were winning the game. There was an awkward pause at the other end of the line and then Trudeau said, 'Oh, I see. What inning are they in?'" (For those who don't know, hockey is played in periods, baseball in innings.)

Like Trudeau, Ed did not accept criticism well. ("Who does?" says Anne Carroll.) Though he won't admit it, and appears in public to have the hide of an armadillo, Ed is thin-skinned and vulnerable. Staff members sometimes felt they had to tread carefully if they were proposing changes in his style or — heaven forbid — intellectual content. But the evidence was overwhelming that he needed help. "No reporters rushed to scrum Broadbent outside the House of Commons after Question Period," wrote Charlotte Gray in *Saturday Night*. "His comments were either irrelevant or too long-winded (among CBC Radio *As It Happens* researchers, he was known as Rent-a-Rant). His advisers had told him not to crack jokes on television after he informed an interviewer who enquired about his religion that he was a Druid."

They would be ready to give up on him and then he'd get out with real people and show them what it was all about. "There's no NDP leader I've met who's as good as Ed at campaigning," says Sears. "He would go to an event where he was only supposed to make a token appearance and he'd be so comfortable, and have such a good time, dancing and talking and meeting everyone in the room, that you couldn't get him out of there. If you're responsible for his management and security, he drives you crazy." Like the time an NDP supporter was leaving an event on a motorcycle and Ed couldn't resist jumping on the back for a ride.

It is an interesting conundrum: Ed thought of himself as an intellectual, yet his handlers valued not so much his cerebral skills as his human touch. Ed didn't seem to understand that he was a natural populist. Jo-Anne McNevin had spotted his knack with people right away when she ran his '72 campaign in Oshawa and insisted that the way to sell Ed Broadbent was not to prop him up behind a podium delivering long, philosophical speeches, but to get him out onto the streets among people. In the successful '79 election, Murray Weppler would observe the same talent and comment: "Ed didn't know what he was good at."

It remains one of the deepest contradictions in Broadbent: deep down, he really wants to explain the merits of blending liberalism and socialism; he believes in the power of ideas. But he slowly learned that politics, in the real world, is dominated by television images and thirty-second clips. Voters make their choices based on a grab-bag of feelings about how politicians look, move, sound. He was startled by this discovery; it was almost as if an egghead found himself in a beauty contest, not sure what to do next.

He had to come to terms with the importance of leadership. As Jeffrey Simpson observed in *Discipline of Power*, "Studies of voting behaviour all point to the same conclusion: party leadership is the most salient motivating factor affecting the success of a political party. A leader is of crucial electoral importance since he personifies the party and acts as the national spokesman for its ideals and principles. On him, should power be won, will rest the hopes of the nation and the responsibilities of high office. . . . But the surrender of political campaigns, and of politics generally, to television has heightened the leader's importance in determining electoral success.. . . . Quite often, the candidates' personalities and physical characteristics become more important than the ideas they express or the point of view they represent. They are judged as performers . . ."

> I'd rather deal with a guy off the street in a back alley than deal with a politician. . . . At least in the back alley, you know where the other guy is coming from. You know where he stands. In politics, you never know, because politicians are afraid to offend anybody. . . . They use experts for everything, how to dress, how to speak, what to say, how to walk. It's crazy. . . . My advice to Mulroney and to any other politician is simple: be what you are, say what you honestly believe. And if you believe what you're saying, if you believe in what you stand for, most of the time you'll win. And even if you still lose, at least you haven't surrendered. In the end, that's why I left. I couldn't surrender that last part of myself. That's what power, that's what politics, does to people. You have to surrender yourself entirely to the system. (Michel Gratton, former press secretary to Prime Minister Brian Mulroney, tells Joe O'Donnell why he quit the PM's office — *Toronto Star*, August 30, 1987.)

Maybe it was Ed's lack of glibness, his awkward honesty, that protected him from being swallowed by the system. Even if he had wanted to become smooth like Mulroney, or polished like Trudeau, he couldn't do it. But his own party expected more passion, and few New Democrats found him inspiring.

Ed was not the only Canadian politician who was not a great orator. Manitoba Premier Ed Schreyer was considered one of the more boring speakers in existence, as was Ontario's Bill Davis — yet both men were phenomenally popular leaders. On the national stage, however, Ed was compared unfavourably with one of the great political showmen of all time, whom he faced every day in Question Period: Pierre Trudeau. No Anglo could compete with the complex charms of this fascinating figure who exhibited, said media guru Marshall McLuhan, the ideal "cool" image for television. In the 1974 election, McCall wrote, the Prime Minister's chief advisers, Jim Coutts and Keith Davey, "scripted" a campaign in which their protagonist, "his expression opaque as a Chinese mandarin's," was transformed into a folksy, loveable, misunderstood guy, a role Trudeau "the consummate actor, was able to play to perfection."

For Ed, nothing played to perfection through the autumn of 1974. He was trying to hold everything together, with no money, few able bodies, and little praise. Life at the top, he found out, was an all-consuming experience, especially with the party at rock bottom. Ed was pulled in ten different directions at once. Jean-Guy Carrier, Lewis's press secretary, had stayed on and was trying to persuade Ed to pay attention to Quebec, which remained *terra incognita* for the NDP. But Ed was needed in more fertile territory, out west and in the Maritimes. At the same time, Michael Decter, the young Winnipeg whiz kid, was engaged in some basic demographic research to figure out who voted NDP. At Harvard, Decter had been influenced by the analytical work of Pat Caddell, who became an adviser to Jimmy Carter; Decter wanted to haul the party that had never been able to afford polls into the modern age. He discovered that one of its few loyal constituencies was old people, thanks to the enduring impact of Stanley Knowles's pension legislation; it was a powerful constituency in electoral terms, given the demographics of the aging population. One of the least loyal was labour; by far the majority of workers did not vote NDP. From 1968 to 1974, according to Desmond Morton, "la-

bour support dropped from 28 per cent to 22 per cent"
and "the labour movement was on the brink of bolting
the party." This reality was far from the myth of a party
dominated by organized labour.

Dreaming up strategies for Ed, Decter became "convinced that Ed could heal the Lewis–Waffle split. Ed's
views weren't far from those of Jim Laxer and he was
close to Lewis. He had brought in Jo-Anne McNevin, who
was a bridge to the B.C. party and organized labour. He
was friendly with Bill Knight, who was back in Saskatchewan working for the party." Decter saw Ed pulling together a coalition that would include the women's
movement, environmentalists, Saskatchewan. . . . But
while Decter was planning all the great things Ed could
do, Ed was suffering. The optimism that fuelled his drive
was uncharacteristically low.

That Christmas, Ed found out that his father had cancer. The disease had started in Percy's throat. He was an
avid cigar smoker, as was Ed. Mary, Ed's mother, was
"petrified," says sister Velma. "She was more upset than
Dad. She was always very much in love with him."

"During the period Dad was sick," says Ed, "we
achieved the greatest closeness, in a way, but I don't
want to talk about it." Ed's protective shield around private family matters is inviolable; but he admits he was
shaken up at the prospect of his father's death. There was
a lot of unfinished business between the two men.
Though father and son had never been intimate, they had
strong feelings about each other.

Mary's distress over her husband's illness was felt by
Ed, who was still very close to his mother. Mary was her
son's greatest booster. She took personally every negative
comment against Ed, and there was a lot of sniping at
him during this period. She read the papers, watched the
news, and would always call to cheer him up if she felt
he'd been hard done by. But she did not know what he
was going through; the family was not prepared for Ed's
sudden withdrawal from the leadership race.

What happened, quite simply, was that New Democrats
were not happy with Ed's leadership, he knew it and

decided to quit. The party was not emotionally prepared to accept the end of an era — and the beginning of a new one. They could not quite believe that thirty-eight-year-old Ed Broadbent, who was far from attaining the saintly heights of David Lewis or Tommy Douglas, would replace these icons whose roots stretched back to the founding of the CCF. Though Ed had been an MP since 1968, he had not grown up in the party. He hadn't been a member of the CCF; he was not an heir of the Saskatchewan radicals, as Tommy was, or of the labour movement as David was — indeed he had alienated both groups. He was not a fiery orator, he wasn't a renowned intellectual, he wasn't a great anything. And he had no powerful allies to fall back on, to pull strings for him.

Tony Penikett, now leader of the Yukon NDP Government, then a member of the party's federal council, expresses a commonly held view. "I didn't immediately leap to Ed's support," says Penikett. "I wanted to see if Schreyer would be interested in the leadership. I was waiting for someone better to come along." Practically everyone was looking for someone better. Party stalwarts were scouring the country for candidates to replace David Lewis; even Eric Kierans, a former Liberal Cabinet minister in Quebec, was approached.

Aware of the desperate search that was going on, Ed made his move. In January '75, at a federal council meeting, Ed advised his colleagues that he would not be running for the leadership. "It was a shock to everybody," says Penikett. "All of a sudden, hey, we thought, we better not lose this guy." But they had lost him — though Gerry Caplan, for one, was skeptical about Ed's declaration that he wanted to stay home with his family and listen to Bach.

After the meeting, Ed offered a ride to Penikett and Wally Firth, the NDP MP for the Northwest Territories and first northern native ever elected to Parliament. (Penikett had managed Firth's campaign.) Penikett remembers how tired Ed looked. "He had big circles under his eyes. He was totally exhausted. He asked me to drive — we were in Montreal, heading for Ottawa — and on the ride home we had our first real heart-to-heart talk about basic stuff about the difficulty of explaining democratic socialism in a culture that regards it negatively, in a North American environment where there is no party of the left. Ed was a great person to talk to about things like that. You'd have an idea and Ed would say, 'Gramsci thought about that in the '20s, he wrote a book about it, you should read it.' He's thought through the basic problems. He has a foundation."

The day after the Montreal meeting, on January 16, 1975, Canadian Press reported that

> Edward Broadbent, parliamentary leader of the New Democratic Party, announced yesterday that he will not seek the party leadership. . . . He had been considerd a front-runner in the leadership race, which will end at a July convention in Winnipeg . . . The announcement from his office stated that 'Mr Broadbent cited his desire for more time with his family as the reason for his decision. . . .'
> Mr Broadbent has been a persistent worker in this Parliament, leading his diminished caucus against a strong majority Government. But after holding the balance of power in the previous minority Parliament, the party has not had the same impact in this session. Although the interim leader has continued to be a strong spokesman on economic matters, particularly in relation to the automobile industry, he has not been able to wield the same clout as Mr Lewis, whose voting support was often necessary to the life of the previous government.

The news reports did not mention that the party's failure to show much enthusiasm for Ed had precipitated his withdrawal.

Says Ed: "I had no illusions. I was a relatively young MP with no great impact on political life. I was well aware of it — coming after the greats in the party, as I did, it didn't astound me that party members didn't come flocking to me. I admired Tommy and David, but I was a

Canadian of a different generation. I knew that my contribution would be quite different. Their speaking capacities were terrific, yet their rhetoric belonged to an earlier era. The activists knew it but they still expected the old messianic fervour. The CCFers grew up with it in the '30s and '40s, but in the '70s and '80s that barn-burning oratory wasn't the lure it used to be. We were in the television age. It's still a function of leadership, I know, to offer inspiration, but I felt the great passion and commitment of Tommy and David were not turning on people of my generation. They were seen by younger people, including myself, as belonging to a generation whose time had passed. I say that as a guy who was initially motivated by Tommy more than by anyone else, and who learned more from David than anyone else."

So what did Ed feel his contribution would be? "I thought then, and I think now, that I would bring an expression in concrete language of what social democracy is all about, without exaggerated rhetoric, and with a sense of joy. There had been a sense of sacrifice about earlier social democrats, a feeling of being outsiders. I'm not an outsider. I was quite comfortable coming into a party that was already established. I didn't have to fight for its existence. It's a profound difference. I feel at home within myself and in my country, as a social democrat. It's a tradition that is now, thanks to Tommy and David, unconsciously embedded in the political psyche of Canadians. It is my task to bring that out, to evoke it, to make it conscious."

But he had not found a way to make his message heard. Outside Oshawa — where he had no choice but to lay off the lectures — he was still treating the public forum as a political science seminar. Deep down, he really wanted to explain how society had evolved and why social democracy was the next step in the progression toward more humane co-habitation. "I believed it was important to talk about the right ideas," Ed says. "I had grown up with George Orwell, Koestler and Camus, with the concept of the anti-hero, with a skepticism about rhetoric."

He was uncomfortable with the rhetorical flourishes of speech writers. His idea of a speech was simple: "Here are the arguments, bang-bang-bang, this is what's unjust, here's what we should do about it." Delivered, he adds, "with a deliberate lack of rhetoric. But I discovered that telling the truth is not enough for a political leader. There is an obligation to arouse commitment." He recognized that he had been inspired by the passion of Tommy Douglas, "and I came to appreciate the importance of feelings in politics, but still I had a great skepticism. I was suspicious of exaggerated emotionalism." He was also, unconsciously, a typical product of Ontario: a little repressed, somewhat prudish, despite his rowdy humour, and quite the upright Anglican boy — though if anyone suggested his image was at all uptight or WASPish he was extremely offended. "That's the last thing I am," he would say, convinced that his personal exuberance, his "politics of joy" were evident in his public persona. Yet in the grand tradition of Ontario politics, he had an intense dislike of extremism in any form which has persisted throughout his career. "Your course of action has to be rationally and ethically justified," he says. "I was interested in convincing people by reason, persuading them of what was rationally desirable and possible. Now I understand a leader has to do more. A leader must move people. I used to think it was wrong to arouse people. Now I feel differently."

In 1974, he could not arouse his own party; nor was his decision to quit the leadership race a stunt designed to attract attention, he insists. "Some people thought I was playing a little game," he says. "One of the interesting things about political life is that people rarely take statements from politicians at face value. But I was quite serious. I hadn't known what was involved in the role of leader, and suddenly I got on-the-job training. It was a shock."

More to the point, perhaps, was the shock of the party's ambivalence toward him. "Ed was hurt the establishment didn't support him," says Decter. "He was wounded deeply. He got mad enough — or strategic enough — to withdraw." Decter figures Ed's decision was real. "I was pretty sure he'd run in the end, but he wouldn't give me any clear assurances so I went back to Winnipeg to work for the Schreyer government." By the time Ed changed his mind and announced that he would be a candidate, Decter was ensconced as a senior adviser to Schreyer's Cabinet planning secretariat, and he was supporting Rosemary Brown for the leadership. It was Brown's campaign — precipitated by feminists more as a grand gesture than a serious shot at power — that would eventually "scare the pants off Ed," according to Kay Macpherson, and force Broadbent to confront feminism.

Sixty days after his withdrawal, during which time he suddenly received outpourings of affection from party stalwarts, Ed was back in the race. On March 27, 1975, *The Globe and Mail* reported that "Edward Broadbent has reversed his decision of two months ago and decided to seek the national leadership of the New Democratic Party. . . . He told a press conference yesterday that he had been assured by leading party figures and his supporters in the caucus that if he wins he will be allowed time for his private life." The same day, *Globe* columnist Geoffrey Stevens wrote about "The Broadbent Dilemma."

"He is kidding himself if he thinks he can be national leader of the New Democratic Party and still enjoy what other people consider a normal family life," observed Stevens. "Suppose the party has a promising candidate in One Hill, Sask., the candidate has some chance of winning the seat and a visit from the leader just might help to tip the balance. Could the leader refuse to make the trip on the ground that it is his weekend to take his wife shopping?" Stevens concluded that what happened between January, when Ed withdrew, and March, when he re-entered, was that New Democrats "approached him not on the basis that he was the least undesirable of an inferior crop of potential leaders, but rather on the basis that they wanted him, Edward Broadbent, as their leader." This more positive view Stevens attributed "to a gradual realization in the party that the old days are gone and cannot be reclaimed. The days of hair-shirt saints have passed. . . . The party is fresh out of J.S. Woodsworths, M.J. Coldwells, Tommy Douglases and David Lewises. Once New Democrats realized this, they were able to view their younger people, particularly Mr Broadbent, in a different, more kindly perspective."

Ed speaks of his own change of heart more pragmatically. He had talked personally to the three western NDP Premiers — Allan Blakeney, Ed Schreyer and Dave Barrett — "to see if they were willing to run. I wouldn't have run if they were available, but they weren't." And he was talked to by the party establishment, which lacked a strong alternative and was finally desperate to get Ed. "I was persuaded," says Ed.

If he was expecting a coronation, he was disappointed. The leadership convention "was not the easy stroll to victory one would expect in the circumstances," wrote Norman Snider in *Toronto Life*. Ed was up against Lorne Nystrom, a Saskatchewan MP; Rosemary Brown, a British Columbia MLA; former MP John Harney; and a fourth, fringe candidate named Douglas Campbell. The three leading men were stunned that the greatest excitement was generated by Rosemary Brown's grass-roots campaign.

Kay Macpherson was one of Brown's early supporters. Then sixty-two years old, Kay had joined the party in 1972, run unsuccessfully in 1974 and was "totally shocked, going to conventions, at how male-dominated it was. The women would have done all the organizing and then on the platform it would be all men."

When the leadership convention was well under way in Winnipeg on July 7, 1975, Hugh Winsor reported in *The Globe and Mail* that Ed Broadbent, "dubbed the establishment candidate," was supported by ten of the sixteen members of caucus and by the three western NDP Premiers. "His campaign, run by veteran organizer Jo-Anne McNevin, has all the marks of a professional organization. Every delegate (there were 1,661) has been entered on huge charts and his [sic] voting preferences noted. Each of fifteen floor directors has the same list in a small book and, as the arguments and buttonholing go on, the status of the potential support is updated every three hours." The convention hall was flooded with Broadbent posters, floor signs and literature, all professionally designed, amid a bobbing sea of orange "Ed" buttons.

The Brown campaign, on the other hand, "is more of a movement than an organization," wrote Winsor. "It is a vehicle for the women's rights issues of day care, income security for home-bound parents and abortion." Brown was also attracting the tattered remnants of the Waffle as well as westerners who saw Ed "as just another Ontario MP," in the words of Vic Schroeder, later a Manitoba Cabinet minister. A Mennonite lawyer who would take over Ed Schreyer's seat, Schroeder remembers most of all feeling "undecided and ambivalent. I didn't think Ed understood the need for strong policies on regional development. I supported Rosemary, though I'm not sure I would have if I thought she was going to win." Brown attracted, in other words, the western protest vote. Stephen Lewis, leader of the Ontario NDP, saw a narrower appeal: "The Brown campaign is a mixture of fundamentalism and feminism — a very potent brew." Desmond Morton rated Rosemary Brown "a second Jim Laxer, with more fire, fewer facts and a dependence on trite platitudes that troubled even some of her own followers." Ed, however, was not critical of Brown's socialist rhetoric. "It's part of her style," he says. "It's not my style — but a lot of what she said was vivid and passionate. She had a huge impact on me. Afterwards, she was very helpful, working with me on women's issues. She educated me about feminism."

Brown was widely regarded as the most charismatic figure in the race. Jamaican-born, she was a passionately eloquent spokeswoman for the party's left wing. Observing her in action at debates prior to the convention, Christina McCall had reported (in the *Globe*, on June 7) that "the main interest came out of the brave and very often brilliant performance of Rosemary Brown, who acted as though she refused to believe what the party sages have been saying since she declared her candidacy in mid-February, that any candidate who's a black, a woman and a British Columbia MLA rather than a member of federal caucus has too much against her . . ." In her speeches, "going easy on the feminist issues and leaning hard on the economic ones, [she] often turned the question period that followed into a personal triumph wherein she displayed a first-rate intellect and a quick perception of the human factor involved in nearly every question." In contrast, Harney was perceived as having lost confidence and charisma after his '74 election defeat; Lorne Nystrom was considered too young and too stolid at twenty-nine; and Ed "appeared on platforms to be merely pedantic, as rigid as his navy-blue blazer and wearier than his thirty-nine years," wrote McCall.

Stephen Lewis said he was supporting Ed because "during the past year I saw an immense development in [him] as Parliamentary leader, and he showed in his [nomination] acceptance speech that, given the opportunity, he will be an effective speaker." (Lewis's endorsement sounded like faint praise.) Willy Parasiuk, later Manitoba's health minister, was a more positive supporter. "I was a Broadbent guy," says Willy. "When Ed was campaigning for the leadership, he stayed at my house and slept in the bottom bunk in my son's room, while my son slept on top. I liked Ed. He was the most open. He could relate to the Waffle. 'Let's bring everybody in,' that was his attitude. He didn't want to exclude anyone."

Nevertheless, Kay Macpherson felt "there wasn't much to choose from between the three men." She remembers the mounting excitement as Rosemary Brown's team — working in a non-hierarchical, consensual fashion, attempting to practise its feminist principles — realized their candidate was gaining momentum. "The whole thing changed from a run-of-the-mill leadership contest," says Kay. In bearpit sessions, she observed, "the language began to change, because of Rosemary. No one had dared say the socialist word, but because Rosemary talked about socialism, the other candidates ended up pounding their fists about socialism. Rosemary talked about affirmative action and feminist issues and it was all new to them, but they started adopting the language.

We really focussed the party on our issues. The men were scared silly. It never occurred to them that this could happen. We were amazed that we got her to the final ballot."

Broadbent's well-organized, well-financed team had not expected Brown's strong showing, especially since she had very little money — she spent only $5,454 compared to Ed's $14,500. She certainly got more bang for her bucks: on the first ballot, Ed headed the list with 536 votes, to Brown's 413. On the fourth and final ballot, Ed won with 948 votes to Brown's 648. "It's a real victory," said a jubilant Brown, when it was all over. "We've managed to shift the party to the left, somewhat." The press concurred.

Ed emerged in good spirits, although the union support that was supposed to line up behind him never fully arrived: only one-third of labour's eligible delegates showed up. On July 8, he announced his strategy: "A national investment plan allocating new capital according to NDP priorities . . . and the organization to win sixty seats in the [next] election," wrote Hugh Winsor. Ed would have trouble delivering on the electoral front, but as leader he at last had the opportunity to move the party "beyond the welfare state," as he put it. As for Ed's political performance, Winsor, who had known Ed as a friend in Oshawa fifteen years earlier, observed gently that, "Although he has always been a warm individual on a personal basis, Mr Broadbent is only slowly learning to be a public person. . . . Unable to muster the synthetic anger that is often the mark of a successful politician, he shies away from anything that smacks of demagoguery . . ." Geoffrey Stevens decreed more bluntly that Ed "excites almost no one in the party or outside it," but conceded that "Ed Broadbent won the leadership because he was the best candidate. . . . Mr Broadbent will not find it easy to instil a sense of direction and purpose in his tired and battered party. He will not excite the Canadian people. But he will be a solid, respectable, responsible leader. He will serve his party well."

A feminist delegate who supported Rosemary Brown observes: "When Ed won, many of us saw him as a caretaker leader, decent, honest, plodding along, holding things together until a more charismatic leader emerged. We didn't foresee that the Canadian public would come to distrust charisma and media flackery and here's uncharismatic Ed, decent and honest at a time when the public is searching for decency and honesty . . ."

Ed's first appearance in the House of Commons as the newly elected leader of the party occurred on July 9, 1975. Prime Minister Trudeau wished him well, "but not too well." Robert Stanfield, who had been plagued by party dissension and would soon be replaced as Tory leader by Joe Clark, brought the House down when he said he hoped Ed would get "the same loyalty and support from his caucus that I have always enjoyed." It was prophetic sarcasm: within five years, the NDP caucus would be torn apart over constitutional reform, and Ed would nearly be dead, in political terms.

In the meantime, the '74–'79 Parliament was a relatively peaceful period for New Democrats, which gave Ed's advisers a chance to work on him, and gave him an opportunity to get a handle on the party. He rode his bicycle to Parliament Hill — it took eight minutes from his Sandy Hill condominium — and he set about getting things organized. "He knew he couldn't do what Douglas and Lewis had done — hold the party together by sheer personality," wrote Charlotte Gray in *Saturday Night*. "He had to give it structure." Terry Grier, appointed head of the election planning committee in 1976, told Gray that Ed's insistence "on a focussed, methodical approach" became "one of his most significant contributions."

In his own office, Ed said farewell to his personal secretary, May Gretton, who had guided him through his early years on the Hill. May retired to travel around the world with her husband; she was replaced by Anne Carroll, whom party workers consider "outrageously devoted" to her boss. Carroll does not disguise her commitment. "I just got hooked," she says. "You work your heart out, you work your soul out, you work till you drop. I thrive on it." The daughter of a Conservative railway worker, Carroll knew nothing about NDP policy when she started canvassing for the party in the early '70s. When she found herself working in Ed's office, she was "a green kid," but she learned fast. "Our job is to keep Ed up, and the way you do it is not with compliments but by keeping things around him running well. Smooth operations — that's all he asks for. Calmness and efficiency. The team has to work together. You don't have fights in front of Ed." Still with Ed after more than a decade, Carroll has become his executive assistant and a figure of considerable influence in the leader's office. Described by a disgruntled former staff member as "the dragon lady who guards Ed's door," Carroll is the tough cop to Ed's nice guy — and heaven help you if Carroll doesn't like you. (When George Nakitsas, the party's research director, moved in the winter of '87 to the position of Ed's chief-of-staff, Carroll's response was, in effect: "Over my dead body." Ed, however, told her to "work it out with George." She did.)

On Parliament Hill, Ed still relied heavily on Stanley Knowles. "Ed treated Stanley with reverence," says Weppler. Stanley advised on procedure, tactics and the intricate rules of Parliament, which the elderly MP knew better than anyone in the House. With the introduction of television into the Commons in 1977, Question Period became an even more significant forum from which the NDP could beam its message out to the country. "A tiger in debate, Broadbent's national recognition began to improve when Canadians began to see the actual confrontation," observed Norman Snider in *Toronto Life*. "Television loves a drama and Broadbent hammering away began to become a staple of the national news." But it took great effort behind the scenes — and Ed's recognition of the need for skilled media advisers — to make it all happen.

Slowly, Ed was adjusting to the job. He was talking about what he wanted to talk about — economic issues, industrial strategy, full employment policy, tax reform. While Trudeau plugged away at his most precious goal — patriating the Constitution — Ed focussed on patriating the economy. On July 12, 1975, he described his cherished national economic plan: "We have to regain control of our own economy; we should begin in the resource sector; we want that sector as the initiation point because then we could develop the secondary industry in Canada." He criticized the concentration of corporate power and he coped with the marked decline of official labour support that had been so obvious at the leadership convention.

Dennis McDermott, Canadian director of the United Auto Workers, was still no fan of Ed's, and Ed knew it. "Dennis never felt comfortable with academics, to say the least," says Ed. "His phrase would have been: 'academic shitheads.'" In the fall of '76, McDermott would muse aloud about the possibility of the unions breaking their ties to the NDP. Courted by the Liberal government, he was invited to join Prime Minister Trudeau's delegation on an official visit to Washington, for talks with U.S. President Jimmy Carter. Ed, of course, could offer no such perks. But the labour–Liberal romance did not last long. In the middle of October, Trudeau unveiled the wage and price controls program that he had denounced when Robert Stanfield advocated it during the previous election campaign.

Ed was launched on the attack: wage and price controls were unfair, he said, because wages were inequitably held down while price or profit controls were "unenforceable." The labour movement scurried to jump on side as Ed ridiculed the Liberals for "abandoning moral commitments"; he went after corporations for gouging ever-increasing profits out of consumers who couldn't afford to pay. He was particularly effective publicizing the massive increase in bank profits which rose as inflation soared, demanding that excessive profits be reinvested to create jobs. Unemployment was moving up to 12 per cent, more than one million people were out of work, and by 1981 interest rates were so high that, said Ed at a Labour Day gathering, his own brother was threatened with the loss of his home. David Broadbent was a ten-year veteran at General Motors, earning about $20,000 a year, with a wife and two children. His mortgage was coming up for renewal, and he was threatened with an increase from nine and three-quarters per cent to twenty-two per cent. "I just don't know how I'll handle it," David said.

Liberal economic mismanagement, Tory ineffectiveness: this was the backdrop against which Ed's leadership formed. And he saw how quickly the Liberals could respond to NDP ideas, if they were desperate. REINVEST HIGH PROFITS TO CREATE JOBS, PM SAYS. This was a *Toronto Star* headline on February 8, 1979. For months previously, REINVEST HIGH PROFITS was a headline attached to Broadbent speeches. Now it had been picked up by Trudeau, following the announcement that profits had increased 21 per cent for the first nine months of 1978, compared to wage increases of 6.2 per cent. Trudeau, however, attempted to deflect Broadbent by saying that, "I know members of the NDP are unhappy that companies make profits." Trudeau then tried to take credit for the situation. "I would even say that the government is largely responsible for the fact that there are profits." Not even the business community could tolerate Trudeau's misplaced arrogance. In September, 1976, the Gallup Poll showed the Liberals had sagged to 29 per cent, their lowest rating in more than thirty years. The Tories under Joe Clark — elected Conservative leader in February — were approaching the 50 per cent mark, and the New Democrats were still trailing below 20 per cent.

Through it all, Ed was travelling — and he no longer complained about life on the road. Newspaper clips from a one-month period reveal a typical schedule: "Broadbent will visit Newfoundland and Nova Scotia on a factfinding tour . . ." "NDP Leader will tour British Columbia for a first-hand look at unemployment in Nanaimo, Powell River and Vancouver . . ." "Broadbent in Windsor and Southern Ontario" and "NDP Leader in Quebec." Quebec visits were exhausting because of Ed's struggle to speak French, but they were essential.

Pierre Trudeau and most of Ottawa were obsessed with Quebec. On November 15, 1976, René Lévesque led the Parti Québecois to victory, eight years after its formation.

"We had won seventy-one seats and the Liberals had lost exactly the same number," wrote Lévesque. "It was more than a sweep, it was a tidal wave, breaking in from everywhere to carry away the joyful crowd of adults laughing with tears in their eyes, children perched on their shoulders . . . the *fleur-de-lys* floating triumphantly . . . it made you think of a very pure, hot first day, the 'beginning of a new age' . . ."

While jubilant Quebeckers jumped for joy, Canada's Prime Minister made plans. Once again, observed Keith Davey, Pierre Trudeau was "the right man in the right place at the right time." The day after the PQ victory, Davey said: "I know this sounds cross and un-Canadian and disloyal and all sorts of things, but the PQ win is the best thing that could have happened to the federal Liberal party." Davey was thrilled. "Instinctively I knew that the overwhelming majority of English-speaking Canadians would be determined to keep Quebec in Canada. Inevitably this would mean once again rallying behind Pierre Elliott Trudeau's leadership. This is exactly what happened."

None of this was good news for Ed. He had watched Trudeau capture the spirit of the '60s and ride the crest of the era's idealism into power; now, eight years later, Trudeau was again the man of the hour: English Canadians trusted him to keep the French in line. As the Québecois celebrated on TV, Ed sat with his Francophone wife Lucille, who understood only too well the allure of Québecois pride that Lévesque had released.

Ed was, however, preoccupied, nursing another, deeper feeling: grief. Only a month earlier, Percy (Ginger) Broadbent died of cancer at Oshawa General Hospital.

More than ten years later, helping his daughter Christine pick up the contents of a drawer she had knocked onto the floor, Ed came across "an exchange of notes with my Dad when he was dying. There was a reconciliation, a couple of days before he died. He was writing messages about wanting to be taken off life-support systems. In one note to him, I said I admired him for overcoming his drinking problem. I told him he had immense courage. I

had never said that to him before, ever. I had never said
I admired anything about him." Ed leaned back on the
sofa in his Parliament Hill office, and smoothed his face
with his hands. "It takes death, sometimes, to bring these
feelings out."

By the fall of '76, the political winds shifted in Ed's favour. He suddenly began to get good press — partly because the competition was looking bad. Pierre Trudeau's
media relations were freezing up; Joe Clark was not making a positive impact. The press can be cruel: on April 24,
1976, a *Globe and Mail* columnist reported: "Shortly after
the Tories announced that their new leader was Joseph
Clark, two veteran New Democratic Party officials attending the Tory convention approached me to pronounce
Canadian socialism's verdict on the new leader of the Opposition. 'Joe Clark,' they collectively said, 'is the only
man in Canada who can make Ed Broadbent look like a
heavyweight.' "

The *Globe* columnist disagreed with the two NDP officials and supplied a list of names, including Liberal Cabinet Ministers André Ouellet, Marc Lalonde, Jean
Chrétien and even Himself, Pierre Trudeau, who "collectively make Honest Ed Broadbent, the forever discounted
politician, look like a man who can put his opponents
down for at least a nine-count, if not a TKO." The main
event was Ed's handling of the so-called "judges affair,"
in which *The Globe and Mail* had obtained letters between Mr Justice Mackay and Justice Minister Ron Bas-
ford. "Mr Justice Mackay alleged in one letter that he
knew of two occasions when Cabinet ministers had attempted to intervene with judges about matters before
the courts and one case when the principal secretary to
Mr Trudeau [Marc Lalonde] attempted to do so." Leading
the charge against the government, "in an affair that has
tarnished the image of our judiciary and our politicians,"
wrote the columnist, "Honest Ed has become the effective
leader of the Opposition. . . ."

After years of being described as dull and boring, it
was Ed's turn for accolades. On September 13, 1976,
under the headline BROADBENT MIXES SOCIALISM AND

LAUGHS, the *Globe*'s John King described Ed in wholly positive terms: "Edward Broadbent likes being a politician. When the workers in an Oakville automobile plant whooped and waved as they spotted him taking a VIP tour last week, his face lit up, his hand stretched out and everyone stopped for a chat. When members of a New Democratic Party riding association had him in a closed-door accountability session, he was in his element. And when his political schedule put him in painter's coveralls at a 'media event' in Hamilton, he was as good a slapstick actor as any politician."

But King took pains to point out that Ed's primary mission was a serious one, that he was "a dedicated socialist" whose real interest was to build up the party. "He is the man in charge of No. 3 who is really trying harder. . . ." Ed told King that he had "a temperamental suspicion" of people who dreamed of becoming prime minister, but he admitted to dreaming "that before long the federal party will form a national government in Canada. . . ." He hoped, he said, that it would happen "during my period of leadership."

He was enjoying a honeymoon that would be abruptly shattered at the beginning of the '80s. But for now, life as the New Democratic chief was glowing. His leadership of the party was confirmed at yet another convention in Winnipeg in 1977 where "the sweet scent of party unity abounded," in the words of the Toronto *Star*'s John Honderich. Ed had managed to create a sense of harmony; the feuding factions had backed off and even the party's left flank seemed content. Jim Laxer was happily present and Rosemary Brown told Honderich that she credited Ed "with cooling out all the groups." Ed even delivered a rousing, ten-minute speech on national unity that surprised delegates and brought them to their feet clapping enthusiastically. "It's the first time he's made listening to David Lewis seem like an anti-climax," quipped a delegate. Yet Honderich wondered whether the Canadian public would bother to listen.

"With Broadbent at the helm for exactly two years," he wrote, "the NDP is firmly embedded in third place in the

Gallup poll — floating somewhere between 17 and 19 per cent of the committed vote. The same poll shows more than half the voters — 57 per cent — don't even know if Broadbent is an asset to his party. Only 27 per cent believe he is. Yet this is the same man who by all accounts won the battle of the Opposition leaders in the House of Commons in his questioning on the recent activities of the Royal Canadian Mounted Police. And the same man who stole the limelight from Opposition leader Joe Clark last year during the "judges affair. . . ." Not only was Ed being seen to perform well in public, and to have mastered the House of Commons, but his imprint on party policies was firm. "No longer is the NDP calling for the immediate nationalization of all banks, oil companies and natural resources," wrote Honderich. "Policies passed at last weekend's convention — including planks to nationalize one oil company, ban junk food advertising, revise the tax system, impose an excess profits tax on petroleum firms, and nationalize Canadian Pacific — could almost sit comfortably with the left wing of the Liberal Party." And here was the crunch; this was Ed's great gamble — that he could transform the party into a modern social democratic organization that was seeking power, without losing its socialist soul.

Murray Weppler, Ed's chief of staff, and Peter O'Malley, Ed's press secretary, were working hard to establish Ed as a media player. "Our objective was to build his profile," says O'Malley. "Whatever story was moving on any given day, we jumped it and put Ed into it. We invented a genre of political communications. Where David Lewis would have made a speech on auto parts and put out a press release afterwards, we integrated the visual elements with the story. We'd take Ed to an auto plant, he'd talk to the guys — which he does very well — and then he'd stand in the plant and talk about auto parts to the TV cameras."

From Weppler, Ed learned to speak in shorter sentences; where Robin Sears tried to tone Ed down, Weppler toned him up. From O'Malley, Ed learned the power of visuals. One example from the period: Ed was still in the habit of riding his bicycle to Parliament Hill. O'Malley set up a "photo opportunity" of Ed wearing a suit, pedalling past the Peace Tower with his briefcase strapped to the back of his bike. It was "the real Ed," it made a great shot and it was picked up by the wire service and slapped in newspapers across the country.

"All I cared about was distilling our message down to fifteen usable seconds," says O'Malley. He found that Ed learned fast. "Put him in the right setting, and he delivers. He's disciplined. He can stay on track." Ed became, in O'Malley's opinion, "a superb performer. As an actor, he's world class."

How Ed had developed in a few short years: he no longer objected to a little TV makeup to hide the raccoon circles under his eyes, he was getting his face on the nightly newscasts, he had learned to speak in short clips, his message was convincingly moderate, his style persuasive and, most astonishing, by 1980 he would top the polls as the political leader with the highest approval rating in the country — a popularity level he holds in 1988.

In a September, 1978, article in *Saturday Night* magazine titled "Ed Broadbent on a Fast Track," Sandra Gwyn led off: "Too bloody many Canadian socialists think having a good time is some kind of horrible crime." She was quoting Ed Broadbent, who was wearing a safari suit and a button in his lapel that read "Save Energy, Boogie in the Dark." Whirling with Ed around the dance floor of Club Loreley in Oshawa during the town's multi-cultural Fiesta festival, Gwyn observed that Ed was a great dancer, that he loved to have fun, did a passable imitation of Johnnie Ray singing "Cry," adored Liv Ullmann and Margaret Laurence and "didn't like the ending of *An Unmarried Woman.*"

"I'm confused," wrote Gwyn. She was not the only one; indeed the double-take she was doing on Ed was a typical reaction. He was the kind of guy who didn't make a splashy first impression, but he grew on you. "The Broadbent taking shape in my notebook just doesn't connect at all with the image of Broadbent I started out with," Gwyn continued. In Ottawa, he was "ponderous," while "here on his home turf, he's a relaxed, engaging guy with unsuspected wrinkles in his personality." Wrinkles in his personality: he was, in other words, a human being with quirks, with character. "Broadbent, I can report, likes whipping down the 401 at forty kilometres over the speed limit in his eight-cylinder, four-on-the-floor Monza hatchback painted British racing green, with a cigar clenched in his teeth in the manner of Jean-Louis Trintignant in *Un Homme et une femme*. Broadbent also turns out to be one-half of one of the sunniest political marriages I've ever observed." The same observation is made about Lucille and Ed in '88: they had somehow survived the political campaigns, the separations and the struggles to bring up their children; they were still, obviously, in love with each other.

Gwyn wrote approvingly that Lucille "doesn't go in for a lot of talk about The Importance of Being Her Own Person," which may have been a dig at flaky Margaret Trudeau's search for identity, "nor does she claim to be Fifty Per Cent of a Team," which was likely a shot at Maureen McTeer's active participation in her husband Joe Clark's political life.

Yet what seems to have most astonished Gwyn was that in Ed she saw a human being she could identify with, a man of her own generation, a middle-class Canadian who was more than a politician. It was about this time that the refrain that has followed Ed ever since began to be heard: "I'd love to vote for you, Ed, and if you were a Tory or a Liberal you'd be Prime Minister."

Ed's increasing popularity was the result of his own hard work, his capacity to grow, a solid team backing him and an ingenious media strategy. But the intensity of commitment — the party had so few people and so little money compared to its competitors — promoted burnout. Robin Sears remembers the incredible strain of the 1977 to 1980 period, which he spent gearing up for, and mounting, two election campaigns that burst explosively, one on top of the other. "It was an awful grind. It exacted an enormous toll," he says. He was out on the road so much that his relationship with Robin Harris — they were not yet married — broke up. (They got back together later.) He was also astonished by the reaction of his leader to this stretch of unrelenting pressure. Ed thrived on it. "Believe it or not," says Sears, "Ed's idea of a good time is an election campaign. He's like a rock star who loves touring. And he had high hopes, he had great expectations, but then he always does."

It didn't take much to get Ed's adrenalin going. In the October 1978 by-elections, fifteen seats were up for grabs. The Tories scored best, winning ten ridings, while the Liberals lost five incumbents and held on to only two seats; the New Democrats also won two, and the Social Credits one. While the Liberals mourned, Ed danced for joy. From Toronto, he'd gained Bob Rae, a hotshot young Rhodes Scholar and lawyer; and in Newfoundland, in a traditional Tory riding, New Democrat Fonse Faour, another lawyer, delivered a stunning upset victory that gave the NDP its first-ever Newfoundland seat.

The upbeat mood continued into the '79 election, where, says Murray Weppler, "we built the campaign around Ed's strengths. He has the one commodity politicians would give their souls for: honesty. We wanted to mainstreet because the guy has a quality of warmth and sincerity. He's open and accessible and he has a physical charisma — he's a big, strong-looking guy with a nice face. I remember we went through the Houdaille plant [an Oshawa bumper manufacturer] and I couldn't believe how well he handled it. He talked only to those who wanted to talk. He didn't thrust out his hand to everyone. He was sensitive. We finally convinced him that this is one of his strongest political attributes — his warmth, his sensitivity, knowing when not to intrude on someone's space. His weak point was still his speeches. It was hard for him to project emotion before a big crowd, though he did it so well one-to-one." Mike Breaugh, Oshawa's MPP, didn't think Ed's lack of oratorical skills was such a handicap. "TV has made Ed Broadbent," says Breaugh. "If this were old-time politics, no question, he'd be nowhere. But TV is an intimate medium and this is where Ed's so good — at the intimate talks, the personal contact.

People want to make contact with politicians and see who they are; through TV, you can see who Ed is."

Thanks to the Election Expenses Act, the NDP for the first time had real money to spend — and Ed's image received some professional polish. For the '79 election, the party would commit more than $1 million to advertising (Conservative expenditures were more than double — almost $2.5 million — while the Liberals spent $1.8 million.) Thirty-second television commercials were a top priority and Ed, at the insistence of a very expensive, hired-gun adman, became the star — to the dismay of party purists who expected the NDP to keep to the high road selling party policy, not promoting the flesh-and-blood charms of its attractive leader.

In search of the right agency to handle the job, Sears watched "more dreadful commercials" than he cares to remember and finally chose Lawrence Wolf. A savvy American advertiser who moved to Canada in 1970, Wolf is a tall, balding, witty professional; his agency is located in a posh, renovated brick house on Prince Arthur Avenue, behind Toronto's Park Plaza hotel, just west of the Yorkville district. A polished bronze plaque beside the front door is engraved "Wolf," and Larry Wolf is something of a loner, if only in the sense that he was not attached at birth to any of the Canadian networks in which he now operates; nor was he a victim of conventional Canadian thinking about political parties. Quite like his new political client, Wolf had staked a claim on new turf — but unlike Broadbent he'd made a lot of money out of it. He and his partner-wife Mary live in a Barton Myers-designed home overlooking a ravine in the centre of the city; their two sons have been attending private schools. And in the driveway of the Wolf, Richards, Taylor agency are parked his Jaguar and her BMW. In the lobby, packages and posters for products they have worked on are proudly displayed: Atlas batteries, Petro-Canada tires, Betty Crocker cake mixes — "We named Betty Crocker's new cake mix Super-Moist to build a pre-emptive moistness position on top of Duncan Hines," crows a Wolf brochure.

Back in '79, Larry Wolf scrutinized Ed, dined with him at various elegant Toronto eateries, argued with him about politics and prepared an award-winning campaign designed to enhance a man Wolf came to see as the most interesting leadership candidate in North America.

"Larry Wolf was the first adman we employed who brought the kind of distance and professional reserve that we needed," says Sears. "Larry was not 'of the faith.' I didn't want a party loyalist who would just feed me back the truisms we were operating under. I wanted cold, professional advice. I got it — and it made a lot of people unhappy."

Wolf assessed the situation and told Sears bluntly: "Your best presenter is Ed Broadbent. Your campaign's gotta be about Ed." Wolf had made his reputation taking new or 'minority' products and selling them into a market dominated by corporate giants. He called his strategy "targeted positioning," which involved identifying a market niche, moving into it and expanding the product's range. He planned to do the same thing for the New Democrats, and insisted the first task was to make Ed Broadbent a household name. Sears approved, though he was later attacked for running a leadership campaign that aped the personality politicking of Liberals and Conservatives.

One of the first things Wolf did was get Ed's hair cut shorter and change his wardrobe, outfitting him in elegant $600 custom-made suits. "It was easy getting Ed into good suits," Wolf laughs. "Ed appreciates good things. He has a wonderfully sophisticated palate. He knows good food and good wine. I remember sitting with him in Auberge Gavroche [a French restaurant] when he discovered the little buttons on the cuffs of his suit jacket actually button and unbutton — which doesn't happen with a suit off the rack. He thought it was terrific. We kibbitzed a lot. I had to find out how he thought — with a guy like that, you don't ignore substance. He's got a lot of substance. We had a wonderful discussion in Fenton's for three hours one evening over dinner, arguing about what had brought England down, with him insisting it wasn't the unions. Another time at Winston's, Johnny Arena [the owner] came out with a genuine Napoleon brandy, on the house — the first time I'd ever had a Napoleon — which we enjoyed with a Davidoff Cuban cigar." Wolf beams, well aware of the irony of enjoying the best of Winston's — the Bay Street boys' favourite hangout, where John Turner always had a special table — with Ed Broadbent. "The best time I've ever had in the advertising business was working with Ed."

What some party members considered the "crass commercialism" of Wolf's approach did not bother Ed. He had learned a harsh fact about modern political life: if he didn't make it on TV, he would never make it. He seems not to have felt squeamish about selling himself. There was a transformation involved here: the socialist philosopher had evolved over ten years into a hard-nosed politician. The young MP who in 1968 was an activist lefty calling on the party to abandon its "gradualism" was now a gradualist seeking power. His two great Canadian teachers, Tommy Douglas and David Lewis, had pointed the way; their influence was reinforced by Ed's experiences in the heady world of the Socialist International.

Rubbing shoulders with the Willy Brandts and Olof Palmes of western Europe and Scandinavia, he entered a world where social democracy was a dominant force. Winning, he now felt, didn't necessarily mean selling out. He had also overcome his existential ambivalence, fostered in his intellectual days by Camus and Koestler. Though he still rejected rhetoric, he appreciated the personal appeal of individual politicians. "The SPD [West Germany's social democratic party] would never have formed a government without Willy Brandt as leader," Ed says. "The personal dimension is an inescapable aspect of political existence. Political theory is an abstraction to most people. They get motivated by the person who believes the abstractions. They like to catch a glimpse of passion, fun and zest — without that, the leader is just a set of abstractions."

Broadbent and Sears never worried that their political message would get lost. Wolf produced a series of commercials that simply showed Ed speaking straight into the camera, talking about the New Democrats' goals. Wolf coached, prodded, questioned, shot and reshot his subject; sometimes thirty takes were required to capture Ed in just the right mood. Ed gamely complied, sweating under hot lights, growing accustomed to the spotlight.

In 1987, no longer working for the New Democrats, Larry Wolf recalls his dominant impression of Ed. "I realized he'd been stuck with an unfortunate label. Ed is a social democrat in the Western European tradition. He is *not* a classic socialist — but at the cocktail parties in Rosedale he's a very, very misunderstood guy. The establishment's perception of Ed is fairly primitive and very inaccurate. He's not anti-business. What he is, more than anything, is a Canadian nationalist in the best sense of the word. He's the only one who's been talking sensibly about a Canadian industrial strategy, saying that Canada has to function more like Japan or Sweden or West Germany, which makes a lot of sense. It means more collaboration between business, government and labour, promoting innovation — that's what Ed likes to talk about."

Wolf came to the conclusion that "Ed is a practical, pragmatic guy. He's sensible. I don't agree with his position on free trade, and some of his tax ideas might be a little more aggressive than I might personally like," he smiles, "but even acknowledging that, he'd be good for this country. And I really believe that if he's properly pitched in the next election, he will become the next Prime Minister."

The reason for Ed's popularity is simple, says Wolf. "Leadership is the big thing with voters. You look at the North American crisis in leadership, at the problems with Gary Hart, in Canada you look at Mulroney and Turner, both have serious image problems, serious credibility problems." If Ed doesn't win, says Wolf, it won't be Ed's fault. "It will be a vote against the party."

Back in '79, winning was not the issue. Reviving the party from its disastrous losses in '74 was the major goal. On May 17, 1979, *The Globe and Mail*'s Geoffrey Stevens, then considered the most influential political writer in the country (and now the *Globe*'s managing editor), wrote a long and glowing article about Broadbent's leadership of his first-ever national campaign. Stevens began with a quote from David Lewis: "No leader has done us more proud than Ed Broadbent in this campaign." And this time out it was a very different sort of New Democratic Party effort. No longer the poor cousin hanging around airports waiting for commercial flights while Liberals and Tories hopped on chartered jets, Ed Broadbent, forty-three, had his own jet, accompanying aides and media gaggle, advertising expertise, elegant suits. According to Stevens, it took some getting used to. "Gone are the familiar meetings in drab church basements. . . . Gone are so-earnest little sessions with the 'brothers and sisters' in smoky union halls."

The absence of socialist fundamentalism precipitated the charge that Ed had sold out — and that made him really mad. New Democrats were accustomed to the commie-pinko-red-menace scare tactics that opposition parties had used on them since the '30s, but now Ed was accused of the opposite, and the charge was coming from within his own ranks: that he was just another Liberal in left-wing clothing, threatening to dissolve the socialist core in middle-of-the-road banalities.

Stevens did not seem to buy 'Ed-as-the-Liberal-menace.' He observed that "unlike some New Democrats, [Ed] does not cringe at being called a socialist." Ed insisted that he was staking out "a relevant left" position and denied adamantly, wrote Stevens, "that under his leadership the NDP is burying its radicalism, abandoning the poor, the elderly and the exploited of society . . ."

Yet there could no longer be any doubt about Ed's push into the mainstream. Nor was Ed apologetic about his intentions. His aggressive stance, says Mike Breaugh, was a direct result of being an Oshawa-based politician. "Oshawans don't care about the fine points of ideology, they want you to get things done. Oshawa politics isn't about theory. It's about getting people elected and getting access to the power structure." Ed's hard-nosed constituents provided him with a constant workout that built up his political muscle. Every trip back to Oshawa, walking through a shopping mall or down the main streets, he'd be accosted by locals demanding to know why he hadn't done this or that. "They'd give him shit, first, then they'd praise him," says Breaugh. "They figured he ought to be Prime Minister and if not they wanted to know why not."

Larry Wolf picked up the refrain that was now a swelling chorus around Ed's appearances and turned it into a television scroll that made for an unusual political ad: "A lot of Liberals and Conservatives believe that Ed Broadbent would make the best Prime Minister," ran the words on a silent TV screen. "They say if Ed Broadbent were the leader of their party, he'd win the biggest landslide in Canadian history. People don't have the same nagging kind of doubts about Ed Broadbent as they have about Trudeau or Clark. Maybe it's time to put aside the old Liberal and Conservative myths and simply vote for the best man. If enough people did that, Ed Broadbent would be the next Prime Minister of Canada."

The Liberals, about to lose power, were playing what Christina McCall termed "the politics of desperation" — while John Turner, the former finance minister who had retired to his corporate law practice in Toronto, waited not so quietly in the wings. Having won a majority in '74, no longer dependent on the NDP to drive them forward, the Liberals seemed to have run out of ideas. Nor was Trudeau's '79 campaign brilliantly conceived. Unpopular in English Canada, he was running under a campaign slogan — A Leader Must Be a Leader — that put him front and centre with not much to say. His major goal of patriating the Constitution seemed no closer to being achieved; his wife Margaret, from whom he was separated, was publishing her memoirs to coincide (perhaps accidentally) with the election; her titillating revelations of escapades with rock stars were deeply embarrassing to him. Trudeau was isolated, alienated, corroded by the struggle to hang on to power — even suggesting that perhaps the death penalty should be restored, a notion that would have horrified his younger self. His chief handlers,

Jim Coutts and Keith Davey, struggled to keep their man in line and worried, says McCall, about his latest "display of excessive candour." She adds that a friend of Trudeau's referred to the problems he was having controlling himself as "the moments when he just can't keep the mask in place any more and his soul jumps out and screams."

The silent scream of a bushwhacked politician, too long isolated in the maze of power — this was the distressing reality that Coutts and Davey tried to conceal. But nothing could be done to reverse the Liberals' slide in the polls as Canadians indicated an intention to switch to Joe Clark — not because they liked bumbling, stumbling Joe, who talked like a chipmunk, but because they were sick and tired of Trudeau. It was the same old Liberal–Tory, Tory–Liberal ping-pong game with the NDP dominating issues, outperforming the old-line party leaders, but stuck in the electoral background: going back to 1957, the Diefenbaker Conservatives had won a minority government (twenty-five CCF seats), followed by the Diefenbaker sweep of '58 (eight CCF), another Tory minority in '62 (NDP nineteen), a Liberal minority led by Pearson in '63 (NDP seventeen), another Liberal minority in '65 (NDP twenty-one), the Trudeau sweep of '68 (NDP twenty-two), a Liberal minority in '72 (NDP thirty-one), a Liberal majority in '74 (NDP sixteen), a Conservative minority in the making in '79. Watching this apparently inexorable pattern, Ed became more determined than ever to break new ground.

Once again, in the tradition of Canadian elections, critics saved their highest praise for the NDP leader. On April 5, the *Toronto Star*'s Richard Gwyn compared how the three leaders were functioning on the campaign trail: "Pierre Trudeau is snappish these days, Joe Clark is tense, Ed Broadbent is thoroughly enjoying himself. . . . Broadbent is saying what he wants to say, while Trudeau and Clark are saying what they think they should." Broadbent told Gwyn: "I really do believe we're at a turning point in our history. We have to gain control of ourselves as a people now — be masters in our own house, if you will . . . what I am really trying to do is to kindle hope in the long-term future of this country."

He was getting his message across via ingenious press "events" that were designed for media appeal. "You've got to hand it to Ed Broadbent," wrote the *Star*'s David Blaikie from Saskatoon on April 18. "He's an innovator when it comes to staging election news conferences. The campaign isn't half over yet and about the only place he hasn't held one is the dark side of the moon." The cameras had followed Ed on a tour of Vancouver harbour, down into the bowels of Sydney Steel Mills, through the high-tech control room of a Saskatchewan potash mine. As the *Star*'s Mary Janigan put it, "these days Ed Broadbent doesn't talk about the issues — he visits them." All in the name of making real and tangible his "Gospel of Industrial Strategy."

On May 13, Ed took on Trudeau and Clark in "The Great Debate" and came out smelling of roses. In Janigan's opinion, "viewers saw Broadbent pummelling Clark on national television, Broadbent holding his own against Trudeau, and then Trudeau trouncing Clark." But she observed the deadly trap Trudeau had laid for Ed, trying to "befriend" Ed — leading voters to fear that perhaps Ed would prop up the hated Trudeau in yet another minority government. For the New Democrats, this perception was the kiss of death. Still, Ed was looking good.

"Mr Broadbent has, in my view, consistently outperformed both Mr Trudeau and Mr Clark," wrote the *Globe*'s Geoffrey Stevens on May 17, five days before the election. "He may not be exciting, but he generally makes sense." The largest paper in Canada, the *Toronto Star*, for the first time endorsed Broadbent's New Democrats, which made the party ecstatic. In two separate editorials prior to the election, the *Star* determined that neither the Liberals nor the Tories were addressing the crucial economic issues: "Ed Broadbent has proposed an industrial strategy which puts heavy emphasis on processing Canadian natural resources, identifying key future technologies and on developing Canadian-controlled companies to do the research and come up with the products. He would also introduce planning agreements like those already used in West Germany, Norway, Sweden, France, Holland and Britain. And he would tie tax incentives and grants to targets for jobs, research, exports and investment. . . . In this election, the NDP is the only party that is taking realistic aim at this essential need."

It was beginning to look as if Ed's gamble might work: throughout the campaign, he made it clear that he was seeking to widen the party's appeal. But the risk was enormous: "By pitching their appeal at the disaffected voters in the centre of the political spectrum, and by adopting the marketing techniques of the old parties, they have blurred their image as the only genuinely progressive federal party; they may have disenchanted their traditional supporters without establishing themselves as an acceptable alternative for most voters," wrote Stevens. If this was socialism — which Ed insisted it was, in its modern form — it did indeed alienate the Saskatchewan radicals and was still a long way from attracting mass replacements. Ed did not espouse public ownership as an essential strategy; his words were moderate, his vision pragmatic.

When asked about the possibility of yet another minority government, Ed told all comers he was running to head a government, not prop one up. Yet the invisible wall separating the mass of Canadian voters from the New Democratic Party was still intact, despite his best efforts. Liberal–Tory ping-pong, it seemed, would cease only when traditional voting patterns dissolved with the maturing of the baby boomers — unless the old-line parties got to the new generation first.

BREAKTHROUGH ELUDES ED, ran the *Toronto Star* headline. On May 22, 1979, Joe Clark's Tories won a minority with 136 seats, though they received fewer votes than the Liberals, who came second with 114 seats. The New Democrats were third with twenty-six — up ten — and the Social Credit party hung on to six seats. Ed had cast a wider net but he'd caught only 18 per cent of the electorate — up from 15 per cent in 1974 but still far from his rivals: the Tories won 36 per cent, the Liberals 40 per cent of the popular vote. Ed felt — temporarily — crushed.

In the early morning hours of election night, Ed met reporters in an upstairs room at the United Auto Workers hall in Oshawa. It was 2 A.M. Ed was "worn out and didn't want to say much," wrote the *Star*'s David Blaikie. But Ed managed a few lines: "We fought this election on issues that I considered to be of great importance to the people of Canada. . . ." Asked how the NDP planned to play its cards against the new Tory minority government, he didn't answer: "He simply disappeared into the night, grateful to be led away by his wife Lucille and party aides. He added nothing for reporters who pursued him as he went, down a fire escape and into a waiting car." After riding so high, having let his hopes soar, Ed's encounter with reality was painfully disappointing — though he would not long remember it. For most New Democrats, the election results represented a crucial recovery. The NDP had attracted more than two million voters, and in less than a year it would inch further into the mainstream. Things were not so bad. And the NDP's rivals were in trouble.

The Tories, out of power since Diefenbaker was defeated in '63, were determined to act as if they had a majority — but they were faced with a serious problem. Joe Clark's Conservatives "were skilled in the politics of the Opposition, but were untutored in the defensive compromises of power," wrote Jeffrey Simpson in *Discipline of Power*. "Repeated electoral defeat engenders an almost desperate desire to develop policies in order to answer every question and so persuade the electorate that the Opposition party is ready to govern. . . . Once in power, the civil service and interest groups start telling the party its policies are wrong. What was so pristine in Opposition becomes clouded by power."

While the Iranian revolution precipitated another round of oil price shocks, Clark's newly elected government spent the summer "feeling for the levers of power," in Desmond Morton's phrase. "Interest rates began to soar. Financiers belatedly condemned the more profligate of Clark's election promises. Alberta's Peter Lougheed proved as intransigent on oil revenues to a fellow Tory as he had been to the Liberals. When Clark made concessions to Alberta, he outraged an equally Tory government in Ontario. Within weeks, the new government's honeymoon was over; by September polls showed Clark lagging far behind the Liberals." But the Liberals, stunned by defeat, unaccustomed to being in opposition, were strangely subdued. Even the most partisan of Liberals, Keith Davey, acknowledged that the official opposition "was laid-back, if not lacklustre." At a convention in Toronto in the fall, wrote Davey, "the party, collectively and individually, was hurting and angry at itself and Pierre Trudeau."

Joe Clark continued to stumble. He had been propelled into the Prime Minister's office not so much because voters were attracted to his policies but because they were disenchanted by Trudeau. Clark's early moves were unpopular, particularly his proposal to sell Petro-Canada — a sale Ed repeatedly stated he would not accept. Not for nothing had the New Democrats put themselves on the line in 1973, threatening to pull the plug on Trudeau's minority government unless it created a national petroleum company. As one of the players in that deal, Ed was determined to save Petro-Canada; Joe Clark, unlike Trudeau, did not appreciate the depths of Ed's commitment — or Ed's capacity to go in for the kill.

CHAPTER SEVEN

Walking through Fire: The Constitutional Wars

From 1980 to 1984, Ed walked through fire, and he came out stronger and wiser. When you go through the dark side, the way he did, you come out of it tough — or you're finished.

Terry Grier.

$\mathbf{E}$d Broadbent's push to topple the faltering Conservative government signalled to the world that the New Democratic Party leader had taken off the gloves. Ed's adrenalin was triggered by the downward slide of Joe Clark's minority government, elected on May 22, 1979. The Tories' muddle was complemented, in Ed's eyes, by the Liberals' disarray. Ed smelled blood.

On November 21, 1979, Ed was attending the NDP's national convention in Toronto when he found out that Trudeau had just announced his retirement. Not wasting a day, Ed hastily called a meeting in his Sheraton hotel room. "He said to come up to his room for a drink," says a staff member. "I asked him what he wanted to talk about. He was very indirect. When I got there, he had assembled about twenty people, plucked them away from the convention, all his key people." Terry Grier, chairman of the election planning committee, was among the group and made a list of attendees: "Ed; Robin Sears, federal secretary; Mary Ellen McQuay, assistant federal secretary; Marc Eliesen, research director; Jo-Anne McNevin, national organizer; Dick Proctor, principal secretary; Peter O'Malley, press secretary; and organizers Penny Dickens (Toronto), Joyce Nash (British Columbia) and Cliff Scotton (former federal secretary)."

Ed "schmoozed around" and then he dropped his bombshell. Grier's notes record, in capital letters, one statement by Ed: "LET'S GO NOW." Ed told his people that "it would be prudent to prepare for the collapse of the government," says a staff member. "He wanted to know how long it would take us to get ready for another election. Well. You could have heard a pin drop. There was total stunned silence. Not even remarks like, 'Gee Ed, I wasn't thinking that way myself.' We were broke, we didn't have a pot to piss in, we were exhausted, we were heading into winter . . ."

Terry Grier says: "The weight of opinion in that room was strongly against an early election. I said I thought the Liberals would gain in Ontario and that we'd gain only marginally in the split. I am struck now by my perspicacity. I also said we should not rule out Trudeau staying to lead the Liberals through another election. I'm giving myself A-plus for that one. But I definitely thought another election right away was not a good idea."

New Democrats were still rejoicing from the '79 campaign, though Ed had been disappointed by the outcome. He thought he'd win forty to fifty seats — even sixty seats, the target he'd announced in the mid-'70s. Still, the party had risen from sixteen to twenty-six MPs, "we felt we'd done a good job and we were glad it was over," says Sears. Yet after the November 21 meeting, he wound up on Ed's side, with a great deal of ambivalence: "We all had dreams the Clark government would come tumbling down, but nobody seriously anticipated the Tories would screw up relations with the Créditistes." It was a volatile situation: the minority government was unstable, the Prime Minister unable to manoeuvre in choppy waters. "Clark was a nerd," says Sears, "and the Liberals were rudderless. With or without Trudeau, they were not functioning at all in the fall of '79 — except for Allan MacEachen, who was a formidable figure."

It was Ed who first spotted the opportunity, Ed who was eager to topple the house of cards. "I could see it," says Sears. "I was amazed. Ed really believed the Liberals were on the run, he thought Clark would self-destruct, and he saw an opportunity for the party to make a breakthrough."

At times like these, argues Gerry Caplan, leaders must be restrained. "This is a characteristic of all leaders: they have no political judgement. They cannot be detached because they're so deeply enmeshed in their cocoon. All leaders believe they represent a whole lot of people, that they know what people want. But they *can't* know what's happening in the real world — that's why they have to rely on their advisers." Robin Sears takes a different tack. "Fundamentally, my conviction is the opposite of Caplan's," says Sears. "You tell the leader it's crazy. You try your best arguments. But if he's still determined, you back him or you quit. Period. You cannot gainsay the leader's decision on the battlefield."

In this instance, Ed's aides succumbed to the force of his dominant will. He miscalculated in terms of the breakthrough, but that is his nature — to seek it, like a camel rider driven further by a mirage in the desert. Even if the oasis isn't there, the vision gets him through. "I believed the breakthrough was out there, absolutely, and I still do," says Ed. "It's a quirk of mine, I suppose. When I go into a situation, I don't like to go in with illusions. I'm optimistic, but I want all the facts. Then, when I've made a decision, I go full force. If the outcome is negative, I get out fast. I forget it, almost literally. I repress bad news. I put it behind me. I move on." Does he remember his disappointment in '79 or '80? "No, I honestly don't." Did he really make an effort to "get all the facts"? He shrugs; he thinks he did. But then, so much of political life is based on instinct — and in '79, after eleven years in the House of Commons, facing two weak political parties, his instincts were howling. He didn't want to give the Liberals time to elect a new leader, and he didn't want to give the Tories time to consolidate their hold on power.

Terry Grier remembers that after the November 21 gathering in Ed's Toronto hotel room, there was no follow-up meeting, just an inexorable sense that something was about to happen — something being driven largely by Ed. Grier, as close as he was to Ed, was in the dark. "There were never any long, thoughtful discussions," says Grier. In hindsight, he realized that "Ed had come to a conclusion and acted upon it in a very short period of time. I was caught off base. I was close to the centre, but I didn't know what Ed was thinking. There were no telephone conversations between the two of us. If we had talked about it, I would have tried to dissuade him. I would have contended that the perceived breakthrough was not about to occur." And that's probably why Ed didn't talk to Grier. "When Ed has made up his mind, he is one stubborn bastard," says a former aide.

By the end of November, Ed's enthusiasm for the task at hand was apparent. "Broadbent's personality change" was noted by Richard Gwyn. "These days, Broadbent almost literally bounces around in high spirits as he goes about calling the NDP 'the true Opposition,' or 'the only real alternative.' " Ed attracted 1,400 delegates — the largest number ever — to a policy convention where TV cameras captured a popular NDP slogan: "Save Petro-Canada; Sell Clark." Ed was in fighting form, his audience moved to rapturous applause at his aggressive stance against Clark and Trudeau. In the House of Commons, he was forever on the attack, aided and abetted by Bob Rae's stinging performance as finance critic. "Zapping the banks and oil corporations," in Gwyn's words, Rae was "a Robin to Broadbent's Batman." The NDP caucus, Gwyn concluded, had "out-talked, out-worked and out-manoeuvred the Liberals."

On December 11, 1979, the Conservatives brought down their ill-fated budget, notable for an additional 18-cent-a-gallon excise tax on gasoline that turned into the kiss of death. Finance minister John Crosbie talked about "short-term pain for long-term gain," while the opposition parties rose up in outrage. Still, the Tories weren't wor-

Maclean's / Michael Sturdy

Broadbent with former mentors, David Lewis (left) and Tommy Douglas (right).

Toronto Sun, UPI

Ed clowning around on Parliament Hill.

Ed and Lucille with daughter, Christine, and son, Paul, in 1977.

Ed, Lucille and Christine skating on the Rideau Canal.

Gail Harvey

Ed and Lucille with Percy and Mary Broadbent.

Oshawa/Whitby This Week/Walter Passarella

Ed riding to work on Parliament Hill.

*Ed with Bob White,
president of the
Canadian Auto
Workers.*

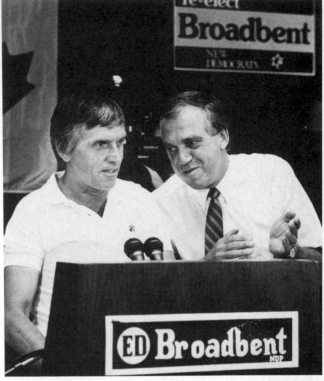

Oshawa/Whitby This Week/Walter Passarella

*Ed and Lucille at a
media event: a dog-
sled ride in the
Northwest
Territories.*

Gail Harvey

*Ed on the campaign
trail, 1979.*

*Ed on the campaign
trail, 1979.*

*With principal secretary
George Nakitsas (left), executive
assistant Anne Carroll and
federal secretary Bill Knight.*

Mary Broadbent.

ried; they figured the Liberals and New Democrats were playing chicken.

On Wednesday, December 12, at the Liberal caucus Christmas party, Trudeau, who had already announced his retirement, was given a symbolic Christmas gift: a chainsaw "to cut down the government," according to the official presenter. The Liberals were prepared to vote against Crosbie's budget, MacEachen having agreed to a text Ed had shown him outlining the NDP's objections. They were playing with fire — but still nobody quite believed that what was going to happen would happen.

The day "it" happened — Thursday, December 13, 1979 — Clark's legislative assistant, Nancy Jamieson, told the Prime Minister his government would be defeated that night. He asked why. "Because we don't have the numbers," she said. Everybody knew he didn't have the numbers. The standings were still the same: 136 Tories, 114 Liberals, twenty-six New Democrats, and six Créditistes, whose support Clark had not secured. Still no one believed it was coming. "To this day," says Sears, "I don't know how the Tories could have let it happen. It's a puzzle. There was a deal to be done between the Tories and the Créditistes . . ." He shakes his head.

That afternoon, Terry Grier landed at the Ottawa airport, arriving for a routine election planning meeting the next day. He was met by Jo-Anne McNevin and Mary Ellen McQuay, which was unusual. Right away he realized something momentous was going on. "They had stricken looks on their faces. 'You've got to do something,' they said. 'They're going to pull the plug tonight.'" Grier was agitated. "I went straight to the Hill and met with Ed. I ranted about 'are we out of our minds?' but eventually — I'm a realist — I saw from his response that the die had been cast."

That night in the House of Commons, NDP MP Bob Rae moved the New Democrats' amendment to the Liberals' non-confidence motion, and the government lost by a margin of six votes. After the vote, Bob Rae stepped into the elevator with Liberal MP Marc Lalonde, who said to Rae: "Is this really happening?" Rae said yes. Lalonde asked why. Rae said, "Read Barbara Tuchman's book, *The Guns of August.* Archduke Ferdinand has just been shot."

In *The Rainmaker*, Keith Davey recalled leaving the House after the vote. "The first person I bumped into on my way out was Jeffrey Simpson of *The Globe and Mail* who said, 'You guys have just made the biggest mistake of your life.'" Davey added: "So much for punditry."

The government fell, and the next day, Grier's routine election planning committee meeting turned into a two-day marathon, kicking off preparations for an election on February 18, 1980. Sears went out and borrowed $1 million from a bank and received a lesson in the workings of capitalism. "We got the money at prime rate plus one-quarter of a point," says Sears, "and I had a fascinating talk with the bank manager about how he charged the highest interest to people who could afford it the least, and charged the least to those who could afford it the most."

Though Sears and Grier leaped into the fray, they were nervous. As Sears puts it, "I'm very conservative about election planning. We had campaign debts left over from '79, we owed money to Larry Wolf, we had people to train — and I don't like going into elections unprepared."

Ed, however, was elated, though he wasn't prepared for the Liberals' game plan. "We didn't know Coutts and Davey would be so successful in positioning Trudeau to the left, in a strong nationalist position," says Sears. Was Ed shocked at the sudden revival of the Liberals, whom he thought to be expiring? "No," says Sears. "He was calm. He wasn't rattled. And the '80 campaign, much to our surprise, went magnificently. We had nightmares of being snowbound but except for a couple of occasions when our DC-9 was stuck in snowdrifts, we were fine." This time out, their man was a household name and more popular than either of his two adversaries.

Larry Wolf was back in action, in charge of the New Democrats' advertising. He devised a clever newspaper ad, in the form of a quiz. It won a prestigious copywriting award and appears in the glossy 1986 annual awards edition of *Studio* magazine, which is crammed with award-winning work by the likes of photographer Annie Leibovitz (who shot Whoopi Goldberg dunking in a bathtub filled with milk), promoting Macintosh computers, Kraft Miracle Whip, furniture, fashion, autos. Suddenly, in the midst of its art-filled pages, a bold, black-and-white headline jumps out: FIND OUT IF YOU'RE A CONSERVATIVE, LIBERAL OR NEW DEMOCRAT. There follows a series of questions on oil prices, Petro-Canada, energy development, unemployment, inflation, medicare, pensions, taxes, small business, mortgages and foreign policy. One sample:

Canadian Resources.

A. We can create jobs by processing Canadian resources into finished products here at home instead of exporting them to other countries.

B. We need to give foreign investors more tax and profit incentives to help us develop our Canadian resources.

C. The best way to maintain our standard of living is to increase the export of our natural resources.

(Turning the page upside down, one discovers that A is the New Democratic position, B is Liberal, C is Conservative.) Testing the quiz on friends, Wolf was amused to observe that "they'd complete the questions and turn upside down for the answer — only to find out to their horror that they were closet New Democrats." Which happily reinforced Ed's fundamental conviction: that his task was to make conscious the social democratic conscience which animated the Canadian spirit.

The strategy of focussing on Ed was repeated for the 1980 election. Larry Wolf was delighted to see that the Liberal and Tory campaigns were based on attacking each other's leader. In *Discipline of Power*, Jeffrey Simpson quotes one of Wolf's statements to NDP staff during the '80 campaign. "Our strategy is really very simple," said Wolf. "The other two parties are hiding their leaders. We're putting ours up front. If you look at the Conservative and Liberal campaigns, it's the only advertising I've ever seen in the history of modern politics where the total focus of the advertising is on what's wrong with the other guy.

"Look at the Liberal commercials, and the subject is Clark. When you look at the Conservative commercials, the subject is Trudeau. That's really an ass-backwards way to advertise. We're proud of our leader. We think he has something to say. He's a positive, rather than a negative option. We feel he's the best of three choices, rather than the worst of three evils."

"Our strategy was obvious," Keith Davey wrote about the Liberals' game plan. "We had to spotlight Joe Clark throughout the entire campaign. Canadians had soured on Prime Minister Clark and our task was simply to reinforce that negative image. However, it was equally clear that this was not the campaign where our leader should be in the front of the window."

While the Liberals and Tories bashed each other, it was Ed Broadbent who again received glowing reviews. On February 13, 1980, *The Globe and Mail* published a long article by Geoffrey Stevens, outlining what he saw as the "three pivotal events in the brief history of the New Democratic Party. The first, obviously, was the founding convention in 1961, when Canada's social democrats closed the books on the Depression-born CCF. . . . The second was the Election Expenses Act which, coming into force just after the 1974 general election, vaulted the NDP into the same financial league as the Liberals and Progressive Conservatives. . . . The third pivotal event was the election of Ed Broadbent as [leader] . . ." In Stevens' view, Ed had "completed the process, begun in 1961, of converting a protest movement into a mainline bourgeois political party, a labour-based party which can vote to break a strike of west-coast grain handlers, a non-militaristic party which can contemplate with equanimity increased defence spending, a reform party which can envisage governing without performing radical surgery on existing social and economic institutions."

One can hear the Saskatchewan radicals' outcries of betrayal, though Stevens defended Ed against such attacks. "This is not to accuse the NDP of having lost its old distinctiveness," he wrote. "There is no surer way, in fact, to goad Mr Broadbent into anger than to suggest his party has become indistinguishable from the Grits and Tories." Indeed, like Ed himself, Stevens figured "this could be the NDP's election, the election that finally produces fifty or sixty NDP seats."

It wasn't; it didn't. The system, from Ed's point of view, was still constipated. The outcome exacerbated the regional divisions that have always plagued Canadian politics. Trudeau won a majority of 147 seats, with not a single Liberal MP west of Winnipeg; Clark's Tories slipped to 103 seats, winning only one in Quebec. Though the New Democrats' position improved somewhat — they attracted almost 20 per cent of the popular vote and gained six MPs, winning a total of thirty-two seats, the highest number ever — it was not the breakthrough Ed was looking for.

Sears remembers election night in Oshawa, sitting with Ed and his family and friends, watching the returns come in. Ed's initial disappointment was lifted by the emotional support he received — with an assist from a box of fancy Cuban cigars Sears gave him — and he quickly "repressed the bad news." The party had picked up an additional nine seats in the west, it had stalled in Ontario, and gone nowhere in Quebec, though its vote had doubled from 5 to 10 per cent in that province. Of the thirty-two-member caucus, twenty-seven came from its traditional western power base; this would spell trouble for the leader from Ontario, who had failed to make gains in his own province. The party had dropped from six Ontario seats in '79 to five in '80.

Within a week of the election, Ed had one of the biggest surprises of his life: invited to meet privately with the Prime Minister, Broadbent was the startled recipient of an offer to become a Cabinet minister. Ed remembers the occasion well. "Trudeau asked if I'd be interested, personally, in coming into his Cabinet. I thought, 'You've got to be kidding,' So I said, jokingly, 'Let's see, I'll take five or six Cabinet portfolios.' Trudeau said, "You've got them.' Suddenly I realized he was serious."

According to Tom Axworthy, then Trudeau's principal secretary, the Prime Minister "wrestled in his soul when he came back [into power] in 1980. We knew what we wanted to do on energy and the Constitution, but however handsome our victory, we had so few western members — just Lloyd [Axworthy, Tom's brother] — that for the sake of moral legitimacy we needed real representation in the west. Trudeau's offer to Broadbent was made with the highest of purposes."

Trudeau held out a tantalizing lure: a vague but sweeping plan for patriating Canada's energy sector that reflected NDP planks on resource development — of all issues the one closest to Ed's heart. Trudeau could not have picked sweeter bait. "He talked about the expansion of Petro-Canada and what became the National Energy Program, which would have a major impact on the west, and it was obvious why he wanted us on side," says Ed.

Trudeau envisaged the New Democrats functioning as ground troops in the west, selling energy policies the NDP had long advocated; indeed, Axworthy believes the Liberals "were bringing in a more radical energy program than anything the NDP would have ever done." The only trouble was, Ed wouldn't accept the offer, and he didn't agonize for long about the decision. "It made no sense for us in terms of power relations," says Ed. "If we differed, we'd be out. They had the majority. They didn't need us in terms of numbers. Accepting Cabinet posts under those circumstances presented no long-term advantage to the party."

Ed told Bob Rae about Trudeau's offer of Cabinet seats "in the washroom of the Primrose Club at my wedding," says Rae. It was five days after the election, on February 23, that Rae married Arlene Perly in Toronto. At the reception afterwards at the Primrose Club, "Ed discussed the situation with me, but he clearly hadn't weighed the idea very seriously, though he'd canvassed a few people, he'd talked to Blakeney about it. But it was never formally discussed in caucus." Senior New Democrats had dismissed Trudeau's initiative as dangerous to the party. "Trudeau and Coutts had always wanted to co-opt the NDP — and wipe us out," says Rae. "It was an old left-Liberal strategy. It was never on." Axworthy insists that Trudeau's offer was sincere. "We knew the reaction in our own party would be bad — suggesting that we take the dreaded socialists into Cabinet — but if Broadbent had shown some interest, we would have had wider consultations to work out the details. We were prepared to do it."

The Liberals' need was great; ultimately, the lack of NDP support for the National Energy Program, introduced in 1980, combined with the Liberals' weakness in the west, contributed to the NEP's downfall, says Axworthy. "Broadbent's support for us on the Constitution was crucial. But the NDP was mute on the energy program. They never did much to help us when the Americans, the multinationals and the Conservatives attacked us. The oil companies used regional discontent for their own corporate interests, and the NDP took a pass. Ed got burned on the Constitution, and I guess he wasn't prepared to fight Trudeau's battles in the west on another issue."

Political economist Stephen Clarkson says that "Ed made a big mistake not accepting Trudeau's offer. Trudeau gave him a chance to implant himself and his party at a more credible level." Clarkson, who is co-writing with Christina McCall a book on the end of the Trudeau era, figures the NDP's refusal to entertain the idea of a coalition was based on "a paranoid response" that was inappropriate to the times. With a handful of NDP Cabinet ministers, says Clarkson, Ed could have changed the course of Canadian political history, had a direct influence on the development of energy policy and, at the same time, taken credit for delivering to western Canada the control over resources which was so important to Allan Blakeney — which Clarkson thinks could have gone a long way to resolving Broadbent's battles with the Saskatchewan premier. But Clarkson underestimates the deep-rooted hostility of western New Democrats to Trudeau's Liberals. At that time, in those circumstances, a coalition wasn't in the cards.

Trudeau's other reason for wanting the New Democrats on side was that he had decided to go for broke on the Constitution. On May 20, 1980, three months after the federal election, the Quebec Referendum was held. The Québecois voted "no" to Premier René Lévesque's carefully worded appeal for support for sovereignty-association; in a sixty–forty split, the majority heeded Trudeau's promise to bring Quebec into a made-in-Canada Constitution that would forever protect the rights of French-Canadians. Separatism was officially dead — but not for long.

"Throughout this period, the Canadian people heard and read largely about an arid wrangle over abstract notions that few understood," wrote Robert Sheppard and Michael Valpy in their book, *The National Deal: The Fight for a Canadian Constitution.* They had covered the fight for *The Globe and Mail,* and in their book they uncovered the story that had never before made it into print. "It was not a juiceless wrangle at all; it was a great and absorbing human drama. . . . It dominated the agenda of every government from sea to sea. It mesmerized the press, touched every major institution in the country — the church, the courts, academia, the legal and business communities. It drew in Canada's ethnic communities, women's groups, aboriginal peoples, and inflamed — almost intolerably at times — the country's twin political crises of the 1970s and '80s: Quebec nationalism and western alienation. One political party, the NDP, was fractured by the issue, the wound still unmended. The Liberals were gravely crippled. . . . Federal Conservatives were pitted against their powerful blood relatives in Ontario. Political friendships were destroyed. . . ." And, they do not mention, the battle nearly finished off Ed Broadbent. "It was war," says Robin Sears. "A bitter civil war. The '80 to '81 period was the worst political experience of my life. It was as nasty and difficult and painful as it comes in this world short of violence — and I mean that."

"The background to the constitutional fight is important," says Bob Rae. "The party was not in good spirits, facing another four years of Trudeau. We were in an awfully tough position. We had been able to slam the Tories over their plans to dismantle Petro-Canada, but now we were up against Lalonde and MacEachen who were busy expanding Petro-Canada." Once again, New Democrats felt the Liberals were speeding ahead on an NDP agenda, and New Democrats were caught in a double bind: did they praise the Liberals for advancing NDP policy, or did they attack them for not doing it properly?

By September, Bob Rae realized a similar dilemma was arising over the Constitution. He was one of the first New Democrats to perceive the danger. "We didn't yet know what Trudeau was going to do, but I said that we'd have to be very careful about attacking a Constitution proposal that was in line with our own policies and was positively viewed by the public." Patriation was popular in Rae's downtown Toronto riding and in similar Central Canadian constituencies that had a high percentage of immigrant and non-WASP citizens, who also tended to support Trudeau. But the country was, as usual, split. In western Canada, antipathy to Trudeau was so great that, as Rae puts it, "westerners felt that if Trudeau wanted something, they wouldn't touch it. Period."

On September 7, 1980, Governor-General Ed Schreyer hosted a working dinner for Prime Minister Trudeau, the ten provincial premiers and their chosen ministers. It had taken fifty-three years of aborted constitutional negotiations to reach this point. "The prime objective," wrote Sheppard and Valpy, was to end the "legal absurdity" that required Canada, "a full-fledged nation — to trudge off to the former colonial power in Britain whenever it wants its constitution amended. No other autonomous state in the world has this problem."

Trudeau was determined to make the breakthrough that had eluded him for more than a decade. The singular driving force of his political career, in Sheppard and Valpy's assessment, was "to bind his people, francophone Canadians, to the rest of the country. . . . He came to

244   ED BROADBENT: THE PURSUIT OF POWER

establish a beachhead in English Canada for the notion that the French minority should have the fundamental right to use its language, to *live* in its language, in every part of Canada. 'You have to give me language. It's my existence,' he told Bill Bennett near the end . . ."

But Trudeau's vision of a bilingual Canada was at odds with the evolving character of the Québecois nation, led by his great opponent René Lévesque, Premier of Quebec. Defeated in the Referendum, caught in a constitutional process in which he did not believe, Lévesque arrived at Schreyer's dinner feeling edgy, out-of-place. He was not alone, however, in his dislike for the Prime Minister. The three western Tory premiers were united by their animosity toward Trudeau and their suspicion of Ontario Premier Bill Davis, who would side with Trudeau. British Columbia's Bill Bennett, Alberta's Peter Lougheed, Manitoba's Sterling Lyon were not in a conciliatory mood. Newfoundland's testy Brian Peckford, another Tory, attacked Trudeau's "socialist tendencies." Saskatchewan's NDP Premier Allan Blakeney, the enemy Trudeau alternately feared and courted with the greatest conviction, held aloof. By the time Blakeney's fifty-fifth birthday cake was ceremonially served, the party mood was demolished. "There is no mood for consensus. . . . Co-operative federalism is as dead as Pearson," wrote Sheppard and Valpy. Trudeau, not bothering to hide his disdain, "with the histrionic gesture of a man overwhelmed by ridiculousness, lays his head down on the table like some forlorn Buddha." Then he left, prematurely early, rudely. As he exited, his RCMP bodyguard leaped up to follow. The Prime Minister was overhead saying to the Mountie: "Fuck off, and don't follow me home." OVERHEARD

Meanwhile, back at Ed's office on Parliament Hill, the New Democratic leader had been engrossed in talking and thinking about the Constitution for many months. The party's position was clear — though many activists felt "we hadn't done our homework, we weren't prepared, it wasn't our issue," according to Tony Penikett, party president from 1981 to 1985. Patriation, a made-in-Canada Constitution, a Charter of Rights — these were

NDP planks, laid down by the party's pioneers in the 1933 Regina Manifesto and in the NDP's 1961 founding statement; but, Penikett would argue, the party had never properly debated constitutional issues. If it had, it would have stumbled upon the reasons for Blakeney's opposition to the Charter of Rights, and open warfare could have perhaps been averted. But hindsight makes obvious what wasn't at the time.

"The NDP decision seemed easy," wrote Desmond Morton. "Summer caucus sessions had explored innumerable scenarios and given Broadbent a mandate to support Trudeau if he acted." Trudeau acted. For Ed, the fateful day was October 1, when he had a long, private talk with the Prime Minister. The two men had a very ambivalent relationship, "a very competitive relationship," says Sears, though "they both respected each other's concern about the greater philosophical issues. They could speak to each other on an intellectual, non-partisan level." Yet it was, for Trudeau, an uncomfortable situation. "He *needed* Ed more than he needed anyone else to make it happen," says Sears. If Ed was ever looking to hurt Trudeau — already so politically isolated — this was his chance. It was also a golden opportunity to score points among western Trudeau-haters. But Ed didn't take it.

With reservations, seeking certain key amendments, Ed gave Trudeau his commitment. He believed he was doing the right thing. What he didn't do, however, was leave Trudeau on hold at the last minute in order to consult his advisers and provincial NDP leaders — which later came to be seen as his major sin. "He should have said, 'Thank you very much, I will take this under consideration and get back to you,'" says a former aide. "Because he didn't, he screwed up." Another insider observes: "Ed failed to massage the party's egos at the critical moment. He forgot about playing politics. And for that he got the shit kicked out of him."

Publicly, on the night of October 2, Trudeau appeared on national television and announced that he was proceeding unilaterally — that is, alone, without the support of provincial governments — to create a Canadian

Constitution. Tory leader Joe Clark came on next, a stern opponent, leading the fight against Trudeau's "divisive" and "damaging" move. Finally, Ed Broadbent appeared and said that he and his party in general supported patriation, with certain reservations that included the need to ensure provincial control over resources — which New Democrats would fight for. Ed was delivering a party position that, says Robin Sears, "was laboured over through the spring of 1980 and represented the best collective wisdom we could come up with." Peter O'Malley believes Ed took the high road — and that he was right. "By supporting Trudeau up front, Ed had power and influence on the process — unlike Joe Clark, who opposed Trudeau from the outset and had no input," says O'Malley. "The Tories contributed nothing to the constitutional process."

Still, Allan Blakeney believes that "Trudeau's high-noon tactics were outrageous. He thought unilateral patriation was the only way to unblock the logjam. I was disappointed that Ed Broadbent supported him. And Ed knew our position — but so be it. We worked with Ed right to the end." Bill Knight, then Blakeney's principal secretary, says the root of Blakeney's opposition was economic. It was about money and power and resources. "The shift came in the early '70s," says Knight, "when the price of oil started to go up." Thanks to OPEC, a barrel of crude rose from $2.50 in 1970 to a high of $35 in 1981. The price shocks stunned the industrialized world, fuelled the recession and rained windfall profits on oil companies and western Canada, where the tar sands and even the Beaufort Sea in the Arctic became economically attractive. Suddenly, Alberta and Saskatchewan were getting rich. Lougheed and Blakeney were using their new-found resource wealth to diversify the economy and pay for social programs. "Within a decade," says Knight, "the resource sector was providing 50 per cent of our revenues, which we were plowing back into the health care system and into our economic programs and reforms. Then we ran head on into the feds in a battle over price and control."

At the height of the boom, the Liberals moved to secure Canadian energy supplies, aiming for self-sufficiency by 1990 and 50 per cent Canadian ownership of a sector dominated by foreign companies. But the view from the west was stormy. The National Energy Program was seen as yet another unilateral move by Central Canada to bleed the west of its wealth. The Liberals were squeezed. Hammering them from the south were the American oil companies and the u.s. State Department. Alexander Haig, then secretary of state, actually threatened retaliation against Canada for attempting to control its own energy supplies. And caught in the middle was Ed Broadbent, watching the energy battle rage while his hands were full of constitutional resolutions, his western-dominated caucus growing increasingly restive.

Blakeney, determined to maintain control over his province's own resource revenues, launched an all-out attack on the Constitution. Much of his ire was directed against a Charter of Rights that would, in effect, give more power to an appointed judiciary and reduce the power of elected politicians. In other words, he trusted politicians more than judges. It was on this issue that Stephen Lewis and his father David Lewis had their first major political dispute: Stephen agreed with Blakeney, David supported Ed, as did Tommy Douglas and Stanley Knowles.

The fight between the pro-Charter and anti-Charter groups was, in Robin Sears's opinion, "unsolveable. It was about different visions of the world. There was no way that we could have found common ground — and god knows we tried. We might only have hurt each other less."

"Those who argued against an entrenched charter," wrote Sheppard and Valpy, "said it would only benefit lawyers and would create unnecessary litigation, most probably by the better organized and wealthier lobby groups, who could afford expensive court battles. . . . As Douglas Schmeiser, a former dean of constitutional law at the University of Saskatchewan put it, 'It is a worrying prospect that five old men, a bare majority on

the Supreme Court, could rule on the great social and political issues of the nation contrary to and regardless of
the wishes of the populace.'" In its favour, a Charter of
Rights protects citizens against the excesses of unruly political or police regimes, asserting fundamental democratic principles: "freedom of belief, expression and
association, the right to a fair trial and legal procedures,
and guarantees against discrimination based on race, religion, sex and ethnic or national origin, as well as the
right to learn and use either of the two official languages." Some of these were, of course, the very rights
that Trudeau had suspended when he imposed the War
Measures Act in 1970.

The key question for Ed is a strategic one: Did he come
on side with Trudeau too soon? He does not hesitate. "It
was essential to break the deadlock," says Ed, reiterating
that constitutional debate had already consumed more
than half a century. "If I hadn't, we would not have a
Constitution today. We had talked in caucus about what
should be in the package, we acted consistently with caucus decisions and party positions; the amending formula
had been previously agreed to by all the provinces. . . . I
knew a difficult period would unfold; I knew it would
produce conflict; what I didn't know was how intense it
would get. But there's a time for leadership that involves
risk-taking."

Ed was dead wrong about the degree of support he
thought he had. Norm Simon, who would arrive in the
middle of the constitutional brouhaha to become chief-of-
staff, remembers Ed phoning him the day of his fateful
meeting with Trudeau. "He said he was happy with the
package and that he'd endorsed it in principle. I asked
him how his folks felt. He said, 'I've talked to them and
everything's fine.'" This was, perhaps, the boundlessly
optimistic Ed speaking, not the rational skeptic.

Still, Ed is absolutely firm on this issue: "I had the
mandate from the party, I believed I was speaking for
Canada and for the party." Sheppard and Valpy support
his contention. Though they question the motives of
Clark and the strategy of Trudeau, they determined that,

"Alone of the three national party leaders, the NDP leader took his position on the Constitution with no secondary agenda tucked in his back pocket." Ed expected his colleagues to do likewise.

He was appalled by the back-room manoeuvring of November 5, 1981 — the so-called "night of the long knives" — when a deal was struck among Canada's English-speaking premiers while Lévesque slept. Lévesque had left the meeting early the previous evening; having heard nothing from the premiers, he went to bed at one o'clock in the morning. At breakfast the following day, Peckford handed Lévesque "a final proposition." Lévesque wrote: "They had taken advantage of our absence to eliminate the most crucial of our demands. . . . It was the stab in the dark." Consumed with outrage, Lévesque went home. Quebec had been excluded from the Constitution that was supposedly being remade for the benefit of the Québecois. "I couldn't find words strong enough," wrote Lévesque, "to express my burning resentment."

The winter of '80–'81 through to debates in the House of Commons in January '82, where physical threats and fist fights were not unheard of, was the worst of times. "It was devastating," says Svend Robinson, the NDP justice critic from Burnaby, B.C. Bilingual, with a law degree from the University of British Columbia and postgraduate studies at the London School of Economics, Robinson sat on the historic Special Joint Committee on the Constitution of Canada. Robinson worked long and hard to strengthen the Charter of Rights. He, too, felt shattered by the events of November 5, 1981. He found out that not only was Quebec absent from the deal, but that the premiers were "selling out" native rights and women's equality; they had introduced the "notwithstanding clause," an escape hatch which allowed anything in the Charter to be overridden. Robinson came out of a meeting, met by the glare of TV cameras, and said he couldn't support the deal. "The price paid was too high," he says.

For Ed, the situation was constantly changing, as clauses were added and dropped, as battle lines formed and broke and reformed. He was at once on the offensive, pushing for improvements, and on the defensive, protecting his hide. Lorne Nystrom, who led the anti-Broadbent Gang of Four (NDP MPs Simon de Jong, Doug Anguish, Stan Hovdebo and himself), remembers "many, many conversations with Ed, at caucus, *ad nauseam*, week after week, one crisis after another." In Nystrom's view, as in Blakeney's, Ed had been partially blinded by his Ontario bias and failed to appreciate that the western point of view did not coincide with Central Canada's. "It sounded good to Ed, Ontario had a veto, but the other provinces weren't treated equally," says Nystrom. Simon de Jong, a former president of the Saskatchewan CCF youth, thought Ed was "too uptight, too cerebral." De Jong wanted a more flexible, futuristic approach that included the right to clean air, clean water, education, jobs. And on it went. Anne Carroll, Ed's executive assistant, would be calling MPs at 7 A.M. while they were still at home in the shower, telling them to arrive on the Hill for emergency meetings. Nelson Riis, first elected in 1980, was "shocked by the process. The Constitution of Canada was not something I'd spent a lot of time thinking about. I couldn't believe the depth of antagonism. I thought there would be more willingness to co-operate among NDP members. Instead, it was a marginal civil war most of the time."

Robin Sears received "late-night, threatening phone calls from party members who said I'd be run out of the party for supporting Ed, that I was destroying my grandfather's legacy." Colin Cameron, his grandfather, had been a CCF pioneer. "I would lie awake nights, feeling torn apart, literally," says Sears. Saskatchewan MP Les Benjamin, who supported Ed, says, "I was as popular as a skunk at a garden party in my own province. Close friends told me they'd never again put my sign on their lawn; they said I was a traitor to Saskatchewan. It was traumatic. I caught hell. Got some pretty vicious mail."

Bob Rae figures they had one thing to be grateful for: "The process went under-reported." The main reason it was so awful, he adds, is that it went on for so long. "We lost control of events and were always having to react to statements by the provincial premiers or the Prime Minister."

"What made it easier for Ed," says Rae, "was that he always felt he was right. He was firmly committed to the Charter, to patriation — and he's not prone to enormous self-doubt or profound second thoughts, at least I never saw him act that way." The downside to Ed's decisiveness was that "he could be difficult to work for, because he was so tough-minded and obstinate," says Norm Simon. If anyone suggested, during this period, that, "Maybe your strategy's not the best one, maybe we should do it another way," he'd say, "No. This is the way it's going to be. Period." What Simon remembers more than anything was "Ed's obsessiveness on the Constitution, though he said he wanted to get back to economic issues. He just stuck in, he held on, he wouldn't budge — I always wished he could have let go a little more. But he never lost control. He handled the stress. 'With all due respect,' he'd say, 'you son-of-a-bitch. . . .' "

At one memorable dinner in a Vancouver restaurant, Ed and NDP MP Ian Waddell engaged in a cussing-and-swearing argument that embarrassed their companions and elicited a round of applause from diners when they left. Waddell, a Vancouver lawyer who had served on the Berger Commission inquiry into the Mackenzie Valley pipeline, was pushing Ed to support a tougher aboriginal rights clause. Says Waddell: "Ed told me if I was so concerned about the Indians I should go out and defend them as a lawyer. I said, 'You asshole, I'm one of your new caucus members and you should be listening to me.' "

There were heated sessions in Ed's office that went on for hours, with caucus members attacking Ed and each other, with native leaders and their lawyers, women's groups and their lawyers, perched on windowsills because there were too many of them for the sofas, arguing over every comma of the aboriginal rights clause/equality rights clause that the NDP finally supported. Indeed the fight for equality rights, documented in Penney Kome's book *The Taking of Twenty Eight: Women Challenge the Constitution*, was all by itself the stuff of history.

Thousands of women participated in a grass-roots lobby culminating on Parliament Hill, that was equivalent to the decades-long U.S. struggle over the Equal Rights Amendment; in Canada, women won their case in two intense years.

Eventually Ed took the Indian and Inuit cause to Trudeau. The Liberals had consistently argued that aboriginal rights could not be enshrined because they couldn't be defined. Ed remembers the debate with Trudeau, detailed later by Sheppard and Valpy: "Trudeau opened Socratically by asking Broadbent to tell him what an aboriginal right was. Broadbent's rejoinder was to ask Trudeau rhetorically, to define what was meant by religious freedom in the seventeenth and eighteenth centuries. . . ." Ed argued that freedom was an evolving notion, as were aboriginal rights, which could be recognized without being carved in stone. He "left the meeting feeling he had made the better argument. But he was irritated because Trudeau never concedes a point — a reason for Broadbent's personal antipathy to the prime minister: he has come to believe that Trudeau likes to argue more than he likes to get the truth, which Broadbent, the political philosopher, considers an intellectual weakness."

One of the most poignant times for Ed was a secret meeting in a hotel in Hull, Quebec, just across the river from Ottawa. David Lewis attempted to bridge the chasm between Blakeney and Broadbent. It was not long before David's death in 1981. He was under medication, feeling vulnerable and emotional — like a wounded animal struggling to protect its young. Tommy Douglas was also there, having fought long and aggressively on behalf of Ed's position. "Broadbent and Blakeney went at each other over the question of the Charter of Rights," says one of Ed's aides. "David got into it — he supported Ed very strongly — and he moved himself to tears in his passionate defence of Ed." Bill Knight, then Blakeney's chief of staff, was there too, and says David was defending not so much Ed but the party itself. Knowing that he was dying, David was suffering terribly over the wrenching battle that was tearing the party apart.

"David articulated the differences between Saskatchewan and the federal party," says Knight, "he analyzed
the whole thing — the room was charged with tension
and emotion — and he aimed his appeal at both Broadbent and Blakeney. He was incredible." Afterwards, the
McLeods wrote in their biography of Tommy Douglas,
"Broadbent came upon David Lewis weeping in the street
outside the hotel, with Douglas standing forlornly at his
side." Lewis felt that "something he and Tommy had
worked for all their lives was coming undone." There is
no more poignant image of the elders of the party fearing
for its future, forced by age and illness to leave its fate in
the hands of the younger generation. The next day, David
called Ed to apologize for "getting so carried away."

Everyone was carried away. The meeting resolved
nothing. Caucus members continued to waver from issue
to issue, from tactic to tactic, as the debate ground on in-
ternally and amongst Liberals, Tories and provincial politicians. Though the CLC was officially on Ed's side, "many
labour staffers were against Ed," says a senior trade
union official. "Trudeau gave nothing on collective rights,
which are political rights and should be dealt with in
Parliament by elected people, not by appointed judges —
but under Trudeau's package, power was being shifted to
the courts, there was nothing about the right to a job. . . .
So there was more off-the-record support for Blakeney's
position in the executive council of the CLC. But the CLC
didn't want to start a public war with Ed."

Finally, the party split three ways: Broadbent loyalists
such as Bob Rae agreed with their leader on substance
and even if they felt he'd mishandled tactics they thought
it was a mistake to say so; Saskatchewan dissidents,
headed in caucus by MP Lorne Nystrom who lined up with
Blakeney, opposed the Charter and the deal's Central
Canada bias; and those in favour of a stronger Charter
fought for women's and native rights.

This is the often false hysteria of a life in politics. The
crises never stop, no matter what. For all the obsessiveness of the Constitutional struggle, Ed had other
obligations to attend to. In the spring of 1981, he was

preparing for a two-week Latin American peace mission that would take him through Central America, into the bloody civil war in El Salvador, and deposit him for seven hours in the company of Cuba's revolutionary leader, Fidel Castro.

The trip began sadly. On May 23, the day of Ed's departure, David Lewis died. Ed was already en route to Mexico, having stopped for a plane change in Atlanta, Georgia, where an emergency call summoned him back to Ottawa for Lewis's funeral on May 26. Ed was stunned. Though he had known Lewis was ill, he was not prepared for "the great personal loss" of his teacher and ally; and he did not fully appreciate the turmoil the Lewis family was enduring. David's children had not been informed about his leukemia until shortly before his death; Stephen, for one, felt bitterly deceived and was estranged from his mother. They were not much comforted by the overflowing crowd that jammed Ottawa's Jewish Community Memorial Chapel.

The object of virulent attack in life, Lewis, in death, was showered with praise. "Death has stilled his voice," said Prime Minister Trudeau, "but his reforming spirit will live on in the lives of countless men and women who, over the years, have been inspired by his ideas and moved by his eloquence." Lewis's funeral was jammed by dignitaries, with Trudeau sitting in the front row. For Ed it was a deeply moving occasion. Lewis had seen the spark in him, trusted him, trained him; Ed was his heir.

But there was no time for grieving. Right after the funeral, he flew to Mexico City and was in El Salvador a day later. The trip was sponsored by the Socialist International, and Ed was to report back to Willy Brandt, president of the SI. Brandt expected Ed to establish the foundation "for an international mediation effort to produce a formula for peace between El Salvador's warring factions," wrote the *Globe*'s Oakland Ross from Mexico City. "Political violence, involving right-wing death squads, Government security troops and insurgent guerrillas, has resulted in the deaths of as many as 20,000 Salvadoreans since the beginning of 1980. The death toll continues to mount relentlessly, with the daily discovery of more corpses, many mutilated beyond recognition, scattered about the capital and the surrounding countryside."

Ed remembers the shock of El Salvador. "Fifty people had been hit by death squads overnight while I was there. I spoke to eighteen-year-old kids waving machine guns — they were government soldiers — saying they were going to keep out the socialists. I met with church people and they drove me down streets that would empty when the government van approached. I saw terror for the first time in my life."

The day after his meeting with Ed, Salvadorean President Jose Napoleon Duarte "pointedly and publicly rejected any possibility of an international effort to end the war," wrote Oakland Ross. And in Cuba, to Robin Sears's alarm, Ed criticized Castro quite harshly for his gunrunning to El Salvador and restraints on human rights — all the while smoking Castro's Havana cigars.

Back at home in his sunny backyard, Ed's political troubles paled in comparison. Clad in shorts and sandals, showing off his tan, he told the *Toronto Star*'s Carol Goar that "this [constitutional] experience has not exactly been an unqualified pleasure to live through." (Less than a year later, on April 17, 1982, the Queen signed Canada's new Constitution Act.)

Goar noted that Ed was "usually pretty good at hiding his feelings behind this kind of wry understatement, but now the sarcasm seems forced, the accompanying smile a trace wan. The last few months have left both the party and its forty-five-year-old leader weary." There was never time to rest. "One of the ever-present headaches of being a socialist," he said, "is that you have to keep plotting new directions all the time because the government of the day keeps catching up to you and taking over your policies." At the same time, Ed was experiencing tensions within his office from party members who were seeking more access to the inner sanctum.

In 1980 Judy Wasylycia-Leis became Ed's executive assistant for one and a half "difficult years." Though the constitutional wars were raging, she remembers most vividly encountering "the tight little group of men around Ed — I found it hard to fit in as an equal. It was such a tight clique." What she terms "the male bunker" had arisen partly because of the need to close ranks defensively against outside attacks; partly it was that politics was still a male prerogative — even in the NDP. As committed as the party was to equality (at the 1983 convention, the NDP would pass a constitutional amendment requiring at least 50 per cent of federal positions and committees to be filled by women) and as much as Ed thought he had learned from Rosemary Brown — his inner circle remained a male bastion, breached only by Anne Carroll.

Judy W-L, as she's known, was an independent-minded young feminist determined to break through at a senior policy level; she went on to bigger and tougher things, becoming a Cabinet minister in Howard Pawley's NDP Government in Manitoba before her thirty-fourth birthday.

"Ed expected a lot of support from his staff," says Judy. "At times I remember being annoyed at things he'd ask me to do, run for this, go for that." She didn't like being directed to do menial tasks; for the previous three and a half years, she had been women's organizer for the federal party, drumming up feminist consciousness across the land and in the leader's office. Dorothy Inglis, an NDP activist from Newfoundland, remembers Judy W-L bringing Ed to women's caucus meetings. "Ed listened to us speak about the issues," says Inglis, "and he learned. He became one of the strongest supporters of the women's movement in the party." Marion Dewar, party president from 1985 to 1987, concurs, noting that by 1988, six of nine vice-presidents were women.

Judy W-L loved her work. "It was wonderful. I would lobby and pester and nag and get through to Ed on the issues. I would show up at daily executive meetings of caucus; I'd have my issues, day care, pensions, reproductive choice, affirmative action; I'd lose more often than I'd win but gradually women's issues began to be raised in

Question Period." And when the NDP did it, she noticed, the other parties followed suit.

But when she was "promoted" to Ed's office, "my role was no longer to raise just women's issues. If I did it too much, I'd lose my credibility. And when I did, it was usually me against the male group. Eliesen and O'Malley tended to see women's issues as 'soft,' detracting from the serious stuff." Ed never knew, says a former (male) adviser, "how rude O'Malley and Eliesen often were to Judy." Still, she felt she made inroads: "Ed came to grasp the issues and be more outspoken," she says.

Ed bristles at the charge that Judy may have felt squeezed out by the men in his office. "I brought her here, on my staff, because of the work she'd done on women's issues," he says. "I wanted that input. I supported her." Their greatest advance, he feels, "was putting women's issues on the agenda at the '84 election."

Looking back, with the wisdom gained from exercising power in government, Judy W-L now feels she can better understand the enormous pressure Ed was under. She observed that under stress, he could be difficult to deal with. When he was sold on something, he would move fast — sometimes too fast, impetuously; the strong hand of a restrainer might be required. "Ed's not great at asking for criticism or taking it," she says. "It's hard to sit Ed down and say, 'You fucked up.' His reaction makes you not want to do it — but now that I've been a Cabinet minister, I have more sympathy for what he was going through. The longer you're in politics, the more you're subjected to such constant scrutiny that you don't want to hear the bad news. Just tell me the good stuff."

Ed's personal life — his marriage to Lucille — was by then the main oasis of "good stuff." According to friends, his relationship with Lucille was the single most important factor in his ability to retain his sanity. Nestor Pidwerbecki remembers that in 1975, when Ed was elected leader, he had insisted that his private life would remain private, that the party had promised to reserve two weekends out of every four for Ed to spend at home with his family. Nestor had laughed. As Ed's constituency organizer, Nestor knew better. The extreme demands placed on an NDP leader — Tories and Liberals could send out Cabinet ministers to functions — would curtail Ed's friendships and his family life. "I knew what was going to happen," says Nestor, "and it did. Ed is always travelling, always working. He has logged hundreds of thousands of miles going coast to coast to coast over the years — we've seen him less and less in Oshawa too — and Lucille has been golden. She's supported him."

Absorbed in caring for their children Paul and Christine and leading her own life, which included some charity work as well as her intellectual and artistic interests, Lucille had reconciled herself to the public role of "the smiling, pleasant wife," a phrase she says with a wry grin. But she had also worked hard to keep the lines of communication open with Ed — an endeavour that became increasingly difficult as his time was taken over by the party and the constant battles. "You have to keep working on your relationship," says Lucille. "You can get into a routine of just living, going to meetings, doing what you have to do. If you're not careful, you don't take time to enjoy each other and you lose touch." She made sure they took the time — cross-country skiing in winter, trips to the Caribbean, just sitting together in the evening, listening to their beloved opera, reading, talking. She speaks about the special qualities of "a love relationship" with such feeling that one understands this is what she has with Ed; their friends have also sensed the spiritual and sensual joys of the Broadbent marriage. "There's real sex appeal between those two," said one. "What they've got together doesn't exist in a lot of relationships, and it's quite extraordinary to find it in political life."

Carol Goar, the *Toronto Star*'s National Newspaper Award-winning columnist, lives in the Sandy Hill district of Ottawa, near Ed's place. Walking home one night, Carol passed the Broadbents' house. "I looked in the leaded-glass windows," said Carol, "and I saw Ed and Lucille together, sitting in front of the fire, reading." Carol smiles wistfully. I can see her, a slender, solitary woman on a cold winter's night, drawn by the strains of music and the warmth of the cosy scene. "It looked very nice," she says.

Lucille is sitting in front of the fire in her living room, on the floor, poring over family albums. There are snapshots of birthday parties at a family cottage, pictures of Ed and Lucille with Paul and Christine, skating on the canal, riding bikes, eating hot dogs. But the family photos are vastly outnumbered by black-and-white stills of political campaigns: Ed in the early '80s riding on a constituency worker's motorcycle (which aggravated the RCMP officer responsible for the party leader's security); Ed twirling ecstatically on the campaign plane; Ed making speeches; Ed, Lucille, Paul and Christine on the platform on various election nights, growing up, growing older. Ed standing on an airport tarmac, watching for a plane, as Lucille stands behind him, with her arms around him, hugging him. Lucille smiling, in the background.

Lucille had to come to grips with "the traditional role" she was playing, while Ed was being trained in feminism. She considers herself a feminist, yet she was living a lifestyle in which there was "no egalitarian sharing of the workload." She was acutely conscious of the gap between theory and practice in Ed's life. "It's all very well for Ed to talk about women's equality when he doesn't have to live it out. I know what people say. He has a wife at home who cooks his meals, does the laundry, cuts the grass. It's very difficult. All the leaders have been criticized for having a wife at home catering to their needs, caring for the children. The wife is criticized for being a princess whose livelihood is provided by someone else." It is a role that causes vulnerability and doubts. "Sometimes I wonder," she says, "if I should have gone back to work when Christine was small. Not that I have any regrets. But . . ." It's a big but — she faced a difficult reality: with her husband entering the prime of his life, fully engaged in politics, she was pondering an uncertain future, not sure what she would do with herself when Christine finished high school. She talked about Susan Riley's book, *The Lives of the Saints*, which depicts

political wives, in Lucille's words, as "well-paid prosti-
tutes." It is not a description she appreciates, nor does
she think it's fair.

"Lucille is a woman of rare value," says her friend
Penny Collenette, a law student who is married to former
Liberal Cabinet minister David Collenette. "She is a feminist in a quiet way. She has no desire, no need for the
limelight. She has experienced a lot of tragedy and difficulty in her life, so she wants to enjoy the good times. I
can't say enough about her. She's decent, kind, a wonderful friend — in my mind, she stands out like a star. She's
a sweetheart. I would do anything for her."

Penny met Lucille in the early '80s and their friendship sprang from their efforts, through the Parliamentary
Spouses Association, to help Soviet Jews get out of Russia. Penny had started a petition. "I needed the signa-
tures of the wives of the three political leaders, and I felt
very shy about it — who was I? I was just a backbencher's wife. But I phoned Lucille at home and she was wonderfully friendly, she told me to come right over and she
jumped right in." With Jane Crosbie, wife of Tory Cabinet minister John Crosbie, Lucille Broadbent and Penny
Collenette became a trio of ardent defenders of human
rights. They met with the Soviet ambassador, travelled to
Washington and London for meetings and, along the way,
became great friends. "We had a ball," says Jane Crosbie.
"In London we stayed at a Labour hotel, because it was
cheap and we didn't have much money, and when they
found out who Lucille was, they were thrilled. We even
went to Downing Street and met Margaret Thatcher. She
was very nice."

That partisan opponents can be friends often surprises
outsiders to Ottawa who see the political scene as defined
by the fire-and-brimstone battle that's acted out in Question Period every day. Lucille describes a political dinner
at which she sat next to Prime Minister Brian Mulroney;
she commiserated with him about the difficulties of quitting smoking, which he had managed to do and she had
not. The next day, Mulroney sent Lucille a package of the
nicotine gum which he said had helped him in his fight

against the weed. Indeed, Lucille and Ed are almost notorious in Ottawa for having good times with non-supporters. "Reporters don't see this," says Penny, "but when we're here in this town, it doesn't matter what party we're in, we've all got the same logistical problems — especially the spouses."

When the Collenettes go to the Broadbents' for dinner, the discussion is always lively and the meal superb, says Penny. "Lucille enjoys having people over, she's like Ed that way. She loves to garden and to cook. The flowers are always artistically arranged, the food wonderfully prepared and their home is a home — a sanctuary. Lucille keeps it beautifully — and she does it all herself."

But Lucille has no desire to present herself as the perfect woman. Her life with Ed has not been all roses. They have had serious disagreements: for instance, Lucille vividly recalls overhearing Ed in the study of their home "making a casual comment that English-only made air traffic safer. I was flabbergasted." Lucille is referring to the 1976 controversy about allowing bilingual air traffic controllers in Quebec to speak French to French-speaking pilots. The Canadian Air Line Pilots Association protested (in favour of English-only), shut down the nation's airports and precipitated what Prime Minister Trudeau called "the worst crisis since wartime conscription."

The Voice of Canada League, an anti-French group, charged that "in its hysterical pursuit of bilingualism at any price, the present government has pursued a racist policy worthy of South Africa." Conventional wisdom had it that English-only was safer — a view which appalled Lucille, who saw it as merely an expression of Anglo dominance. To hear it coming out of the mouth of her own husband shocked her. "I was very upset," she says. "I realized Ed was just reacting to the idea of air safety, but I thought it was obvious safety would be enhanced if people could speak to each other in their own language." Which was, of course, the view that ultimately prevailed. "I was wrong," says Ed. "My research was bad." On all matters related to Quebec and the French language, Lucille feels familial ties — and exerts a powerful influence on her husband. "I have always felt very strongly about Quebec, but it seemed to take Ed a long time to see what the Québecois had gone through," she says. "Growing up in Ottawa, the discrimination against Francophones was obvious. I guess you have to live the experience to fully understand."

Robin Sears observed that Lucille's "moral influence" could be felt in her husband's office; she is always a force to contend with, though her power is subtle. Indeed it is difficult to convey Lucille's impact. The way she speaks is perhaps the best clue: her voice is rich and strong, her articulation of ideas precise, her convictions passionately held. Her friends talk about how sweet and kind she is, but when it comes to intellectual and moral concerns, she is quite strict. At the same time, she is adamant that "in a relationship, neither individual should feel any coercion to give up what they desire to do. Every individual must be respected. I would never tell Ed — or any friend of mine — what to do. I might suggest there are pros and cons, but no, I would not try to impose my own views on someone else." Ed and Lucille have, however, influenced each others' thinking. On abortion, for instance: "I'm opposed to abortion in the sense that I'm opposed to capital punishment," Lucille says. "I cannot see myself terminating a life — but I have come around to realizing that it's a decision that must be taken by the woman. I have accepted this. I have altered my point of view. At the same time, Ed is much more understanding of the dilemma, of the feelings of the pro-life people. Before, he couldn't see why anyone wouldn't support the right to abortion. For him, it was simple. Now, I would say, he is more tolerant of people who oppose abortion — of people in his own caucus who have a different opinion. He hasn't changed his own position, but I'm happy to see he's more understanding."

On broader matters, Ed has felt the sting of Lucille's principles. Initially attracted to him by his idealism, she grew concerned, as his political career developed, about how he was changing. "Ed's pursuit of power," she says, pondering, "it took me a long, long time to feel comfortable with it. I was against compromises. I thought it was very important to stick to one's basic principles. I saw a shift in Ed. I saw indications his idealism was being deflated; it disturbed me. I was concerned about what was happening to him as an individual." Lucille and Ed had many long discussions about power, principles, compromise. They debated late into the night. "It's the moral issues that spark discussions in our relationship," she says. And like Ed, Lucille is unstoppable when she's got a moral issue between her teeth; this one caused some friction between the two. Finally, Lucille says she was persuaded by Ed's argument that "in politics, you have a moral obligation to pursue power. Only if you have power can you make the changes you believe in. In order to get power, you have to make compromises." She realized, she says, that she had viewed the pursuit of power as a dangerous course. "'Now I accept it." She was comfortable that Ed was "finding the balance between power and principles."

He desperately needed this balance going in to the party's biennial convention in Vancouver in July, 1981. A messy showdown was looming and it was "the last thing [Ed] needed to wrap up a year which has tried his patience, his authority and his pride," wrote Carol Goar. "He's doing his best not to be bitter about it. He will soon know whether his party is ready to meet him in the same spirit."

It wasn't. "Defying appeals for party unity, a group of Saskatchewan New Democrats stubbornly remained seated during an opening day salute to national leader Ed Broadbent," wrote Goar on July 3. "Nearly 1,000 delegates from across the country looked on in shocked embarrassment as the hostile Saskatchewan group refused to salute Broadbent. . . ." Coups were springing up everywhere; a leadership challenge was in the air. "Ed would have been gone, except for one thing," says an anti-Broadbent delegate: "We didn't have a horse [candidate]."

Robin Sears, federal secretary, tried to downplay the sound of knives sharpening by telling reporters that this was just a typical debate engaged in by people who cared about issues. He remains convinced to this day that he and Bill Knight "stage-managed" the clash of the titans — Broadbent vs. Blakeney — in order to allow for "controlled dissent." Others dispute the degree of control wielded by party organizers.

"It was bloody," says Tony Penikett, who was elected as party president in the middle of it all. "The staffs of Broadbent and Blakeney weren't speaking to each other. There was an attempt by the western leaders to do a Lady Macbeth gang-up on Ed." It took some heavy duty negotiating to keep the troops in line. With the help of Penikett, Bob White and the party saints — Tommy Douglas and Stanley Knowles — Ed pulled it off, finally, with some skillful manoeuvring in backroom strategy sessions. This little episode, involving a few trade-offs around foreign policy and the Constitution, demonstrates the new wily Broadbent.

B.C. New Democrat John Brewin tells one part of the story. The son of Andrew Brewin, a revered Toronto NDP MP, John had been a campus CCFer at the University of Toronto in the mid-'50s, when Ed was there. He is now a lawyer in Victoria, B.C., where his wife Gretchen is the city's mayor, and he will be running for the NDP in the next election. President of the B.C. party in 1978–79 and co-chair of the NDP's international affairs committee in the early 1980s, John Brewin had participated in protracted debates on foreign policy. He strongly supported the resolution calling for Canada to pull out of NATO — a move that was popular with the B.C. party. Brewin was well aware that he was opposing "the instincts" of Ed and some of his key advisers who did not like the anti-NATO resolution.

Prior to the Vancouver convention, there was considerable backroom skirmishing in an effort, says Brewin, "to work out a trade-off. Ed agreed to back off the fight about NATO to ensure our support on the more important issue — for him — of the Constitution. He recognized that to pick a fight with the B.C. party on NATO was not very sensible in the circumstances." Dave Barrett, former Premier of B.C. and still the very popular leader of the party, lined up with Ed on the Constitution; and Ed, when asked about pulling out of NATO, "would roll his eyes heavenward," says Brewin, "and state: 'This is party policy and I support it.'" (Ed would quietly continue, however, to try to modify the NATO policy — behind the scenes.)

In advance, the opposing forces had agreed on lists of designated speakers who would line up at the microphones to speak for or against the constitutional resolution. One Broadbent aide who was "part of the task force working to control things," remembers that "the senior people on both sides had figured out how we were going to get through it. It was orchestrated. We didn't exchange scripts, but we made sure the whole thing wasn't going to blow up." Still, the atmosphere was tense. On the morning of the great constitutional debate, one delegate remembers seeing Robin Sears outside the locked convention hall hissing into his walkie talkie, frantically trying to locate Mary Ellen McQuay, the assistant federal secretary who was inside the hall. It turned out they were on opposite sides of the same locked door, getting ready to make sure the stand-ins for their speakers lined up at the right microphones.

"The dramatic moment of the debate," wrote Desmond Morton, "came when a gaunt, sober-suited Stanley Knowles followed [Lorne] Nystrom. . . . Half a century of oratory had taught Knowles how to seize and hold an NDP audience." Then Knowles was followed by John Rodriguez, a former MP from Ontario, who made the mistake of attacking Knowles. "Delegates booed him," wrote Morton. "The tide turned. The vote, when it came, upheld Broadbent by almost two to one."

Ed emerged intact. "You have to give it to Ed," says Norm Simon. "His persistence turned the corner. He won the vote at the convention. If he'd lost, it would have meant fatal weakness."

Back in Ottawa, Ed's staff clipped convention stories displayed under headlines such as this one: BROADBENT CALLS TO HEAL WOUNDS. But despite Simon's optimism, things were going to get worse before they got better.

There was one ray of hope in 1981 — Howard Pawley's New Democrats defeated Sterling Lyons's Tories in Manitoba — but it was shadowed by the defeat of the Blakeney government in Saskatchewan a year later. Nineteen eighty-two wasn't much fun for anyone, though it was the year that Ed brought former Wafflers Jim Laxer and Gerry Caplan back into the fold. Laxer, as research director, and Caplan, as federal secretary, were joined by a deceptively mellow, roly-poly hayseed from the enemy camp: Saskatchewan's Bill Knight became Ed's principal secretary.

Knight knew more than any of them about exercising power and he would outlast them all. Only twenty-three years old when he was elected in a '71 by-election, he was David Lewis's whip during the minority government; defeated in '74, he became secretary of the Saskatchewan party until '79, when he was chosen chief of staff to Premier Blakeney, a job he held until the party's defeat in '82. Throughout the years of Blakeney's battles with Broadbent, Bill Knight was a chief commander on the western front. Now he had switched sides. His new role was to defend Broadbent and build up the federal team — "riding shotgun," as Knight puts it. "In Saskatchewan, I was considered the fed symp — the moderate. In Ottawa they'd say, 'Here comes the radical from Saskatchewan.'" Widely considered one of the shrewdest political advisers in the country, Knight's attitude to the constitutional collisions best expresses his style: "When anyone asked me about it, my line was, 'What was that all about, anyway?' To Ed, I'd say, 'What were you doing, anyway?' All I want to do is win elections."

Knight's personal political views were always hard to pin down. He charmed party conservatives and left-wingers alike, and he even maintained warm relations with Jim Laxer and Gerry Caplan during the crises that would develop.

Ten months before Caplan became federal secretary, Jim Laxer took charge on the policy end as research director. A dozen years earlier, Laxer and Caplan had been young radicals tilting at the establishment, while Ed was a junior MP; now they were in control of the party. Caplan was a seasoned organizer and administrator, having guided Stephen Lewis through seven years as leader in Ontario; Ed had been caucus chairman under David Lewis, and national leader for seven years; Laxer was something of a star in a field of expertise not often considered an NDP strength: the economy.

Laxer had settled in as a professor of political economy at York University. He was the Canadian counterpart to the Kennedy School's Robert Reich, whose advocacy of industrial strategy for America caused *Esquire* magazine to label Reich "one of Washington's hottest gurus." Laxer, the Mr Industrial Strategy of Ottawa, had been writing about the same issues for more than a decade: "When the Americans pick up on industrial strategy, as soon as it takes off south of the border, it'll be acceptable here," he said.

Laxer had written seven books — about foreign control of the economy, resource development, oil and gas, economic planning — in which he applied Swedish, European and Japanese models to his own vision of an independent Canada. With a reputation as a popularizer of complex economic ideas, exuberant and absorbed in the issues uppermost in Ed's mind, Jim seemed to Ed like the right man at the right time.

Their early months together were fruitful. Laxer was marvellously adept at explaining the whys and wherefores of Ed's favourite economic plans. Where Ed sounded ponderous — and indeed polls showed the NDP had not succeeded in selling its economic proposals — Jim was bright and snappy. "We have to hammer away about why foreign control of our economy is no good," he said. "The Americans buy us out with our own money. It's a mug's game. The Tories say we need more foreign capital. The fact is that foreign companies borrow their capital from Canadian banks, import their product design and R&D from head office, so the net result is destruction of job potential. In the long run, we have to initiate here to create jobs here."

Laxer was always talking about long-term, as opposed to quick-fix, solutions. As research director, he did the background work, preparing a series of packages on economic development that Ed would present at every opportunity. Ed was excited about his collaboration with Laxer and eager to talk. What was the NDP selling? "The economy, peace and social programs," said Ed. Nationalization, he pointed out, "is no longer considered a panacea by socialists. Sweden and Austria have relatively little public ownership, but they've developed techniques to control foreign ownership and make sure the economy is run first and foremost for the benefit of their own citizens."

Ed would go on for hours about economic planning. "We want to build on what we've got, where we have comparative industrial advantages," he said. "For instance, we've got one of the largest fisheries in the world in a protein-short era. People want our fish but we're not marketing it worldwide." He moved on to machinery related to resource extraction. "We had a $1.3 billion deficit in mining and forest products equipment last year. We should be using our resource base as a foundation for our manufacturing, so that we become a world leader in these fields." In this manner he covered the country, the regions, the resource industries, farming, the manufacturing sectors. He was full of ideas — though he failed to get the media to pay attention. By and large, the press continued to report that the NDP had nothing new to say.

Ed pondered the "loss" of Petro-Canada, an NDP concept which had been usurped by the Liberals. "It was a figurehead for us. We need a new symbol to tie the package together. You can talk about industrial strategy but it might as well be porridge unless people can see what you mean."

Then, on October 19, 1982, Ed delivered his famous Hamilton speech, which contained, wrote Richard Gwyn in the *Toronto Star* (on October 23, 1982), "the most dramatic change in party policy since its founding. . . ." Ed must have felt a little like Alice in Wonderland — he hadn't really said anything so dramatically different yet his world turned inside out. In his Hamilton speech, he described "the unravelling of our national economy," the global shifts that had triggered the decline of the American empire and the rise of Japan and Europe. It was standard stuff. He quoted a *Harvard Business Review* study which "concluded that the key weakness of North American business was its unwillingness to make long-term investments," because of its fixation on short-term profits. This was motherhood. "Economic planning is the key," he said, to the success of America's competitors, and it could work equally well for Canada. He outlined an industrial strategy that would not increase the deficit. He detailed proposals for tax reform that would increase revenues and stimulate economic development particularly in the high-tech, research and development areas that were so crucial to achieving international competitiveness. He emphasized that he would not increase the deficit.

BROADBENT MAKES HISTORY said the *Star* headline. Richard Gwyn waxed philosophical: the NDP, he wrote, "has more than justified its existence by performing as what historian Desmond Morton has called 'a conveyor belt' of new ideas into our political system. . . . But for the CCF we wouldn't have unemployment insurance. But for the NDP we wouldn't have medicare." However, "As an idea machine the NDP has been running down for some years. . . . Abruptly, NDP leader Ed Broadbent has dragged his party into the centre of the economic debate. His speech in Hamilton this week represents the most dramatic change in party policy since its founding. . . ." The change, as Gwyn saw it, was that Ed, in his new-found concern for deficits, was talking about wealth creation, not just wealth redistribution.

Ed thought the fuss was a tempest in a teapot — "I'm not sure it was such a big deal," he says — but it precipitated more dissension in party ranks and caused him some embarrassing moments when reporters tried to pin him down on just exactly what he meant. It was during the aftermath of the Hamilton speech that Caplan arrived in Ottawa to take on his duties as federal

sccretary. Caplan determined that Laxer "had been pushing Ed too far, too fast. Jim was throwing overboard all
the Keynesian stuff about stimulating the economy,"
which was so dear to the hearts of organized labour, especially during a time of high unemployment. "The party
wasn't ready for it, Ed wasn't ready for it," says Caplan.

Yet the Hamilton speech was not so different from
other speeches Ed had made on industrial strategy; nor
was he out of line with the frugal, profit-oriented approach of western NDP governments. The Canadian social
democratic tradition is fiscally prudent: Al Johnson, for
twelve years Tommy Douglas's deputy treasurer and a
chief architect of Saskatchewan's economic miracle, observes that "we did it without ever once creating a deficit." Johnson's approach was, by clever management and
control over resource wealth, to stimulate the economy,
provide services, generate economic activity and balance
the budget. On the other side of the world, Bob Hawke,
former president of the Australian Council of Trade
Unions, would lead the social democratic Labour Party to
victory in 1983 and set about to slash Australia's $9 bil-
lion deficit. Hawke would indeed go further: establishing
a labour–business "accord," he would eventually succeed
in balancing the budget for the first time since 1970.

Laxer insists that his ideas about how to reform government spending without increasing the deficit were
shared by other key Broadbent advisers. Bill Knight, Ed's
principal secretary, was in favour of the "new, realistic
approach to economic issues." Knight liked to say that
"Ed is our first federal leader who is truly post-Depres-
sion, who talks a contemporary language."

Peter O'Malley, now a communications consultant in
Ottawa, also recalls that their "basic thrust was to dig
the party out from the old-time religion of economic stim-
ulation and establish 'The One Real Thing' — an economic policy that made sense. The polls kept showing
that the party had great credibility on social justice issues and no credibility on economic issues. We wanted
the NDP to get real about the economy."

"Before the Hamilton speech," says Laxer, "Bill Knight, O'Malley and I met with Ed. We went over the substance of the speech, we recognized that the labour movement would react, but Ed said he felt comfortable with what he was saying. He said he knew there would be criticism and that he could handle it. Well, he couldn't handle it, and without consulting us he eventually reversed himself. I realized, gradually, that I had no input anymore."

O'Malley figures that one reason Ed backed off was that "he'd taken a shit-kicking over the Constitution, he was just coming out of it, and the last thing he needed was another fight. After Hamilton, the flack was immense. The labour guys — the research guys in the CLC and the UAW — went crazy." As in the beginning of his political career, when Ed espoused industrial democracy, he again outraged the labour establishment. Sam Gindin, the influential chief economist of the United Auto Workers and a close adviser to Bob White, was appalled when Ed's Hamilton speech combined deficit reduction with an emphasis on achieving "international competitiveness." To Gindin, the combination conjured images of "workers having to accept wage concessions, decreases in social services, a shift in the tax structure to help certain companies — and who's paying? Workers. It's a dead-end street."

Marc Eliesen, the party's research director from 1976 to 1981, was more sympathetic. He had moved on to Manitoba, where he was appointed deputy minister of energy in Pawley's new regime. Working for a tight-fisted NDP government that was interested in industrial development, Eliesen appreciated what Ed was trying to do in the Hamilton speech. Still, Eliesen figured, "Ed was strategically wrong to have made that speech at a time when unemployment was high and we still hadn't recovered from the recession. In politics, timing is everything."

Caplan's timing, coming on the scene when he did, was just as unlucky. Before Stephen Lewis stepped down as Ontario NDP leader in 1978, Caplan had taken off for Africa. From '77 to '79, he lived in Nigeria and ran CUSO

(Canadian University Service Overseas); back in Canada, he worked for more than two years as the head of Toronto's Health Advocacy Unit. When he was approached by Ed in 1982 to come to Ottawa as federal secretary, he was initially delighted; but the manner in which he won the job was less pleasing. The federal council, which votes on such appointments, was deadlocked over Caplan's candidacy; he was finally approved on October 21, 1982, by only one vote over the western favourite Cliff Scotton. "It was so hurtful," says Caplan. "It was a blow to win it in that way." He did not realize that the deadlock represented the divided state of the party.

Caplan started a gruelling regimen, travelling across the country, meeting with party officials; in the first year he figures he spent only three weekends at home in his Ottawa apartment. He was quickly enveloped in "stories of treachery, venom and betrayal." He learned to walk very delicately around Grant Notley, leader of the Alberta party, who was "poisoned" against Ed; and he had to be very, very careful how he trod in Saskatchewan. These were not auspicious times. By December, 1982, the recession was deepening and the Gallup Poll showed support for the New Democrats had slid to 20 per cent among decided respondents, down one point from the month before, down three points from the summer and down six points from a record high in February. "I simply don't understand it," Ed told Canadian Press. He joked "that his wife Lucille put it all down to the movement of the planets."

Gerry Caplan responded to reporters' queries about the party's future in a manner that annoyed Ed. Whereas Ed always gave out his most optimistic assessment for public consumption, Caplan acknowledged that things weren't looking too good. It was "inescapably true," he admitted, that the party's message wasn't getting across. Caplan's proclivity for what Ed saw as pessimistic pronouncements would increasingly strain their relationship. For his part, Caplan was having a hard time treating Ed with the deference due a boss. The two men were peers and Caplan had no sense of "looking up to the leader," which is usually helpful in a federal secretary. They started to rub each other the wrong way.

Broadbent was in trouble. Uneasy with Caplan, the party's chief executive officer, losing touch with Laxer, his research director, Ed lacked the resources to quell the western rebellion that was still brewing. It was a painful period, leading up to the party's fiftieth anniversary convention in Regina at the beginning of July, 1983. Planned as a celebration, the Regina convention threatened to repeat the Vancouver '81 conflict — but this time round the prospects were even more dismaying, given the symbolism of the occasion. "On the one hand we were euphoric about celebrating our fiftieth anniversary," says Caplan, "on the other, we were riven in pieces by dissension. It was a bizarre experience."

Preparing to return to the party's spiritual home, Ed was weary. Elected leader in '75, he had enjoyed a glorious honeymoon in which he had been praised for unifying the party and leading it up in the polls; eight years later, the good stuff was forgotten, and Ed was blamed for all the turmoil and bad polls. "Our message isn't getting out," he finally acknowledged, in the style of Caplan, when the party dropped to 16 per cent in the Gallup Poll before he arrived in Regina. WHO NEXT WILL HEAD THE NDP? asked a *Toronto Star* headline a week before the convention that "may well be Ed Broadbent's last." The *Star*'s Bob Hepburn figured that Ed would be forced to step down after the next election. Conventional wisdom had it that Ed Broadbent was finished.

In Ed's Parliament Hill office, paranoia was rampant about the behind-the-scenes manoeuvring of Grant Notley, Blakeney and his former attorney general, Roy Romanow. On the eve of the convention they produced "a statement of principles" about the creation of "a new social contract," with an emphasis on co-operation among labour, business and government. It wasn't a new idea, but it was a challenge to Ed.

"The party had its beginnings in the west," said Notley, "and as we return to Regina we should be looking more to the west. . . . I don't mean that we're anti-

Ontario. . . ." But of course they were. With a leader from
Ontario, with "eastern technocrats" running the party,
the NDP had failed to make the crucial breakthrough in
Ontario and had lost touch with western Canada. The
thirty-two-member caucus included twenty-seven western
MPs; many of them were sick of watching Ontario "screw
things up." And they were driven, deep down, by a powerful, traditional resentment: "We westerners hate the
banks, the railways, and Ontario," says Al Johnson, the
Saskatchewan financial wizard. Johnson points out that
westerners have always had a hard time appreciating
Ontario culture. "Ontario is a very civil society," he says.
"There's a very narrow margin of expression tolerated in
Ontario. The premiers of Ontario all look the same and
sound the same: civilized, moderate, progressive but not
too progressive. Ontario is an extraordinary place. The
downside, for a westerner, is that you never know what
the hell's going on. You can talk to people in Ontario and
you never know if they love you or hate you, because
they hardly seem to react." Westerners, like Quebeckers,
were not so repressed; they didn't mind letting their anti-
pathies show.

Caplan, who as federal secretary should have been
aware of what was going on, was shocked to arrive in Regina and discover "the disruptive activities of western in-
surgents." Caplan was appalled that Blakeney and
Notley worked against the federal leader "and never told
Ed what they were doing. They had people all across the
country — snakes-in-the-grass — contributing to their
manifesto. They surely could have phoned Ed and said,
'We're not happy, we want to talk.' It was a case of
friends and colleagues moving clandestinely — and it
reflected the bitter aftermath of the Constitution fight."
Still, Caplan tried to keep the lid on it, and again the
party's senior leaders worked behind the scenes to reach
a compromise.

Even so, "Ed was treated badly at that convention,"
says Bob Rae. "The westerners sprung their statement on
him at the last moment. Nobody ever talked to me about
it. I asked Grant Notley why he hadn't called me. He

said, 'Oh, you Central Canadians are all together, there's no use to talking to you.'" Rae asked another western enemy of Ed's: "Why are you doing this? We're heading into an election and you have no candidate to replace Broadbent." Rae was told: "We don't want to kill him. We just want to wound him."

On July 2, the *Globe*'s Charlotte Montgomery reported from Regina: "The carefully crafted show of unity of the federal New Democratic Party convention here disintegrated yesterday when one MP publicly acknowledged that he had seriously considered challenging the leadership of Edward Broadbent and another said he was approached but flatly refused." The first was Saskatchewan MP Doug Anguish, the second B.C. MP Nelson Riis.

The search for candidates to replace Ed was so intense it reminded one New Democratic gourmet of "pigs excitedly sniffing for truffles." Party stalwarts like Lloyd Shaw, father of Nova Scotia NDP leader Alexa McDonough, were scouring the country for likely prospects. Roy Romanow was asked many times, but bowed out. Shaw tried to enlist Stephen Lewis, but Lewis refused — all under cover. Tony Penikett, still party president, was once again the frantic go-between, running back and forth among enemy camps that would not be reconciled. As a "hinterland" politician, he well understood western complaints and he supported Blakeney's opposition to the Charter; but he was a Broadbent loyalist. "At Vancouver in '81, the debate was more principled and high-minded," says Penikett. "At Regina in '83, it was more of a grudge match. The wolves had started to circle; there weren't many of us defending the camp."

Then there was Tommy Douglas's great speech. "Douglas had been wheeled into the hall on a golf cart which pulled an enormous cake, made up to celebrate the fiftieth anniversary of the Regina Manifesto," wrote the McLeods. After the Saturday night banquet, Tommy stood up, looking small and frail — he was dying of cancer — and delivered his swan song. It was an epic aria that electrified his audience. "It was wild," says Caplan. "Two thousand people desperately grabbing at his words in an attempt to re-establish the old magic — and he was magnificent." Penikett remembers that "Tommy took us back to the roots of the party, to remind us where we'd come from, what we'd achieved, how far we had to go. The journey wasn't completed. He linked the past to the future. We knew it was the last great performance of one of our founders — David had died, Stanley had his stroke — but Tommy was still fresh and exciting." When Tommy finished, the crowd cheered and applauded for "twenty minutes," says Caplan. Bob Rae remembers being overcome: "People were crying and jumping up on tables — all the anger and emotion was released. It was incredible." Rae says the ovation lasted for half an hour; another delegate says it was forty minutes long.

The day before Tommy's speech, Jim Laxer and Peter O'Malley were driving from the Agribition (agricultural fairgrounds) into downtown Regina when they saw a little old man walking alone through an industrial district of huge, deserted warehouses and railway tracks. Dark clouds rumbled across the sky, threatening a thunderstorm. As Laxer and O'Malley pulled closer, the old man stooped down, picked up some garbage and stuffed it behind a water spout. "I couldn't believe it," says Laxer. "It was Tommy, about to be deluged in a thunderstorm, twenty-four hours before he was to deliver his last speech to his people, and there he was, cleaning up garbage. We had come upon him totally unawares. We picked him up. He was as cheery as ever, jaunty, optimistic — though he knew what the party was going through. He talked, and we felt inspired as you always did when you talked to Tommy. He was a believer. It was the last time I ever saw him." (Tommy Douglas died on February 24, 1986.)

On July 4, as delegates headed home, "the usually congenial Mr Broadbent was unsmiling as he fielded reporters' questions . . . ," wrote Charlotte Montgomery in the *Globe*. Ed tried to shrug off stories about dissatisfaction with his leadership; he tried to pretend everything was fine. He had escaped the ambush; somehow, with the support of the party's establishment outside Saskatchewan, he had headed his enemies off at the pass. Watching him survive yet another gang-up, one can only wonder at his tenacity. Still, there was little joy going home. Tommy's speech hadn't solved the problems. "The morning after," wrote Desmond Morton, "both the nostalgia and the bitterness remained."

Back in Ottawa, in the heat of summer, Ed didn't have a chance to recuperate.

> Obituary, Toronto Star, Aug. 21, 1983: Mary Broadbent, mother of federal New Democratic Party leader Ed Broadbent, died of cancer early yesterday morning at Toronto General Hospital. She was 72. . . . Canon David Peasgood of St George's Anglican Church in Oshawa . . . called Mary Broadbent "a fine, deeply caring person. She was involved in the church and in the Simcoe Hall Women's League, a settlement house assisting people in need. She was concerned about helping people, the down-and-outs of the community."

The *Star* added that "Ed Broadbent has cancelled plans to leave today to campaign for an NDP by-election candidate in the Mission – Port Moody riding in British Columbia."

Torn apart by his mother's death — though Mary Broadbent had cancer, she had not been in terminal condition and the family suspected medical malpractice — Ed was not in great shape. Anne Carroll, Ed's executive assistant, remembers driving to Oshawa with Bill Knight for Mrs Broadbent's funeral. "I walked into the funeral home, took one look at Velma (Ed's sister), and started to cry," says Carroll. Ed, too, was in tears. "Because he is who he is," says Carroll, "you don't expect him to feel the same feelings you do. He was terribly sad." Ed remembers his mother's funeral for the motley crew of people who attended: the local mayor, his political friends from Ottawa mixed with Oshawa relatives and ordinary people — kids from the Boys and Girls Club, bridge partners, down-and-outers — who'd all been touched by Mary Broadbent's kindness. Robin Sears recalled: "The sense of calm and reverence when Ed stepped through his mother's front door made me so envious — it seemed an impossibly unconflicted love between mother and son."

Back in Ottawa, Richard Gwyn was writing about the upcoming by-elections. Should the NDP lose Mission – Port Moody, "one of the party's safest seats, [it] could mean the end of Ed Broadbent's political career. His resignation sometime this winter would become a definite possibility and perhaps even a probability."

"If we lose Mission – Port Moody," an NDP insider said, "and if our rating in the Gallup Poll doesn't get back above 16 per cent, we're going to have a very rumbly fall with consequences that won't be predictable." A caucus rebellion was imminent; the insider suggested that Ed would be too vulnerable to resist.

Little more than a week after Mary Broadbent's death, on August 29, the party lost the Mission – Port Moody seat, vacated by New Democrat Mark Rose, to the Tories; and in a by-election on the east coast, newly chosen Tory leader Brian Mulroney won himself a seat in the House of Commons, sweeping the Nova Scotia riding of Central Nova.

"It was inevitable, given our standing in the polls, that there would be discussion about Ed stepping down," says Terry Grier. "Ed knew the talk was going on. He undertook some cautious canvassing of people he respected, I did some on his behalf . . . and there was definite unrest. Of course Ed was affected by it. He was demoralized." Robin Sears advised Ed to stay on "only as long as he was still having fun." Sears felt it was crucial that Ed control the decision to stay or to leave. But the point had been reached that Ed's friends were worrying about the manner of his exit.

As the party continued to sink in the polls, Ed tried not to show how deeply shaken he was. "The polls affect him," says Lucille, "I *know* they affect him, even though he tries to push them to the back of his mind." Anne Carroll says that Ed was suffering, "but he would never let it show. You could *feel* what he was going through, but he's not the kind of person who asks for sympathy. You have to remember that through it all, he still had to go to Question Period every day, he had to run things, meet people, make decisions. It's more painful when you look back. At the time, we had our daily tasks; no matter what was happening, we took it day by day."

Publicly, Ed was as cheerful as ever. In Oshawa, for the benefit of reporters, he exuded an optimism observers thought admirable and puzzling. Ed said how lucky he was, what a wonderful childhood he'd had, and so on. Adversity, he said, was nothing new to New Democrats.

Nestor Pidwerbecki, Ed's constituency representative for a decade, watched his leader with some amazement. Then 48, the same age as Ed, Nestor is a Ukrainian-Canadian who had campaigned in his youth for former Tory MP Mike Starr, also Ukrainian; but when Ed first ran in 1968, Nestor liked what he saw and switched sides. By now Nestor was as close to Ed as anyone — and Ed is a man who doesn't let his guard down easily. Nestor recalls, during that period, feeling "surprised Ed kept going and didn't just quit. He had lots of excuses, starting with his back." Ed had a chronic disc problem that was exacerbated by constant travelling. He would fly to Vancouver for the day, return to Ottawa, head out immediately for Newfoundland, return, fly to Whitehorse, on and on. "Gruelling," is the word from Ed's former press secretary, Peter O'Malley. "I was a young guy," says O'Malley, "and I was exhausted." It was Weppler and O'Malley who had devised the media strategy that required Ed to be constantly out in the field, in auto plants, in forests, on seashores, at oil rigs, talking in the right places about the right issues. It was a strategy that had won TV coverage, before the Constitution and the Liberal and Tory leadership races obliterated everything else, and it was a strategy that promoted burnout. Ed had to be everywhere, himself, in person.

In the fall of '83, after Ed's mother's death, before Ed had the operation that cured him, Nestor would pick Ed up at the Toronto airport for the drive to Oshawa, "and even just sitting in the car, he was in pain," says Nestor. "A normal individual would have said, 'I'll knock off and take it easy until I'm feeling better.' Not Ed. He insisted on keeping going. We'd do the rounds in Oshawa, he'd go to the constituency events and see all the people, he'd be smiling and shaking hands and talking and being his usual cheerful self, and then he'd literally lie down on the floor of my house to get the tension off his back. I was really worried about him. I don't know why he didn't quit."

Ed remembers the pain. In November, he went into hospital for an injection into his spine that was supposed to cure him but it didn't work. Before Christmas of '83, the pain got so bad that when he finally went to see his doctor in Ottawa, "she phoned to get me in [to the hospital] that day. Then she drove me in her little car across town at 6 P.M. on a winter's evening. I got the CAT-scan then and there. It showed I needed an operation fast. I got it, and everything's been fine since."

But the political pain persisted. In January, 1984, a confidential and very critical report on NDP economic policy was released to the press by Jim Laxer, "orchestrated by O'Malley following his dismissal," says a party insider. Things were getting nasty. O'Malley was bitter about being fired; Laxer about being frozen out of the inner circle. This was their revenge: "NDP locked in past . . . out of touch with reality . . . needs total overhaul," crowed the headlines. In Laxer's opinion, "the oddly unsatisfying quality of social democratic pronouncements in Canada in recent years" was based on the NDP's outdated reliance on stimulating the economy in order to promote consumer spending. Going into the '90s, he argued, two revolutions had to be recognized: technological and global. The industries of the future are high tech; the American Empire has declined, overtaken by its rivals in western Europe, Scandinavia and Japan. As a result, it was no longer possible to jog along in the same old ruts. Laxer proposed yet another version of an industrial strategy that he had been working on with Ed; it was not radically different on many points from what Ed had been saying all along.

Ed was infuriated, however, by Laxer's behaviour. "I don't say negative things about staff people," Ed says, "but Jim was supposed to do the report for *me*." Caplan called Laxer's leak "a heinous crime. Jim chose to give this document to the media in a way that was without honour — and before giving it to Ed. Not only did Jim display disloyalty, but his message was perverse. He said in effect that we have not been doing what we have in fact been doing."

Laxer's response was that if he'd quietly delivered his report to Ed, it would have been buried. Laxer did not attack Ed personally. "I care more about ideas than I do about party loyalities," says Laxer bluntly. He acknowledged that he wasn't a team player; he returned to York University and continued to push his ideas publicly, through a TV series and another book on global economic restructuring, *Decline of the Superpowers*. By 1988, alienated from the NDP, though still friendly with Caplan, Laxer would be flirting with the Liberals, attached to a cluster of ex-New Democrats who were touted as the new wave of Liberalism. There were also rumours that Laxer would run for the Liberals in the next election. Since parting before Christmas 1983, Laxer and Broadbent have not spoken — an unusual state of affairs for Ed. Even with Blakeney he has remained on cordial terms. Not with Laxer.

For Ed, the "Laxer episode" was just more bad news. Battered by another public exposé of a family squabble, Ed plowed on, struggling to attract positive press. No one would let him forget reality. "So why is that man smiling, anyway?" the *Star*'s Joe O'Donnell asked.

"You got me," confessed Ed Broadbent. "That's a very good question. Maybe only a psychiatrist can answer it." O'Donnell noted that the party was still dropping to all-time lows — about 12 per cent in the polls; that Broadbent had been stung by Laxer's report; that Ed had been grounded by back problems; that his leadership was shaky. "And there was the same Ed Broadbent, with every reason to be miserable, sort of chortling his way around Metro and environs last week during a five-day,

three-city swing to launch his party's pre-election campaign. 'That's laughable,' Ed told a TV reporter who said
he had heard Broadbent's job was on the line. And sure
enough, Ed Broadbent laughed."

Sandwiched between the enormous publicity generated
by the Tory leadership convention in June '83 and the
Liberal media blitz that attended John Turner's coronation as leader in June '84, the New Democrats disappeared from view — and sank in the month leading up to
the election to as low as 9 per cent in one poll.

"As the Chinese say, it was an interesting experience,"
says Ed. "You have to keep it in perspective. Look at
what Tommy and David went through to found this
party. Look at what people in totalitarian countries go
through, struggling for basic human rights. That's suffering. If your ultimate goal is to get to the top of some ladder, these aggravations can be much more serious than
they were for me. Being leader of a political party is not
my goal in life. I'm in this to make my community a better place when I leave than it was when I arrived. But
I'm not a Utopian. [George] Orwell attacked socialists for
setting up false expectations. It's important to know the
limits of what we can do politically."

Did he feel, perhaps, that he had reached his own personal limits? "No. In no sense was I ready to pack it in. I
didn't think the party's problems were due to me. I never
felt overwhelmed. I think I must have inherited a good
batch of genes. Things never overcame my mother." Putting aside the question of ego and ambition, of which Ed
undoubtedly has his fair share, I asked if he remembered
the darkest nights, say, the Christmas of '83. Finally, for
the first time in six months of talks, he admitted to having felt low. "Yes, I was tired. I was very sad about my
mother's death — that was a huge gap in my life. But I
had the tiredness of someone who feels he's right. If I felt
I was on the wrong side of the battle, I would have been
destroyed. Democratic politics is the most difficult thing
you can do, it's a life that challenges your intellectual,
physical, spiritual stamina. If you don't believe in what
you're doing . . . ." He throws up his hands, momentarily

at a loss for words. "What sustains you is the belief that you're doing what's right, not doing something just to get to the top. If that was the driving force, I could have been in despair. But I never was."

CHAPTER EIGHT

Breaking Through the Barriers

In the past, there was no need for the NDP in Quebec. In 1961, Lesage came to power, bringing Lévesque into the Cabinet, and Lévesque was a social democrat. He had the NDP philosophy. Then in '76, Lévesque became premier. Now Lévesque is dead. Quebeckers are fatigued with Liberals and Conservatives. There is a unique opportunity in Quebec for the NDP to take forty seats — if the campaign is properly organized.

Eric Gourdeau, former economic adviser to René Lévesque, now a New Democratic organizer and candidate in Quebec.

In the first six months of 1984, a casual observer of the political scene would have concluded that Ed had hit the wall — for sure, this time. The press was writing off the party, talking about its "annihilation," about Broadbent's imminent execution. "I remember those caucus meetings, just before the election, when we were down at 9 per cent in the polls," says Bill Blaikie, a Winnipeg MP and United Church minister. "The amazing thing was, we never broke down, and Ed never lost his sense of humour." Coming out of a caucus meeting one day when most of the MPs were feeling terribly blue, Blaikie recalls Ed quoting from Thomas Aquinas, "something about having to keep faith." Ed never seemed to lose it, at least not in front of caucus. And as spring turned to summer, Ed's tough old soul and battered body were renewed from some invisible spiritual source; he had retreated into a cocoon — not a coffin — from which he would emerge transformed.

In the spring, the *Star*'s Val Sears (father of Robin) asked: "Why have Canadians turned away from a party that pioneered medicare, pricked and goaded a federal government into creating the welfare state, gave Parliament a conscience? The answer, the frightening, frustrating answer, is that New Democrats don't have the faintest idea." Robin Sears, meanwhile, working for the Socialist International in London, was receiving late-night phone calls, outpourings of grief and torment from anguished party members.

Val Sears directed his question at Gerry Caplan and was answered with another question: "How can we create a strategy," said Caplan, "when we don't know what the problem is? We are trying to get ready for an election and find our own soul at the same time. It's awful." Terry Grier, chairman of the election planning committee, blamed the party's ailments on the recession and a worldwide shift to the right, exemplified by U.S. President Ronald Reagan, elected in 1980. "Socialism is in the shadows," said Grier. Broadbent took a similar tack: "These are bad times. In bad times people become conservative, resistant to change. We are the party of change." However, Caplan undermined his leader's message by hanging out his fears: "We have lost women, we have lost the peace movement, we have lost youth. Nothing persuades people we are new . . ."

Then, in the midst of the misery, Ed Broadbent got lucky; in 1984, John Turner was elected leader of the Liberal Party, to Ed's joy, and John Turner decided to run with favourable polls into what he thought was the embrace of the Canadian public.

"Within seventy-two hours of Turner calling the election," says Gerry Caplan, "Ed was transformed into a great fighting figure — articulate, funny, energetic. He should have been surly and bitter and depressed. He wasn't. It was incredible. He has never looked back."

In early July, on the very day that Turner announced an election for September 4, 1984, Ed had an accident that could have ended everything. Lucille Broadbent re-members the scene at home. "We had been sitting up on the roofdeck, listening to music, reading, when it started to rain. We came downstairs but then Ed realized he'd left the radio on the deck. He went up to get it — he was wearing a dressing gown and thongs [plastic sandals]. The wood on the steps was slippery from the rain; he fell and slid all the way down the stairs on his back. It was awful. His back was completely bruised. I thought he'd damaged himself — he'd had that operation — and I figured, well, this is it. He won't be able to campaign."

It was surely the end. Even Ed, ever the stoic, admits, "it was an agonizing fall. Boy, did I go! I was all bruised from stem to stern." Lucille applied ice packs to the swelling welts on her husband's back and kept her worst thoughts to herself. She had watched "the troubles" from the sidelines, during the past four years, and she was aware of what she terms "the political nastiness" Ed had endured, though "he tried not to rehash things at home." As she soothed her husband's wounds, assessing them with the practised eye of a nurse, she wished she could "relieve some of the pain, carry some of the burden," but she knew there was nothing she could do. Did she want him to quit? She shrugs. "Ed is so *determined*," she says. "He would never have left when things were in a mess, no matter what his condition."

The day after his fall, Ed was raring to go — no serious damage done, no one any the wiser as to his accident. He told reporters he was "delighted" by Turner's announce-ment of a general election and called his opponents "the Bobbsey twins of Bay Street," a felicitous phrase that was picked up by the media and set the tone of the New Dem-ocrats' very clever campaign.

"Ed told me," says Nestor Pidwerbecki, "that he'd go through the election and if he didn't turn things around, that would be it. In the meantime, he said he'd give the campaign 110 per cent, and he did."

Lynn McDonald, who won Bob Rae's Toronto seat in a 1982 by-election (Rae had become leader of the Ontario NDP), recalls her sense of having "joined a sinking ship."

With a Ph.D. from the London School of Economics, author of *Social Class and Delinquency*, McDonald had a
long and distinguished career in non-electoral politics;
she was a member of the LeDain Commission (a federal
enquiry into the non-medical use of drugs, including mar-
ijuana) and a former president of the National Action
Committee on the Status of Women. Embarking on the
'84 election, she figured her Parliamentary career would
be, in contrast, "a very short one indeed," given the party's standings and its internal wranglings. "But Ed never
lost courage," says McDonald, who is not part of Ed's inner circle and not given to praising him unnecessarily.
Though she had been irritated by his propensity to smoke
cigars in caucus meetings — she won that battle — she
admired his response to the worst of times. "He kept
calm. There were no recriminations, no 'woe is us.' He
was a pillar of strength. He told us not to worry, that
things would get better when we got equal time in election coverage. He was right."

On July 31, 1984, Jeffrey Simpson wrote in *The Globe
and Mail*: "In this most difficult election campaign to
read, one of the key mysteries is the state of the New
Democratic Party. A month ago, the conventional wisdom
insisted that the NDP was down for the count, knocked
cold by self-inflicted punches. For eighteen months, the
NDP had scraped the bottom of the polls, falling as low as
nine and a half per cent in one national survey. . . . Suddenly . . . old Ed is bouncing with life, jabbing and weav-
ing better than either Mr Turner or Mr Mulroney. By
general consensus, he more than held his own in the English television debate. . . . But is it all too late?"

Is it too late? There was a terrible poignancy to that
question, and — behind the scenes — a terrible despair
that Ed refused to admit into his consciousness. In April,
Susan Riley had written in *Maclean's* that "the NDP still
has to grapple with the threat of annihilation in the approaching election." Ed joked to Riley that, "We don't
want to peak too soon." But other New Democrats took
the threat more seriously. Gerry Caplan, pondering the
situation, had set his thoughts down on paper in yet

another "confidential" report that was later leaked — again, to Ed's outrage — to the press.

"CONFIDENTIAL: Election 1984 — The Strategic Overview." Thus Caplan began his harsh assessment of party fortunes. "It is critical that all our planning for the coming campaign be conceived and executed with an explicit awareness of the advantages and disadvantages for the NDP of the current political situation. We face disturbing problems which, if not minimized, could lead to unhappy electoral consequences . . . ."

Nick Hills, who directed Southam News' coverage of the '84 election, got his hands on this memo and wrote in a subsequent article that no impartial observer "would have disagreed with Caplan before the campaign began. The NDP had spent more than two years going through hell." Actually, it was four years, dating back to Ed's support for Trudeau on the Constitution. Scanning the party's woes, the attacks on Ed's leadership at the '81 and '83 conventions, the disaffection of western New Democrats, Hills wrote that "in the summer months before the election call, they were stuck at a level of public support which suggested they would lose more than half their thirty seats. To make matters worse in the public's perception, the party's own pollster, Larry Ellis, had taken a major sampling of public opinion in British Columbia, Saskatchewan, Manitoba and Ontario, and come up with the same sort of results, made his recommendations and then been fired. It looked as though the NDP couldn't face up to the facts, so it shot the messenger. The best that Caplan could say, in the downside of his internal analysis, was 'We can avoid the apocalypse some predict for us, but it is by no means inevitable that we will.' "

What intrigued Hills, given this scenario of certain doom, was that "less than three months later, the New Democrats not only avoided apocalypse, but were returned to Parliament with more seats in English Canada than the Liberals. . . . The achievement of the New Democrats in basically holding on to what they had won in 1980, in the face of such a gigantic political tide to the Conservatives, can never be underestimated."

How did it happen? Partly it was organization: Caplan devised a survival strategy that focussed on four dozen key, winnable ridings, highlighting the essential role the NDP played defending the interests of ordinary people. "Canadians don't want the NDP to disappear from the national scene," he said. "Whatever their political views, a significant number believe that our role as advocate for the underprivileged, as conscience of the nation, help make this a more decent country. . . . [They] would be dismayed if they woke up one day after the election to learn that the NDP had inadvertently been decimated. This is an important but subtle strength of the national party . . . ."

Caplan's analysis showed that "half of all Liberal voters may be persuaded to switch their allegiance." Crucial to winning their support was the performance of the leader. Under enormous pressure, Ed delivered — with gusto. His memory of the '84 kickoff is vivid. This is something he likes to talk about — he was the clear underdog, the darkest of dark horses, and he surprised everyone. "I was viscerally up," he says, "I wanted to get off the mark fast, I intuitively felt we were going to do well." As he tells the story, he gears up and is transformed from a subdued politician into a fighter. I have met him in his fifth floor office in the centre block on Parliament Hill. The sun is beaming in the corner windows which face onto the Ottawa River. In the background, the Gatineau Hills in Quebec undulate across the horizon. In the foreground, Ed, wearing an elegant dark-gray suit, loosens his tie and leans forward on the sofa, hunching over, punching one fist into the palm of his other hand. His dark brown eyes shine and he is filled with energy. "I wanted it to be an aggressive, populist campaign," he says. The idea of kicking off on Bay Street was his, as was his description of Turner and Mulroney as "the Bobbsey twins of Bay Street." It was his coinage of the phrase "ordinary Canadians" that carried the campaign, though behind the scenes Gerry Caplan had some fierce arguments with Ed about sticking to issues in which the party had credibility — which meant downplaying Ed's favourites, economic policy and industrial strategy. "It was a great blow to Ed," says Caplan, "when our own polls showed that we had no credibility on economic issues. It was the party's old problem: people loved us for our heart and didn't trust, or weren't interested, in our head. The secret of '84 was that we played it to the heart."

Pulling the party's act together was, however, no easy task. There were "internal battles and deep divisions," says Caplan, "about what kind of campaign to run." Election strategy sessions were snakepits filled with *angst*. Before the campaign started, "it was all going to ratshit, an endless escalator on the way down," a party activist told Hills. "We were becoming inconsequential. Every one per cent [we dropped] in the opinion polls meant another 100,000 voters lost." After Larry Ellis was fired, he told the press that, based on his numbers, the New Democrats might win zero seats, none at all; at his most optimistic, Ellis figured the party would take one or two ridings. The party's dead saints rolled over in their graves.

Says Caplan: "We were terrified about what was going to happen." Worse, Caplan let his fear show, which riled Broadbent. Ed is a stoic; few people have ever seen him "blow." He is stubborn, he gets impatient, he rants, he glares, he swears, but he rarely "loses it." He expects the same self-control from his staff people. Caplan, too, normally exuded a professional detachment, but the pressures of this particular election got to him. He remembers that his own anguish led to "a little collapse" in the spring of '84. "At an election preparation meeting with party and [Parliament] Hill staff, I was so frustrated that I started shouting and screaming. I lost it [control]. I went home to bed for a few days. I was really upset. I had always prided myself on being a little bit detached. Norm [Simon] had said to me, 'You're the guy we look to, to be cool.' But this time I couldn't pull myself out from the centre of the maelstrom."

At the crux of the matter was the fear — repeatedly underlined by the press — that the party "could wither and die," in the words of Val Sears. "Should they fail to elect twelve members, the NDP would cease to exist in the House of Commons. They would lose the privilege of asking questions during Question Period. They would lose the party leader's salary and an office budget for some thirty staffers ($879,000)." Richard Gwyn rubbed it in, describing "Some nightmare scenarios. . . . The step beyond invisibility could be oblivion, as happened to the Créditistes in the 1970s."

It is no wonder that Broadbent and Caplan irritated each other — though they were equally devoted to the party, in their own distinct fashion, and they were pulling off the impossible. Ed disliked what he termed "Gerry's bleeding in public." Gerry thought it was "intellectually dishonest" for Ed to tell reporters he was shooting for victory. "How the hell was an 11 per cent party going to form a government?" Caplan would ask. Broadbent would be infuriated — though he avoided making proclamations about what he was going to do when he became Prime Minister. He was the one who had to compete on the hustings with Turner and Mulroney, "the corporate clones," and he refused to give them an inch, in public. He would not play a supporting role; psychologically, he needed to feel he was competing on the same turf — certainly he considered himself at the very least an equal opponent — and indeed he was so perceived.

Again, Ed received rave reviews for his performance, while Turner stumbled — there was the bum-patting incident — and Mulroney faltered. As a good leader should, Ed presented a calm, united front; he didn't let the party's internal discord show. "Mr Broadbent has run the smoothest campaign of the three," wrote Jeffrey Simpson. "He has not made gaffes, as have Mr Turner and Mr Mulroney. He has got his facts right, unlike Mr Turner, and he hasn't been plagued by a loose tongue, unlike Mr Mulroney. He has been carefully spacing out NDP policy pronouncements — women's issues last week, tax reform yesterday in Vancouver. His party's theme — defending the interests of ordinary Canadians — seems just right in a campaign against parties led by two lawyers-cum-businessmen."

Even Gerry Caplan rebounded. He told reporters in mid-July that he was "thrilled and delighted beyond my wildest expectations." This election was, it should be noted, Caplan's first working directly with Broadbent; Caplan didn't know about Ed's great love for campaigning, and his great skill. Ed was also taking Caplan's advice: Ed was *not* promising to form a government nor was he introducing grand industrial strategies. NDP pollster Vic Fingerhut, based in Washington, D.C., reinforced Caplan's message. "You've got your slogan — Fighting for Ordinary Canadians," said Fingerhut. "It's working. Stick to it."

Ed's performance was highlighted by his opponents' troubles. Mulroney was being roasted for campaign promises that would cost $20 billion — a figure inadvertently leaked to the press by Tory MP John Crosbie, who left open a document that was seen by an *Ottawa Citizen* reporter. Mulroney then denied Crosbie's numbers, said he'd never seen them, they weren't official, and that the real costs would be much lower though he couldn't say by how much.

Turner, meanwhile, was being hounded by Mulroney — in an attack that would come to haunt Mulroney — about patronage. Turner had processed a series of plum patronage appointments that Pierre Trudeau appeared to have left on the books in order deliberately to embarrass Turner. At first Mulroney had responded to the patronage issue by indicating that the Tories would feed at the pork barrel until they were satiated — and the Tories were starving. Later, Mulroney changed his tune: "I undertake today that all political appointments will be of the highest unimpeachable quality. I'm going to send out a dramatic sign of renewal in this area of Canadian life."

Broadbent was well launched on his attack against the "Bobbsey twins," arguing that there was no difference between the Liberals and Tories. He advocated a minimum tax on wealthy Canadians who were paying no tax at all. He said he would abolish the Senate, a costly "patronage home" for Liberals and Tories, and he predicted that both Turner and Mulroney "would scrap the Foreign Investment Review Agency and gut the National Energy Program, allowing even more energy resource ownership by foreign-owned multinationals." Mulroney later fulfilled these predictions.

Richard Gwyn applauded: "For a man about to be hanged, and at the very least to be quartered, New Democratic Party leader Ed Broadbent is looking remarkably cheerful these days. He's trotting steadily and smoothly along at the same time as Progressive Conservative leader Brian Mulroney has been tripping over his own shoelaces and Prime Minister John Turner has been lunging around with his track suit still on. . . . He made an inspired campaign opening (it was his own idea), smack in the middle of Bay Street, with the TV cameras panning up from him to the corporate towers around him." Gwyn accepted Broadbent's contention that "he is leading what amounts to Canada's effective opposition party." Indeed, he observed, the polls were showing that voters believed Liberals and Conservatives, "no matter which of them happens to win, will, as soon as the election is over, walk and look and quack in exactly the same way. . . ."

By late August, the NDP was back from the brink. It had risen to 18 per cent in the polls, while the Tories and Liberals changed places: the national fervour for getting rid of Trudeau, at first appeased by Turner's presence as Liberal leader, was still not satisfied. Turner was increasingly viewed as a re-tread; he had lost his touch. He went into the election with 49 per cent in a *Globe*–Crop poll conducted at the end of June, which showed the Tories at 39 per cent and the NDP at 11 per cent. By the week before the election, the Tories were up to fifty, the Liberals had slumped to twenty-eight, and the NDP was up to nineteen.

The dismal fate foreseen for the New Democrats did not occur: the NDP won thirty seats, two less than in 1980. The Liberals' humiliation was not foreseen and did occur: they went into the election with 147 seats and came out with forty, the worst result in party history. With 211 seats, the Tories won the largest majority ever recorded, a victory widely attributed to the depth of antipathy toward Pierre Trudeau.

The new Prime Minister was a political neophyte. Brian Mulroney had won the Conservative leadership on June 11, 1983 — "a man who had never been elected to anything, yet wanted to start at the top," wrote Claire Hoy in *Friends in High Places.* Little more than two months later, on August 29, he won the Central Nova by-election in Nova Scotia. He held a seat in the House of Commons for only a year before he became Prime Minister. Parliamentary procedure, the rules of the House, the functioning of government — it was all new to him. As a business man, his main claim to fame was that after losing the Tory leadership to Joe Clark in 1976, he had joined the Iron Ore Co. of Canada, a subsidiary of Hanna Mining Co. of Cleveland, Ohio. Appointed president in 1977, he presided over the company's demise, closing down the town of Schefferville, Quebec, in 1982. Mulroney took pride in the generous severance arrangements he made for employees. However, Michel Nadeau, then the economic writer for *Le Devoir*, examined Mulroney's activities at IOC and reported, in 1981, that instead of re-investing profits in the company during three of its most profitable years, IOC had transferred to its owners $97 million in 1979 and dividends of $82 million (U.S.) in 1980. Canadian Press reported in 1982 that in the previous two years alone, IOC's shareholders had taken out of the company "roughly the total amount invested . . . since operations began in 1949." In *Friends in High Places*, Claire Hoy noted that Mulroney promised to "launch [Schefferville] on a new economic course." Though Mulroney presented great plans for its future, today Schefferville is "a desolate ghost town," in the words of the *Montreal Gazette*'s Claude Arpin.

If Mulroney's business career was hardly inspiring, as a politician he presented a clean slate — though a memo written by one of the organizers of his '83 leadership campaign revealed back-room concerns about his style.

People don't trust Mulroney, wrote Toronto businessman John Thompson, "because of the slickness, smoothness, pat answers, feeling that there is no substance, plastic image and the feeling that you are someone's candidate — big business or Conrad Black." Still, Mulroney was an unknown quantity; he had no track record. But he promised to clean out Liberal corruption, scandal and patronage; he promised a new age of good government. Only time would tell.

Ed Broadbent emerged from the election rejuvenated. And since 1984, he has been sailing on smooth seas, sweeping three by-elections in July of 1987, from St. John's, Newfoundland to Hamilton, Ont., to the Yukon. Although intermittent squalls have threatened the voyage, he has retained firm control of his party, displaying "a new maturity and self-confidence, without a lot of ego inflation," says Marion Dewar, who wasn't having such an easy time of it. Behind-the-scenes battles bubbled to the surface and were contained, as both Broadbent and the New Democrats entered a new phase.

One of the struggles that never exploded in the media focussed around Marion Dewar's presidency of the party from 1985 to 1987. The former mayor of Ottawa, a tall, charismatic woman in her late fifties, Dewar was determined to shake the cobwebs out of the organization. "I never worked so hard in my life," she says, describing the part-time, volunteer position which she turned into a full-time job — not without generating a lot of resentment. Because there was no office for the president in Woodsworth House, the party's old brick house-headquarters in downtown Ottawa, she was seated at a makeshift desk behind the Xerox machine — until Tommy Douglas retired and she was given his office. Instead of being welcomed, she found herself increasingly shut out by the old guard on federal council.

"I like to think I was an agent of change," she says. She was aiming to strengthen the party's links with the grass-roots movements — women's organizations, environment and peace groups — that infused the party with vigour. Instead, party officials "seemed to think I was going to ruin everything. From their perspective, they'd worked hard all these years and they saw me as this smart alec, coming out of nowhere, who thought she was a big shot because she was the mayor of Ottawa." Anne Carroll, Ed's executive assistant, says with affection that Dewar had "an overabundance of enthusiasm" for her task. Dewar drew up organizational flow charts, ordered a management study, supported a move into modern offices and the sale of the old house — it literally had bats in the attic — and ran into a brick wall.

Her predecessor as president, Tony Penikett, had been unable to continue in the job because of his own political success. He led the Yukon NDP into power in 1985 — a dramatic achievement for a man who a few years earlier was the only visible New Democrat in the region. From the commanding heights of the Yukon Government, he observed the dissension in Ottawa. "I gather they had a trying time," he says, ever the diplomat. "My sense of it is that most of Marion's problems came from her perception of her role. She may have thought the party president was some kind of deputy leader, that the staff ought to report to her, instead of to the federal secretary." The scene became tense. "The federal secretary is the chief executive officer," says Penikett, "and you can't function in a small office where there are two bosses." Though Dewar denies that she was "out to get" Dennis Young, then federal secretary, Young was eventually forced out. "Marion can't be blamed for Dennis Young's demise," says a member of the federal council. "Dennis didn't have the organizational know-how, and he was no friend to women." Young's supporters claimed, however, that he was the victim of a coup.

These sorts of internal conflicts would have shaken an inexperienced party leader. But Broadbent stayed out of the fight, which seems hardly to have dented his serenity. "Marion and Dennis had legitimate objections about each other," he says. "The party was going through serious growing pains, and it was my task to ensure the job [of expansion] got done. It was a reflection of our maturity that we kept the difficulties to ourselves, right to the end." Ed was kind to Dewar, encouraging her to use his office resources when she had trouble getting things done at party headquarters, supporting her efforts to develop women candidates; at the same time, the Dewar–Young polarization ultimately strengthened Ed's hand, and the party's effectiveness. Young "resigned," triggering a series of shifts that by the beginning of 1988 had reshuffled the cast of characters.

Marion Dewar ran in the '87 by-elections — she won in Hamilton — and was replaced as president by Johanna den Hertog, 36, who is already being touted as a potential leader of the party. Tall, attractive and articulate, fluent in four languages (French, German, Dutch and English), den Hertog will be running in the next election in Vancouver Centre against Tory Cabinet minister Pat Carney; some B.C. Tories are worried. Raised in Edmonton, educated at McGill University in Montreal, den Hertog was a young Vancouver feminist when she moved into NDP politics in the mid-'70s. A co-founder of Vancouver Rape Relief, she became chair of the B.C. NDP's policy committee and organized Vancouver mayor Mike Harcourt's successful bid for the provincial party leadership in 1987. Her husband Ron Johnson is an NDP activist and party official. They have a son, Alexander, who is almost three years old.

Den Hertog's initiation onto the federal scene went smoothly, and by early '88 the sense of order — after so many years of discord — was striking. Having made serious errors in his choice of staff in the past, Ed seemed to know what he wanted. His principal secretary Bill Knight took over as party CEO — a widely heralded move. Knight is credited by many activists for orchestrating the harmony that is evident at headquarters, despite the strains of growth.

"Knight's the kind of guy," says Nancy Riche, executive vice-president of the Canadian Labour Congress and a vice-president of the party, "that when I get frustrated at an executive council meeting, I can go and sit down with him, crack jokes, kibbitz and get what's bothering me off my chest. I always come away from a talk with

Knight feeling good — and then the next day I'll think, 'Hey — what's Knight going to do about it? What does he really think?'"

That's the way it should be, says Knight, sipping red wine in the bar at the Château Laurier, after his evening swim. He is plump, blond and benign. He trots around Ottawa in the winter in an old brown tweed overcoat with an orange NDP tuque pulled down over his ears. People call Knight the invisible mender; for sure he doesn't like attracting too much attention to himself. "I hate all that Coutts and Davey insider shit," says Knight. "It's a tragedy if someone like myself becomes the party. We found a way of killing this idea of all the king's men — the entourage, the insiders." He focusses his attention on leadership. "Politics is a tornado. The eye of the storm is the leadership. It drives the mass of energy forward but it's got to be calm at the centre. Ed's the talent. We're into team playing and letting Ed be himself. It's our job to get it in motion and keep it light so he can do his thing. His fundamental power is his optimism. He's naturally competitive and aggressive. My job is to ensure that everything's working so he can give a maximum performance. It's important he doesn't do the analytical work. The demands are too great. He can't get fragmented. If you ever start consuming the leader's energy, it's not working. Everything has to be geared so he can concentrate on his performance. No matter how good all the people around him are, when those cameras flip on they're pointed at one person. He has to do it. The great thing about him is: what you see is what you get."

How does Knight deal with party purists who consider his approach crass? Knight shrugs. "There's some people that want us to stay in a certain place forever." He positions his hand down low, then moves it up high. "We're building a base. We're going for power. That's what we're doing. I'm looking at 100 seats. I think we can form the government. If you're from Saskatchewan, you think there's only one route to go and that's straight to the goal line. Why not?" He speaks in a quiet and steady voice; he makes it sound like it's going to happen.

Knight's major limitation is that he speaks lousy French, but his replacement as principal secretary, George Nakitsas, is linguistically advanced (French, English, Greek). "The boys," as Nancy Riche refers to them, complement each other nicely, representing the developing alliance between Quebec (Nakitsas's home) and Saskatchewan (Knight's).

Nakitsas, who had functioned so well as research director since the hasty, bitter departure of Jim Laxer, is a 37-year-old Montrealer of Macedonian (Greek) ancestry, married with two young children; his parents were machine operators in the Montreal fur industry. An economics graduate of McGill University, Nakitsas was pursuing a Ph.D. (on technological change and employment patterns) when he started working for the Canadian Labour Congress in 1976. He moved from research into the CLC's political education department and worked closely with the NDP as labour campaign co-ordinator, playing an active role in elections in Manitoba and British Columbia. The thrust of his efforts, he says, "was getting beyond partisan politics and talking about the need for political involvement. We weren't telling people how to vote; we were trying to get them to look closely at what the parties stood for."

Nowadays, Nakitsas has "a finger in every pie," as he puts it, "sending out signals, keeping in touch. We've moved beyond the survival mode of '84. We're running a maximum-growth strategy." Nakitsas is a soft-spoken, self-effacing man — and to Broadbent, a pillar of strength. "George is extraordinary," says Ed. "I have never met a man who combines such ability with such an absence of ego."

Under Knight and Nakitsas, the party is mushrooming, building organizations in every one of the country's 282 ridings (295 after redistribution takes effect in mid-July '88), trying to cope with surges of growth in new territories: in Alberta, the breakthrough in the last provincial election netted the NDP an unprecedented sixteen MLAS and combined with the nurses' strike of February '88 to galvanize public support, drawing 1,300 people to an NDP nomination meeting in Edmonton; in Halifax, Alexa McDonough, leader of the Nova Scotia NDP, topped the polls as the most popular provincial politician, and her influence is promising new gains for the federal party; and in Quebec, where 250 Quebeckers have been jostling for nominations in seventy-five ridings, ex-Liberals and jaded Péquistes have been streaming into NDP headquarters looking for "the new alternative."

Stepping into these swelling seas on February 1, 1988, was the new research director, whose job it is to feed Ed with information for Question Period every day and keep him plugged in to the major issues in every region. Eyebrows were raised in certain circles when Nakitsas's old job was filled by Arlene Wortsman, the newest member of Ed's team — a gutsy choice, given that Wortsman is not an old-style party player.

A tall, quick-witted woman, 38 years old, Wortsman was brought up in middle-class Toronto and canvassed for the Liberals when she was twelve years old because her father liked Lester Pearson. Engaged in student politics while studying history and political science at the University of Toronto, she did postgraduate work at York University's Faculty of Environmental Studies and then found herself supporting the nomination of a fellow U. of T. grad in a 1978 by-election. Her pal from student days was Bob Rae. When he was elected to the House of Commons, he asked her to come to Ottawa as his executive assistant — which is one of the reasons why Rae looked so good as federal finance critic. Wortsman had a fresh curiosity, a knack for getting to the heart of issues, a non-traditional approach — and she could make sense of arcane documents like the Bank Act. Because she wasn't raised in NDP politics, she didn't know the dogma. She was always asking, "Why?"

Then she found herself lured to Manitoba by Michael Decter, a former aide to Broadbent. As clerk of the Executive Council, Decter was Manitoba's equivalent to Ottawa's Michael Pitfield, then clerk of the Privy Council. Decter hired Wortsman as a policy analyst. Within a year, she was running Pawley's policy group, where she

stayed until 1984. Back in Ottawa by 1985 as acting director of economic policy for the federal Status of Women
department, she had a baby, took French immersion, and,
as her maternity leave was expiring, landed the job as
NDP research director, an appointment that won special
plaudits from feminists. When she took the job, she asked
Ed if it would be all right if she brought her year-old son
along on the campaign plane, when the election was
called. Ed shook his head and said no, that wouldn't be
possible. "Why not?" she asked, as she explained to Ed
how it would work — she would bring a baby sitter to
look after the child while she was briefing Ed on issues.
Finally Ed looked at her and grinned: "You're right. Why
not?"

Arlene is very persuasive; she is also the living embod-
iment of new-wave New Democrats. "I don't have the
deep philosophical base that Ed has," she says, with no
hint of apology. "I'm just looking for a better world that
treats people equally, with a sense of justice, and this is
the party I'm most comfortable with — though the NDP is
certainly not perfect. I have no dogma. I'm pragmatic. I
have worked in government, and the main thing I
learned is that to be in government in the '90s is going to
be tough, because there's no money. You can't do everything you want to do. It's not a matter of add-ons; it's a
question of trade-offs."

In his own sphere, Ed's pragmatic grasp of trade-offs
was already apparent. His skillful handling of the Meech
Lake Accord — signed on June 3, 1987, by the Prime
Minister and the provincial premiers after an all-night
session that brought Quebec into the constitutional
agreement — showed that he had learned his lesson from
the constitutional wars.

Meech Lake could have been a bomb — its opponents
said it *should* have exploded — but Ed approached the
matter carefully. Instead of jumping in to support the
deal, as he had done with Trudeau's constitutional proposal, he conducted long, thoughtful caucus meetings and
heard everyone out, going round the table, drawing forth
opinions, making notes, articulating the pros and cons.

No mutiny occurred, though there was serious opposition to the Meech Lake process; the deal had been concluded behind closed doors by the Prime Minister and provincial premiers, delivered with a "take it or leave it, all or nothing" flourish that cut off efforts to improve it. More contentious was the substance: B.C. MP Ian Waddell, who had pushed Ed so hard to strengthen aboriginal rights, was strongly opposed to Meech on the grounds that it impaired the ability of the federal government to act decisively in the best interests of the nation and infringed on aboriginal and women's rights. "Mulroney gave half the federal government's power to the provinces in the Meech Lake deal," says Waddell, "and he wants to give the rest away to the Americans through free trade. What are we going to do when we decide we made a mistake and that we want a strong national government again?"

This was the concern that inspired former Prime Minsiter Pierre Trudeau to denounce the deal. Ottawa had given to the provinces a constitutional veto that would, Trudeau argued, make the provinces more powerful than the federal government. He called Mulroney "a weakling" whose deal "will render the Canadian state totally impotent. That would destine it, given the dynamics of power, to eventually be governed by eunuchs." Strong stuff — and difficult for many to ignore.

When Waddell publicly opposed Meech, he was responding to the B.C. party, which later repudiated the deal; he was also cognizant of the "rumblings" in Manitoba and in the north. Tony Penikett, leader of the Yukon NDP government, angered that territorial leaders were barred from Meech Lake discussions, was outraged when the deal gave each province the power to veto the admission of new provinces. Winnipeg MP Bill Blaikie, who had, like Waddell, held a dissenting opinion on the Constitution, was deeply concerned about the inadequacies of Meech — as was Ed. "To reform the Senate, bring in new provinces or change any federal institution, the deal requires unanimous consent," says Blaikie. "Mulroney is assuming there won't be a stalemate. It was a tough decision to support it. But Ed felt — and finally we shared his point of view — that we should agree because of Quebec. Recognition of Quebec's special status is a long-held NDP position, and we couldn't turn our backs on that. People accused us of selling out because of political opportunism. That's bull."

Ed continued to hammer at the same points: no, the deal was not perfect; yes, he would continue to work on improving it; but above all "we have to rectify the injustice of Quebec's exclusion from the constitution and this is a beginning." Not everyone admired his position. In an editorial on April 13, 1988, the *Toronto Star* mocked him for coming down "solidly on both sides" and asked: "When will Broadbent stop weaseling on this issue?" He was doing what he'd done back in the early '70s, when he supported both federalism and Quebec's right to self-determination — and was also mocked. Seventeen years later, his Quebec position (transformed into the official term, "distinct society") was enshrined in the Constitution, via the Meech Lake deal, and Ed wasn't about to back down.

"Ed's bad years, when the daggers came out — and there were a lot of daggers, believe me — those struggles were a blessing in disguise," says Marion Dewar. "When you go through the kind of battles he experienced over the Constitution, you either get bitter and cynical, or you grow. Ed grew." Her comment was reminiscent of an observation made by former Prime Minister John Diefenbaker in 1979. "Leadership's a funny thing," he said. "It makes some fellows grow, and others swell. Ed's growed."

If Broadbent had some respect for former Prime Minister Pierre Trudeau, he seems to have little regard for the current Prime Minister. On December 17, 1984, and again on May 28, 1986, Broadbent was thrown out of the House of Commons for saying Mulroney had "deliberately misled the House," and, on the second occasion, for refusing to retract a statement that the Prime Minister had lied. Mulroney, for his part, returns the hostility. "Prime Minister Brian Mulroney seems especially venomous toward Ed Broadbent," wrote Southam News columnist Don McGillivray on February 9, 1988. "When Broadbent asked Mulroney a question in the Commons Monday, the prime minister almost spat across the floor of the House" in replying to the NDP leader.

"Mulroney's bitterness toward Broadbent," McGillivray suggested, could be related to Broadbent's political prospects: Ed "seems to be able to sail serenely above the battle, at least in the opinion polls . . . it's no wonder Mulroney's grabbing every chance to try to cut Broadbent down to size." Mulroney's real fear, McGillivray proposed, was that the New Democrats might be "poised for a comeback," and that "the political situation is shaping up like the one that boosted the NDP to the top of the polls" during the summer of '87. With the Tories scanning the political horizon for a stretch of favourable weather in which to call an election, tensions were mounting.

Most troublesome — for the Conservatives — was the state of affairs in Quebec. The Tories, so recently outcasts in Quebec — they won one seat in the 1980 election, and then took fifty-eight in 1984 — could not help but feel nervous about the volatility of the electorate. The key to national power is Quebec — where the New Democrats have never elected an MP. But through the winter and spring of '88, Broadbent's équipe québecoise (Quebec team) received increasing attention. In a full colour photograph on the front page of the Montreal Gazette, Ed Broadbent arm-wrestled Paul "the Butcher" Vachon, brother of wrestler Mad Dog Vachon. Paul was running for the NDP and he was a popular candidate, active in community education on such issues as child abuse and wife battering. If some people joked about the Vachon brothers, no one was scoffing at the party's burgeoning membership lists and new candidates. The Star's Robert McKenzie, formerly a skeptic about the NDP's chances in Quebec, bubbled over with enthusiasm in April about "Broadbent's prize catches." His list included: "François Beaulne, an international finance expert and former vice-president of the National Bank; Paul Cappon, a medical doctor and McGill University professor who is to chair an international convention in Montreal in June of some 5,000 doctors opposed to nuclear arms; Phil Edmonston,

U.S.-born, Montreal-based consumer-protection activist; Rémy Trudel, outgoing rector of the University of Quebec campus in Abitibi; Philippe Bernard, a university administrator who is a former PQ treasurer; Pierre Hetu, internationally known orchestra conductor; Maria Peluso, regional director of the Canadian Council of Christians and Jews; Claire Brassard, a labour relations lawyer; Ruth Rose, a University of Quebec economics professor."

At the NDP's new headquarters in east-end Montreal, former Liberals and Péquistes were settling in as New Democratic workers. "We had 418 members at the beginning of 1987, and by January '88 we had 12,000," said Donald Houle, the party's new federal organizer. "We got 2,000 new members in the last week of February alone, and by the end of May we had 20,000 members." Houle's story alone is evidence of a new mood in Quebec. Houle is a former Quebec Provincial Police officer with twenty-three years' service under his belt. He drives around the province in a Honda equipped with a telephone; he's never out of touch. Until a little over a year ago, he had never heard of the NDP. Head of security for the 1976 Montreal Olympics and for the Pope's visit in the early '80s, Houle was director of the QPP's drug squad and chief of criminal investigations in Montreal, where he was responsible for supervising 600 to 700 men in some cases. He was also what he calls "a nut for politics." Having retired almost two years ago to his home town, Rouyn-Noranda, in northeastern Quebec, Houle and his best buddy, Michel Lemire, were the most powerful Liberal organizers in the region. Lemire runs his own interior decoration business, Michel Draperies, but his major passion for twenty years has been political organization.

In 1986, Houle and Lemire were looking for a hot Liberal candidate to run in the next federal election. They checked around town; the name on everyone's lips was Rémy Trudel, president of the University of Quebec at Rouyn-Noranda. Dr Trudel — he has a Ph.D. in the philosophy of administration — is renowned for having created a very special university (with a $10 million annual budget) that has taken education to the people of

Quebec's north. He pioneered teaching Cree Indians and Inuit in their own languages, and contributed to the booming prosperity of the region, where 80 per cent of its mining operations are now run by Quebeckers and unemployment is down to five or six per cent. A community activist, with an impressive network, only 39 years old, a native of Trois Rivières, Rémy Trudel was attractive, eloquent, the man of the hour — and so Houle and Lemire paid a visit to see him in November, 1986.

Trudel picks up the story: "Imagine the situation," he says, sipping a glass of wine in a Montreal hotel bar. "There they were in my university office — Donald and Michel. I've known them for years. We worked together on the election of the mayor of Rouyn-Noranda. They live for politics. It's their addiction."

Houle and Lemire told Trudel they'd done a survey and that "you are the best candidate for the federal election."

"Really?" said Trudel. "I'm curious. Tell me, what colour [party] will I be?"

Houle and Lemire laughed at Trudel's joke. "What a question," they scoffed. "Of course you'll be red [Liberal]."

Trudel, a former Péquiste, shrugged. "There's only one thing I'm sure of. I'll never be a candidate for the Liberal party. You want to know why? It's not a party, it's a collection of interests. You ask me what about the Tories? It's also just a group of interests, not a party with ideas. If one day I run, I'll be with the NDP."

"The ND-what?"

"Look at the polls," said Trudel. "The NDP, without any organization whatsoever in Quebec, is getting 25 per cent support. Think what the NDP could do with some organization."

Houle and Lemire went away and promised to think about it. Trudel himself was not so sure what his own decision would be, but he'd read some NDP literature, its book of policy resolutions, and liked the party's program. Two weeks later, Houle and Lemire came back to see him. "Rémy, we don't understand anything about the NDP. Maybe you have a good idea here, but we'd like to meet someone from the NDP." It was as if they were requesting a meeting with a creature from another planet.

"Sure," said Trudel. "I'll arrange for you to meet Mr Broadbent." Trudel was bluffing but he figured it was worth a try.

Houle and Lemire were surprised — they had heard of Ed Broadbent, they knew he was *le chef* but they had never thought of going straight to the top. Nor had Trudel, until that moment. His only contact with the party came at its Montreal convention in March 1987, where as an interested observer he casually met George Nakitsas, then the party's research director. After the convention, Trudel contacted NDP headquarters in Montreal, was given the phone number of Ed's Parliament Hill office, and reached Nakitsas, who did not let Trudel slip through his fingers. He invited Trudel to bring his friends to Ottawa for a meeting at the beginning of May — the earliest date Trudel could make because he was then involved in organizing the International Symposium on Northern Development, which included delegates from the Soviet Union, China, and the Scandinavian countries.

On May 1, Trudel and his Liberal pals arrived at Le Soupçon, a sophisticated Ottawa restaurant which the Broadbents frequent — it is located near their house and owned by Lucille's niece. Ed Broadbent, Nakitsas, Michel Agnaieff, the party's chief spokesman in Quebec, Rémy Trudel, Donald Houle and Michel Lemire embarked on a leisurely, lively meal. Lemire, on meeting Broadbent, felt like "a kid at his first communion — I fell down on my chair. I was surprised, I didn't expect it. I felt his charisma. It was really something — we're just a couple of small guys from Rouyn-Noranda, and Mr Broadbent talked with us for three hours." Just themselves occupying centre stage in the restaurant, which had opened specially for the Broadbent party, they ate and drank and talked. Trudel, Houle and Lemire peppered questions at Ed. Most of their questions were about business — the topic that dominates Quebec politics. Having gained considerable control over their economy in the last twenty-five years since the Quiet Revolution began, using the

levers of government to promote economic development
and investment in local entrepreneurs, Quebeckers are
avidly pursuing the growth of small and medium-size
businesses — the corporate sector that produces the vast
majority of new jobs.

Not beating around the bush, Michel Lemire demanded
to know: "What's your party going to do for small and
medium-size businesses?" Lemire, Houle and Trudel are
not woolly ideologues; a political party, Trudel likes to
say in the pragmatic tone common to Quebeckers, "is,
after all, only a tool. When you want to do something for
your community, you want the best tool." If the tool
doesn't work — like the Liberal or Tory parties, in his
view — get rid of it; if the "new tool" is the New Democrats, use it. To make a long story short, when they had
drunk the last glass of wine, Houle and Lemire were very
impressed. "Geez, what a good guy," said Lemire. "Broadbent is a simple man, warm, sincere, I like him." Trudel
was equally moved. "He didn't make big promises. He
kept saying, 'If it's possible, we will . . . .' He has a good
feel for reality." If they worried about one thing it was
that the NDP was the party of centralization. Ed reassured
them that his policies — and his party — were dedicated
to decentralization and grass-roots development.

They went home to Rouyn-Noranda and told their
friends they were forming an NDP riding association and
that Trudel would be running for the NDP nomination.
"Our friends were happy," says Leimire. "We explained
that the NDP is the new alternative, and people understood. Mr Broadbent told us his party is left-of-centre, not
extreme, and that's where we sit." Houle and Lemire had
never voted PQ. "We were never separatist," says Lemire.
"We love Canada and we love Quebec in Canada. We
have a nice big, rich country and we want to keep it that
way." Trudel says he voted PQ in the past, "not because I
was anti-Canada but because I was for the affirmation of
the French people. We needed the PQ to give us control of
our economy and our destiny." Now that the PQ was in
decline, it was clear to Trudel that the tool best suited to
the purposes of Quebec's people was the NDP.

As Houle and Lemire set to work in Rouyn-Noranda, Ed's staff kept an eye on their activities and realized that not only were they serious about politics but they were good. In September, they organized a sold-out dinner – 450 people, mostly Liberals and Conservatives, at $50 a head — and had Ed up to speak. By October, 1987, Donald Houle and Michel Lemire had been persuaded to set up shop in Montreal, commuting to Rouyn-Noranda and spanning out across the province. "I thought about it a lot," says Houle. "I was retired, I liked my life up north, I have a house near the lake, a ski-doo, I like hunting and fishing, I have Hereford cattle . . . but this seemed more important. Rémy Trudel has the best chance of anyone in Quebec to win a seat in the next election, and I think it's a good contribution for me to come to Montreal, where I lived and worked for so many years, where I know so many people." He figures the party's prospects are strong in twenty to thirty ridings, out of a total of seventy-five. "The best organization will win the most seats. The more time we have, the better organization we will create. I want to make a *big* organization." Every week he hits the road, driving out to yet another community to sell "the new alternative" and round up workers. "The Liberals were a good party, but under Turner, no way," he says, unrepentant about his switch.

In the boardroom of NDP headquarters, just beyond Houle's office, the NDP election platform committee is meeting. A distinguished gray-haired pin-stripe-suited executive co-chairs the meeting with a young, elegant, dark-haired corporate lawyer. Eric Gourdeau and Claire Brassard represent two new wings of the Quebec NDP: he is a businessman and elder statesman whose networks reach back into the Quiet Revolution and forward into the new society created by René Lévesque's Parti Québecois, whose government Gourdeau served as a senior deputy minister for almost a decade. She is a self-described "feminist socialist" — which she says "is very particular to the feminist movement in Quebec. We had certain political pretensions." She joined the NDP in 1985, "when Lévesque left the PQ and the PQ went right-wing." Her

first opportunity to get a feel for Broadbent came two
years later, at a meeting of the NDP's Quebec committee
just before the Montreal convention. The meeting was notable for the visible tension between Jean-Paul Harney
and Ed Broadbent, former leadership rivals (twice they
ran against each other). Harney, former leader of the
Quebec NDP, now living near Quebec City, was thinking
about running federally in the next election. (Later, he
would announce his candidacy.)

The occasion was also "historic," says Claire Brassard,
for resolving the Quebec group's desire to have their
province recognized as a "distinct society." Brassard recalls how it went: "Ed arrived on time, very calm, self-
possessed. He was very warm and friendly with us. He
didn't drink coffee. He sat down with a blank sheet of paper in front of him and a gold pen — very neat, well prepared. Jean-Paul Harney was late, very nervous, very
aware of Broadbent's charm." As the meeting proceeded,
Brassard was surprised that Broadbent "let the committee discuss and didn't intervene for the first hour and a
half. I kept waiting for him to interrupt, but he didn't.
He listened, made notes, and when he finally spoke, he
had a very clear idea of what the resolution should be.
Right away, without having to fight, he gave us more
than we thought we'd get [on the "distinct society"] —
and we were so surprised we didn't know what to do."
Harney, whom some Quebec NDPers saw as trying to "out-
Québecois the Québecois" in terms of presenting a very
aggressive brand of French nationalism, was silenced.

At about the same time, Brassard was delighted when
the party found its first "godfather" figure — and she
found a mentor: Eric Gourdeau, whom Robert McKenzie
described as "an energetic sparkplug of a man . . . [his]
blue-gray eyes sparkle behind his glasses and his shock
of thick, graying hair seems to bristle in anticipation
when he's asked about the coming election. . . ." Gourdeau embodies the "sympathetic" link between Lévesque's Parti Québecois and the New Democratic Party.
Descended from ancestors who settled near Quebec City
in 1623, Gourdeau was raised in a progressive family; his

mother's sister had a son, Robert Cliche, who became a prominent Quebec lawyer and the Great French Hope for the NDP in the '60s. Gourdeau, an engineer and economist, was educated at Laval University and set up his own consulting business specializing in forestry, energy, northern development and environmental issues.

Despite Gourdeau's many years working for Liberal and Parti Québecois governments, he had never joined a political party until March of 1987, when he sent in his application to join the NDP. "It took me four months to get my card," he says with a smile. "I had to phone them three or four times to remind them." A man who enjoys blazing new trails — with Michel Bélanger, now chairman of the National Bank, he was a key figure in the nationalization of Quebec's private power companies — Gourdeau was looking for the next big challenge of his life. He found it in the NDP. When his membership card finally arrived, it came with a list of party members in his Montmorency-Orleans riding on the outskirts of Quebec City. "We have 45,000 voters, and there were six NDP members," he says wryly. Undeterred — the Québecois are accustomed, after all, to long shots — he thought deeply about federal politics, and decided he wanted to meet Broadbent.

It was again at Le Soupçon, the Ottawa restaurant, that Broadbent and Gourdeau met in the fall of 1987. Gourdeau was impressed. "I liked Broadbent right away. I thought he was a simple man. I felt he still belonged to the milieu he came from, and he gave me the impression he wanted to know more about Quebec." Know more? Broadbent was ready to climb the highest mountain to make connections in Quebec. Indeed his strategy — as yet unnoticed in the media — was to link Quebec and western Canada, creating a corridor to power that was shaped like a rainbow. And in the person of Gourdeau he had the man who understood the historic common ground between Quebec and Saskatchewan.

In 1960, at the dawn of La Révolution tranquille, Eric Gourdeau was a chief economic adviser to René Lévesque, then Quebec's minister of Public Works and "Hydraulic

Resources" — an "afterthought," as Lévesque put it, that would become "the goose that laid the golden eggs." In his *Memoirs*, Lévesque wrote: "July, 1960: one newspaper spoke of the next month as the thirty days that shook Quebec . . . we were being carried by an irresistible whirlwind of enthusiasm, appetite for life, and limitless confidence in our own capacity to move things forward." One evening during this period Lévesque visited Father Georges-Henri Lévesque, "the man who was the liberating conscience of our generation." As they walked together to the edge of the waterfall at Montmorency, "probably inspired by the deafening roar that seemed to fill one's very being, my companion turned toward me: 'Hurry up!' he shouted. 'What's happening is a revolution. Don't let it slip through your fingers.' "

"Lévesque was a socialist, there's no doubt about it," says Gourdeau. "And when we looked for models, naturally we looked to Saskatchewan, which was the first province to understand the role of the state in development and to make it work." Gourdeau and his Quebec colleagues received help, behind the scenes, from Tommy Shoyama and Al Johnson, the Saskatchewan civil servants who'd been brought to Ottawa in the '60s. Shoyama served the Saskatchewan government from 1946 to 1964, and then successive federal governments for another quarter century. In the mid-'70s, he replaced Simon Reisman as deputy minister of finance.

Today, Al Johnson is ensconced in serene quarters at Massey College at the University of Toronto, where he teaches public policy. In his sixties, with a Ph.D. from Harvard and a truly illustrious career behind him — culminating with the presidency of the CBC from '75 to '82 — he still carries the exuberance of the Saskatchewan revolution. "Quebec and Saskatchewan had the same experience, though the character of each place is so different," he says. "The cause was manifest. We both had grand visions. We understood each other. Both societies moved from nothing to an advanced social democracy. We faced the same problem: how do you develop a province economically in a market situation that's not helpful to you?"

He well remembers that the Quebec–Saskatchewan connection was made in Ottawa in the '60s "through the public service. It wasn't a case of Jean Lesage meeting with Tommy Douglas. The Lesage government was moving towards social democracy and province-building; in Saskatchewan we had done what the Quebec government was interested in doing. The occasion for conversation was substantial."

The key to success in both provinces, says Johnson, was the strength of the political leadership combined with a collective vision for the society.

"Tommy Douglas cared more about creativity — and humanity — than anything else," says Johnson. "He gave us space, he created a climate of experimentation — we were so young — and yes, it was a brilliant public service, animated by the freedom Douglas imparted. We had a cause, and it liberated the energies of the people." Gourdeau similarly describes the atmosphere in the Quebec government through the '60s as a time of "experimentation, adventure and achievement." It was based on a principle that was articulated in 1962 and became the slogan for both the Quiet Revolution and the Parti Québecois: *Maître Chez Nous*. Masters in our own house.

In 1968, about the time that Lesage's Liberals were faltering and René Lévesque quit the party to found the PQ, Gourdeau resigned from the government to resume his consulting business. He continued to work on resource development projects for private clients, many of them American energy corporations, and became familiar with the Washington scene. After the Parti Québecois victory in 1976, Lévesque asked Gourdeau to return to government as deputy minister for economic development; Gourdeau agreed, though he was never a separatist, and later moved on to direct a new secretariat concerned with Inuit and Indian development. He remained in Lévesque's inner circle until 1985, when the Parti Québecois was defeated by Bourassa's Liberals. "I stayed on under Bourassa until 1986, but I could not work for Bourassa," says Gourdeau. "Lévesque and I were on the same wave length. I could not communicate with Bourassa."

So Gourdeau took a year off to play golf, listen to music, read — and think about what he wanted to do with the rest of his life. On October 9, 1987, three weeks before Lévesque's death, Gourdeau met with his old friend. Gourdeau told Lévesque he had joined the NDP and was thinking of standing for a federal nomination. "Lévesque thought profoundly about it," says Gourdeau, "and then he said, 'That's a good idea.'" With Lévesque's blessing, Gourdeau was off and running. He started calling his old friends and acquaintances. He told them he wanted to come and talk to them about his ambitions in federal politics. He didn't tell them which party he was attached to. They were happy to see him and, somewhat to his surprise, had guessed he was talking NDP.

In order to establish a federal riding association, Gourdeau needed ten members. He rounded up ten friends, and then discovered that in order to hold a nomination meeting he needed 150 members. "I went out and got them too, no trouble," he says. Old friends who were organizers for the other major parties showed up and bought memberships. "Actually, I was amazed," he says. He need not have been: the Gourdeau networks run wide and deep. Apart from his "official" career, he was chairman of the local school board for five years, his wife is known throughout the community for her good works, and their five children have been active around town. By the spring of '88, Gourdeau was co-chair of the Quebec platform committee and was working with new party members across the province "to bring the Quebec perspective into the national program." His secret agenda was to reconcile Ed Broadbent and Jean-Paul Harney. "They were rivals," Gourdeau shrugs. "It's time they were friends."

Gourdeau smokes his cigarette — Buckingham plain, the same brand Lévesque smoked — and thinks out loud: "In the past, there was no need for the NDP in Quebec. In 1961, Lesage came to power, bringing Lévesque into the Cabinet, and Lévesque was a social democrat. He had the

NDP philosophy. Then in '76, Lévesque became Premier. Now Lévesque is dead. Quebeckers are fatigued with Liberals and Conservatives. There is a unique opportunity in Quebec for the NDP to take forty seats — if the campaign is properly organized."

CHAPTER
NINE

The Pursuit of Power

The next election will be about motive.
Who do I trust? Spontaneity, emotion, mo-
tive: these are the touchstones of the new
era.

Allan Gregg, pollster, February 1, 1988.

Ed's steady progress leading the party began to be noticed; everyone started to talk about how Broadbent had
changed. Ed's best friend in Ottawa, Joe Levitt, was
amused. A gray-haired peacenik (Veterans Against Nuclear War) and professor emeritus at the University of
Ottawa (where he taught Canadian intellectual history),
Levitt is currently writing a book on Lester Pearson and
the Canadian role in nuclear disarmament between 1946
and 1957.

Seated in the living room of his old (as in renovated)
brick house in Ottawa's Glebe district, Joe Levitt talks
about his friendship with Ed. Levitt is a big man who ex-
udes an almost electric enthusiasm for life and ideas. His
hair sticks out from his head and his laughter bounces off
walls. He first met Ed Broadbent when they were both
pursuing their doctorates at the University of Toronto in
the '60s. Levitt's thesis was on French-Canadian history,
focussing on Henri Bourassa, the Quebec patriot who was
also the hero of Jim Laxer.

Levitt is fifteen years older than Ed and considers himself "an old-fashioned socialist. My generation had an attachment to nationalization. Ed doesn't have any of that;
never did. He rejected Marxism in the '60s. He doesn't
like commies. He's not anti-business. Ed loves General
Motors. He doesn't talk about an evil ogre exploiting the

workers; he talks about a marvellously efficient corporation that makes the best cars in the world — that's a lot
of bull, but he's a GM man." How does Levitt, an old leftist, accept Ed's moderate stances? Levitt shrugs happily.
"A Broadbent government would be a right-wing, social
democratic government. The socialist agenda has shifted
to peace, foreign policy, the environment, women, child
care. . . . He'd bring in some reforms but the idea that
he'd do anything to cripple the economy — no way. He
doesn't dream of turning Canada into Tanzania."

Levitt laughs, eyes shining with delight. "Can you
imagine the fun I'm having? I met a student in 1964, he
was my best man when I got married to Marnie [his second wife] in 1971, and twenty-four years later he's a con-
tender for Prime Minister — and we're still friends.
We're both political junkies."

Levitt's wife, Marnie, a high school teacher who considers herself a strong feminist, drops in to interject that
"my son takes potshots at Ed — thinks he isn't left
enough. But Ed's always up for a good argument. We all
love to fight around here."

Levitt continues: "Ed and I don't agree on everything
but we love talking politics. In the old days it was abstract, intellectual stuff. Nowadays Ed likes talking practical politics, about how to win elections. If you told him
he was going to remain in opposition for the rest of his
life, I think he'd quit. He told me once, 'I want to be
where the action is. You can't change things unless you
have power.' What makes Ed different is that he wants to
change the world and he feels he must seek power in order to do it — it's a moral duty for him. The real politics
start when you get a mass audience — many socialists
don't understand this. Ed does. He's an unusual combination: moral fibre, strong principles, very tough, wants
power. Politics is a very tough game, it's a very serious
fight, like a war, you need tough people who can take it."

"Ed is like a very interesting crystal," says Marnie.
"On the one hand he looks very clear, but he has a lot of
sides to him. He has good vibes, a high energy level, an
unusual capacity to make contact with many different

kinds of people." Has she ever seen his demanding, perfectionist side? "Let's say Ed is very firm, so you have to
be very firm yourself if you want him to see your point.
He has a very strong personality, an acerbic sense of humour. He doesn't lose his cool. He is *so* self-directed —
not that he's selfish — but it would be a struggle to keep
up your own personality with him." How has Lucille
managed? "On matters of principle, Lucille is just as
strong as he is. She's gutsy. They're a healthy combination."

Has Ed changed? Says Joe: "When the NDP was at 10
per cent in the polls, all I ever heard was what a drip
Broadbent was. Now that he's hit 40 per cent and moved
the party into contention, he's a genius. Ed hasn't
changed; the people have."

There is no doubt that the public's affection for Broadbent has been reinforced by Mulroney's scandal-prone
Cabinet and Turner's troubles. Did Ed get better? Keith
Davey says yes, in one respect. "Ed Broadbent has finally
learnt to stop shouting in the House of Commons and has
become far more effective," Davey wrote in *The
Rainmaker*. "I wish he was a Grit. Ed's a closet intellectual who skilfully champions many causes which he can't
possibly believe in. Anyway, I like him."

The people who don't like Ed are mostly to be found
within the New Democratic Party. According to a couple
of disgruntled ex-advisers, he's superficial, stubborn and
pig-headed. Says one: "He's dull. He has no new ideas. He
earns more than $100,000 a year and fancies himself a
statesman-like figure; in our party that doesn't always go
down too well. He plays it safe. You're never going to get
any daring moves from Ed. He's predictable."

Tom Axworthy, former principal secretary to Pierre
Trudeau, suggests that Ed hasn't changed, but the scenery has. "Ed is Ed. I always liked him. We used to talk
political philosophy, and that was fun. I didn't think he
was a hero or a wonderman, but he did a good job knitting his party together after the Lewis/Waffle split —
people forget how deeply divided the NDP was, as bad as
the Tories under Clark or the Libs under Turner. Ed was

always a straightforward guy in the House. But he paled beside Trudeau, who was a bit of a giant. Trudeau was a big tree, and Ed was overshadowed. Ed's out of the shadows now. The country is giving him a closer look. He's seen to be blooming because he's being compared to pygmies."

For the new Prime Minister, the bloom came off the rose — inevitably. By mid-February, 1987, the Tories had slumped to 22 per cent, with the Liberals leading at 41 per cent and the New Democrats rising to 32 per cent. By July, an astonishing thing had happened: continuing dissatisfaction with Mulroney was not being picked up by the Liberals, as was the traditional pattern. Disenchantment with Liberal leader John Turner gave Ed an opening, and the NDP soared to a record high of 44 per cent in the summer of '87 while the Liberals dropped back to 35 per cent. Though the New Democrats' rating moderated into the low-30s range and held there through the spring of 1988, with the three parties running neck and neck, the NDP had broken new ground. They were in the mainstream.

Broadbent's pleasure was heightened by his perception that, as he puts it, "the caucus has been wonderfully disciplined, working together as a team." He felt his MPs had matured; they were keeping their cool in the midst of Tory scandals and Liberal shifts to the left. At caucus meetings he spoke repeatedly about "not being spooked by the Liberals. If we find them moving onto our turf, taking over our positions, we don't have to start talking like comic-book leftists. We remain a credible social democratic party." The seas were choppy, but Ed was steering a calm ship.

His second-in-command, NDP House Leader Nelson Riis, was exuding confidence. "My guess from reading history is that the Tories will commit political hari-kiri, soon enough that people will remember the Liberals — and we will form the next government." Riis's optimism was startling. The blond-haired, former finance critic is a quiet-spoken, solid guy not given to outbursts of reckless enthusiasm. Within caucus, he is known as the conciliator, head of a leadership team in which Ed places great trust.

In Canadian cultural circles the Riis name is best known attached to Nelson's younger sister. Sharon Riis is one of the great literary talents to have emerged from western Canada — author of *The True Story of Ida Johnson*, screen writer of *Loyalties*, recent winner of a Gemini Award for *The Wake*, a film series on Métis women. Nelson and Sharon's Norwegian-born parents settled in Northern Alberta and then moved to British Columbia, where Nelson grew up working as a deckhand, timber cruiser and fisherman in order to finance his university studies through to a post-graduate degree in geography from the University of British Columbia. His springboard onto the federal scene was municipal politics in Kamloops; his eclectic interests would serve him well in NDP caucus — which includes former Tories and Liberals in the team. Bill Blaikie, the tall, bearded Winnipeg MP who co-chairs the international affairs committee, is a former leader of the Young Tories of Manitoba. Rod Murphy, NDP whip, is a former Young Liberal and protégé of Tom Axworthy, who lured Murphy into attending Liberal events while at high school in Winnipeg. At university, Murphy studied political science under Lloyd Axworthy, Tom's older brother, now a leading left-Liberal MP.

"There was a shift at the end of the '60s," says Murphy, a cheerful, pink-cheeked teacher whose home base is Thompson, Manitoba. "Our generation got interested in the Liberals as a progressive force, but then we saw them retreating on economic issues, and we switched to the NDP. Schreyer came to power [in 1969] and we saw what an activist government could do." Rod and Nellie — as he calls Nelson Riis — are feeling chipper these days about Liberals being weak and Tories crumbling. Surely, as westerners, they're concerned about the strength of the hard-core Tory vote? "Those legendary Tory voters," Rod Murphy muses. "What happened to them in Ontario? I think they died in the last Ontario election. If Tories aren't happy, they stay home — that's one of the reasons why Joe Clark lost in 1980."

The third member of the caucus core, Iain Angus, a former Ontario MPP, represents Thunder Bay, Ont. In the spring of '88, he was adjusting to one of the harsh but commonplace realities of political life: marriage breakdown. His wife is a party vice-president and they are sharing custody of their two children; it is a painful period for him. So why doesn't he quit? "I worked hard to get into this business, and I like it too much." As caucus chairman, Angus is Ed's chief management honcho, in charge of ensuring that weekly caucus meetings run smoothly. In the businesslike climate that Ed has been promoting, Angus has proved adept at putting out brush fires of dissent. On Meech Lake, for instance, "Ed made it clear what would happen if anybody broke rank on the issue," says Angus.

The new sense of discipline and team playing has put some noses out of joint: Ian Waddell was stripped of his caucus role for opposing Meech Lake; Svend Robinson was castigated for "interfering" in Jim Fulton's British Columbia riding, where Robinson joined a Haida Indian protest against logging in the environmentally sensitive South Moresby region of the Queen Charlotte Islands off the B.C. coast. Though Robinson was regarded with some caution as a "loose cannon on deck," he was later supported by caucus members when he announced publicly that he was gay.

Once-fractious New Democrats no longer approve iconoclastic behaviour. Jim Fulton is alleged, on his first day in caucus, to have jumped up on the table and "mooned" Ed, but such shenanigans are now rare. Privately, an MP accustomed to the bad-old-days will admit to missing the open spill of dissent, but this is a team that is gunning for bigger game; its members are determined not to be sidetracked.

They are well aware that their fortunes have been boosted by the scandals and bumblings that have shaken the Conservatives — "the gang who can't shoot straight," as Keith Davey has described them. Since 1984, eight Tory Cabinet ministers have been fired or resigned. Robert Coates, defence minister, quit after the *Ottawa*

Citizen revealed he had visited a strip club while on an official visit to West Germany. John Fraser, fisheries minister, resigned over the so-called "Tunagate" fiasco; he had deemed good for sale canned tuna that department officials had rejected as tainted. Suzanne Blais-Grenier, environment minister, stepped down after an uproar about alleged excessive spending on limousines and travel during an official European trip. Sinclair Stevens, minister of regional industrial expansion, became the target of conflict-of-interest allegations and resigned. After a multi-million-dollar inquiry, the judge ruled Stevens "had violated the terms of the blind trust into which he placed his business dealings," according to *The Globe and Mail*, and "been in conflict with existing [Cabinet] guidelines fourteen times." Stevens is appealing.

Marcel Masse, communications minister, stepped down when he became the target of an RCMP investigation into irregularities in campaign spending. Although he appeared to have been exonerated and rejoined Cabinet as minister of energy, his case blew up again in February, 1988, when a letter from the election commissioner surfaced, stating that Masse had indeed violated the law, but that no charges would be laid. André Bissonnette, minister of state for transport, was fired in January 1987 after allegations of corruption regarding the purchase of land by Swiss-based Oerlikon Aerospace, which paid more than $3 million for a site that was priced at $800,000 before it was sold three times in eleven days; Bissonnette and his business/political associate Normand Ouellette were charged with corruption relating to bribes. Roch Lasalle, minister of state, resigned after attending a dinner with a group of businessmen who paid $5,000 each for their meal on the understanding they were enhancing their chances for a shot at Government contracts; then the RCMP began investigating other activities Lasalle may have been connected with while he was a Cabinet minister, including land deals near Mirabel Airport in Quebec, where a local Conservative organizer was shot dead in December.

Then in February 1988, when Tory fortunes had started to improve — the Government had wrapped up a free-trade package with the United States, though it was not yet ratified, and had brought Quebec into the constitutional agreement via the Meech Lake deal — suddenly there were more explosions. Bissonnette and Ouellette lost an attempt to have breach-of-trust charges against them dropped, and they came to trial in the first week of February on charges of conspiracy, breach of trust and fraud; Ouellette, who managed Bissonnette's blind trust, would be found guilty of fraud and ordered to repay Oerlikon more than $1 million. Bissonnette's best friend for twenty-five years, Ouellette had invested the profit from the sale of land to Oerlikon in term deposits "opened in the names of four holding companies owned by himself, his wife, Bissonnette and Bissonnette's wife, Anita Laflamme," Canadian Press reported. Bissonnette, however, was found not guilty and Ouellette is appealing.

There was more to come: the same month, Tory MP Michel Gravel "lost a bid to have the Supreme Court of Canada quash fifty counts of corruption, bribery and breach-of-trust charges against him," the *Toronto Star* reported. The charges against Gravel involved alleged kickbacks worth at least $232,000. And another Quebec Cabinet minister was fired: Michel Côté, supply and services minister, already demoted for overspending by $90 million his budget as minister of industry, was forced out when it was revealed that he had borrowed $250,000 from a Quebec businessman and violated conflict-of-interest guidelines by not reporting the loan.

On February 3, the *Toronto Star*'s front page said it all: PM FIRES MINISTER MICHEL CÔTÉ was the main headline. Beneath it, at the center of the front page, ran another bold headline: HONESTY, OPENNESS WILL HELP THE NDP WIN VOTES, POLL SAYS. Martin Cohn, of the *Star*'s Ottawa bureau, reported that "the New Democratic Party is in the best position to gain voter support because of its reputation for honesty and integrity among the Canadian electorate, according to a poll released today. . . . Thirty-six per cent of voters chose the NDP as the most honest, compared with

18 per cent for the Liberals and 14 per cent for the Progressive Conservatives. . . . And six in ten Canadian voters said honesty in government 'will be the single most important factor in their deciding which party to support in the upcoming election,' pollster Angus Reid said."

That morning, Ed took the *Star*'s front page in to the caucus meeting. He was elated. "Since the 1984 election, this has been the best piece of news for me," he said. "Our message is getting across. We've been fighting for fairness and integrity in government, and finally there seems to be a conjunction — I don't know how long it will last — between what we stand for and what the Canadian people are looking for. The truth about the NDP is what wins us votes — not disguising what we are, but getting people to know us. Our opponents have said, 'Wait till people find out what the NDP really stands for.' I say, I can't wait for people to find out. Here we are."

For the Tories, the turmoil was devastating. They tried to ease the pain. "In Quebec, we were fifty-eight inexperienced, new politicians who were elected," said Cabinet minister Benoît Bouchard. "We would like to avoid that reality, but we have to face it." Sinclair Stevens blamed the media. "The media are trying to capitalize on something that is ridiculous by sensationalizing trivia," he said. But the heat didn't let up. On February 4, 1988, the Prime Minister was drawn into quicksand by Stevie Cameron's story in the *Globe*. Cameron connected Michel Côté's undeclared loan — for which he was fired — to a personal loan Mulroney had received "from Progressive Conservative Party coffers for $324,000 worth of home furnishings." She noted that this sum was "in addition to about $800,000 in Government funds spent on furnishings and maintenance of the [Sussex Drive and Harrington Lake] residences in the same time." In a year and half, the Mulroneys had spent about $1.2 million of Government and party money to enhance their lavish lifestyle. When Cameron questioned whether Brian Mulroney had declared his loan, she was rebuffed. Later that evening, TV news programs showed Government spokesmen declaring that the loan was not a loan but "an advance." Little more than a month later, Cameron would report that funds donated to the Conservative Party for political purposes had been used to pay for a $3,234 Bulgari necklace for Mila Mulroney.

Ed Broadbent said it was "sad" that the House of Commons was continually diverted from economic and social policy matters by Tory scandals; John Turner said: "This is the most dishonest government in memory."

Though the Tories' problems benefited their opponents, Liberals were not as happy as they should have been. As the Liberal party maintained a shaky lead in opinion polls, John Turner sank to the bottom of the leadership rankings. Nowadays, many Liberals will only speak off the record about what Montreal journalist Jean Pelletier describes as the Liberals' "suicide mission." Penny Collenette, a former organizer who supported Jean Chrétien's failed leadership bid against Turner, says: "The frustration is terrible. We feel like champagne that's been corked. If we did get a new leader, we'd be bursting with energy. As it is, I feel like I'm watching the disintegration of the party." Tom Axworthy observes, however, that the party's problems are of its own making. "Liberals love to win — that's their strength and their weakness. They thought Turner looked like a winner and they fooled themselves. It became evident quite soon after he was chosen in '84 that this wasn't the Turner we remembered. He was more than rusty. You're talking about the Titanic sinking here." Keith Davey could only shake his head, convinced that "there is a real danger the Liberals under Turner will finish third in the next election. If that happens, we run the risk of becoming like the British Liberal party. We're in debt $6 million, we need $7 to $10 million for an election. . . . I'm not optimistic." Davey took seriously the threat posed by Broadbent's New Democrats. "If nothing changes," he said, "Broadbent could form a minority government."

Throughout this period, Tory pollster Allan Gregg watched the unfolding of "a new '80s phenomenon, a new climate, where people recognize that politicians aren't deities and governments can't solve all our problems." If you're a politician, says Gregg, "the population wants a glimpse into your soul. They want to know what your motive is. They care less about slick performance and more about the human being. You can say, 'I made a mistake,' or, 'I don't know.' In today's climate, honesty is a tremendous positive."

Part of Gregg's work involves sitting around with "focus groups" watching randomly selected TV clips of politicians. Gregg listens to his groups' reactions. Turner, says Gregg, elicits such uniformly negative responses that people in the focus groups have accused Gregg of deliberately choosing clips that show Turner in the worst possible light.

In this new era, which "turns on its ear everything we were taught about political presentation," says Gregg, Ed Broadbent has emerged as the contemporary figure, the modern politician — a man of depth. Brian Mulroney "presents" like a politician from an earlier era. Though he's three years younger than Broadbent and comes from the same class (lower-middle), Mulroney's image harks back twenty years to the negative persona that Gregg terms "the consummate politician," a figure voters don't trust.

"Spontaneity, emotion, motive — these are the touchstones of the next election," says Gregg. "Turner's got nothing — on strength of character, on empathy, it's almost sad. Mulroney is seen to be gaining in competence and strength, partly because he's had the resolve to stick it out through the heat, but there's still the suspicion that he tells people what they want to hear, that his only motive is to win." Comparing Broadbent and Mulroney, their strengths and weaknesses stand in stark contrast: Ed is "very strong on the personality stuff," where Brian is weak. "Broadbent has a well-defined personality for people, he scores well on empathy and strength. You hear, 'This is a guy I can relate to, a guy of courage and conviction.' His motives are well established. And this next election, I would say, will be about motive."

Martin Goldfarb, the Liberal pollster, shows similar findings. "People think Ed is honest, bright and competent; he's straight. He speaks from the heart; that's his big strength. His weakness is inexperience in government. Mulroney's weakness is that fundamentally he's not trusted. Part of that is patronage, part is that they see Mulroney prepared to give away a lot just to get a deal. They think he's politically opportunistic, that he would do anything to win whether it's for the good of Canada or not. The problem people are struggling with is: what's the alternative? They like Ed, but they're nervous about the NDP because of its ties to labour. That's his Achilles' heel. Ed has to convince the country he's not in the clutches of labour. The NDP is more acceptable in a coalition government. People like the balance of the NDP and Liberals. Minority governments have served us well."

Ed says the NDP's own polling does not show the same suspicion about the labour movement, partly because union leaders like Bob White have become national heroes; nor is he prepared to dump on organized labour. "I wouldn't have been elected in 1968 had Local 222 not built up support for the party in the union," he says. As to charges that labour has not delivered for the NDP, he says, "That's not true. If you look across the country at regions where unions are strong — from Oshawa through to Windsor, Sudbury, Kenora, Rainy River and in Manitoba and British Columbia, we win seats."

Certainly the party's relationship with the labour movement has entered a new phase. With the CLC's Nancy Riche, and CAW's Bob White, sitting as NDP vice-presidents, the new generation of union leadership is strongly supportive of Broadbent. Could that mean, however, that Ed is unduly influenced by what some people see as the conservative, or conflict-prone, hand of the trade union movement? No, he does not accept that characterization: "If you see working people on TV, it's usually because they're in a conflict situation, out on strike. The reality is that most union members are not involved in strikes. It's a false image." (Labour Canada statistics show, for 1987, "the percentage of work time lost to labour stoppages at one of the lowest levels in the past quarter-century," according to *The Globe and Mail*.) Ed goes further: the labour movement, in his view, represents "a progressive force in society," having shown special leadership on the issues of economic nationalism, opposition to free trade, health and safety and women's equality.

And if Ed takes a position to which union leaders object, what then? "In some instances, you have to be prepared to take on certain people," he says. "If some union leaders are not prepared to be internationally competitive, I have to say too bad. On workers' rights, they must set the priorities; but in areas like international competitiveness, we have an obligation to show leadership. I want to see more co-operation between management and labour, which I really do believe can be profitable, and I'd like to see Crown corporations begin to set standards for the private sector. Instead of CN being a source of discontent, it would be nice to see it as a model of industrial relations."

And he's off to the races on industrial democracy and worker participation, "giving people greater control over their lives, which is good for business. Efficiency is good for profit margins and it's good for human enjoyment. Workers want to be efficient. You know the old saying, 'an inefficient worker is an unhappy worker.' It's true." Which gets him going on the Scandinavian and Japanese models for integrating workers into industrial management systems. "They beat us because their management techniques were better for workers and made their companies more profitable. There's nothing wrong with that." That leads to compliments for his favourite car maker, which in the late '80s has begun applying ideas about industrial democracy that were first articulated by Ed in the late '60s. "GM spent $2 billion modernizing one plant, and out of that there were only a couple of hundred new jobs. Workers understood that the investment was necessary to stay competitive, because they were involved in the process. Now GM sends workers — not just management — to see the setup in Europe and Japan and tells them, 'We want you to understand what they're doing. You're part of the process, not just an object.' I don't want

to romanticize this, but it's a beginning, involving workers in decision making, and GM in Oshawa has done a
marvellous job."

That kicks off his vision of a social democratic society,
wherein the private and public sectors are equally respected, equally viable. "In Sweden, the president of
Volvo was a member of the social democratic party. I an-
ticipate the day when you'll find people like that in
Canada, presidents of corporations — not all of them, but
a few — accepting the party that's working for a more
equitable mix, even if it means checks on corporate
power. My kind of social democrats are Olof Palme
[former Prime Minister of Sweden] and Gro Brundtland
[Prime Minister of Norway]. I like their intellectual openness, desire to avoid clichés and take on problems — not
symbols — to work in concrete ways to transform society." The European and Scandinavian social democratic
leaders speak in similar terms: Brandt of "common survival," Palme of "common security," Brundtland of a
"common future."

Coalition: it's the C-word that nobody in Ottawa wants to
speak out loud. The Oxford dictionary defines coalition as
a "temporary combination for special ends between parties that retain distinctive principles." The purpose of a
coalition is for parties to unite to form a government.
John Turner has already uttered "it" in public and
Broadbent has said "it" would not be excluded from wide-
ranging discussions depending on the outcome of the next
election. But "it" is hypothetical and premature, say both
party leaders, as they look to elect as many MPs as they
can. Outside the inner circles, some Liberals are openly
enthusiastic, for obvious reasons. "There have been successful coalition governments all across Europe," says
Tom Axworthy. Are Canadian voters sophisticated
enough to appreciate the concept? "Sure. You've got the
baby-boom generation that's accustomed to boutique-
shopping in all aspects of life. They're not attracted to big
department stores any more. They like to pick and
choose. They're discriminating." But would the partners

in a coalition lose their identities? "If our baby boomers can distinguish between twelve different kinds of potato chips, they can distinguish between two different parties in a coalition."

Mention the C-word to Ed and his mouth shuts firmly. This is a potentially divisive issue on which New Democrats are split: there's the hard-line faction led by Stephen Lewis which is irrevocably opposed to a coalition with "the enemy," and for this group, the Liberals are indeed the enemy. Then there are NDP MPs like Pauline Jewett, Ian Waddell, Lynn McDonald, Marion Dewar and Simon de Jong who think the idea is worth considering. On Ed's home front, Lucille Broadbent believes Ontario NDP leader Bob Rae, who flirted with the idea of coalition in 1985, "should have gone one way or the other, either with some MPs in Cabinet or full opposition." Her husband is known for feeling uncomfortable, to say the least, with Ontario's 1985 NDP-Liberal Accord, which vaulted the Liberals into power, gave them an opportunity to shine and resulted in a 1987 Liberal landslide that buried the NDP.

On May 2, 1985, the Ontario election resulted in a stunning upset. The reigning Tories under Frank Miller were reduced to a minority of fifty-two seats. David Peterson's Liberals won forty-eight seats and 35,000 more votes overall than the Conservatives. The New Democrats were disappointed with their results: twenty-five MPPs elected. The province was clearly in the mood for a change, and "Rae didn't want to go down in history as the man who extended the life of the [Tory] dynasty beyond its forty-two-year hegemony," wrote Rosemary Speirs in *Out of the Blue: The Fall of the Tory Dynasty in Ontario*.

Eager to find a new way out of an old scenario, Bob Rae discussed the various options with Broadbent "all the way through the process," says Rae. "Ed was supportive." Ed was also very interested. He had his own unforgettable experience with minority government, when the NDP had propped up Trudeau's Liberals and been trounced. As caucus chair under David Lewis from 1972 to 1974, Ed helped the NDP push for the creation of Petro-Canada, pension reform and all manner of progressive, popular policies for which the party received no credit in the '74 election, when David lost his seat and the NDP caucus shrank from thirty-one to sixteen MPs.

Bob Rae faced the same dilemma — how to handle minority government effectively, without demolishing the party. He says he "explored the idea of a coalition with people in the party and realized there wasn't enough support to do it." Which is putting it mildly. "Saying the word coalition was the equivalent to saying 'fuck' in the confessional," says one New Democrat who was close to the discussions. "If you said the word, the reaction was so intensely negative you felt like you were supposed to leave the room and wash out your mouth with soap."

Rae was confronted by former party leaders Donald MacDonald and Stephen Lewis, who told him coalition "was absolutely unmanageable," a conviction shared by Gerry Caplan. Rae felt overwhelmed by the opposition. "There was I, a thirty-six-year-old leader, being advised that one-third of the party's members would tear up their cards if I did it. Coalition was such a taboo subject that it had never been discussed. If Stephen had formed a coalition with the Liberals in 1975, when the New Democrats came second, he could have been Premier — but it wasn't considered. My mentioning the idea — in private — was the first time an NDP leader initiated a discussion about coalition government. I think we have a responsibility to make minority government work. Those who see a conflict between morality and power are making a big mistake. This idea that the party can only be in opposition, that it must remain the conscience of the nation, is frustrating. Ultimately, the party wants power and responsibility. Why not take responsibility? Why not try to make things work? If we can't discuss coalition, we're consigned to living in the past, repeating old patterns. I have absolutely no doubt that Tommy Douglas and David Lewis would have confronted this question." In the end, however, Rae's party held him back from breaking with tradition. "The two-year accord I persuaded the Liberals to sign was the best I could do in the circumstances," he says.

The opposition to partnership with the Liberals was based, says Rae's principal secretary, Robin Sears, on "brand competitiveness. Parties or products closest to each other often feel the most contempt for each other because they're competing in the same market." Sears sits at his Queen's Park desk beneath a framed poster of Willy Brandt, former chancellor of West Germany. "Brandt first came to power," says Sears, "through a coalition, and in Europe that has been the route to power for most social democratic parties." Coalition governments, he adds, tend to be stable: "[Former] Italian Prime Minister Bettino Craxi, a socialist, formed a coalition which became the most stable government Italy's had in forty years." Still, for a whole lot of reasons, he says: "I doubt that coalition is on our short-term agenda."

It is definitely *not* on Stephen Lewis's agenda: "We don't have anything in common with Liberals," he says. "They are the apotheosis of opportunism. It was Liberals who put Japanese-Canadians in jail, Trudeau who imposed the War Measures Act, Trudeau who didn't speak out on South Africa in the United Nations for four years. I have personally found it easier to get on with Tories — at least I know where they stand." Some of Lewis's friends argue that his relations with Tories have in reality come very close to crossing the invisible line that Sears characterizes as "the difference between heavy petting and consummation. Stephen's relationship with Bill Davis was very close. Even an informal minority arrangement involves constant deal-making behind the scenes."

Another friend of Lewis's observes: "By accepting Brian Mulroney's offer to become Canada's ambassador to the United Nations, Stephen in effect accepted a 'Cabinet position' and exercised power within the confines of a right-wing, Tory government. A lot of people accused Stephen of selling out, but he's always insisted he hasn't compromised his integrity, and I believe him. If Stephen can do it, why can't the party?"

Among the NDP's senior caucus members, Pauline Jewett — who will not run in the next election — has no problem with coalition but does have differences with her leader over other issues, notably NATO. A former president of Simon Fraser University, Jewett was a Liberal MP who quit her party to join the New Democrats in 1970 after Pierre Trudeau imposed the War Measures Act. She considers herself a left-winger, and says she has "always seen Ed as a centre person. He's become more polished, more aware of the universe of issues, but his politics haven't changed."

First elected as a New Democrat from British Columbia in 1979, Jewett was chosen by Ed as external affairs critic. "The first thing we talked about was NATO. Ed wanted to take another look at our NATO policy." He hoped, she says, that she "would lean toward a more sympathetic position toward NATO." Until 1969, the NDP had supported membership in the North Atlantic Treaty Organization. That year, at the Winnipeg "Waffle" convention, some 1,500 delegates decided that NATO was an obsolete institution formed in a post-war, cold-war climate; that Canada had no influence on NATO decisions and would be best advised to spend its efforts and money defending its own territories. Jewett shared these views. "We can recall," she says, "Trudeau's very caustic remarks about what really went on at NATO meetings. At a seminar in Switzerland, a year before he retired, Trudeau indicated that NATO meetings were merely rubber stamps for what the Americans wanted with a few concessions to the Brits and West Germans." In 1969, Trudeau had toyed with the idea of withdrawing Canadian forces from NATO.

The NDP is not the only group that views NATO with a jaundiced eye. "NATO always seems to be in turmoil," wrote *The Globe and Mail*'s Jeff Sallot on February 13, 1988. Describing the North Atlantic Treaty Organization as "an alliance of sixteen countries with sometimes conflicting loyalties," Sallot noted that French President Charles de Gaulle "had pulled the French military out of the integrated NATO command, while remaining in the political side of the organization. . . ." In 1988 France extended its activities outside NATO by forming an exclusive army brigade in partnership with West Germany, anticipating the possible U.S. withdrawal of NATO troops, adding an extra strain to an already chaotic alliance.

At the New Democrats' federal council meeting at the Château Laurier hotel in Ottawa starting on Friday, April 15, 1988, a group of 120 party officials met over the weekend to decide the party's NATO position. The international affairs committee had, over a period of two months, hammered out a proposal that was, in many ways, a typical Broadbent compromise — Ed got what he wanted, and the others got the promise of what they wanted — though the leader was careful to distance himself from the discussions. "We tried to steer clear of the committee so it didn't look like Ed Broadbent was pushing for this," said one of Ed's aides. What Ed got was a recommendation, endorsed by council, that an NDP government would not withdraw from NATO in its first term. At the same time, the party's credibility on military affairs received a boost with the announcement that Major-General Leonard Johnson, a former defence department strategist, would be running for the NDP in Kingston, against Tory Cabinet minister Flora MacDonald. *The Globe and Mail* reported that "General Johnson, who has been a high-profile crusader for nuclear disarmament . . . acknowledges that his military credentials — unprecedented for an NDP candidate — will be used by the party to blunt charges that the NDP is 'soft' on defence issues, and to shore up what is widely perceived to be its most vulnerable policy area." Ironically, Major-General Johnson "favours the withdrawal of Canadian NATO forces from Europe."

Ed's personal commitment to NATO, shared by the majority of Canadians, has been influenced by his friends in the Socialist International. Says Jewett: "Ed meets with the leaders of Europe's social democratic parties, they're all in NATO and they want Canada in." True. In the winter of 1987, Thorvald Stoltenberg, the foreign minister of Norway, arrived in Ottawa to attend a conference on social democracy and to meet privately with Broadbent.

Stoltenberg, in his late fifties, is a great friend of Ed's and a persuasive proponent of belonging to the NATO club, especially in the new climate of detente — not that his remarks, he emphasized to me, were in any way intended to intrude on Canadian affairs. From Ottawa, Stoltenberg was flying to Brussels for a meeting with George Shultz, Reagan's secretary of state, who would be briefing NATO's foreign ministers on the progress of disarmament talks in Geneva with Soviet foreign minister Eduard Shevardnadze. Stoltenberg felt the presence of social democratic ministers at such a meeting was important. "This will be the first real disarmament agreement to take away a whole system of nuclear weapons," he said, "and if I've done my homework, I can have some influence on how it develops."

Stoltenberg's pragmatic, internationally minded expression of democratic socialism has had a major influence on the evolution of Broadbent's thinking since Ed became active in the Socialist International in the mid-'70s. In Scandinavian circles, Marxism is passé. It played a historic role but is not considered part of the contemporary debate. Scandinavian socialists have come to terms with capitalism in the sense that they have supported the growth of a strong, profitable, private business sector that operates within a socialist framework designed to benefit the whole community. "Co-operative capitalism" is one term used to describe an approach, practised also in West Germany and Japan, that allows governments to co-ordinate long-term industrial planning and scientific research and development that are crucial to success of the so-called "sunrise industries."

"Our weakness," says Stoltenberg, "is that by the '40s and '50s, in our eagerness to create equality, we developed too much bureaucracy, too many rules and regulations that made people feel stifled. It's only right we should have been criticized. Our work now is to reform the reforms. But I'm not talking ideology. I'm interested in practical solutions, which evolve out of specific problems." Social democrats, he says, do not carry about a pre-ordained blueprint, nor do they pretend to have all the answers.

Social democracy he describes as "the counterweight to survival of the fittest. It's the strength of togetherness — you feel it in the Nordic countries. The climate forces us to co-operate with each other in order to survive. The strongest entrepreneur is dependent on collective society — the car maker needs good roads to drive on and people to buy the cars. I was raised in a conservative family, but when I got to university I wanted to oppose the arrogance of the strongest, the arrogance that you can stand alone. I don't believe in it. I don't want that sort of society. It's not enough for the strongest to help the weakest through charity. It's not a good foundation, and it doesn't work."

He points to America, where charitable organizations are strong and social services weak. "Of course the greatest critic of America is one of my best friends, and he knows more about poverty than most of us." Stoltenberg is referring to Michael Harrington, co-chair of the Democratic Socialists of America, which operates in the Democratic Party. A slender, gray-haired Irish-American Catholic, active in the Socialist International, Harrington is the source of what Stoltenberg and Broadbent consider some of the most progressive thinking in the world. In the 1988 U.S. presidential primaries, Harrington has been writing speeches for Jesse Jackson.

"As I said to Harrington, you've got the thinkers and we've got the movement." Ed Broadbent.

With right-wing Reaganites and their massive deficits discredited, slammed by the worst stock market crash in history, surrounded by urban blight and rural bankruptcies, there is a sudden burst of opportunity for what Michael Harrington calls *The Next Left* — which is also the title of his fourteenth book. It was twenty-six years ago, in 1962, that Harrington's *The Other America* was published to an unexpected acclaim that would carry its astonished author toward the inner sanctum of power, into the orbit of President John Kennedy.

Sadly, the poverty Harrington described so vividly in *The Other America* has not diminished. Despite the Democrats' War on Poverty, a strategy adopted from Harrington by the Kennedy Administration and taken up by Lyndon Johnson after Kennedy's assassination, the gap between rich and poor has only widened. The Third World characteristics of this First World nation are everywhere starkly visible, especially in New York City, where Harrington lives.

In the winter of '87, a week before going into hospital for an operation on his throat — he has cancer of the larynx, which proved inoperable — Harrington walked the streets of New York surrounded by the grim evidence for his conviction that U.S. capitalism is self-destructing. Strolling along Central Park South, where condo-apartments cost $2 million, coiffed, jewelled, fur-coated ladies pampered silky-haired pets that trotted past the silent, lurking shadows of the homeless, who appeared everywhere, creeping, searching through garbage, or just sitting, endlessly waiting, in the splendour of wealth.

The United States, he wrote in *The Next Left*, is "in social terms, the most left-wing nation on earth. We often fail to recognize that fact because the United States is, in political and legislative terms, the most backward of advanced societies. It is the only developed capitalism without a significant socialist movement; its welfare state was not only the last to emerge in the West, but remains the meanest and cheapest, the only one without a national health system."

America's refusal to care collectively for its people, allowing its education system to crumble, is now, he says a threat to the nation's future. He writes that "the unconscious premise since the Industrial Revolution, so well summarized by John F. Kennedy — 'A rising tide lifts all boats' — is no longer operative." The nature of economic growth, he says, has altered drastically.

Growth no longer means more jobs. The phenomenon of "de-skilling" is a downhill ride, and it is happening throughout the industralized world: relatively well-paid, skilled blue-collar jobs are disappearing by the hundreds

338 ED BROADBENT: THE PURSUIT OF POWER

of thousands, replaced by low-wage, no-skill service sector jobs. The shipbuilder reduced to wrapping hamburgers at McDonald's is no longer upwardly mobile; and without the upwardly mobile American dream, says Harrington, America is in trouble. It is essential, he writes, "to work out a new public philosophy that will make social decency once again a practical imperative." Poverty and unemployment, he points out, are expensive to maintain; productive people enhance the economy. Describing the New Deal for the '90s, he talks about progressive taxation, full employment, a national investment bank, emphasis on education and retraining — all NDP policies.

Bringing the issues back home, Broadbent connects Harrington's analysis of American woes with his own opposition to free trade, the major economic issue that has dominated Canadian politics since the 1984 election. The ground on which Ed stakes his political career is the need for government–business–labour co-operation in order to promote national economic development; it is precisely this concerted form of action, predominant in the most successful economies in the world, that would be outlawed by a Conservative deal that rejects a role for government. "What social democrats do," says Al Johnson, "is they civilize the market economy at the same time as they support its development. The big difference between a guy like Ed Broadbent and a guy like Mulroney is this: they both believe in a free economy, but Ed also believes there's a role for government to play, civilizing the market, which is what we've always done in Canada, with medicare and pensions and on down the list."

"I'm in favour of expanded trade and I'm for the reduction of tariffs, but Mulroney's deal is something other than a trade deal," says Ed. He is speaking to a crowded lecture hall, packed with students at Durham College, located in the outskirts of his Oshawa riding. He starts off positioned behind a wooden podium at the front of the room. As he warms to his subject, he moves forward, closer to the kids, standing in between the armrests of a front row seat which is pushed up against its back. At first his audience seems startled by his easy informality and overwhelmed by the mass of trade information he showers on them, speaking spontaneously, without notes. But as they warm to him, they are transformed from passive watchers into active questioners.

"Mulroney is not a stupid man," says a student. "He's putting his political life on the line for this deal. He's got to be thinking there's something good in it."

Ed nods. "Sure. Mulroney believes there will be an expansion in trade with the U.S."

Student: "Isn't this good? Don't you think this is opening up the door to Canadians to expand in the U.S. market? There's got to be one point about it you like."

Ed: "There's normally a whole range of issues on which politicians agree at least 50 per cent. Every once in a while there's a bill or an issue which you're totally against, like capital punishment. Free trade is like that. It impinges on our capacity as a nation to make our own decisions, to control our own economic development. It takes away a whole range of options without giving us guaranteed access to the American market. And if we get into more disputes, as we will, as we did over softwood lumber, shakes and shingles and steel, the dispute settlement mechanism is worse than what we have now. The U.S. will still have the authority to keep out Canadian softwood lumber. We can't change U.S. laws, even if they are unfair to us. And under this deal, we are restricted from supporting regional development, because the Americans would view government support as an illegal subsidy. They get our energy, and we're restricted from controlling foreign investment. What's going to happen to western Canadians? They desperately need to diversify their economies. Under the deal, the Americans have equal access to western energy resources, and the western provinces lose the ability to control these resources for their own benefit."

Student: "But what about the Auto Pact? That's free trade and that's been good to us."

Ed: "The Auto Pact is not a free-trade agreement. It's the opposite. It's managed trade. The presidents of the Big Three signed a deal committing themselves to a level of production in Canada, in exchange for duty-free access to the Canadian market. What Mulroney's done is he's gutted the Pact. We've lost the safeguards that made sure the Big Three invested here. You don't have to assume the Americans are big bad guys — and I don't — I just assume that they're looking after their own interests the way we should be looking after ours."

Student: "But why should American companies have to invest here? We're being unfair to them, making them invest here." (Audience groans.)

Ed: "The idea is that this is our country, not theirs. They're welcome to make a profit here, that's fine, but there's gotta be a net benefit to us from companies coming in here, using our people, our resources. We have to remain in control of our own destiny as a people. Pierre Trudeau used to stand up to the Americans. There was a sense that we could co-exist and from time to time differ. That's okay. We're friends. I like Americans. I've met George Bush. I know American politics. But we've got to look out for ourselves. A bad deal is worse than no deal at all."

At the end, driving back to Toronto to the airport for a return flight to Ottawa, Ed talked about the problem of explaining what's wrong with free trade in a world of simplistic solutions. "Like that one student said," Ed observed, "what's wrong with expanded trade? It sounds so nice. How do you explain that what Mulroney is doing strikes at the very heart of the nation's capacity to act in its own self-interest?"

Glimpses into the future hinted at more changes: in February, 1988, in Newfoundland, Richard Cashin's fishermen's union, which had broken away from its international body, voted to affiliate with Bob White's Canadian Auto Workers. Cashin, a lawyer, was considering running for the NDP in the next election. A poll in St John's, trade minister John Crosbie's turf, showed the NDP running ahead of the Tories and just behind the Liberals. In Quebec, at a series of nomination meetings, where only a handful of NDPers had turned up in '84, it was now customary for 600 people to pack the halls.

At the end of February, the Liberal Party, still more than $5 million in debt, had trouble meeting its payroll. Canadian Press reported that "a senior Liberal official had to go to the bank and make 'a frantic plea' for money to pay its employees." A month later, a former organizer said the party was "on the verge of bankruptcy. It hasn't paid rent for its office building for three months." Through May and June, John Turner was still ducking the sniper fire of bitter discontent from within his own ranks, but he was hanging on.

Meanwhile, their war chest overflowing, the Tories were saying they would spend about $10 million on the next election. The chairman of Elections Canada announced, however, that the spending ceiling was set at $7.5 million. The NDP wasn't worried; it had no debt, said Bill Knight, and fundraising was well in hand. (In the '84 election, the NDP spent $4.7 million, compared to $6.3 million by the Liberals and $6.4 million by the Tories.) As the polls jumped up and down, pundits were declaring the next election a three-way horse race, for the first time in Canadian history. George Nakitsas, Broadbent's principal secretary, said he'd be "quite happy going into the election with one-third of the electorate behind us."

Across the continent in British Columbia, where John Turner's hold on his Vancouver riding was considered shaky, a poll showed the New Democrats holding 53 per cent of the committed vote, well ahead of the Liberals at 27 per cent and the Tories at 20. In Manitoba in April Howard Pawley's NDP government was defeated, and

Pawley resigned as provincial leader, indicating he might run federally in the next election. Allan Blakeney, former premier of Saskatchewan, "left the door open" about a possible entry into federal politics, as did former Governor General Ed Schreyer.

In Oshawa, Mike Breaugh was getting excited. "This is our time to go for it," he said. "I mean *go*, like we do in Oshawa, by getting rid of the old nursemaids who hang around wringing their hands. This is like playing football and suddenly the line opens up for a crack of a second. If you're in the right place at the right time, and you run fast enough, you can get through. Ed has the power to drag the party through."

In politics, timing is everything, and in '88 Ed got lucky. The trends shifted in his direction. *Newsweek* magazine declared in its January, 1988 cover story that THE EIGHTIES ARE OVER. It defined the decade as "a time when avarice got respectable, poverty expanded and wealth became a kind of state religion." President Ronald Reagan — by then a lame-duck leader facing retirement — was the figurehead of the era. The "unembarrassed extravagance" of the Reagans, who spent $800,000 redecorating the White House — equal to the sum spent by the Mulroneys on their living quarters — was no longer something of which to be proud. The money culture had exploded. It was "no longer chic to flaunt wealth," in the words of Tom Wolfe. Ivan Boesky, Wall Street's King of Greed, was in jail, the stock market was staggering and gurus were warning that a recession lurked around the corner.

Jules Feiffer captured the shift in a 1987 cartoon in the *Village Voice*: "I've been there before," says a bleary-eyed guy at a bar. "A smug generation of young people. Educated. Over-confident. Cut off from the real world. Along comes a crisis. It threatens their way of life. It undermines their faith. Overnight, their values change. Last time it was Vietnam. This time it's Wall Street. Here it comes . . . the radicalization of the Yuppies."

Tracking down the new mood in America in the wake of Black Monday, the stock market crash of October 19,

1987, I travelled from New York City to the Long Island community of Syosset, to visit American journalist and author Barbara Ehrenreich. Her economic analyses in the *New York Times* have demonstrated that she is looking down the road to the future. Educated as a scientist at Rockefeller University, an elite institution in Manhattan, she became well-known in the '60s as an anti-war activist. Co-chair of the Democratic Socialists of America, with Michael Harrington, Ehrenreich's vision of the world jibed with Feiffer's.

"We've been through a bad time," she said, sitting with her feet up in her Syosset living room, which overflowed with books, magazines, disarray and dog hairs. "It's been eight years of the most right-wing president ever, and it got depressing. But we're coming out of it. The revival is upon us. The right has lost moral and economic credibility. I do a lot of travelling to campuses on speaking engagements, and I can sense a new mood. You must remember, we have reason for optimism. We have seen the world change. We saw the American people go from 90 per cent in favour of the Vietnam war to 90 per cent opposed." It was Ehrenreich's generation that stopped the war. Having matured in the past twenty years and moved into positions of power, can they start the new era?

It has already begun. Well on its way for the next decade, according to historian Arthur Schlesinger, Jr., is the generational change that will make the '90s look like the '60s. Schlesinger predicts a great wave of "pent-up idealism" will radically alter North American society. Heading into the '90s, the world as we know it is being transformed. How will these vast shifts be acted out on the Canadian stage? What political leader and party will capture the mood of the times — as Pierre Trudeau and the Liberals did so sweepingly in 1968?

Quebec journalist Lise Bissonnette, former editor-in-chief of *Le Devoir*, doesn't know what to make of the Broadbent/NDP prospects — especially in Quebec. She has interviewed Ed Broadbent many times in the last decade, and observed how much Quebeckers seem to like him. "If

I sit with him in a café, people always stop by. They're happy to see him. They want to touch him. There's something about the man that is appealing, as much here as in other parts of the country." It's not that he speaks French well. "Broadbent mangles the language," she laughs, "but people don't seem to mind, and they like it that he insists on speaking French." She remembers a recent interview with him. She told him she would conduct it in English. "He absolutely insisted like mad that he had to do it in French — he was charming about it — but afterwards when I listened to my tape it was a disaster, trying to figure out what he was saying."

In her years as a political writer she has not had much luck, she says, in predicting election results, so she has taken to listening to her seventy-five-year-old father. "My father is like the majority — he can switch from one party to another. He goes with the wind. Lately, he's been telling me he can't listen to John Turner, and as for Mulroney, there's pride involved. Mulroney's gang seems to be a bunch of crooks, he says, and he doesn't want to be associated with crooks. He's not proud about that. Now he's saying, 'I like this guy Broadbent. I'll vote for him. I trust him.' "

As Bissonnette spoke, Ed was back in Jonquière, Quebec, for his third "immersion" stay. During the day he attended classes at the local CEGEP (junior college) along with all the other students, who were surprised to find a man of his eminence in their midst; and every evening, he went "home" for dinner with the Carons, the elderly couple he has boarded with since first studying at Jonquière in 1979. Monsieur Caron was the town's undertaker before his retirement; the Carons are a religious family. Their home is located right next door to the Catholic church. In their kitchen is a large cross; in the living room, a tall statue of Jesus that lights up. They raised seven children and now enjoy the company of students. When Ed first stayed with them, he couldn't speak a word of French. Now when he comes, they all rattle on together at a tremendous rate.

My last conversation with Ed concerned the Carons. I received an urgent message to contact him. I finally reached him late at night; he was very excited. I figured something big must have happened — a new party position on NATO, perhaps? No — Ed wanted to talk about having breakfast with the Carons on the last day of his visit. The three of them had been sitting at the breakfast table, chatting, when Madame Caron said that she wanted Ed to get cards for her and her husband. "Cards?" said Ed, oblivious. "What kind of cards?" Mme Caron said they wanted cards so they could belong. Finally Ed figured out, to his astonishment and joy, that they wanted to join the NDP. This small victory, it seemed, gave him the greatest pleasure. It really made his day.

AT THE END OF THE DAY

Peter O'Malley, Ed's former press secretary, is burned out after seven years on the road with Ed, disillusioned about the political meatgrinder that turns real human issues into plastic commodities. Yet like many who have participated in the heightened passions of political life, O'Malley is still somewhat obsessed with "the way it was." It was all-consuming. "You wake up and your day, your entire life is dictated by what's on the top of the political agenda for those twenty-four hours. It's a weird way to live. What amazes me, finally, about Ed is his adaptability. He's survived it. He's still a human being."

Bob Rae suggests that Ed's survival is related to his "self-sufficiency. He's like Tommy Douglas that way. He's not as vulnerable as David Lewis was. He's good at compromising but at a deeper personal level, he's not malleable. By that I mean he thinks for himself. There's a real person in there. He reads for himself. He still re-writes speeches. He has his own perspective. The system hasn't managed to grind him down." Nestor Pidwerbecki says it's Ed's convictions that keep him going. "When he's convinced he's right, look out," says Nestor. "You've got a tiger by the tail. Ed doesn't stop, and he won't let go."

Ask Lucille how her husband has endured and she shrugs. "His books and his music." After twenty years bound up in the all-consuming intensity of politics, Ed still goes home at the end of the day — that is, when he gets to go home — and sits with Lucille, by the fire, reading novels, listening to music. This is his meditation, his salvation. Lucille has always been struck by his remarkable ability to clear his mind, relax, and cut out the static of extraneous worries. "I'm the kind of person," she says, "if I have something on my mind, I think about it until I've resolved it. Ed has taught me to leave a problem on the back burner and concentrate on what I'm doing at the moment. He knows how to live in the present. He's lucky that way."

"What makes Ed remarkable to me," says Carol Goar, who has covered Ottawa for more than a decade, "is that he is one of the most personally secure people I have ever met — and there are surprisingly few people like that in this town. Mulroney has so many personal insecurities he could keep a psychiatrist busy for thirty years; Turner is a bundle of unresolved conflicts." Mulroney she describes as a tough fighter, a survivor, a man who got where he is through "sheer force of will. But he doesn't have a deeply rooted sense of Parliament or what government is all about." Mulroney she sees as a plant with glossy leaves "and weak roots, compared to Ed, who has very deep roots." Ed is like an oak tree, strong at the base, not easily toppled over. Carol observes that journalist Val Sears has said that Ed's lack of sharp edges makes him uninteresting, "the charisma problem. Maybe what Ed lacks for a journalist is an element of surprise. Ed is never going to do anything dangerous or reckless or terribly inconsistent. With Mulroney and Turner you have to brace yourself for the outside chance of disaster."

Paul Broadbent, Ed's son, says his father is "a man out of time, in a way. He tends to look at the more practical considerations of life as intrusive. He's a perfectionist, very demanding, with high standards. He's completely absorbed in his political world. He still loves to travel, to go out for a meal, to go to the cinema, but he's always recognized. I remember once we were in Germany at the top of a tower in a remote castle and what happens? We bump into some Canadian tourists who fall all over him. At home, he used to sit out on a lawn chair with a glass of wine and a cigar, reading a book. Now he would get a crowd gathering. I guess his books and his music are the last of his little pleasures. Basically, he never stops. When he wants something, he goes after it. Drive, drive, drive, that's my father."

Ambitious, tough, demanding, driven: these are the deeper qualities that propel the nice guy of Canadian politics. The idealist who so attracted Lucille grew into a pragmatist, pursuing power. Out of his academic studies he developed a vision of social democracy that embraces capitalists and socialists. He has imprinted this vision on his party. For him the art of politics is a balancing act. And after twenty years in the business, he has, according to friends and opponents alike, blossomed into one hard-nosed politician. "Ed Broadbent can play the political game," says his Liberal friend David Collenette, "but when you strip him down, he's as straight as they come. Deep down, he's a honest guy."

Ed's deeply rooted stability is derived from many elements: his mother's love, his intellectual education, his marriage to Lucille, his own genetic optimism. His social democratic convictions are strongly felt. He really believes he is doing what is right and beyond that, he doesn't seem to worry. Others may say he is stubborn, power-hungry, superficial, too moderate, bereft of ideas. . . . He works like a dog, then he goes home. He listens to Callas. He reads. He turns off the light, goes upstairs, and sleeps the deep sleep of a man content in his work. Tomorrow, the sun will rise and the breakthrough will be one day closer — he really believes. And if it isn't? That is one question he is not ready to answer.

Chronology

1630   The first traceable artifact owned by the Broadbents: a teapot still in the family today.

1709   Albertus Schreiber, Ed's direct ancestor on his mother's side, emigrates from Germany to New York City.

1800   Jacob Scriver dies in Adolphustown, the United Empire Loyalist landing place near Kingston, Ontario.

       The Scriver farm already established in Prince Edward County.

1860s   Town of Broadbent founded just east of Parry Sound, Ontario.

1866   Robert McLaughlin moves the family carriage company from the village of Tyrone to nearby Oshawa.

1872   Adam T. Broadbent, Ed's great-grandfather, settles in Broadbent.

1884   Jack Broadbent, Ed's grandfather, is born in England.

1886   Albertha (Bert) Tait, Ed's grandmother, is born near Parry Sound.

1901   McLaughlin Carriage Co. produces 25,000 carriages a year.

1904   Tommy Douglas born in Falkirk, Scotland.

1905   Jack and Bert Broadbent are married.

1907   McLaughlin Carriage Co. starts manufacturing motor cars.

1909   Aug. 14: Percy Broadbent, Ed's father, is born near Parry Sound.

       David Lewis born in Svisloch, Poland (now Russia).

1911   Aug. 17: Mary Anastasia (Scriver) Welsh, Ed's mother, is born in Tweed, Ontario.

       Nov. 18: C.B. Macpherson born in Toronto

1915   McLaughlin Motor Car Co. starts making Chevrolets.

1917   "Parkwood," the McLaughlin's mini-Versailles estate in Oshawa, is completed.

1918   Col. Sam McLaughlin, Robert's son, sells out to General Motors, becoming the first president of General Motors of Canada.

1919   The Winnipeg General Strike.

Tommy Douglas's family moves to Canada, settling in Winnipeg.

Pierre Trudeau is born in Montreal.

Mackenzie King succeeds Sir Wilfrid Laurier as Liberal leader, holding the position until 1948.

1921   Mary Scriver Welsh's mother dies and Mary is sent to an orphanage.

1921- Mackenzie King is Prime Minister.
1930

1922   René Lévesque is born in Quebec.

1927   Jack and Bert Broadbent, with their nine children, settle in Oshawa where Patrick Welsh, Mary's father, has found work at the Motors.

Jack Broadbent starts working at GM, followed by his sons Oren, Arnold, Aubrey, Reuben, Bill, and later Percy.

1929   Mary Welsh, a secretary at Oshawa Wholesale, meets Percy Broadbent, a supersalesman at the same company.

1930   Oct. 29: Percy Broadbent marries Mary Welsh and they move into his parents' house.

1930- R.B. Bennett's Tories defeat Mackenzie King's Liberals
1935   and form the government; Percy Broadbent, an ardent Tory, is delighted.

1931   Aug. 10: Velma Broadbent, Percy and Mary's first child, is born.

1932   David Lewis wins Rhodes Scholarship to Oxford University.

1933   The Regina Manifesto is adopted, signalling the creation of the Co-operative Commonwealth Federation.

1935– Mackenzie King is Prime Minister.
1948

1935   Tommy Douglas elected MP, joins CCF leader J.S. Woodsworth in House of Commons; the CCF has 7 members.

C.B. Macpherson starts teaching at the University of Toronto.

1936   March 21: John Edward Broadbent born in Oshawa.

David Lewis becomes national secretary of the CCF.

1937   In March, the United Auto Workers union organizes the GM plant in Oshawa; in April, the Oshawa Strike lasts 15 days and Ontario Premier Mitch Hepburn sends in armed troops against strikers.

1943   CCF forms official opposition in Ontario and the party leads polls nationally.

1944   Tommy Douglas leads the CCF to victory in Saskatchewan and begins his 17 year reign as Premier.

1948   Mackenzie King retires and is succeeded by Louis St. Laurent, who takes over as Liberal leader and P.M. until 1957.

1950   Percy Broadbent hits rock bottom, losing his job at Oshawa Wholesale, and goes to work at the Motors.

Oshawa's Central Collegiate opens and Ed Broadbent enters grade nine.

Cité libre founded with Trudeau and Pelletier on its editorial board, opposing Quebec Premier Duplessis.

1951   Founding Congress of Socialist International in Frankfurt; CCF attends.

1952   General Dwight Eisenhower elected president of the United States, defeating Ed's hero, Adlai Stevenson.

1953   Ed Broadbent, in grade 11, chosen president of the student council.

1955   Ed Broadbent, valedictorian, graduates from Central Collegiate, and enrolls in philosophy at Trinity College, University of Toronto.

1956 John Diefenbaker elected Conservative leader.

1957 June 10: *General election*: Dief's Tories win minority government (112 seats to Liberals 105, CCF's 25 and Social Credit 19).

Lester Pearson wins Nobel Peace Prize for negotiating a peacekeeping operation in the Suez Canal.

1958 Lester Pearson elected Liberal leader.

General election: Dief's Tories win biggest majority in Canadian history to date, 208 seats to Liberals' 49.

Pundits predict death of Liberal Party.

CCF elects only 8 MPs; party leader M.J. Coldwell defeated along with Stanley Knowles and Colin Cameron. Fate of CCF also in doubt

1959 Ed Broadbent, disinterested in party politics, graduates from U. of T. and returns to Oshawa for a year to teach high school English; he meets Lucille and Louis Munroe.

1960 Jean Lesage leads the Liberals to power in Quebec and the Quiet Revolution is underway.

René Lévesque elected MNA, becomes minister of water resources, responsible for creation of Hydro-Quebec.

Ed Broadbent wins a Canada Council scholarship, embarks on an M.A. in the philosophy of law at U. of T. and encounters his major intellectual mentor, political theorist C.B. Macpherson; he also meets Yvonne Yamaoka.

1961 Ed Broadbent marries Yvonne Yamaoka.

At NDP founding convention, Tommy Douglas becomes leader.

Broadbent joins the NDP.

Brian Mulroney is studying law at Laval University in Quebec City.

Pierre Trudeau is teaching law at the University of Montreal.

John Kennedy becomes president of the United States.

1962   Publication of C.B. Macpherson's most famous book, *The Political Theory of Possessive Individualism.*

General election: Diefenbaker's Tories shrink to minority status, with 116 seats to Liberals' 100, Social Credit 30, NDP 19.

Tommy Douglas loses his seat due to Saskatchewan doctor's strike over the province's medicare scheme, implemented while Douglas was Premier.

David Lewis is first elected to the House of Commons.

The Carter Royal Commission on Taxation announced by Diefenbaker.

1963   *General election*: Liberals, led by Lester Pearson, win minority government, with 129 seats to Tories 95, Social Credit 24, NDP 17.

Tommy Douglas is re-elected, David Lewis loses his seat, Walter Gordon becomes finance minister.

Trudeau attacks Pearson for advocating nuclear warheads on Canadian soil.

Lucille Munroe switches from the Liberals to the New Democrats.

U.S. President John Kennedy is assassinated in Dallas, Texas.

1964   Pearson, against Douglas's and Dief's opposition, approves nuclear warheads moving into Canada.

Ross Thatcher, former CCF MP, now leader of Saskatchewan's Liberals, defeats NDP Government.

1965   *General election*: Liberals go for a majority and again get only a minority of 131 to Tories 97, NDP 21, Social Credit 14.

Trudeau elected MP in Westmount, defeating Charles Taylor, whom Trudeau had supported in previous elections.

Canada-U.S. Auto Pact signed, with safeguards ensuring production in Canada by the Big Three.

Walter Gordon resigns from Trudeau's cabinet, denouncing Canada's colonial status.

George Grant's *Lament for a Nation* is published.

Louis Munroe dies and Lucille moves to Ottawa with her son Paul.

1966 Legislation for a national medicare program based on the Saskatchewan model is passed.

1967 Ed Broadbent's marriage to Yvonne Yamaoka ends.

Lévesque quits the Quebec Liberal party.

At Conservative leadership convention, Robert Stanfield defeats Diefenbaker to become Tory leader.

Pearson shuffles cabinet, introduces three new ministers: John Turner, Jean Chretien and Pierre Trudeau, the new minister of justice.

1968 April 6: Liberal leadership convention, Turner loses to Trudeau.

General election: Trudeaumania; Trudeau becomes Prime Minister with a Liberal majority of 155 seats to Tories 72, NDP 22, Social Credit 14.

Ed Broadbent is elected MP from Oshawa, defeating the Tory incumbent by 15 votes.

Mel Watkins releases Watkins' report on foreign control of economy.

René Lévesque founds the Parti Quebecois.

1969 Jim Laxer, Gerry Caplan, Mel Watkins and Ed Broadbent form the Waffle, a left-wing group within the NDP.

Broadbent withdraws from the group, opposed to its rhetoric.

Manitoba election: Ed Schreyer leads NDP to victory.

NDP Waffle convention in Winnipeg in October; the party is at war; Broadbent tries to unite opposing factions, champions industrial democracy and is ignored.

1970 The October Crisis: British trade commissioner James Cross kidnapped in Quebec; Oct. 16: Trudeau imposes the War Measures Act, the next day Quebec labour minister Pierre Laporte found dead.

1971 After a decade as NDP leader, Tommy Douglas steps down; Broadbent, the first to declare his candidacy, comes fourth as David Lewis is elected leader.

Ed Broadbent marries Lucille Munroe.

Saskatchewan election: Allan Blakeney's New Democrats defeat Thatcher's Liberals.

Trudeau, 52, marries Margaret Sinclair, 22.

1972 *British Columbia election*: Dave Barrett's New Democrats defeat W.A.C. Bennett's Social Credit regime.

Oct. 30: *General election*: Liberal minority of 109 seats to Tories' 107; NDP wins 31 seats, the most ever; Broadbent re-elected by 824 votes and becomes caucus chairman; David Lewis supports Trudeau in return for legislative achievements that include the creation of Petro Canada.

1974 *General election*: Liberal majority of 141 seats to Tories 95, Social Credit II, NDP reduced to 16 seats; David Lewis defeated; Ed Broadbent, re-elected with a 10,000-vote majority, is chosen interim NDP leader.

1975 Jan. 16: Ed Broadbent announces he will not seek the leadership; on March 26, he is persuaded to re-enter the race.

July 7: Ed Broadbent elected leader of the New Democratic Party.

Sept. 10: John Turner resigns as Liberal finance minister and moves to Toronto to practise corporate law.

Ontario election: Tory Premier Bill Davis wins minority with Stephen Lewis's New Democrats coming second, forming the official Opposition.

British Columbia election: Barrett's NDP government defeated by Bill Bennett's Social Credit party.

Trudeau announces wage and price controls, says the free market isn't working, and is charged with being a socialist.

1976 Tory leadership convention chooses Joe Clark over Brian Mulroney.

Liberals hit 30-year-low in the polls, 29 per cent.

Percy Broadbent dies of cancer.

Nov. 15: *Quebec election*: the Parti Quebecois forms the government, René Lévesque becomes Premier.

1979 Tommy Douglas retires.

John Diefenbaker dies.

General election: Joe Clark's Tories win a minority government that will not last a year: Tories 136, Liberals 114, NDP 26, Social Credit 6.

Nov. 21: Trudeau retires and Broadbent believes the breakthrough is at hand; he pushes for a fast election, uniting with the Liberals to defeat the Clark government on Dec. 13.

1980 For the first time national polls show Broadbent as the most popular political leader in the country.

General election: Trudeau's Liberals win a 147-seat majority, Tories 103, NDP 32.

Trudeau offers Broadbent cabinet seats, seeking western support for the National Energy Program; Broadbent refuses.

May 20: Quebec Referendum on sovereignty-association; Lévesque's forces are defeated; Trudeau announces he will proceed with unilateral patriation of the constitution; Broadbent gives his support in principle, seeking certain amendments, and outrages Saskatchewan NDP Premier Allan Blakeney; the Constitutional Wars erupt and Broadbent enters the worst period of his political life.

Ronald Reagan elected President of the United States.

1981 May 23: David Lewis dies from leukemia; Ed Broadbent, en route to Central America, returns to Ottawa for Lewis's funeral and then flies back to El Salvador to continue his peace mission on behalf of the Socialist International.

In July, at the NDP Vancouver convention, party organizers try to stage-manage the Broadbent vs. Blakeney showdown over the constitution.

Quebec election: Parti Quebecois re-elected.

Trudeau reaches a deal on the constitution with 9 premiers on Nov. 5, the "night of the long knives," excluding Levesque.

Manitoba election: Howard Pawley's New Democrats defeat Sterling Lyons' Tories.

1982   April 17: Queen signs the new Constitution Act on Parliament Hill.

Saskatchewan election: Blakeney's NDP government defeated by Grant Devine's Tories.

1983   June 11: Brian Mulroney elected Tory leader.

July 2-3: NDP Regina convention, Broadbent suffers vicious attack.

August 20: Broadbent's mother dies.

NDP loses Mission-Port Moody (B.C.) to Tories in a by-election as Brian Mulroney wins Central Nova by-election.

November 17: Broadbent enters hospital for back pain.

December 21: Broadbent undergoes back surgery.

1984   Jim Laxer, former NDP research director, releases report denouncing NDP economic policy.

NDP drops to 13 per cent in polls in February.

Feb. 29: Trudeau resigns.

In April, NDP support sinks to 11 per cent in polls.

June 16: Liberal leadership convention, John Turner defeats Jean Chretien and becomes Prime Minister.

In July, NDP support drops to 9 per cent in polls.

General election: massive Conservative majority, 211 seats; Turner's Liberals shrink to 40 MPs, New Democrats to 30.

Stephen Lewis appointed Canada's ambassador to the
United Nations.

1985- Marion Dewar, former mayor of Ottawa, becomes NDP
1987 president; internal battles as the party modernizes.

1985 *Ontario election*: NDP leader Bob Rae signs accord with
David Peterson's Liberals that vaults Peterson into
power.

1987 June 3: Mulroney and the provincial premiers sign
Meech Lake Accord.

In July, three by-elections swept by New Democrats.

July 21: C.B. Macpherson dies.

In August, NDP soars to 44 per cent in one public opinion poll, a record high; Broadbent again the most popular
political leader in the country.

Ontario election: massive Liberal landslide.

Oct. 5: Canada and the U.S. release proposed free trade
agreement with no final text.

Oct. 19: Black Monday: the stock market crashes.

Dec. 10: Simon Reisman, Canada's chief trade negotiator,
presents Mulroney with 314-page text for free trade deal.

1988 The year of Conservative scandals and Liberal troubles
as John Turner's leadership is under constant attack.

April 15: NDP federal council settles NATO policy,
promising that an NDP government would not withdraw
Canada from NATO in its first term.

Manitoba election: Howard Pawley's NDP government
falls to Gary Filmon's Tories.

The polls show Canada's three national political parties
in a three-way race, for the first time in history.

Select Bibliography

Books

Abella, Irving, (ed.) *On Strike: Six Key Labour Struggles in Canada 1919-1949* (Toronto: James Lorimer and Co., 1975).

Davey, Keith, Senator, *The Rainmaker: A Passion for Politics* (Toronto: Stoddart, 1986).

Frizzell, Alan and Westell, Anthony, (eds) *The Canadian General Election of 1984: Politicians, Parties, Press and Polls* (Ottawa: Carleton University Press, 1985).

Harrington, Michael, *The Next Left* (Toronto: Henry Holt & Co., 1986).

Hoy, Claire, *Friends in High Places* (Toronto: Key Porter Books, 1987).

Kome, Penney, *The Taking of Twenty-Eight: Women Challenge the Constitution* (Toronto: The Women's Press, 1983).

Laxer, James, *Decline of the Superpowers* (Toronto: James Lorimer & Co., 1987).

Levesque, Rene, *Memoirs* (Toronto: McClelland and Stewart, 1986).

Lewis, David, *The Good Fight: Political Memoirs, 1909-1958* (Toronto: MacMillan of Canada, 1981).

Macpherson, C.B., *The Political Theory of Possessive Individualism: Hobbes to Locke* (Toronto: Oxford University Press, 1962).

Macpherson, C.B., *The Real World of Democracy* (Toronto: CBC Enterprises, 1965).

Marsh, James H., (ed.) *The Canadian Encyclopedia* (Edmonton: Hurtig Publishers, 1985).

McCall, Christina, *Grits: An Intimate Portrait of the Liberal Party* (Toronto: MacMillan of Canada, 1982).

McDonald, Lynn, *The Party That Changed Canada: The New Democratic Party Then and Now* (Toronto: MacMillan of Canada, 1987).

McLeod, Thomas H., and McLeod, Ian, *Tommy Douglas: The Road to Jerusalem* (Edmonton: Hurtig Publishers, 1987).

McQuaig, Linda, *Behind Closed Doors: How the Rich Won Control of Canada's Tax System . . . And Ended Up Richer* (Toronto: Viking, 1987).

Morton, Desmond, *The New Democrats, 1961-1986: The Politics of Change* (Toronto: Copp Clark Pitman, 1986).

Sheppard, Robert and Valpy, Michael, *The National Deal: The Fight for a Canadian Constitution* (Toronto: Fleet, 1982).

Simpson, Jeffrey, *Discipline of Power* (Toronto: Personal Library Publishers, 1980).

Speirs, Rosemary, *Out of the Blue: The Fall of the Tory Dynasty in Ontario* (Toronto: Macmillan of Canada, 1986).

Stevens, Geoffrey, *Stanfield* (Toronto: McClelland and Stewart, 1973).

Thomas, Lewis H., (ed.) *The Making of a Socialist: The Recollections of T.C. Douglas* (Edmonton: University of Alberta Press, 1982).

Vallieres, Pierre, *White Niggers of America* (Toronto: McClelland and Stewart, 1971).

Articles

"Ed Broadbent on C.B. Macpherson," Broadbent, Ed, *This Magazine*, November 1987.

"On the March," Gessell, Paul, with Clark, Marc, *Maclean's*, August 3, 1987.

"The Importance of Being Ed," Gray, Charlotte, *Saturday Night*, March 1988.

"Ed Broadbent on a Fast Track: This Time the NDP Goes for Broke," Gwyn, Sandra, *Saturday Night*, September 1978.

"The NDP Survivors," Hills, Nick, *The Canadian General Election of 1986: Politicians, Parties, Press and Polls.*

"Lucille Broadbent: Portrait of a Very Private Political Wife," Labreche, Julianne, *Chatelaine*, April 1982.

"My Eighty Years on Wheels," McLaughlin, R.S. as told to Eric Hutton, *Maclean's*, September 15, October 1, October 15, 1954.

"The NDP's Fight for Survival," Riley, Susan, *Maclean's*, April 23, 1984.

"Ol' Brown Eyes: The Sentimental Love Song of J. Edward Broadbent," Snider, Norman, *Toronto Life*, February 1988.

"The Soul of Man Under Socialism," Steed, Judy, *Toronto Life*, December 1980.

Special thanks to Geoffrey Stevens for his innumerable news stories, features and columns about the national political scene in *The Globe and Mail*; many are quoted in part in this book.

Index